Imagining the Balkans

Updated Edition

Maria Todorova

OXFORD
UNIVERSITY PRESS

2009

OXFORD
UNIVERSITY PRESS

Oxford University Press, Inc., publishes works that further
Oxford University's objective of excellence
in research, scholarship, and education.

Oxford   New York
Auckland   Cape Town   Dar es Salaam   Hong Kong   Karachi
Kuala Lumpur   Madrid   Melbourne   Mexico City   Nairobi
New Delhi   Shanghai   Taipei   Toronto

With Offices in
Argentina   Austria   Brazil   Chile   Czech Republic   France   Greece
Guatemala   Hungary   Italy   Japan   Poland   Portugal   Singapore
South Korea   Switzerland   Thailand   Turkey   Ukraine   Vietnam

Copyright © 1997, 2009 by Oxford University Press, Inc.

First published by Oxford University Press, Inc., 1997.
Updated edition published 2009.
198 Madison Avenue, New York, New York 10016

www.oup.com

Oxford is a registered trademark of Oxford University Press

Library of Congress Cataloging-in-Publication Data
Todorova, Maria Nikolaeva.
Imagining the Balkans / Maria Todorova — updated ed.
p. cm.
Includes bibliographical references and index.
ISBN 978-0-19-538786-5
1. Balkan Peninsula—Historiography.   I. title.
DR34.T63 1997   96-7161
949.6—dc20

9 8 7 6 5 4 3 2 1

Printed in the United States of America
on acid-free paper

Imagining the Balkans

To my parents,
from whom I learned to love the Balkans
without the need to be proud or ashamed of them.

Preface

The hope of an intellectual is not that he will have an effect on the world, but that someday, somewhere, someone will read what he wrote exactly as he wrote it.

Theodor Adorno

This book, more than any other project I have worked on, has been with me forever. Therefore, it is difficult to arrange in any meaningful way (chronologically or by importance) all the different individuals, works, and events that have shaped my thinking on the subject. Since, in the course of this work, I have, of necessity, repeatedly trespassed into fields where I have little or no expertise, I might fail to acknowledge important influences. This is by no means the result of intellectual arrogance but is chiefly the result of the wild and often unsystematic forays into unknown territory that have, however, always been informed with curiosity and deference for the achievements of others.

The ambitiousness of what I am trying to address in this book is apparent. It presupposes an immensely elaborate secondary literature as well as the fullest possible primary source coverage. In its ideal form, this should be the undertaking of an interdisciplinary team of scholars and the result of long periods of discussion. That this is impossible for the practical purposes of the present project is quite clear. I am compelled to begin with one of a great number of proleptic remarks with which this work is fated to abound, namely that I am clearly and painfully conscious of being unable to produce what, to me, has for a long time been the ideal scholarly work, a complex tapestry of captivating and meaningful design executed with full and rich embroidery in all details. Of necessity, I will have to resort to patches, cursory compositions, and eclectic style. I see my principal task as construing an acceptable framework and suggesting possible lines of debate. Even if it merely triggers argument, this book will have fulfilled its purpose: I am convinced that the problem merits a whole genre of works on "balkanism."

It is part of the *comme il faut* manner of many American academic books to begin with theory, to situate themselves consciously at the outset of their work so as to additionally frustrate their readers' efforts: not only will they have to cope with the flow of the author's narrative or argument, but they are also bound to be (at least unconsciously) vigilant as to how much the professed theoretical context is genuinely internalized, how much is simply an indication of intellectual sympathies and political loyalties, how much is just lip service, the citation syndrome. Mercifully, readers follow their own strategies. Some skip the theory claims entirely and look for what they consider to be the sound substance; others, quite in reverse, read only the theory and treat the rest as trifling empirical illustration. Only a handful of dedicated and intrepid professional readers approach the work *as is* in its professed or manifest intertextuality.

I am only partly conforming to this style tongue in cheek (I am not quite sure whether the stress should be on *conform* or on *tongue in cheek*). This is not because I am not serious about theory: on the contrary, I hold it in enormous respect. However, to do an exhaustive and honest self-analysis of one's eclectic "Hotel Kwilu," to borrow Mary Douglas's metaphor for grand theory, requires a tortuous and possibly futile investigation. I will confine myself here to simply acknowledging my debt to many theorists from whom I have absorbed and applied a number of useful notions, or who have given me solace with their clear articulation and masterful treatment of many hazy doubts that have befallen me. I hope that how I have used them or how they have discreetly influenced my own argument does them much more credit than reiterating their main points, especially insofar as I neither wish to have followed, nor claim to have mastered, their thought in toto: Ernest Gellner, Eric Hobsbawm, Benedict Anderson, Tom Nairn, and the whole rich exchange of ideas around nationalism, modernity, and "the invention of tradition"; the work on the phenomenology of otherness and stereotyping; Erving Goffman on stigma and the wide and fruitful discussion his work triggered among his followers; Mary Douglas on everything from culture through objectivity, skepticism, and wager to libel and especially liminality; the growing literature on marginality; the whole postcolonialist endeavor, with all my due admiration for it but mostly for forcing me to articulate more intelligibly to myself my main points of skepticism and disagreement with the help of Arif Dirlik and Aijaz Ahmad; Fredric Jameson about his overall orientation in what he calls the "era of multinational capital" and "the global American culture of postmodernism"; the latest literature on empire and imperialism from Richard Koebner and Helmut Dan Schmidt to Wolfgang J. Mommsen; Pierre Bourdieu on describing, prescribing, representation in general, and particularly the political power of "naming"; the new writings on taxonomy (categories, naming, labeling, similarity, projection); notions like "discourse" and "knowledge as power," which by now have become so powerfully entrenched that it would be superfluous to invoke the larger framework of Michel Foucault; and, above all, David Lodge whose *Changing Places, Small World*, and especially *Nice Work* have been the best introduction to the world of critical theory, semiotics, metaphor, metonymy, synecdoche, aporia, and the perpetual sliding of the signified under the signifier.

Because I am situating myself within the rich and growing genre of "the invention of tradition" and because of the obvious analogies between my endeavor and "orientalism," early on in my work I was advised to avoid direct intellectual alignment with Edward Said so as not to carry the baggage of the increasing criticism against his ideas. Not least because of an inborn anarchist streak, I wish at this point to acknowledge my intellectual indebtedness to Said. I would certainly not declare that his has been the single most stimulating or most fruitful influence but it has been undeniably important. I think I have distanced myself enough and have shown the basic distinctions (but also correspondences) in the treatment of my own concept of "balkanism" from Said's "orientalism." It would be, however, a sublime intellectual dishonesty not to acknowledge the stimulating and, indeed, inspirational force of Said's thought or emotion. His impassioned critique has produced followers as well as challengers, which in the end is supposed to be the effect of any genuine intellectual effort. There has appeared, in the past few years, a whole body of important studies on the region informed by the same or similar concerns as my own. Some of these studies have been written by friends, and I have profited from the fruitful dialogue with them; others are the work of colleagues I have not met but whose scholarship I admire. I have duly recognized their influence in the text. It goes without saying that, in the end, I am solely responsible for all the errors of commission and omission.

To acknowledge means also to confess. My motives in writing this book have been complex and diverse but, first and foremost, this is not supposed to be a morality tale, simply exposing Western bias in a framework either of imperialism or orientalism (although something could be said in favor of each perspective). By reacting against a stereotype produced *in* the West, I do not wish to create a counterstereotype *of* the West, to commit the fallacy of "occidentalism." First, I do not believe in a homogeneous West, and there are substantial differences within and between the different "western" discussions of the Balkans. Second, I am convinced that a major part of Western scholarship has made significant, even crucial contributions to Balkan studies. Biases and preconceived ideas, even among those who attempt to shed them, are almost unavoidable, and this applies to outsiders as well as to insiders. Indeed, the outsider's view is not necessarily inferior to the insider's, and the insider is not anointed with truth because of existential intimacy with the object of study. What counts in the last resort is the very process of the conscious effort to shed biases and look for ways to express the reality of otherness, even in the face of a paralyzing epistemological skepticism. Without the important body of scholarship produced in the West and in the East, I would not have been able to take on the topics in this book. It will not do justice to all those scholars who have been valuable in shaping my views to mention but a few and it is impossible even to begin to enumerate them.

Nor is this an attempt to depict the Balkan people as innocent victims, to encourage "a sense of aggrieved primal innocence."[1] I am perfectly aware of my ambiguous position, of sharing the privilege and responsibility to be simultaneously outside and inside both the object of inquiry and the process of attaining knowledge about it. In *The Rhetoric of Empire*, David Spurr uses the example of Jacques Derrida and Julia Kristeva who come from "places that define the outer limits of Western European culture: Derrida in colonial Africa, where the French empire fades into the great open space of Africa; Kristeva in Bulgaria, crossing-ground of the Crusades and the historical territory of contention between Christianized Europe and the Ottoman Empire. In such places it is possible to live both in and beyond the West, knowing the boundaries of its language, and looking southward or eastward as if toward regions of the unthought."[2]

I invoke this example not in order to claim authority by analogy (especially as I have not profoundly studied the work of these authors, nor do I share some of their central postulates) but to partake in the awareness of "the danger and the freedom of the boundary situation." I am acutely aware of (and at the same time tremendously savor) my own marginality vis-à-vis both my country of birth — Bulgaria — and my country of adoption — the United States. It is not a newly acquired awareness; its geography has simply expanded. Even back in Bulgaria, the consciousness of mixed ethnic background and my vocation — exploring and teaching about the hybrid society of the Ottoman Empire in the conditions of the dominant discourse of the nation-state — had conferred on me the luxurious feeling of intellectual exile. Had I remained in Bulgaria, I would not have written this particular book, although its ideas and empirical material would have informed my teaching and my behavior. I would have felt compelled to write a different one, one that would have explored and exposed the internal orientalisms within the region, that would have centered on the destructive and impoverishing effects of ethnic nationalism (without necessarily passing dogmatic strictures on nationalism as such), and that, far from exhibiting nostalgia for imperial formations, would have rescued from the Ottoman and the more recent Balkan past these possibilities for alternative development that would have enriched our common human culture. Maybe I will still write it.

But, as it happens, I live *here* and *now*, and for the moment it is to *this* audience that I wish to tell a story, to explain and to oppose something that is being produced *here* and has adverse effects *there*. Of course, it is very uncertain whether we ever reach the audience we speak to; it is equally uncertain whether whom we think we speak for will actually recognize or accept it. My second proleptic remark professes that I do not mean this work to be an exercise in what Peter Gay calls "comparative trivialization"; in a word, I do not want to exempt the Balkans of their responsibility because the world outside behaves in a no less distasteful manner; nor do I want to support the erroneous notion of what Hans Magnus Enzensberger has defined as "no protagonists, only string pullers." I am not writing on behalf of a homogeneous Balkan abstraction. By now, I have realized well the limits of control one can maintain over one's own text and that it is impossible to impose rules on how one should be understood or how one should be used. Rather, I am speaking for this part among Balkan intellectuals who think about the problems of identity and have internalized the divisions imposed on them by previously shaped and exclusionary identities. In doing this, I am trying to emancipate them not only from the debilitating effect of Western aloofness but also from the more emotional rejection of their partners in the East European predicament of yesterday.

My special and deep gratitude goes to the Woodrow Wilson International Center for Scholars, which awarded me a fellowship for the academic year 1994–1995 and where most of this book was written. At a time when the Balkans have generated strong emotions and when the quest for quick fixes has promoted investment predominantly in politically expedient projects, the Wilson Center decided to support a purely speculative effort that can only seem abstruse, convoluted, and *recherché* to the lovers of uncomplicated and straightforward recipes. I profited enormously from the broad knowledge and critical insights of the commentators at my seminar (Larry Wolff and Şerif Mardin), and from the long and friendly conversations with the other fellows at the center: Ljiljana Smajlović, Matej Calinescu, Amelie Rorty, Gregory

Jusdanis, Brook Thomas, Geoffrey Hartman, Joel Kuipers. Special thanks are due my interns Debbie Fitzl and Angeliki Papantoniou.

At different scholarly meetings I have benefited from critical remarks and friendly advice. In personal conversations or correspondence, Milica Bakić-Hayden, Robert Hayden, Vladimir Tismaneanu, Olga Augustinos, Gerassimos Augustinos, Elizabeth Prodromou, Engin Akarli, Pascalis Kitromilides, Stefan Troebst, Theodore Couloumbis, Rifa'at Abou El-Haj, Diana Mishkova, Philip Shashko, Boian Koulov, Evelina Kelbecheva, and Bonka Boneva have shared with me information, valuable views, and critical comments. Mark Thurner and my other colleagues from the postcolonial history and theory reading group at the University of Florida helped alleviate the doubts I had about venturing into unknown waters. Special acknowledgment to Alice Freifeld, who struggled with the whole manuscript at a time when it needed radical surgery. The original manuscript for this work was longer by one third. Abbreviation, necessitated by considerations of size and price, did, in some cases, contribute to more disciplined and clear-cut formulations and the removal of some interesting material that was not, however, central to the argument. For urging me to do this, I thank my editors at Oxford University Press. Yet I regret the contraction of the endnotes, which, in their initial form, contained polemic deliberations and extensive historiographical characteristics. The "art of the footnote" may be losing ground, but I wish at least to document my nostalgia for it. As always, my chief debt is to my family. My husband has always been encouraging and filled with more respect and higher expectations for my profession than I have ever had. I have been thrilled to observe how, for Anna and Alexander, to carry multiple identities has not been a burden but an embellishment. Finally, this book is dedicated to my parents and written for my friends.

Gainesville, Florida   M. T.
February 1996

Contents

Imagining the Balkans

Introduction

Balkanism and Orientalism:
Are They Different Categories?

A specter is haunting Western culture—the specter of the Balkans. All the powers have entered into a holy alliance to exorcise this specter: politicians and journalists, conservative academics and radical intellectuals, moralists of all kind, gender, and fashion. Where is the adversarial group that has not been decried as "Balkan" and "balkanizing" by its opponents? Where the accused have not hurled back the branding reproach of "balkanism"?

By the beginning of the twentieth century, Europe had added to its repertoire of *Schimpfwörter*, or disparagements, a new one that, although recently coined, turned out to be more persistent over time than others with centuries-old tradition. "Balkanization" not only had come to denote the parcelization of large and viable political units but also had become a synonym for a reversion to the tribal, the backward, the primitive, the barbarian. In its latest hypostasis, particularly in American academe, it has been completely decontextualized and paradigmatically related to a variety of problems. That the Balkans have been described as the "other" of Europe does not need special proof. What has been emphasized about the Balkans is that its inhabitants do not care to conform to the standards of behavior devised as normative by and for the civilized world. As with any generalization, this one is based on reductionism, but the reductionism and stereotyping of the Balkans has been of such degree and intensity that the discourse merits and requires special analysis.

The "civilized world" (the term is introduced not ironically but as a self-proclaimed label) was first seriously upset with the Balkans at the time of the Balkan wars (1912–1913). News of the barbarities committed in this distant European Mediterranean peninsula came flooding in and challenged the peace movements that not only were gaining strength in Europe but were beginning to be institutionalized. The Carnegie Endowment for International Peace, founded in 1910, established an international commission "to inquire into the causes and conduct of the Balkan wars." The report of the commission, which consisted of well-known public figures from France, the United States, Great

3

Britain, Russia, Germany, and Austria-Hungary, was published in 1914. This is a magnum opus that looked into the historical roots of the Balkan conflict, presenting the points of view and aspirations of the belligerents, as well as the economic, social, and moral consequences of the wars, and their relation to international law. The report included an introduction by Baron d'Estournelle de Constant reiterating the main principles of the peace movement: "Let us repeat, for the benefit of those who accuse us of 'bleating for peace at any price,' what we have always maintained: War rather than slavery; Arbitration rather than war; Conciliation rather than arbitration."[1]

De Constant differentiated between the first and the second Balkan wars: the first was defensive and a war of independence, "the supreme protest against violence, and generally the protest of the weak against the strong . . . and for this reason it was glorious and popular throughout the civilized world." The second was a predatory war in which "both victor and vanquished lose morally and materially." Still, for all their differences, both Balkan wars "finally sacrificed treasures of riches, lives, and heroism. We cannot authenticate these sacrifices without protesting, without denouncing their cost and their danger for the future." While not optimistic about the immediate political future of the region, the commission concluded: "What then is the duty of the civilized world in the Balkans? . . . It is clear in the first place that they should cease to exploit these nations for gain. They should encourage them to make arbitration treaties and insist upon their keeping them. They should set a good example by seeking a judicial settlement of all international disputes." De Constant reiterated:

> The real culprits in this long list of executions, assassinations, drownings, burnings, massacres and atrocities furnished by our report, are not, we repeat, the Balkan peoples. Here pity must conquer indignation. Do not let us condemn the victims . . . The real culprits are those who by interest or inclination, declaring that war is inevitable, end by making it so, asserting that they are powerless to prevent it.[2]

In 1993, instead of launching a fact-finding mission, the Carnegie Endowment satisfied itself with reprinting the 1913 report, preceding its title with a gratuitous caption, "The Other Balkan Wars." Also added was an introduction by George Kennan, ambassador to the Soviet Union in the 1950s and to Yugoslavia in the 1960s, best known as the *padre padrone* of the U.S. policy of containment vis-à-vis the USSR. Entitled "The Balkan Crises: 1913 and 1993," this introduction was in turn preceded by a two-page preface by the president of the Carnegie Endowment, Morton Abramowitz, which recounts his almost serendipitous idea to reopen the eighty-year-old report. It convinced him "that others should also have the opportunity to read it. It is a document with many stories to tell us in this twilight decade of the twentieth century, when yet again a conflict in the Balkans torments Europe and the conscience of the international community." Abramowitz considers Kennan the person to best bridge the two events and instruct the conscience of the international community (which seems to have been tormented primarily by the Balkans throughout the twentieth century). We "all now benefit from his insight, his sure sense of history, and his felicitous style."[3]

Kennan's introduction began with a praise of peace movements in the United States, England, and northern Europe that sought to create new legal codes of international behavior. Although the initiative for an international conference on disarmament came from the Russian Tsar Nicholas II, it was "immature dilettantism, . . . elaborated by the characteristic confusions of the Russian governmental establishment of the time, . . . not a serious one." Its unseriousness notwithstanding, it was "seized upon with enthusiasm" by the proponents of peace who convoked the two Hague Peace Conferences and other international initiatives. Having separated the serious men from the dilettante boys, thus retrospectively essentializing cold war dichotomies, Kennan described the historical context at the turn of the century, the outbreak of the Balkan wars, and the report of the Carnegie commission.

> The importance of this report for the world of 1993 lies primarily in the light it casts on the excruciating situation prevailing today in the same Balkan world with which it dealt. The greatest value of the report is to reveal to people of this age how much of today's problem has deep roots and how much does not.[4]

Confirming thus his belief in the maxim "Historia est magistra vitae," the second part of Kennan's introduction analyzed analogies with the past and the lessons of these analogies, its approach indicated by the slip "the same Balkan world." The newly created Balkan states were summed up as monarchies whose leaders were "as a rule, somewhat more moderate and thoughtful than their subjects. Their powers were usually disputed by inexperienced and unruly parliamentary bodies,"[5] leaving one to wonder which was the rule and who were the exceptions. The Bulgarian Tsar Ferdinand, "Foxy Ferdinand," plunged his country into the second Balkan war, despite better advice, to achieve his wild ambitions (not Balkan, but Central European, more particularly Saxe-Coburg-Gotha) to enter Constantinople as a victor; he accomplished the loss of his crown, and the unruly parliamentary body ruled that he was never to set foot in Bulgaria again. The "moderate" Milan Obrenović humiliated Serbia in an adventurous war with Bulgaria in 1885, used by George Bernard Shaw to produce his own "peacenik" variation on a Balkan theme. Kennan could have used the bloody assassination of the last pathetic Obrenović, Alexander, in 1903, to illustrate typical Balkan violence had he not been of royal birth. Finally, the Hohenzollern-Sigmaringen dynasty of Romania was moderation incarnate, especially the soap-opera Carol II, but then his mother was the beautiful Queen Marie (a "regular, regular, regular, regular royal queen" according to a caption of the 4 August 1924 *Time*), the favorite granddaughter of Victoria and an intimate friend of the Waldorf Astors.[6]

The explanation for the Balkan irredenta, for dreams of glory and territorial expansion, was summarized in one sentence: "It was hard for people who had recently achieved so much, and this so suddenly, to know where to stop." No mention that the recent Balkan upstarts under the "moderate" guidance of mostly German princelings were emulating the "frugal" imperial behavior of their western European models. Critical of the original report in that "there was no attempt to analyze the political motivations of the various governments participating in the wars," Kennan stressed that the strongest motivating factor "was not religion but aggressive nationalism. But that nationalism, as it manifested itself on the field of battle, drew on deeper traits of character inherited, presumably, from a distant tribal past. . . . And so it remains to-day." And he continued:

> What we are up against is the sad fact that developments of those earlier ages, not only those of the Turkish domination but of earlier ones as well, had the effect of thrusting into the southeastern reaches of the European continent a salient of non-European civilization which has continued to the present day to preserve many of its non-European characteristics.[7]

Had Kennan's essay introduced the original report, written a whole year before the outbreak of World War I, one could empathize with its moral outrage even while overlooking its conceptual inaccuracies: at the time, it seemed that with little effort La Belle Époque would endure forever. Mary Edith Durham was disgusted with what she saw of the Balkan wars but she was confident that this could not befall the human species inhabiting the lands to the west of the Balkans:

> The war was over. All through I used to say to myself: "War is so obscene, so degrad-ing, so devoid of one redeeming spark, that it is quite impossible there can ever be a war in West Europe." This was the one thing that consoled me in the whole bestial experience. War brings out all that is foulest in the human race, and the most disgusting animal ferocity poses as a virtue. As for the Balkan Slav and his haunted Christianity, it seemed to me all civilization should rise and restrain him from further brutality.[8]

Kennan, on the other hand, had full knowledge of the butcheries of the two world wars, or else one should assume that the spirit of Mary Edith Durham went to rest in 1913 and was reincarnated following an innocent amnesia between 1913 and 1989. Although at least technically it is indisputable that the spark for the powder keg came from the Balkans, very few serious historians would claim that this was the cause of World War I. World War II, however, had little to do with the Balkans, which were comparatively late and reluctantly involved. It is probably because of the total in-ability to attribute World War II to anything Balkan that Kennan does not even men-tion it: "Well, here we are in 1993. Eighty years of tremendous change in the remain-der of Europe and of further internecine strife in the Balkans themselves have done little to alter the problem this geographic region presents for Europe." Indeed, there is something distinctly non-European in that the Balkans never quite seem to reach the dimensions of European slaughters. After World War II, it is arrogant to hear the benign admission that "these states of mind are not peculiar to the Balkan people, . . . they can be encountered among other European peoples as well. . . . But all these distinctions are relative ones. It is the undue predominance among the Balkan peoples of these particular qualities."[9]

Kennan has been echoed by a great many American journalists who seem to be truly amazed at Balkan savagery at the end of the twentieth century. Roger Cohen exclaimed "the notion of killing people . . . because of something that may have hap-pened in 1495 is unthinkable in the Western world. Not in the Balkans."[10] He was quite right. In the Balkans they were killing over something that happened 500 years ago; in Europe, with a longer span of civilized memory, they were killing over some-thing that happened 2,000 years ago. One is tempted to ask whether the Holocaust resulted from a "due" or "undue" predominance of barbarity. It occured a whole fifty years ago but the two Balkan wars were even earlier. Besides, Kennan wrote his essay only a year after the "neat and clean" Gulf War operation. In seventeen days, American technology managed to kill, in what Jean Baudrillard claimed was merely a television event, at least half the number of total war casualties incurred by all sides during the two Balkan wars.[11] If this is too recent, there was the Vietnam War, where even according to Robert McNamara's *In Retrospect* "the picture of the world's greatest superpower killing or seriously injuring 1,000 noncombatants a week . . . is not a pretty one." With the ease with which American journalists dispense accusations of genocide in Bosnia, where the reported casualty figures vary anywhere between 25,000 and 250,000, it is curious to know how they designate the over three million dead Vietnamese.[12] Whether the Balkans are non-European or not is mostly a matter of academic and political debate, but they certainly have no monopoly over barbarity.

It is not this book's intention merely to express moral outrage at somebody else's moral outrage. The question is how to explain the persistence of such a frozen image. How could a geographical appellation be transformed into one of the most powerful pejorative designations in history, international relations, political science, and, nowadays, general intellectual discourse? This question has more than a narrow academic relevance. It is the story of (1) innocent inaccuracies stemming from imperfect geographical knowledge transmitted through tradition; (2) the later saturation of the geographical appellation with political, social, cultural, and ideological overtones, and the beginning of the pejorative use of "Balkan" around World War I; and (3) the complete dissociation of the designation from its object, and the subsequent reverse and retroactive ascription of the ideologically loaded designation to the region, particularly after 1989.

While historians are well aware that dramatic changes have occurred on the peninsula, their discourse on the Balkans as a geographic/cultural entity is overwhelmed by a discourse utilizing the construct as a powerful symbol conveniently located outside historical time. And this usage itself is the product of nearly two centuries of evolution. There has appeared today a whole genre dealing with the problem and representation of "otherness." It is a genre across disciplines, from anthropology, through literature and philosophy, to sociology and history in general. A whole new discipline has appeared—*imagology*—dealing with literary images of the other.[13] The discussion of orientalism has been also a subgenre of this concern with otherness. Orientalism has found an important and legitimate place in academia as the critique of a particular discourse that, when formulated by Said, served to denote, "the corporate institution for dealing with the Orient—dealing with it by making statements about it, authorizing views of it, describing it, by teaching it, settling it, ruling over it: in short . . . a Western style for dominating, restructuring, and having authority over the Orient."[14]

Almost two decades later, Said reiterated that his objection to orientalism was grounded in more than just the antiquarian study of Oriental languages, societies, and peoples, but that "as a system of thought it approaches a heterogeneous, dynamic and complex human reality from an uncritically essentialist standpoint; this suggests both an enduring Oriental reality and an opposing but no less enduring Western essence, which observes the Orient from afar and, so to speak, from above."[15] Orientalism has had a tumultuous existence, and while it still excites passions, it has been superceded as a whole. This is not the case in the Balkans. On the one hand, Said's book has not been translated and published in the relevant Balkan languages and thus has not yet entered the mainstream discourse. On the other hand, the notion has been introduced and is popularized by intellectuals who find that it describes adequately the relationship of the Balkans with the West. Insofar as there is a growing and widespread concern over this relationship, the discourse is becoming circumscribed in the category of orientalism, even when not explicitly stated. This book argues that balkanism is not merely a subspecies of orientalism. Thus, the argument advanced here purports to be more than a mere "orientalist variation on a Balkan theme."[16] Given the above-mentioned anticipation of a growing influence of orientalism in the Balkans, the category merits a closer discussion.

Inspired by Foucault, from whom he not only borrowed the term "discourse" but the central attention devoted to the relation of knowledge to power, Said exposed the dangers of essentializing the Orient as other. He was also strongly influenced by Antonio Gramsci's distinction between civil and political society, especially the notion of cultural hegemony that invested orientalism with prodigious durability. This is quite apart from how exactly Said's thought relates to the general Foucauldian or Gramscian oeuvre.[17] Predictably, the response to Said's book was polarized: it produced detractors as well as admirers or epigones. It involved hefty criticism on the part of modernization theorists or from classical liberal quarters. It entailed also serious epistemological critique, an attempt to smooth off the extremes and go beyond Said, and beyond orientalism.[18]

Some of the more pedestrian objections were made on the ground that Said was negating and demonizing the work of generations of honest and well-informed orientalists who had made prominent contributions to human knowledge. Said's professions that he was not attributing evil or sloppiness to each and every Orientalist but was simply drawing attention to the fact that "the *guild* of Orientalists has a specific history of complicity with imperial power" were insufficient to assuage the outcry that the very idea of disinterested scholarship had been desecrated.[19] Even less distinguished objections judged his work on the basis of how it was appropriated in the Arab world as a systematic defense of the Arabs and Islam, and imputed to Said a surreptitious anti-Westernism. There have been more substantial and subtle critiques of Said's endeavor aimed at refining rather than refuting his work. They concerned his nonhistorical, essentialist inconsistencies; the overgeneralization of Western attitudes on the basis of the French and British paradigm; mostly, and justly, Said was reproached for the lack of social and economic contextualization, for his concentration on textuality, for his manifestly idealist approach.[20] It was also charged that by positing the falseness of the orientalist representation, Said did not address the logical consequence "that there has at least to be the possibility of representation that is 'true.'" Yet, like most impassioned renunciations, there was an inevitable element of reductionism. Said had successfully addressed the charge that his negative polemic was not advancing a new epistemological approach.[21]

Despite his later strong declarations against imputing essentialism and ahistoricism to his category, Said overgeneralized speaking of a generic Orient that accommodated Aeschylus, Victor Hugo, Dante, and Karl Marx. Maybe he could not resist the display of literary erudition, but the treatment of Aeschylus's *The Persians* or Euripides's *The Bacchae* at the beginning of a European imaginative geography articulating the Orient, brilliantly insightful as they were, were not helpful in protecting him from charges that he was essentializing Europe and the West.[22] The appropriation of ancient Greek culture and its elevation to the founding status of Western civilization was only a gradual and controversial historical process, whereas Said's sweeping account of the division of East and West suggested a suspicious continuity.

This Saidian fallacy is rooted in the tension between his attraction to Erich Auerbach (as a thinker and existential role model of the intellectual in exile) and Said's simultaneous, and incompatible, attraction to Foucault. Despite lavishly adopting Foucauldian terminology, Said's ambivalent loyalty to the humanist project is essentially irreconcilable with Foucault's discourse theory with its "Nietzschean anti-humanism and anti-realist theories of representation." Moreover, his transhistorical orientalist discourse is ahistorical not only in the ordinary sense but is methodologically anti-Foucauldian, insofar as Foucault's discourse is firmly grounded in European modernity.[23] Still, maybe one should listen more carefully to Said's latest self-exegesis with its recurrent insistence on Islamic and Arabic orientalism, without even an honorary mention of his detours into antiquity and the Middle Ages. When he says that "the reason why Orientalism is opposed by so many thoughtful non-Westerners is that its modern discourse is correctly perceived as a discourse originating in an era of colonialism,"[24] I am inclined to see in the qualifying slip — "its modern discourse" — the hubris and weakness of the academic prima donna who has to accommodate defensively, though discreetly, his past faults and inconsistencies rather than openly admit to them. Then, it would be possible to ascribe his literary digressions (which, anyway, fill only a small part of his narrative) to a tension between his professional hypostasis as a literary critic and his growing identity as Palestinian intellectual, something that might explain the foregoing of theoretical rigor for a profound emotive effect.

Despite distinguished and undistinguished objections, the place of *Orientalism* and of "orientalism" in academic libraries and dictionaries has been secured. In a more narrow sense, it acquired an enviable although contested prestige in avant-guardist cultural theory; in a broader sense, it indicated possible venues of resistance and subversion. Said undoubtedly succeeded in crystallizing an existing concern at the proper moment, in the proper mode.[25] It is healthy to react against the iconlike status Said has acquired both among his apostles and his opponents. To deny, however, or even downplay a connection with Said resembles (although on an incomparably more modest level) the efforts to disclaim any connection with, and even profess aversion for, Marx, while, quite apart from the consequences of where his self-professed followers led, deeply internalizing and unconsciously reproducing Marx's immense contribution to how we theorize today about society. The continuing resonance of Said's category is perhaps best explained by the growing awareness of students of society "of the role of their academic disciplines in the reproduction of patterns of domination."[26]

In a broader context, Said's attack on orientalism was a specific critique of what has since become known as the general crisis of representation. More significantly, he posed the question not only in epistemological but also in moral terms: "Can one divide human reality, as indeed human reality seems to be genuinely divided, into clearly different cultures, histories, traditions, societies, even races, and survive the consequences humanly?"[27] No other discipline has been as strongly affected by this crisis as anthropology since the ontology of separateness, difference, otherness is its methodological basis. Anthropologists have been long aware of what in physics is known as the Heisenberg effect: the notion that, in the course of measuring, the scientist interacts with the object of observation and, as a result, the observed object is revealed not as it is in itself but as a function of measurement. It is a problem that led anthropology as the par excellence discipline studying the alien, the exotic, the distant in faraway societies and the marginal in nearby ones into its present deep theoretical crisis. It led it to the articulation of an often honest, but verbally helpless solipsism; as Wittgenstein remarked "what the solipsist *means* is quite correct; only it cannot be *said*, but makes itself manifest."[28] But this need not be the case. The realization of the limits of knowledge that accompanies the self-conscious act of acquiring it should not necessarily produce a paralytic effect. Carrier, who has focused on essentialization not merely as an unconscious attribute of anthropological studies but as an inevitable by-product of thinking and communication, sees the problem as a "failure to be conscious of essentialism, whether it springs from the assumptions with which we approach our subject or the goals that motivate our writing."[29] Maybe the feeling of philosophical impotence in anthropology and other disciplines affected by the examination of their own techniques will be dissipated simply by getting used to or learning to live with it: familiarity breeds a healthy ignoring of the final philosophical implications of theory, but by no means erases the necessity for rigorous and responsible adjustment of the methodology of observation. This is what happened in physics despite and over the objections that Heisenberg's philosophy of knowledge encountered in no less formidable figures than Einstein, Schrödinger, and Louis de Broglie.

Already in *Orientalism*, Said warned that the answer to orientalism was not occidentalism, yet neither he nor his followers paid enough attention to the essentialization (or, rather, self-essentialization) of the West as the hegemonic pair in the dichotomy. While "East" has become less common recently, this has not affected the casual usage of "West": "Even theorists of discontinuity and deconstruction such as Foucault and Derrida continue to set their analysis within and against a Western totality."[30] It took James Carrier to accost this problem:

> Seeing Orientalism as a dialectical process helps us recognize that it is not merely a Western imposition of a reified identity on some alien set of people. It is also the imposition of an identity created in dialectical opposition to another identity, one likely to be equally reified, that of the West. Westerners, then, define the Orient in terms of the West, but so Others define themselves in terms of the West, just as each defines the West in terms of the Other. . . . Of course, the way I have cast this privileges the West as the standard against which all Others are defined, which is appropriate in view of both the historical political and economic power of the West.[31]

Insofar as the discourse describing the relationship of the Balkans to a putative West is considered, there is an increasing tendency to treat it as a structural variant of orientalism. Introducing the notion of "nesting orientalisms," Milica Bakić-Hayden prefers to treat the discourse involving the Balkans as a variation of orientalism because "it is the manner of perpetuation of the underlying logic . . . that makes Balkanism and Orientalism variant forms of the same kind." The same approach is employed by Elli Skopetea.[32] One can readily agree that there is overlap and complementarity between the two rhetorics, yet there is similar rhetorical overlap with any power discourse: the rhetoric of racism, development, modernization, civilization, and so on. My aim is to position myself vis-à-vis the orientalist discourse and elaborate on a seemingly identical, but actually only similar phenomenon, which I call balkanism.[33] What are, then, if any, the differences between these categories?

In the first place, there is the historical and geographic concreteness of the Balkans as opposed to the intangible nature of the Orient. In his preemptive afterword to the new edition of *Orientalism*, Said explicitly insists that he has "no interest in, much less capacity for, showing what the true Orient and Islam really are." This is premised on a justified conviction that Orient and Occident "correspond to no stable reality that exists as a natural fact."[34] Said's treatment of the Orient is ambivalent: he denies the existence of a "real Orient," yet, by attacking texts or traditions distorting or ignoring authentic characteristics of the Orient, he gives it a genuine ontological status.[35]

Indeed, the opposition between an abstract East and West has been as old as written history. The ancient Greeks used Orient to depict the antagonism between civilized and barbarians, although their main dichotomy ran between the cultured South and the barbarous North (Thracian and Scythian). The Persians to the east were in many ways a quasi-civilized other.[36] From Diocletian's times onward, Rome introduced the East-West division into administration and considered Orient the dioceses of Egypt and Anatolia. In the medieval period, the division was used in the narrow sense to depict the opposition between Catholicism and Orthodoxy, and in a broader sense to designate that between Islam and Christianity. In all cases, the dichotomy East-West had clearly defined spatial dimensions: it juxtaposed societies that coexisted but were opposed for political, religious, or cultural reasons. East was not always the pejorative component of this opposition: for Byzantium, the unrivaled center of the civilized European world for several centuries after the fall of Rome, the West was synonymous with barbarity and crudeness. Only after the fall of Constantinople in 1453 and the eclipse of the Orthodox church, but especially with the unique economic takeoff of Western Europe, was East internalized also by the Orthodox world as the less privileged of the opposition pair.

As Larry Wolff has convincingly shown, the conventional division of Europe into East and West is a comparatively late invention of eighteenth-century philosophes responsible for the conceptual reorientation of Europe along an East-West axis from the heretofore dominant division into North versus South.[37] This new division, although also spatial, began gradually to acquire different overtones, borrowed and adapted from the belief in evolution and progress flourishing during the Enlightenment. Because the geographic east of Europe and the world situated to the east was lagging behind Europe primarily in economic performance, East came to be identified more often, and often exclusively, with industrial backwardness, lack of advanced social relations and institutions typical for the developed capitalist West, irrational and superstitious cultures unmarked by Western Enlightenment. This added an additional vector in the relationship between East and West: time, where the movement from past to future was not merely motion but evolution from simple to complex, backward to developed, primitive to cultivated. The element of time with its developmental aspect has been an important, and nowadays the most important, characteristic of contemporary perceptions of East and West. Thus, since the ancient Greeks, the East has always existed as an elastic and ambiguous concept. Everyone has had one's own Orient, pertaining to space or time, most often to both. The perception of the Orient has been, therefore, relational, depending on the normative value set and the observation point.

Even had Said been more historically minded and rigorous and had spoken merely of the Near East and Islam, instead of the Orient (as he is increasingly doing in his later works), he still would have had a problem with two very broad and shifting categories. Not only are the Near and Middle East amorphous and ascriptive terms devised by the West,[38] but one would have to deal with Ottoman and Turkish orientalism as quite apart from Arabic orientalism, and would have to distinguish between different Arabic orientalisms. Likewise, the notion of Islam as an entity is problematic, both in a geographical and chronological sense.[39] To try to fend off criticism, Said would have had to be what he is not, circumspect and precise, and organically, not only verbally, devoted to the notion of historical specificity, to the idea that "human reality is constantly being made and unmade." Then he would have spoken cautiously of the orientalism of the Arabic Islamic Near East in the relatively short era affected by expanding French and British imperialism before the fragmentation of a putative Arabic identity. Then he would not have written *Orientalism*.

The Balkans have a concrete historical existence. If, for the Orient, one can play with the famous mot of Derrida: "il n'y a pas de hors-texte," the question whether they exist cannot be even posed for the Balkans; the proper question is "qu'est-ce qu'il y a de hors texte?" While surveying the different historical legacies that have shaped the southeast European peninsula, two legacies can be singled out as crucial. One is the millennium of Byzantium with its profound political, institutional, legal, religious, and cultural impact. The other is the half millenium of Ottoman rule that gave the peninsula its name and established the longest period of political unity it had experienced. Not only did part of southeastern Europe acquire a new name—Balkans—during the Ottoman period, it has been chiefly the Ottoman elements or the ones perceived as such that have mostly invoked the current stereotypes. Aside from the need for a sophisticated theoretical and empirical approach to the problems of the Ottoman legacy, it seems that the conclusion that the Balkans are the Ottoman legacy is not an overstatement. While, in the narrow sense of the word, the presence of the Ottoman Empire in the southeast European peninsula had a lifetime spanning from the fourteenth to the early twentieth centuries, the Ottoman legacy bears first and foremost the characteristics of the eighteenth and nineteenth centuries. In practically all spheres in which the Ottoman legacy can be traced (political, cultural, social, and economic), a drastic break occurred at the time of secession and was largely completed by the end of World War I. In the demographic sphere and the sphere of popular culture, the Ottoman legacy has had a more persistent and continuous life. It also has had a prolonged existence as the legacy of perception, constantly invented and reinvented, as long as historical self-identity will be deemed crucial in Balkan societies.

There is a widespread notion that the Balkans began losing their identity once they began to Europeanize. That this phrasing implies their difference from Europe is obvious. Far more interesting is the fact that the process of "Europeanization," "Westernization," or "modernization" of the Balkans in the nineteenth and twentieth centuries included the spread of rationalism and secularization, the intensification of commercial activities and industrialization, the formation of a bourgeoisie and other new social groups in the economic and social sphere, and above all, the triumph of the bureaucratic nation-state. From this point of view the Balkans were becoming European by shedding the last residue of an imperial legacy, widely considered an anomaly at the time, and by assuming and emulating the homogeneous European nation-state as the normative form of social organization. It may well be that what we are witnessing today, wrongly attributed to some Balkan essence, is the ultimate Europeanization of the Balkans. If the Balkans are, as I think they are, tantamount to their Ottoman legacy, this is an advanced stage of the end of the Balkans.

Closely linked to the intangible nature of the Orient, in contrast to the concreteness of the Balkans, was the role the oriental image served as escape from civilization. The East, in general, was constructed for the West as an exotic and imaginary realm, the abode of legends, fairy tales, and marvels; it epitomized longing and offered option, as opposed to the prosaic and profane world of the West. The Orient became Utopia, "it represented the past, the future, and the Middle Ages." It was the admiration of the romantics, which produced Byron's *Child Harold*, the *Ghiaour*, and *The Bride of Abydos*; Goethe's *Westöstlicher Diwan*; Chateaubriand's *Itinéraire de Paris à Jérusalem*; Victor Hugo's *Orientales*; Heinrich Heine's *Romanzero*; and the works of Pierre Loti, Théofile Gauthier, Samuel Coleridge, Thomas Moore, and so forth. The Orient nourished the imagination of the romantics, but it became also an escape for liberals and nationalists who felt stifled by the rise of conservatism and reaction after the Napoleonic wars, when the Orient "became a symbol of freedom and wealth."[40]

This last component, wealth and, inseparable from it, excess, made the Orient the escapist dream of affluent romantic conservatives, too. English gentlemen found desirable models of behavior and dress that they readily emulated. "Men smoking was a custom much associated with Turkey, Persia, and the rest of the leisurely-inhaling domain of North Africa." Benjamin Disraeli spoke in praise of the "propriety and enjoyment" modeled on the lives of Turkish pashas that allowed him the luxury of smoking in repose. "Western would-be sultans retired to smoking rooms after dinner to enjoy the social license of a men's society akin to that of the Arab world. They wore banyans and robes, informal attire that corresponded with Western undress."[41] The imagined Orient served not only as refuge from the alienation of a rapidly industrializing West but also as metaphor for the forbidden. "Confected from Western desire and imagination," the East offered a sumptuous wardrobe and an even more extravagant nudity. There was an explicit relationship between the Orient and the feminine, and it has been argued that oriental discourses involve a theory of sexuality and sensuality in the disguise of a theory of asceticism.[42] Alongside "eastern cruelty," a main theme in orientalist descriptions and painting, came also another component with a strong appeal, lust:

> Scenes of harems, baths, and slave markets were for many Western artists a pretext by which they were able to cater to the buyer's prurient interest in erotic themes. . . . Such pictures were, of course, presented to Europeans with a "documentary" air and by means of them the Orientalist artist could satisfy the demand for such paintings and at the same time relieve himself of any moral responsibility by emphasizing that these were scenes of a society that was not Christian and had different moral values.[43]

The Balkans, on the other hand, with their unimaginative concreteness, and almost total lack of wealth, induced a straightforward attitude, usually negative, but rarely nuanced. There was some exception at the time of romantic nationalism in the words and deeds of philhellenes or slavophiles, but these efforts were extremely short-lived and usually touched on the freedom component, totally devoid of the mystery of exoticism. Even the one exception that espoused Balkan romance was of a distinctly different nature. In 1907, an American, Arthur Douglas Howden Smith, joined a Macedonian cheta organized in Bulgaria. He left a lively account that opened with reflections on the prosaic character of modern civilization depriving its populations of the picturesqueness of days bygone. Resolved to pursue his call for adventure in "lonesome corners of the earth, [where] men and women still lead lives of romance," Smith decided to head for the Balkans, which had long interested him.

> To those who have not visited them, the Balkans are a shadow-land of mystery; to those who know them, they become even more mysterious. . . . You become, in a sense, a part of the spell, and of the mystery and glamour of the whole. You contract the habit of crouching over your morning coffee in the café and, when you meet a man of your acquaintance, at least half of what you say is whispered, portentously. Intrigue, plotting, mystery, high courage, and daring deeds—the things that are the soul of true romance are to-day the soul of the Balkans.[44]

As with the Orient, there is the mystical escape to the Middle Ages but without a whim of the accompanying luridness and overtly sexual overtones of orientalism. It is a distinctly male appeal: the appeal of medieval knighthood, of arms and plots. In Belgrade one got, wrote Smith, the first feeling of the Balkans: "Intrigue is in the air one breathes. The crowds in the Belgrade cafés have the manner of conspirators. There are soldiers on every hand."[45] Still, Smith's is one of the few examples where the "maleness" of the Balkans received a positive account. In practically every other description, the standard Balkan male is uncivilized, primitive, crude, cruel, and, without exception, disheveled. Herbert Vivian's chapter on "Brigandage" in Macedonia, written at the same time as Smith's account, began by introducing the Balkans as still medieval; brigands to him were an appropriate medieval topic and he felt "like meeting the ghost of Sir Walter Scott and extracting fresh tales of a grandfather." The chapter ended on a nostalgic note that the next generation might view all this as a myth of the Middle Ages: "No doubt the world will plume itself upon the uniformity of civilisation, but the traveller's last opportunity of romantic adventure will be no more." The photograph he chose, however, to illustrate this properly controlled discourse was a close-up of a staring, disheveled Macedonian brigand displaying two equally disheveled heads of either his foes or his friends.[46] Unlike the standard orientalist discourse, which resorts to metaphors of its object of study as female, the balkanist discourse is singularly male.

The one woman who excited Smith's imagination did so because of qualities ostensibly held for masculine in this period, despite his insistence that she was "feminine to the core." She was the Bulgarian Tsveta Boyova, born in a Macedonian village, who had graduated in medicine from the University of Sofia and, after having lost her husband, father, and two brothers in a Turkish raid, had offered her services as nurse and doctor to the Macedonian bands. Smith was enchanted to be served a three-course meal by a woman who, lacking enough silverware, washed it after each course:

> To a man who had almost forgotten what civilization meant, and who would have been prone, like his companions, to stare in dull amaze at a frock-coat, it was like an essence from the blue, to have coffee in the afternoon at five o'clock, served by a woman who knew Tolstoy, Gorki, Bebel, Carl [*sic!*] Marx and the leaders of Socialism, from A to Z, to whom Shakespeare was more than a name, and who had ideas on the drama and modern society, revolutionary, but interesting.[47]

Describing her as a sui generis Joan of Arc, Smith was evidently taken by the indefinable quality of Boyova: "I have never met a man or a woman who was her equal in pluck. There was a quality about her, indefinable in nature, that made her striking."[48] Yet, even in the rare exception of Smith, the mystery of the Balkans was incomplete. On arriving in Sofia in 1907, he found the city lighted by electricity, with trolley cars and telephones and well policed, a situation that might "dissatisfy the tourist who is looking for the picturesque." Yet, the disappointment was only superficial:

> Sofia has not been entirely civilized as to lose its Old-World charm, its spicy aroma of the East. The veneer of civilization is only skin-deep in some respects, and in others it has not made an appreciable difference. You feel, instinctively, as you step from the corridor train onto the platform of the low, clean, yellow station at Sofia, that Europe is behind you; you stand in the shadow of the Orient.[49]

It is, thus, not an innate characteristic of the Balkans that bestows on it the air of mystery but the reflected light of the Orient. One is tempted to coin a new Latin phrase: "Lux Balcanica est umbra Orientis." Apart from the above solitary example of romanticizing the Balkans, the images they evoked were for the greatest part prosaic. Durham, too, had approached the Balkans to "forget home miseries for a time," but from the outset she had not seen or expected from the Balkans more than "a happy hunting ground filled by picturesque and amusing people, in which to collect tales [and] sketch." Her favorite refrain was that the Balkans were an opéra bouffe written in blood.[50]

What practically all descriptions of the Balkans offered as a central characteristic was their transitionary status. The West and the Orient are usually presented as incompatible entities, antiworlds, but completed antiworlds. Said has described his own work as "based on the rethinking of what had for centuries been believed to be an unbridgeable chasm separating East from West."[51] The Balkans, on the other hand, have always evoked the image of a bridge or a crossroads. The bridge as a metaphor for the region has been so closely linked to the literary oeuvre of Ivo Andrić, that one tends to forget that its use both in outside descriptions, as well as in each of the Balkan literatures and everyday speech, borders on the banal. The Balkans have been compared to a bridge between East and West, between Europe and Asia. Writing about the Greeks, a British author at the beginning of the century summarized the status of the Balkans:

> A Greek says he is going to Europe when he is going to France and Italy. He calls Englishmen, Germans, or any other Western people who happen to visit or reside in Greece, Europeans in contradistinction to the Greeks. The occidentals in Greece do likewise. They are Europeans, and by implication, the Greeks are not. . . . The Greek is racially and geographically European, but he is not a Western [*sic*]. That is what he means by the term, and the signification is accepted by both Greek and foreigner. He is Oriental in a hundred ways, but his Orientalism is not Asiatic. He is the bridge between the East and West. . . .[52]

The Balkans are also a bridge between stages of growth, and this invokes labels such as semideveloped, semicolonial, semicivilized, semioriental. In a short passage, a veritable masterpiece in conveying the English feeling of forlornness and aversion for the Balkan backwaters, and in discreetly depicting the civilized straightforwardness of British diplomats who found semi-Orientals distasteful, Durham wrote in 1925:

> A Balkan legation is to an Englishman a spot which he hopes soon to quit for a more congenial atmosphere in another part of Europe. As for a Consul, he often found it wiser not to learn the local language, lest a knowledge of it should cause him to be kept for a lengthy period in some intolerable hole [. . .] To a Russian, on the other hand, a Balkan post was one of high importance; the atmosphere of semi-Oriental intrigue, distasteful to an Englishman, was the breath of his nostrils; nor did any Slavonic dialect present any difficulty to him.[53]

The issue of the Balkans' semicolonial, quasi-colonial, but clearly not purely colonial status deserves closer attention. Admittedly, the categories of colonialism and dominance or subordination can be treated essentially as synonyms. For W. E. B. Du Bois, the legalistic distinction between colonized and subordinate was ephemeral: "[I]n addition to the some seven hundred and fifty million of disfranchised colonial peoples there are more than half-billion persons in nations and groups who are quasi-colonials and in no sense form free and independent states." The designation "free states" was a fiction that disguised a reality of oppression and manipulation: "In the Balkans are 60,000,000 persons in the 'free states' of Hungary, Romania, Bulgaria, Yugoslavia, Albania, and Greece. They form in the mass an ignorant, poor, and sick people, over whom already Europe is planning 'spheres of influence'."[54]

It is this discourse that makes the notion of orientalism appealing to a number of Balkan intellectuals who hasten to apply it as a model inclusive of the Balkans. The issue of the legalistic distinction, however, should not be underestimated. It is not only a predisposition to historical specificity that makes me resistant to the conflation of historically defined, time-specific, and finite categories like colonialism and imperialism with broadly conceived and not historically circumscribed notions like power and subordination. For one, the formal difference is crucial in explaining why the Balkans have been left outside the sphere of discussion on orientalism and postcolonialism. But the real question is, even if included, whether the methodological contribution of subaltern and postcolonial studies (as developed for India and expanded and refined for Africa and Latin America) can be meaningfully applied to the Balkans. In a word, is it possible to successfully "provincialize Europe" when speaking about the Balkans, to use the jargon for epistemologically emancipating non-European societies? To me, this is impossible, since the Balkans are Europe, are part of Europe, although, admittedly, for the past several centuries its provincial part or periphery. In the case of the Balkans' European allegiance, the discrepancy is based on the different territorial span between the geographic, economic, political, and cultural Europe. But eurocentrism is not a banal ethnocentrism; it is "a specifically modern phenomenon, the roots of which go back only to the Renaissance, a phenomenon that did not flourish until the nineteenth century. In this sense, it constitutes one dimension of the culture and ideology of the modern capitalist world."[55]

Second, not to be ignored is the self-perception of being colonial or not. Despite howling Balkan conspiracy theories and the propensity to blame one or the other or all great powers for their fate, the sensibility of victimization is much less acute. There is always present the consciousness of a certain degree of autonomy. Even the nominal presence of political sovereignty has been important for the ones who have felt subordinate, dominated, or marginalized; therefore, the coinage or appropriation of this otherwise meaningless category "semicolonial." Meaningless as it is as a heuristic notion, it is indicative both of the perception and the self-perception of the Balkans insofar as it emphasizes their transitionary character.

Unlike orientalism, which is a discourse about an imputed opposition, balkanism is a discourse about an imputed ambiguity. As Mary Douglas has elegantly shown, objects or ideas that confuse or contradict cherished classifications provoke pollution behavior that condemns them, because "dirt is essentially disorder." These confusing or contradicting elements Douglas calls ambiguous, anomalous, or indefinable. Drawing on a general consensus that "all our impressions are schematically determined from the start," that "our interests are governed by a pattern-making tendency," she holds that "uncomfortable facts, which refuse to be fitted in, we find ourselves ignoring or distorting so that they do not disturb these established assumptions. By and large anything we take note of is pre-selected and organized in the very act of perceiving." Although Douglas recognizes the difference between anomaly (not fitting a given set or series) and ambiguity (inducing two interpretations), she concludes that there is no practical advantage in distinguishing between the two. Thus, ambiguity is treated as anomaly. Because of their indefinable character, persons or phenomena in transitional states, like in marginal ones, are considered dangerous, both being in danger themselves and emanating danger to others. In the face of facts and ideas that cannot be crammed in preexisting schemata, or which invite more than a single interpretation, one can either blind oneself to the inadequacy of concepts or seriously deal with the fact that some realities elude them.[56]

It is this exasperation before complexity that made William Miller exclaim at the end of a paragraph on an extraordinary medley of races and languages where "the Bulgarian and the Greek, the Albanian and the Serb, the Osmanli, the Spanish Jew and the Romanian, live side by side": "In short, the Balkan peninsula is, broadly speaking, the land of contradictions. Everything is the exact opposite of what it might reasonably be expected to be."[57] This in-betweenness of the Balkans, their transitionary character, could have made them simply an incomplete other; instead they are constructed not as other but as incomplete self. Enlarging and refining on Arnold van Gennep's groundbreaking concept of liminality, a number of scholars have introduced a distinction between liminality, marginality, and the lowermost. While liminality presupposes significant changes in the dominant self-image, marginality defines qualities "on the same plane as the dominant ego-image." Finally, the lowermost suggests "the shadow, the structurally despised alter-ego."[58] The reasons that the Balkans can be treated as an illustration of the lowermost case, as an incomplete self, are two: religion and race.

One of the versions of the East-West dichotomy played itself out in the opposition between Greek Orthodoxy and Catholicism. It is Catholicism and not Western Christianity in general that is part of the dichotomy, because it was the political and ideological rivalry between Rome and Constantinople that created a rift between the two creeds and attached to Orthodoxy the status of a schismatic, heretic deviation (and vice versa.) The Reformation made unsuccessful attempts to reach an understanding with the Orthodox church in a common fight against papal supremacy. The notion of a general Western Christianity as opposed to a putative Eastern Orthodox entity is not a theological construct but a relatively late cultural and recent political science category, as in Toynbee or Huntington, that appropriates religious images to legitimize and obfuscate the real nature of geopolitical rivalries and boundaries. In the Catholic discourse, there has been a strong ambiguity, and in some extreme cases one can encounter rhetoric where Turks and Greeks were lumped together, yet this was the flagrant exception. Serious attempts at reconciliation and common language between Orthodoxy and Catholicism have emanated precisely from the religious establishment. Orthodoxy, for all the enmity that it evoked among Catholics, was not seen as a transitionary faith to Islam; what was usually emphasized was the unbridgeable boundary between Christianity (even in its Orthodox variety) and the Muslim religion.

Said's orientalism is very distinctly identified with Islam. Skopetea, who has studied Balkan images at the end of Ottoman rule in a framework of Saidian orientalism, contends that there is no difference in the treatment of the Islamic and the Christian East, that there is no Christian monopoly in the Western tradition, and, accordingly, she defines the Balkans as "the west of the east."[59] It seems that Skopetea conflates two different Western attitudes and rhetorics that were grafted on each other: one of religion and the other of class. Whereas the treatment of Islam was based on an unambiguous attitude toward religious otherness (ranging from crusading rejection to enlightened agnostic acceptance), there was an ambiguous attitude toward the Ottoman polity that invited a very distinct class attitude of solidarity with the Muslim Ottoman rulers. This was in stark contrast to the poor and unpolished, but Christian, upstarts, who have been described in a discourse almost identical to the one used to depict the Western lower classes, a virtual parallel between the East End of London and the East End of Europe.

The racial component offers a more complex analysis. On the one hand, there exists a discourse that describes that Balkans as a racial mixture, as a bridge between races. From a pervasive but not explicit theme about the mongrel nature of the Balkans in travelers' accounts until the end of the nineteenth century, it adapted itself neatly to the dominant racial discourse of the twentieth century and resorted to overt racial slurs in the interwar period. On the other hand, despite the presence of the theme of racial ambiguity, and despite the important internal hierarchies, in the final analysis the Balkans are still treated as positioned on this side of the fundamental opposition: white versus colored, Indo-European versus the rest. This also comes to explain the preoccupation with the war in Yugoslavia in the face of more serious and bloody conflicts elsewhere on the globe. As shown by sociological studies on stigma, "difference is an essential part of the process of typification. Put most simply, differences are variations between or within types."[60] It is my thesis that while orientalism is dealing with a difference between (imputed) types, balkanism treats the differences within one type.

What I define as balkanism was formed gradually in the course of two centuries and crystallized in a specific discourse around the Balkan wars and World War I. In the next decades, it gained some additional features but these accretions were mostly a matter of detail, not of essence. In its broad outlines, it was and continues to be handed down almost unalterable, having undergone what Clifford aptly defines as "discursive hardening" and Said explains by introducing the category of "textual attitude," that is, the fallacy "of applying what one learns literally to reality."[61] Long before that, Nietzsche had given his own description of this process:

> The reputation, name, and appearance, the usual measure and weight of a thing, what it counts for—originally almost always wrong and arbitrary, . . .—all this grows from generation unto generation, merely because people believe in it, until it gradually grows to be part of the thing and turns into its very body. What at first was appearance becomes in the end, almost invariably, the essence and is effective as such.[62]

The balkanist discourse, rampant as it is, has not equally affected intellectual traditions or institutions. It is present primarily in journalistic and quasi-journalistic literary forms (travelogues, political essayism, and especially this unfortunate hybrid—academic journalism), which accounts for its popularity. These genres have been the most important channels and safeguards of balkanism as an ideal type. Speaking of racist attitudes, Roland Barthes remarked on how frozen collective representations and mentalities can be, kept stagnant by power, the press, and reigning values.[63] For the Third World, while the press continues to cling to normative views of civilization formed during the colonial era, anthropology and cultural criticism have questioned the consequences of such views. This has not happened for the Balkans, possibly because their noncolonial status has left them out of the sphere of interest of postcolonial critique and cultural criticism, and because Balkan, and in general European anthropology, has been somewhat marginal. Although dealing with facets of the academic discourse, I am extremely hesitant to go into generalizations. The problem of the academic study of the Balkans is a significant theme and deserves separate and profound investigation. I am not trying to avoid it but at this point my research is insufficient to commit myself to a more definite opinion. Tempting as it is to see academic study as partaking in the overall balkanist discourse, the relations between scholarly knowledge and ideology and propaganda are not so straightforward: "[I]t seems in the end that the two forms of discourse remain distinct, that the production of scientific knowledge moves along a line that only occasionally intersects with the production of popular mythology."[64] Still, it would be fair to maintain that academic research, although certainly not entirely immune from the affliction of balkanism, has by and large resisted its symptoms. This is not to say that a great number of the scholarly practitioners of Balkan studies in the West do not share privately a staggering number of prejudices; what it says is that, as a whole, the rules of scholarly discourse restrict the open articulation of these prejudices.

Balkanism evolved to a great extent independently from orientalism and, in certain aspects, against or despite it. One reason was geopolitical: the separate treatment, within the complex history of the Eastern question, of the Balkans as a strategic sphere distinct from the Near or Middle East. The absence of a colonial legacy (despite the often exploited analogies) is another significant difference. In the realm of ideas, balkanism evolved partly as a reaction to the disappointment of the West Europeans' "classical" expectations in the Balkans, but it was a disappointment within a paradigm that had already been set as separate from the oriental.[65] The Balkans' predominantly Christian character, moreover, fed for a long time the crusading potential of Christianity against Islam. Despite many attempts to depict its (Orthodox) Christianity as simply a subspecies of oriental despotism and thus as inherently non-European or non-Western, still the boundary between Islam and Christianity in general continued to be perceived as the principal one. Finally, the construction of an idiosyncratic Balkan self-identity, or rather of several Balkan self-identities, constitutes a significant distinction: they were invariably erected against an "oriental" other. This could be anything from a geographic neighbor and opponent (most often the Ottoman Empire and Turkey but also within the region itself as with the nesting of orientalisms in the former Yugoslavia) to the "orientalizing" of portions of one's own historical past (usually the Ottoman period and the Ottoman legacy).

The Balkans

Nomen

Jaques: I do not like her name.
Orlando: There was no thought of pleasing you
when she was christened.

> Shakespeare, "As You Like It"

The Naming of Cats is a difficult matter,
It isn't just one of your holiday games;
At first you may think I'm as mad as a hatter
When I tell you a cat must have
THREE DIFFERENT NAMES.

> T. S. Eliot, "The Naming of Cats"

As befits the obsession of present Western academic culture with language, the Balkan specter that haunts it is not a character but a name, a signifier. In a Ferdinand de Saussurean system of thought, the signifier is directly related to the signified, as both are elements of a unity. While insisting on their distinction, Ferdinand de Saussure emphasized the precarious balance between the two, the reassuring equilibrium and correspondence between propositions and reality. Poststructuralism introduced a hierarchy by conferring the dominant part to the signifier. For someone like Derrida, there can never occur a coincidence between word and thing or thought. Instead, signifiers and signified are continually detaching themselves from each other and are then reattached in new combinations.[1] Within this perspective, it is predictable that the signifier "Balkan" would be detached from its original and from subsequent signified(s) with which it enters into a relationship. In fact, this is a simultaneous process: at the same time that "Balkan" was being accepted and widely used as geographic signifier, it was already becoming saturated with a social and cultural meaning that expanded its signified far beyond its immediate and concrete meaning. At the same time that it encompassed and came to signify a complex historical phenomenon, some of the political aspects of this new signified were extrapolated and became, in turn, independently signified. That this is an ongoing process would be only a trivial conclusion within a Derridian vision. Indeed, it

might be interesting to approach "Balkan" as an exercise in polysemy, the technical
term used to describe "the way in which a particular signifier always has more than
one meaning, because 'meaning' is an effect of differences within a larger system"; the
utility of this notion is in its ability to show "how particular individuals and communities can actively create new meanings from signs and cultural products which come
from afar."[2] Against such background, it is essential to retrace the odysseys of consecutive attachments and reattachments of the signifier, in a word to perform an exercise
that in the nineteenth century would have been simply and clearly designated as
Begriffsgeschichte.

What, then, is the story of the name "Balkan"? In 1794, the British traveler John
Morritt, then freshly out of Cambridge, set off on a journey through the Levant. His
fervor for the "wrecks of ancient grandeur" led him from London and across Europe
to Constantinople, and from there to the sites of Troy, Mount Athos, and Athens.
On his way from Bucharest to Constantinople, he crossed the Balkan Mountains at
the Shipka Pass in Bulgaria and wrote in a letter to his sister: "We were approaching
classic ground. We slept at the foot of a mountain, which we crossed the next day,
which separates Bulgaria from Romania (the ancient Thrace), and which, though
now debased by the name of Bal.Kan, is no less a personage than the ancient
Haemus."[3] It is only natural that for one of the "Levant lunatics" and future prominent member of the Society of Dilettanti, the territories of the Ottoman Empire
were first and foremost "classic ground" and any reminder of the present was, to say
the least, mildly annoying and debasing the illustrious ancient tradition. Yet, later
accretions were a fact, no matter how displeasing, to be dealt with, and they were
duly recorded.

This was one of the very first times the mountain chain that divides Bulgaria from
east to west and runs parallel to the Danube was called the Balkans in the English-
language travel literature. Practically all British passersby before Morritt and many
after him had used only the ancient term Haemus (Aemus for the ancient Greeks and
Haemus for the Romans).[4] The ones who went beyond merely mentioning the name
accepted the ancient Greek descriptions that went unchallenged for nearly two millennia. Edward Brown, the medical doctor and traveler from Norwich, author of
popular and influential travels in 1669, maintained that Haemus continued to the
west, separating Serbia from Macedonia, and that, under different names, it stretched
between Pontus Euxinus (the Black Sea) and the Adriatic.[5]

Like the English, most European travelers before the nineteenth century preferred
to use the classical term Haemus, but they were earlier aware that this was not the only
designation of the mountain range. The earliest mention of the name Balkan known
to me comes from a fifteenth century memorandum of the Italian humanist writer
and diplomat Filippo Buonaccorsi Callimaco (Philippus Callimachus, 1437–1496).
Persecuted by Pope Paul II, Callimaco settled in Poland and became a close adviser
to the Polish king. He was the author of a history of the deeds of Wladyslav III
Warnenczyk, in which he left a short description of the Haemus, which he saw when
he visited the Ottoman capital on diplomatic missions. In his 1490 memorandum to
Pope Innocent VIII, Callimaco wrote that the local people used the name Balkan for
the mountain: "quem incolae Bolchanum vocant."[6]

In 1553, the future Habsburg emperor Ferdinand I sent a diplomatic mission to the Sublime Porte with the task to negotiate a truce with the Ottomans and secure recognition of Habsburg control over Hungary and Transylvania. The mission was entrusted to Anton Vrančić, bishop of Pecuj since 1549. A Dalmatian, Vrančić came from a notable Bosnian family that had fled the Ottoman conquest, and had been Transylvanian bishop under János Zápolyai before offering his services to the Habsburgs. An accomplished humanist, he was the author of numerous historical and geographical treatises. During his visit to Istanbul in 1553, Vrančić kept a diary of his travels between Vienna and Adrianople where he referred exclusively to *Haemus* and *Haemi montes*, and quoted as authorities ancient authors whom he found amazingly accurate. Although aware of Strabon's objection, Vrančić cited as plausible Polybius and other geographers who maintained that from the highest mountain peak one could observe the Black Sea, the Adriatic Sea, and the Danube River. Over a decade later, in 1567, Vrančić was sent on a second mission to the Porte to sign the peace treaty with the new sultan Selim II. He kept notes, later united and published during the nineteenth century: "Diarium legationis nomine Maximiliani II" and "Ratio itineris, quod est a Viena ad Constantinopolum." The second was a detailed itinerary, marking distances between settlements and interspersed by geographic and other comments, where Vrančić mentioned the Bulgarian Slavic name *Ztara Planina* (i.e., Stara Planina, Old Mountain) for Haemus. The Italian Marco Antonio Pigafetti, who travelled with Vrančić in 1567, also referred to *Stara planina* as the Bulgarian name of *Emo*.[7] In fact, Vrančić was the first traveler to give the Bulgarian name, no doubt because he understood some of the local vernacular, Croatian being his native tongue. *Stara Planina* is a name that rarely appeared among Western accounts, Gerard Cornelius Driesch (1718–1719) being one of the few exceptions.[8]

The German Salomon Schweigger passed through the Balkans in 1577 as priest in the diplomatic mission of Emperor Rudolf II to Sultan Murad II. He stayed for three years in the Ottoman capital and is best known for his efforts, alongside Stephan Gerlach, to bring about a rapprochement between the Lutherans and the Orthodox church, and even reach an alliance against the Pope. An alumnus of the University of Tübingen, he translated into Italian the short catechism of Luther, since many Christians of the Ottoman Empire understood Italian. After his return to Germany, he published a German translation of the Qur'an. Schweigger kept a journal of his travels in the 1570s, which was published in 1608. In it, he gave a detailed description of the Haemus, for which he employed the terms *Emum*, *Hemo*, and *Hemus*. He was the first traveler, after Callimaco, to communicate the Turkish name of the mountain, *Balkan*, thus documenting the spread of the name in the region. He was also the only traveler to mention a Bulgarian Slavic name (which he called Croatian), *Comonitza*, for the mountain:

> [Haemus] is 6,000 feet high, i.e. one and a half German miles (Pliny, bk.IV). In the histories one can read that King Philip of Macedonia, the father of the great Alexander, climbed the mountain Haemus in four days and descended in two, in order to see the countryside around the mountain. It was believed that from the peaks of this mountain one could see the river Danube, the Adriatic Sea, and also Italy and Germany, something which would be a great wonder, since the Vene-

tian or the Adriatic Sea is at more than 100 miles from the said mountain; Germany likewise is more than 100 miles afar. Haemus is known for the silver mines it once had, and the Italians therefore call it the Silver Mountain. The Turks call it Balkan, and the local population call it in the Croatian language Comonitza.[9]

Balkan was again used by Martin Grünberg in 1582, although he ascribed it to the Rhodopes.[10] Reinhold Lubenau, who in 1628 completed the manuscript of his travels between 1573 and 1587, apparently used Schweigger's information and mentioned both names in the forms *Balban* and *Komoniza*.[11] *Balkan* was used in 1608 by the Armenian traveler Simeon trir Lehatsi.[12] Among the French, the name was mentioned first, although erroneously, in the 1621 journal of the ambassador extraordinary Luois Deshayes de Cormanin: "This mountain, which separates Bulgaria from Romania [the medieval designation of ancient Thrace], is called by the Italians 'Chain of the world,' and by the Turks Dervent, the name given to all mountains, covered with woods, just as Balkan is a name for bare cliffs, i.e. what the ancients knew by the name of Haemus."[13] This was a solitary mention and elsewhere Deshayes used the ancient Haemus.

Throughout the eighteenth century, Haemus and Balkan were increasingly used side by side or interchangeably. Caiptain Schad in 1740 specified he was writing about "the Balkan, or the mountain Haemus" or "Haemus which the Ottomans call Balkan."[14] Ruggier Boscovich, a native of Dubrovnik and an eminent European scientist and scholar (whom Dame Rebecca West in a characteristic slip described as "a wild Slav version of the French encyclopaedists") crossed the mountains in 1762. As a Dalmatian, he recognized in Bulgarian a Slavic dialect, and preferred to use the designation Balkan although he was also aware that this was the ancient Haemus.[15] Baron François de Tott was consistent in using *Balkan* in the 1770s, while in the next decades Count D'Hauterive, Felix Beaujour, and François Pouqueville used both *Balkan* and *Haemus*.[16] The Armenians from the mechitharist congregation in the eighteenth century used almost exclusively *Balkan*, although they were aware also of the ancient name *Emos*. The famous twelve-volume "Geography of the Four Directions of the World" by Hugas Indzhekian and Stepanos Agonts described the Balkans as the mountain range crossing Bulgaria in the middle, and beginning at the border with Venice; it also supplied a name for one branch of the mountain not encountered among other travelers: Chenge.[17]

Both forms for the mountain continued to be used during the nineteenth century. In the Austrian cartographer Franz von Weiss's 1829 map of European Turkey, the mountain was designated as *Mons Haemus oder Veliki Balkan Gebirge*, while the branch between the Iskîr River and Pirot was indicated as *Stara planina*.[18] During the 1820s, Balkan became the preferred although not yet exclusive term alongside Haemus among British travelers, and A. W. Kinglake's *Eothen* used only "Balcan."[19] Among Russian travelers not so burdened by classical toponymy, Balkan was the preferred term for the mountain chain. In 1808, during the Russo-Turkish war, Captain Alexander Krasnokutskii was sent to Constantinople to negotiate with the grand vizier Mustafa Bayraktar. He crossed the mountain twice—at Sliven and through the Shipka Pass—and left an astonishing account of the beauty and majesty of *Balkanskiya gory*.[20]

The increasing preference at first affected only the name of the mountain. In 1827, Robert Walsh repeated the earlier erroneous perception that Haemus, the formidable mountain chain, stretched for over 500 miles, beginning at the Bay of Venice and reaching the Black Sea. Now this chain was called Balkan, which meant a difficult mountain. It is symptomatic that none of the travelers used Balkan as a common denomination of the peninsula. It was applied exclusively as a synonym for the mountain Haemus. The first to coin and use the term "Balkan Peninsula" (*Balkanhalbeiland*) was the German geographer August Zeune in his 1808 work "Goea." The first collective use of Balkan as a description of the whole peninsula by a British traveler was by Walsh in 1827, who mentioned that the bishops in this region were always Greeks, and used their own language as the liturgical language "in the Balkans," entirely in the southern parts and predominantly in the northern parts.[21]

The reason why Balkan became one of the most often used designations (alongside Southeastern Europe) has little to do with precise geography. In fact, for over two millennia geographers reproduced the dominant ancient Greek belief that the Haemus was a majestic mountain chain linking the Adriatic and the Black Sea, with a dominant position in the peninsula, serving as its northern border. The name was Thracian and was transmitted to the Greeks, like so much of Balkan toponymy, through the contacts between Greek colonists in the harbors of the Aegean and Black Seas and the Thracians inhabiting the immediate hinterland. It appeared among the Logographoi as "Aimon to oros." While Herodotus in the fifth century B.C. was the first to give some more detailed knowledge about the mountain range, his information was still obscure. During the next century, Theopomp of Chios reported that the peninsula was so narrow that from the highest mountain peak one could see both the Adriatic and the Black Seas. This story became known and reproduced among ancient writers after it appeared in Polybius, the second century B.C. geographer from Megalopolis. Polybius's text is reported only through fragments. As it appears in Strabon (63 B.C.– A.D. 26), it seemed as if Polybius's was an eyewitness account. In the work of Titus Livius, Strabon's contemporary, on the other hand, Polybius's text gives the story of King Philip climbing the mountain Haemus. This picturesque account, although often reproduced even in the modern period, was given little credence: already Strabon had successfully criticized it. Strabon himself stressed the significance of the mountain as a water divide, considering it, at the same time, the natural border between the Thracian–Hellenistic world and the barbarian lands along the Danube.

Among the Romans, the oldest preserved Latin geography of Pomponius Mela from the first decades of the common era, "De chorographia," reproduced the notion of the visibility of the two seas. Pliny reported the height of the mountain at 6,000 feet, and in Ptolemy it was mentioned as the frontier between the provinces of Thrace and Moesia. Ammianus Marcellinus, at the end of the fourth century, likened the mountain to the semicircle of a majestic natural theater that framed Thrace to the north. Not only did the notion of the Balkans as the northern mountain chain linking the Black Sea and the Adriatic persist during the Byzantine period, but Anna Comnena, the great Byzantine writer and princess, believed that, though interrupted by the Adriatic, it continued on the other shore further to the west. Most likely, it was from Anna Comnena that the Italian humanist Jobus Veratius acquired this notion, and in 1553 he spoke of the majestic "catena mundi" that stretched from the Pyrenees to the town of Mesembria on the Black Sea. All throughout the Renaissance and later, the geographies of ancient writers were edited and printed in numerous editions, and not only were their ideas uncritically replicated, they were consciously introduced and referred to as the greatest authority. Italian humanist geographers spoke of the "catena mundi" or "catena del mondo," the chain of the world, a notion involving the belief of the Balkan Mountains as part of a mountain chain that traversed all of Europe, and linked to it somewhere in Croatia. Although at the beginning of the eighteenth century the expanse of the Balkan Mountains was questioned (by Count Luigi Marsigli and the geographer Driesch), and correctly limited only as far as the Timok River, this could not overturn the dominant opinion.[22]

In 1808, August Zeune, the name giver of the peninsula, still stuck to this belief: "In the north this Balkan Peninsula is divided from the rest of Europe by the long mountain chain of the Balkans, or the former Albanus, Scardus, Haemus, which, to the northwest, joins the Alps in the small Istrian Peninsula, and to the east fades away into the Black Sea in two branches."[23] It was the erroneous belief of the Balkan Mountains as the northern frontier of the peninsula that inspired Zeune to name it Balkan, besides his desire to use a name analogous to the Appenine and Pyrenean (Iberian) Peninsulas.[24] At the same time, despite this grand error, already by the eighteenth century travelers were well and precisely acquainted with the concrete geography of the mountain, its main passes and peaks. In the 1830s, the French geologist and geographer Ami Boué authoritatively and definitively destroyed the widespread perception and correctly described the mountain, which ran for 555 kilometers from west to east (from the Timok Valley to the Black Sea), and whose breadth ranged from 20 to 60 kilometers. He also provided a detailed overview of the peninsula, calling it *La Turquie d'Europe*.[25]

Even as the name *Balkan* increasingly entered the vocabulary of observers and commentators, few were aware of its exact meaning. Morritt did not (and most likely could not) expound on the "demeaning" appellation of the ancient Haemus. The word *balkan* is linked to mountain: most Ottoman and Turkish dictionaries explain it as mountain or mountain range, some specify it as wooded mountain, some as a pass through thickly wooded and rocky mountains; *balkanlik* is described both as thickly wooded mountains or rugged zone.[26] Even today it is used in northwestern Turkey for "stony place".[27] According to Halil Inalcik, the Ottomans first used *balkan* in Rumeli in its general meaning of mountain with additional names or adjectives to specify the exact geography. Thus, Emine-Balkan were the easternmost slopes of the Balkan range descending into the Black Sea; Kodja-Balkan (the big mountain) was the main range; Küčük-Balkan (the small mountain) was the spur running north of Shumla (Shumen in Bulgaria); Ungurus Balkan (the Hungarian mountains) was the name for the Carpathians, and so on.[28] The combination Emine-Balkan is actually the literal Ottoman translation of "Haemus-mountain": from the Byzantine "Aimos," "Emmon," and "Emmona," the Ottomans derived their "Emine." Without any specification, the name was gradually applied to the Haemus of the ancient and medieval geographers. Thus, in a document from 1565 preserved in the Başbakanlik Arşivi,

Balkan is used as the name of the mountain where a new *derbentci* village was founded, to become the present day Bulgarian town of Tryavna.[29]

It has been widely accepted that "balkan" is a word and name that entered the peninsula with the arrival of the Ottoman Turks. Of the different etymologies, Inalcik has favored Eren's Persian-Turkish one, deriving the word from mud (*balk*) with the Turkish diminutive suffix *-an*. There has been no documented mention of the word from the pre-Ottoman era, despite the fact that Turkic or Turco-Iranian tribes had settled or were passing through the peninsula: the Bulgarians in the late seventh century who created the Bulgarian state, the Pechenegs, Uz, and Kumans between the eleventh and thirteenth centuries, the latter playing an important part in Hungarian, Bulgarian, and Romanian history. On the other hand, the term *Balkhan* exists as the name for two mountain ranges in the area east of the Caspian sea, heavily populated with Türkmen tribes from the eleventh century on.[30] This has given rise to the less popular hypothesis that the name might be pre-Ottoman (with a possible etymology derived from the Persian "Balā-Khāna," i.e., big, high, proud house), and brought to the peninsula in the eleventh and twelfth centuries by Kumans, Pechenegs, and other Turkic tribes, who were reminded of the Balkhan ranges and applied it to the Haemus.[31] Finally, there exists also the unscholarly assertion that the name is of proto-Bulgarian origin. This deserves mention simply because it is revived today and because it illustrates the important place that the notion has among the Bulgarians.[32]

At the time the ancient geographical error was established, Balkan had not yet become the dominant or exclusive designation. Only by the middle of the nineteenth century was it applied by more authors to the whole peninsula, while not even contending for primacy alongside the preferred appellations evoking its ancient or medieval past: "Hellenic," "Illyrian," "Dardanian," "Roman," "Byzantine," "Thracian." Until the Congress of Berlin in 1878, the most often used designations were deriva-tive from the presence of the Ottoman Empire in the peninsula, such as "European Turkey," "Turkey-in-Europe," "European Ottoman Empire," "European Levant," "Oriental Peninsula." Ethnic designations also began to be increasingly used: "Greek Peninsula," "Slavo-Greek peninsula," "South-Slavic Peninsula," and so on.[33] Within the region, too, Balkan was not the widespread geographical self-designation. For the Ottoman rulers this was "Rum-eli," literally "the land of the Romans," that is, of the Greeks, "Rumeli-i şâhâne" (Imperial Rumelia), "Avrupa-i Osmâni" (Ottoman Europe).

Still, it was too late to overthrow the name entirely. In the second half of the nineteenth century "Balkan Peninsula" or simply "Balkans" was affirming itself in place of "European Turkey." Felix Kanitz published his seminal "Donau-Bulgarien und der Balkan" in 1879, and if W. Tomaschek in 1887 was still insisting on writing about the *Hämus-Halbinsel*, this looked increasingly like a scholarly eccentricity.[34] Another author, the American minister plenipotentiary to the Ottoman Empire in the 1880s, Samuel Cox, distinguished between the two and writing about the numerous and majestic mountains of the empire mentioned "the Atlas and the Caucasus, . . . Pelian and Haemus, the Carpathian and Balkan ranges," but then geography has never been the Americans' strongest point.[35]

In 1893, and again in 1909, with the intention to rectify Zeune's mistake, and indicating the new and correct geographical knowledge of the Balkan mountains, the German geographer Theobald Fischer proposed that the peninsula should be named *Südosteuropa*. The term "Südosteuropäische Halbinsel" had been actually introduced in 1863 by the renowned Balkan specialist, scholar, and diplomat Johann Georg von Hahn, but nothing came of his initiative, although William Miller, most likely quite independently, used the two notions—Balkan peninsula and South-Eastern Europe—as synonyms. Miller also called the lands of the peninsula "the Near East," while clearly considering them an inextricable part of Europe despite being aware of the Balkan inhabitants' habit to refer to their own travel to the west as "going to Europe."[36] The American journalist Edward King in 1885 used the designation Balkan Peninsula but wrote mostly of "South-Eastern Europe," a name he employed alongside, but which he preferred, to Turkey-in-Europe.[37] As late as 1919, the Albanian Christo Dako used Near East as a synonym for the Balkans when he referred to "Albania to be the master Key to the near East; the coveted apple between Italy and Austria and between the other Balkan nations."[38]

By the turn of the century, Balkans began to be increasingly filled with a political connotation. So widespread was its use that in 1918 the Serbian geographer Jovan Cvijić, much as he was aware of the incorrect employment of the term, used it himself in his seminal work on the peninsula. After 1918, the term "Balkan Peninsula," under attack for some time because of its geographic inadequacy and its value-ridden nature, began to fade away but not disappear, notably in the German language literature. In 1929, the geographer Otto Maull reinforced the argument for "Southeastern Europe" as the adequate designation of the peninsula.[39] In the words of Mathias Bernath, *Südosteuropa* was to become the "neutral, non-political and non-ideological concept which, moreover, abolished the standing historical-political dichotomy between the Danubian monarchy and the Ottoman Balkans that had become irrelevant."[40] The 1930s and 1940s, however, witnessed the complete discrediting of this supposedly neutral term in its German usage. *Südosteuropa* became an important concept in the geopolitical views of the Nazis, and had its defined place in their world order as *Wirtschaftsraum Grossdeutschland Südost*, "the naturally determined economic and political completion" of the German Reich in the southeast.[41]

In the United States, too, the idea to substitute a compromised category (Balkan) for a neutral one (Southeastern Europe) had been taken up in the interwar period by a Bulgarian author in a book about the Balkan Union.[42] Its leitmotiv was the debalkanization of the Balkans, which was used to describe the movement for Balkan understanding at the time of the Balkan conferences in the 1930s. Both Theodor Geshkof and the American author of the foreword used Balkans and Southeastern Europe as synonyms but with the clear indication that "Balkans" and its derivative "balkanization" had become terms of reproach. It is ironic that this attempt to resort to an ostensibly neutral "Southeastern Europe" coincided with the period when its German counterpart "Südosteuropa" was disgraced by the Nazis. What it shows, among other things, is how much the different linguistic traditions of the putative West were developing independent of each other, not aware of the evolution of concepts in the separate discourses.

In 1936, delineating the program of the future Institute of Balkan Studies in Bucharest, Victor Papacostea wrote passionately that the ones whose beliefs had nourished the theater and music of ancient Greece and the thought of Plato, the ones among whom St. Paul had achieved his greatest victory of the spirit and had given Rome so many emperors and dignitaries, would never understand how their regions could be named with a Turkish word and after a relatively insignificant mountain, "such an unjust designation." Yet, Papacostea conceded that "despite our criticism and our reservations, the change in the name seems almost impossible." He reviewed the other possibilities for naming the peninsula and concluded that "the term Balkan peninsula will persist. After all, the term 'mountainous peninsula' corresponds to the geographic reality of this peninsula, the most mountainous of all European peninsulas."[43]

It was most likely the misuse of the term by the Nazis that rendered it undesirable in the immediate postwar period. Thus, the Yugoslav geographer Josip Roglić's appeal in 1950 to reintroduce the term Southeast European peninsula was in vain.[44] On the other hand, despite the fact that the term had been compromised, a number of German scholars continued to use it without any trace of the meaning it had acquired during the interwar period.[45] In the rest of Europe and the United States, Southeastern Europe and Balkan have been used, as a rule, interchangeably both before and after World War II, but with an obvious preference for the latter. In certain cases, one can discern a difference in the geographic scope but most often they are employed synonymously.[46]

The one differential interpretation of Southeastern Europe and the Balkans belongs to the German language literature and has to do with differences in the criteria for definition, but even there it is neither pervasive nor unanimous. The broadest interpretation of Southeastern Europe, put forward by Karl Kaser, professes to be based chiefly on a geographical approach, delineating its borders with the Carpathian Mountains in the north, the Black Sea in the east, the Aegean Sea in the south, and the Ionian and Adriatic Seas to the west. It thus encompasses Slovakia (but not the Czech lands, even before the separation of Czechoslovakia), Hungary, Romania, the former Yugoslavia, Albania, Bulgaria, Greece, and European Turkey. In this interpretation, Southeastern Europe can be approached as a comprehensive entity, of which the Balkans are only a subregion.[47] Defining Southeastern Europe as a unity, an object of world history "in the field of tension between Rome and Byzantium, the Habsburgs and the Ottomans, and between the hegemonic claims of the modern great powers in the East and in the West," Bernath included Hungary, Romania, Yugoslavia, Albania, Bulgaria, Greece, and European Turkey.[48] Most often, definitions of Southeastern Europe concern the treatment of Hungary. As a rule, Hungary is included in German surveys of Southeastern Europe but is omitted from the Balkans. Sometimes, although not too often and with qualifications, it is considered also as part of the Balkans. This is mostly the case when the two notions, Southeastern Europe and Balkans, are treated as synonyms. However rarely, this has been done often enough to produce strong reactions from the Hungarians who "resent being called Balkanites."[49] In certain cases Romania, too, has been excluded from treatments of the Balkans proper, and has been covered by the broader notion of Southeastern Europe.[50]

Thus, the concept Balkan has been treated as either synonymous to or narrower than Southeastern Europe. Most generally, the definition of Balkan has followed a set of geographic, political, historical, cultural, ethnic, religious, and economic criteria, and most often a combination of criteria. Although how geographers, historians, and others define the Balkans reflects a classificatory effort, it is briefly surveyed here for two reasons. First, the classificatory attempts of geographers and historians are still closely related to the immediate physical characteristics of the region and are, consequently, more removed from the subsequent decontextualization of the notion. Second, this is the proper place to state who is going to be treated as Balkan in this text, in a word to define my own parameters of the Balkans.

As a rule, geographers accept that the peninsula is well defined by seas to the east, south, and west, and concentrate their disputes over the northern and northwestern border. This is where historical and cultural criteria enter their discourse, although it is often masked by professed geographical considerations. According to Cvijić, the Danube and Sava Rivers should be considered the northern borders of the Balkan peninsula. This effectively put Romania outside his magisterial if controversial survey. On the other hand, Cvijić made an exception when he discussed the South Slavs, and included political and anthropological criteria so that Croats and Slovenes were part of what he called Balkan civilization.[51]

George Hoffman, on the other hand, who spoke synonymously of "the Balkan, or Southeast European, Peninsula," employed a mixture of criteria to come up with an essentially geopolitical interpretation that reflected the cold-war period when his account was written. He defined as explicitly Balkan only three countries: Albania, Bulgaria, and Yugoslavia. Hoffman recognized that Greece and Romania (especially Wallachia and Moldavia) had to be included in a discussion of the "Balkan core," but he did not survey them. In the case of Romania, although allowing for the Danube to be only a symbolic border, he accepted it as a sufficient reason for excluding the country. In the case of Greece, he posited a highly problematic and mechanistic opposition of Northern Greece to the areas south of the Vlorë–Thessaloniki line. According to Hoffman, Greece was a Mediterranean country, and only its parts in Thrace and Macedonia could be included conditionally to the Balkan core. Hungary, while deeply affected by Balkans events, had more important ties to Central Europe; "in addition, its people have traditionally considered themselves western in their attitudes and greatly superior to the Slavic people of the Balkans." That Slovenes and Croats shared the same sentiment was insufficient for Hoffman to even mention their claims: they were included in the core.[52]

The standard approach of geographers distinguishes between a *stricto sensu* physico geographical definition, and one employed for more practical purposes. The first accepts as the undisputed eastern, southern, and western borders the Black Sea, the Sea of Marmara, the Aegean, Mediterranean, Ionian, and Adriatic Seas. The northern border is most often considered to begin at the mouth of the river Idria in the Gulf of Trieste, following the southeast foothills of the Julian Alps, and coinciding with the Sava and the Danube Rivers.[53] Accordingly, some geographers treat as Balkan, besides Albania, Bulgaria, Greece, and all countries of the former Yugoslavia, only the Dobrudzha part of Romania and the European part of Turkey. Others, well aware that the political-geographic and physical-geographic boundaries do not coincide, tend to include all of Romania (sometimes even Moldova), but Turkey is excluded.[54]

This latter, essentially political, approach has been favored by the majority of historians who add historical and cultural considerations. They cover, as a rule, the histories of Greece, Bulgaria, Albania, the former Yugoslavia, and Romania. Most often, the former Slavic territories of the Habsburg domain (Slovenia and Croatia) are surveyed, although there are some exceptions. Likewise, a précis of Ottoman history is usually included, but not the history of modern Turkey. There exist also narrower definitions: Fritz Viljavec, although seeing in the Balkans a political unity with common cultural morphological characteristics formed during the periods of the Byzantine and the Ottoman Empires, effectively excluded from his treatment Romania and Greece, which had developed a distinct cultural physiognomy.[55] On the other hand, one can encounter also broader treatments of the Balkans that include all of the former Yugoslav republics, Albania, Greece, Bulgaria, Romania, Turkey, and Cyprus.[56] Immediately after the Balkan wars and on the eve of World War I, Tomáš Masaryk made an interesting distinction in a paper he read in Munich about Austrian policy in the Balkans. He maintained that until the first Balkan war, the Balkans were not considered to cover Romania, seldomly included Greece, and even Bosnia, Hercegovina, and Dalmatia were often excluded. After the second Balkan war, however, the notion Balkan included the whole peninsula with Romania and Greece.[57]

With all due refinements that some regions are more Balkan than others (in an epistemological, not moral sense), this book covers as Balkan Albanians, Bulgarians, Greeks, Romanians, and most of the former Yugoslavs. Slovenes, *pace* Cvijić, are not included, but Croats are, insofar as parts of Croat-populated territories were under Ottoman rule for considerable lengths of time. Vassal territories, such as Dubrovnik, although only nominally Ottoman, exerted such an important influence on the Balkan Peninsula that their history cannot be severed from the Balkans. With some qualification, Turks are also considered insofar as they are partly geographically in the Balkans and most prominently shared in the Ottoman legacy and, in fact, dominated the Ottoman experience.

The use of Balkan as an ascriptive category in different languages allows some conclusions about the relative importance of the concept. In the main European languages that have been decisive in forming a "hardened" Balkanist discourse (above all English and German, and to a lesser extent French), or in the ones whose interest in the Balkans has been prominent (Russian and Italian), the noun appears only in one form (either singular or plural). The one exception is French where it is used in both: *le Balkan, les Balkans.* In German, *der Balkan* designates both the mountain range and the Balkan Peninsula. It appears also in two adjectival forms: as a qualifier in compound nouns (e.g., "die Balkanländer," "die Balkanhalbinsel," "der Balkanpakt," "Balkansprachen," and so on), and in the adjective "balkanisch," which can have a pejorative or neutral connotation. Both English and Russian use only the plural form (*Balkans, Balkany*) as a name for the peninsula and its political formations. In English, *Balkan* in its singular form is employed only as an adjective, used both with a neutral (alongside the much rarer *Balkanic* or *balcanoid*) and a disparaging meaning. In Russian, both the noun and the adjective *balkanskii* have an exclusively neutral sense. Italian employs the plural form, *Balcania,* to designate the region; its adjective, *Balcano,* is mostly neutral but can acquire a negative connotation. In

French, the singular noun, *le Balkan*, is used for the mountain range; the plural, *les Balkans*, as a name for the peninsula. There is also the neutral adjective "balkanique," although it can occasionally become a pejorative.

In the Balkan languages themselves, the use of the name is varied. To begin with Turkish, which brought the word into the peninsula, it exists today in two nounal forms: as a neologism, a personal noun in the plural, "Balkanlar," to designate the states of the Balkan Peninsula; second, as an archaic common noun, "balkan," meaning mountain, but with a rare and regional usage. It is employed also as an adjective, as in "Balkan yarım adası" (the Balkan Peninsula). The name has a neutral meaning and is not used as a pejorative. Greek and Romanian have only the plural noun: "ta Valkania" and "Balcani" to designate the states of the peninsula; the respective adjectives are "valkanikos," like in "valkanikii laoi" (the Balkan nations) and "balcanic." In Serbo-Croatian and Albanian, on the other hand, the noun appears only in the singular: "Balkan" and "Ballkan" as names for the region, with accompanying adjectives "balkanski" and "Ballkanit." In Albanian, the name as a rule does not have a derogative meaning. In Greek, Romanian, and Serbo-Croatian, both noun and adjective are used in a neutral sense and as pejoratives, standing for uncultivated, backward, disorderly, and so forth. Serbo-Croatian has also the derivative noun used in everyday speech as a self-criticism when one would resignedly acknowledge one's Balkan belongings: "Balkanci smo."

Bulgarian has three nounal forms for Balkan. As a common noun, "balkan" can be used as a synonym for mountain mostly in the vernacular and in some dialects, but much more often than it is in Turkish. The singular personal noun with a definite article—"Balkanît"—is the other widespread name for the mountain range alongside "Stara Planina." As personal noun in the plural—"Balkani"—it is employed to designate the Balkan region. While "balkanets" (pl."balkantsi") can have a pejorative connotation, the derivative "balkandzhiya" (female "balkandzhiika") indicates someone who possess a special ethos: independence, pride, courage, honor. In all languages, with two exceptions, Balkan is used with an emotional ingredient varying from neutral to derogative. The first exception is Turkish where Balkan does not have the pejorative component; the second is Bulgarian, which has all the range from negative through neutral to positive.

The most important word and notion deriving from Balkan is "balkanization." By the end of the nineteenth century, Balkans began to be increasingly used with a political connotation, rather than in a purely geographical sense, to designate the states that had emerged out of the Ottoman Empire: Greece, Serbia, Montenegro, Romania, and Bulgaria. There was hardly a trace of disparagement at that time. It is symptomatic that the word "balkanization," which is most often used to denote the process of nationalist fragmentation of former geographic and political units into new and problematically viable small states, was not created in the course of the 100 years when the Balkan nations gradually seceded from the Ottoman Empire. When the term was coined, at the end of World War I, only one Balkan nation, Albania, was added to the already existing Balkan map; all others had been nineteenth-century formations. The great proliferation of small states as a result of the Great War was triggered by the disintegration of the Habsburg and Romanov Empires and the emergence of Poland, Austria, Hungary, Czechoslovakia, Latvia, Estonia, and Lithuania.

To this post-World War I legacy should be added Yugoslavia, whose creation was, technically speaking, the reverse of balkanization. The falling apart of the Austro-Hungarian and Russian Empires resembled the previous disintegration of the Ottoman Empire and the term "balkanization" was employed as a comparison. It was not applied, of course, to denote that the Balkan nations had been a sort of political vanguard in the denouement of empires that Central and Eastern Europe were emulating: by that time, or more correctly at that time, the Balkans had acquired a thoroughly negative connotation.

Thus, while Eric Hobsbawm was right in equating balkanization with *Kleinstaaterei*, he wrongly attributed it to the disintegration of the Ottoman Empire: "the word *Kleinstaaterei* (the system of mini-states) was deliberately derogatory. It was what German nationalists were against. The word 'Balkanization', derived from the division of the territories formerly in the Turkish empire into various small independent states, still retains its negative connotation. Both terms belonged to the vocabulary of political insults."[58] Not only German nationalists were opposing ministates; liberal political thought shared their disdain. Likewise, the aversion of nineteenth-century socialists against the "Völkerabfälle" in the Balkans can be explained not only by their antipeasant bias but also in terms of their derision of "Kleinstaaterei."[59]

Nor was Hobsbawm alone in wrongly dating "balkanization." Many contemporary dictionaries and encyclopedias, misled by its etymology, have made the same anachronistic mistake: the verb "se balkaniser" denotes the process of "nationalist fragmentation" of former geographic and political units into new small states "like the Balkans after the First World War," despite the fact that all Balkan states, except Albania, had existed from several decades to a century before World War I; "balkanisieren" is the process of state fragmentation and disorderly political relations "as the Balkans during the Balkan wars 1912/13," and "Balkanisierung" is a political term for unjustified fragmentation with accompanying political instability; "balkanize" means "to break up into small, mutually hostile political units, as the Balkans after World War I."[60] The *Oxford English Dictionary* at least stretched the time frame back but still attributed the employment of the term to the Balkans. Only Norman J. G. Pounds was careful enough to word it as generally as possible: "The term balkanization has been used to refer to the breaking up of a geographic area into small and often hostile units."[61] The Italian modern dictionary did not even evoke the meaning of state fragmentation but explained it entirely as a synonym for despotism, revolutions, counterrevolutions, guerrilla warfare, and assassinations, "frequently found in the Balkans countries (and elsewhere)."[62]

The expression "balkanization" appeared in the aftermath of World War I: the first entry for the term in the *New York Times* falls on 20 December 1918. Under the title "Rathenau, Head of Great Industry, Predicts the 'Balkanization of Europe,'" the paper published an interview with the famous head of the German Electrical Company AEG (Allgemeine Elektricitäts-Gesellschaft). In the next four years before his assassination in 1922, Walther Rathenau, a leading proponent of the idea for a Central European economic union, was the spokesman for a solution to the reparations problem and was instrumental in the signing of the Treaty of Rapallo. Already in 1918, he had begun actively campaigning against the impending harsh terms of the peace treaty:

Germany is ruined for generations to come. It is the greatest calamity that has happened in any country in 2,000 years. . . . Black ruin will face us, and there will be
a great tide of emigration probably to South America and the Far East and certainly
to Russia. It will be most dreadful, and the result will be the Balkanization of Europe. The disappearance of Germany from a position of importance will be the
most dangerous fact in history. Sooner or later the Eastern powers will press on the
Western civilization.[63]

"Balkanization" was used by Rathenau to convey an expectation of nearly apocalyptic devastation. His statement did not have any concrete meaning for "balkanization" except to imply that only a strong and powerful Germany could be the counterbalance to this dreadful prospect. It was used, however, as an effective specter to wave
in the face of the Western allies, playing on the fear of an imminent clash between
East and West. What is most significant, it was clearly used as something widely
recognizable as menacing. Apart from this early newspaper mention of 1918, "balkanization" entered the political vocabulary after the system of treaties following
World War I sealed the new divisions of Europe. The *Nineteenth Century* reported in
1920 that France had accused Great Britain of "pursuing a policy aimed at the
Balkanisation of the Baltic provinces." *Public Opinion* in the same year lamented
that "In this unhappy Balkanised world . . . every state is at issue with its neighbours."
S. Graham's *Europe-Whither Bound* described how Hungary in 1921 mourned a large
stretch of its territory being balkanized. In 1922, Arnold Toynbee in *The Western Question in Greece & Turkey* gave his definition of balkanization: "The word . . . was coined
by German socialists to describe what was done to the western fringe of the Russian
Empire by the Peace of Brest-Litovsk."[64]

Balkanization's first extensive treatment came in 1921, when the European correspondent of the *Chicago Daily News*, Paul Scott Mowrer, published "a frankly
journalistic book": "In order that whatever of value it contains might be placed at
the disposition of the public without more delay, I have had to sacrifice the satisfac-
tions of slow composition and conscientious revision, and write over-hastily."
Mowrer occupied himself with several countries—Austria, Hungary, Bulgaria,
Czechoslovakia, Poland, Romania, Yugoslavia, and Greece—whose population he
characterized as "an inextricable medley of disparate races whose identity has been
fully preserved down through the centuries"; this was the region that "has now been
'Balkanized'." He specified what he meant by "balkanization": "the creation, in a
region of hopelessly mixed races, of a medley of small states with more or less backward populations, economically and financially weak, covetous, intriguing, afraid,
a continual prey to the machinations of the great powers, and to the violent
promptings of their own passions."[65] The element of foreign interference in the
affairs of small countries has been so pervasive as to motivate a later writer to define
"balkanization in the strict sense of the word [as] the constant interference of foreign powers (Russia, Austria-Hungary, Germany, France and Great Britain) aimed
at preserving or maintaining their spheres of interest."[66] "Balkanization" thus entered the lexicon of journalists and politicians at the end of World War I when the
disintegration of the Habsburg and Romanov Empires into a proliferation of small
states reminded them of the secession of the Balkan countries from the Ottoman
polity that had begun much earlier.

A second round in the use of "balkanization" emerged with the beginning of the decolonization process after World War II.[67] In a splendid aside in "Color and Democracy," Du Bois showed how the notion of "balkanization" was being used to perpetuate a sense of disgrace and dishonor among the luckless people of the earth, while rationalizing the practice of the dominant western powers to keep smaller countries within their sphere of influence: "The free nations tend to sink into 'spheres of influence' and investment centers, and then often succumb into disfranchised colonies. All this has been rationalized by universal sneering at small nations, at 'Balkanization' and helpless Haitis, until the majority of the world's people have become ashamed of themselves."[68] With the secession of Black Africa from the French Community, "balkanisation" entered widely the French political vocabulary, to designate the frustrating problems facing the eight independent African states (called "entities without reality") carved out of the former *Afrique occidentale française* after 1960.[69] It was also employed by the English press: in 1960 *The Economist* wrote that "[t]he African leaders owe it to themselves . . . to grasp what there is in the majority report for them before they opt for balkanisation"; *The Listener* concurred in 1962: "There are all the makings of a 'Balkan situation' in West Africa."[70]

At about that time, "balkanization" began to be increasingly detached from the context of international relations. An Austrian, Alexander Vodopivec, described his dissatisfaction with Austrian institutions in the mid-1960s in a book on "The Balkanization of Austria": "Balkan—this was once a synonym for unreliability, lethargy, corruption, irresponsibility, mismanagement, blurring of the competencies and borders in the order of law and much else. The term was initially limited to the southeast European states. An annoying development has taken it outside its geographical borders." A West German journalist, Klaus Harpprecht, was also exacerbated by what he called "the muddling and throttling" of the institutions in his country in the mid-1960s that he characterized as "charmless balkanization": "If someone encounters the Bundesrepublik after a long absence, in a couple of weeks he would ask in a bleak moment whether the center of Europe has not become the Balkans without the symptoms of charm, a Bulgaria without garlic, a Romania without Bucharest, music, Gypsies and Swabians."[71]

Still, even in a different context, the term was not entirely divorced from its geographic origins. This has happened increasingly during the past decade, especially on this side of the Atlantic, where the reference to "balkanization" has become entirely detached from the Balkans and is simply paradigmatically related to a variety of problems; the relation of "balkanization" to the Balkans has become what the smile of the Cheshire cat is to the cat. While a significant part of the American reading public would find it difficult to demonstrate even a remote geographical competence on the Balkans, it clearly understands the allusion to balkanization as the antithesis to the melting pot ideal, when Americans are urged "to discard social policies that encourage Balkanization of our society."[72] In a recent review Richard Grant wrote about the chasm between what C. P. Snow called the Two Cultures and James Joyce described in his embodiments of the scientific and artistic temperaments—Leopold Bloom and Stephen Dedalus. While demonstrating the difficulty of making the stretch from one to the other "in our increasingly Balkanized society," Grant gave his readers detailed explanations about Snow and Joyce while apparently assuming that they were quite at home with the notion of a "balkanized society."[73] Even John Steinbeck, searching for America in his "Travels with Charlie," complained that his country was balkanized: "The separateness of states, which has been bitterly called Balkanization, creates many problems. Rarely do two states have the same gasoline tax."[74] The *New York Times*, in a typical move of journalistic Americana, announced a contest for defining the post-post-cold war era: "Are we already in the Age of Global Communication? Of Balkanization? Of Religious War? Of Social Austerity? . . . The main event of our age, its consequences as yet ungrasped, could be the carnage in the Balkans, the rise of Islamic fundamentalism or the unraveling of European unity."[75] Patrick Glynn of the American Enterprise Institute had already announced that ours was the "Age of Balkanization" and that "the ferocious war in the Balkans is but one manifestation of a reemergent barbarism apparent in many corners of the earth." Here the disengagement of "balkanization" from the Balkans is so complete that one can feel the specter of an abstract "balkanization" revisiting the Balkans.[76]

The term has been used in the world of academia by exponents of different and often opposing political views: multiculturalism has been equated with balkanization, it is the name for excessive specialization, a metaphor for postmodernism and postcommunism.[77] Harold Bloom introduced "balkanization" to mourn everything he detested in his discipline: the proliferation of the ideologies of gender and various sexual persuasions, multiculturalism unlimited, the clones of Gallic-Germanic theory: "After a lifetime spent in teaching literature I have very little confidence that literary education will survive its current malaise. . . . We are destroying all intellectual and aesthetic standards in the humanities and social sciences, in the name of social justice. . . . The Balkanization of literary studies is irreversible."[78] Here balkanization is not simply parcelization, the creation of small entities at war with each other; it becomes synonymous with dehumanization, deaesthetization, destruction of civilization. Had Bloom not dismissed so summarily *any* radical critique, he might have agreed with the opinion that "to mistake fragmentation in one realm [the academic] with fragmentation in the other [the political] ignores the possibility that ideological fragmentation may represent not the dissolution of power but its further consolidation."[79] On the left, too, Balkan has become a welcome and easy metaphor: "Every intelligence agency is its own Balkan country, a geography of impasse, capable of believing anything, full of historical grudges against Turkey and its own siblings, playing deadly cold war games, dangerous to civilization. But then, so is every terrorist sect a Balkan country and secret service, self-referential and self-infatuated."[80]

Why, in the face of such richness of notions, words, sounds, is "Balkan" snatched from its ontological base and recreated as an abstract demon? Why has it been turned into a linguistic weed? This rhetorical question is built on the belief that Balkan ontology is not coincidental with the notion that emanates from the use of the adjective "Balkan" and the verb "balkanize" in today's political and cultural vocabulary. On the other hand, the complete decontextualization of the term and its reverse application have followed a fairly simple pair of syllogistic devices. The first is of an extrapolative nature: the Balkans as reality have acquired a reputation that is far from laudatory (quite apart from questions of how deserved or adequate this reputation is); there exist a multitude of undesirable and unsavory phenomena that resemble patterns from Balkan realities or most often from the constructed image of the Balkans; ergo, we can name these phenomena Balkan. The second syllogistic pattern is essentially interpolative: "Balkan" is a harmful attribute; there exists somewhere a little or insufficiently known reality designated as Balkan; this reality must correspond to the loaded designation, thus projecting back to it the autonomous workings of the signifier.

In many respects "Balkan" is a *nomen nudum,* the taxonomical term used to denote a name "which has no standing because it was introduced without publication of the full description demanded by the rules governing botanical and zoological nomenclature." True, the name is used nowadays within a cultural and political nomenclature, but the problem is that it was and is continually used also to denote a concrete geographical and historical reality with its flora and fauna, thus conforming to the rules of the botanical and zoological nomenclature. According to taxonomical rules, it is permissible to label a new species (in this case the abstract cultural demon) with a name that already exists as a *nomen nudum,* one that has no standing because it never has been validated by a description. This is, however, most distinctly not the case with "Balkan." One would wish, unrealistically, that the users of *Balkan* as a derogation would implement Heidegger's device to cross out *Being* while leaving both the word and its superinscribed deletion stand, because the word is inadequate yet necessary. At least the sign of deletion would caution against the metaphorical utilization of the term.

"Balkans" as Self-designation

I will not blot out his name out of the book of life.

Revelation, 3:5

Given the inglorious coverage the Balkans have had in the West, what is the experience of being called Balkan? How do the ones defined as belonging geographically or historically to the Balkans deal with the name? Do they consider themselves Balkan and what is meant by this? Several qualifications are in order. This is not a historical survey of the process of creating self-identities and self-designation. Rather, it aims at conveying an idea of present images and emotions as they are articulated in the region. As such, it has some of the advantages and all the drawbacks of an impressionistic painting. Since it deals with problems of present-day identification in reference to the Balkans, it would seem at first glance that the place of this account should follow chronologically the exploration of the evolution of the term "Balkan." Yet, I am doing it in a conscious breach of seeming methodological consistency for the sake of making a methodological point: introducing already at this point the most important component in this analysis of naming, classification, interpretation, and evaluation—the people of the Balkans. I want to make the reader cognizant of the dominant self-perceptions in the Balkans, so that proceeding through the subsequent chapters would be informed by a conscious awareness of this fact.

It is virtually axiomatic that, by and large, a negative self-perception hovers over the Balkans next to a strongly disapproving and disparaging outside perception. I am acutely aware that resorting to a notion like "the Balkan people" and how they think of themselves smacks distinctly of "national character," a category that I oppose passionately on both methodological and moral grounds. Therefore, lest I commit the same fallacy of essentialism I claim to oppose, I would like to introduce the stipulation that the phrase "how the Balkans think of themselves" should be understood to mean how the ones among the educated elites of the Balkan nations who are charged with or are at least conscious of their ethnic, national, religious, local, and a variety of other multiple identities define (i.e., reject, accept, are ambiguous about, or indifferent to) their link to a putative Balkan identity. As Erving Goffman, commenting on stigma as a basis for self-conception, remarked: "representatives are not representative, for representation can hardly come from those who give no attention to their stigma, or who are relatively unlettered."[1]

Where does this self-perception originate: is it an independent product of self-reflection or has it been prompted and shaped exclusively by the outside view? Although they have been passive objects in the shaping of their image from without (not in the sense that their frantic activities have not contributed to its formation but that they have had no active participation in the articulation and spread of the discourse), the Balkan peoples have not been the passive recipients of label and libel. This book emphasizes the extent to which the outside perception of the Balkans has been internalized in the region itself. At the same time, it is possible to demonstrate that the critical self-reflection was, at least initially, a relatively independent component provoked by comparison and informed by expectations, values, and ideals shared by both external and internal observers, but by means of common cultural sources, not through direct exchange. Therefore, many of the critical self-evaluations predated the hardening of the Balkanist discourse in the second decade of the twentieth century.

The most popular literary image linked with the name "Balkan" is Bay Ganyo Balkanski, the immortal literary hero of the Bulgarian writer Aleko Konstantinov (known simply as Aleko) (1863–1897). The short stories about Bay Ganyo began to appear in the literary magazine *Misîl* in 1894 as feuilletons and were published in 1895 as a collection, subtitled "incredible stories about a contemporary Bulgarian." Bay Ganyo, the counterpart of Tartarin and Schwejk in French or Czech literature, and the derivative noun "bayganyovshtina" (Bay Ganyo-ness) has become the most popular byword created by Bulgarian literature, standing for boorishness, crudeness, grossness. It would not be exaggerated to assert that this is the one literary name and the book that every single Bulgarian knows and has read. To a great extent, the history of Bulgarian literary criticism has evolved around this literary hero because his interpretation has been rightly perceived as equivalent to national self-analysis. The great divide that has passionately polarized Bulgarian literary criticism in the course of a whole century is the ethnic versus the social approach, that is, whether Bay Ganyo should be analyzed as a biological, racial, national, cultural, civilizational type or as a distinctive sociohistorical type without an indispensable ethnic/national specificity, belonging to a definite transitional period in the development of backward societies and having a concrete class profile.

The best contemporary interpreter of Bay Ganyo Balkanski, Svetlozar Igov, contextualized him in a Balkan setting and introduced the notion of *Homo balkanicus*. Aleko articulated the profound disillusionment of "the first post-liberation generation of intellectuals for whom the clash between the lofty ideals of the revival period and the rapid bourgeois corruption of 'free' Bulgaria" reverberated particularly painfully. He followed a cherished model in the moralistic European literature of the Enlightenment—the savage among civilized—that was employed to criticize the hypocrisy of European mores; only Aleko transformed it to convey his scathing critique of the Balkan parvenu among Europeans. There is also an important additional nuance. While Bay Ganyo is simply a comic primitive buffoon in the first part of the book that follows his exploits in Europe, he becomes the authentic and dangerous savage only on his return, among his own, where he is the nouveau riche and newly hatched corrupt politician; "at the beginning he is the funny oddball of the Balkan province, by the end he is a political force, in complete control of the situation, a triumphant social vehemence, the man-mob."[2]

There is no doubt that by creating Bay Ganyo, Aleko was targeting vulgarity and anticulture in opposition to a notion of civilized Europe. He was exposing a phenomenon that he loathed: the superficial mimicry of civilized behavior without the genuine embrace of real values. Bay Ganyo, who sets on his voyage to the West in his peasant costume, returns in European attire, but the disharmony between his appearance and his character is even more comic. William Miller, writing at the same time that Bay Ganyo was created, commented on this issue: "This question of costume is, in the Near East, of more than merely artistic interest; for I have observed that the Oriental is apt to deteriorate morally when he assumes Western garb. . . . The native of the Balkans seems not infrequently to 'put off' his primitive faith and his simple ideas when he puts on a black coat. The frock-coated Balkan politician is not by any means the same ingenious person as the peasant, who is of the same stock as himself, and the silk hat too often converts an unsophisticated son of the soil into a very poor imitation of a Parisian man-of-the-world."[3]

Compare this lengthy quote with its implicit romanticizing of the simple peasant to the economy of Aleko's famous opening of his book: "They helped Bay Ganyo take off the Turkish cloak, he slipped on a Belgian mantle, and everybody decided Bay Ganyo was already a complete European."[4] The central element in Bay Ganyo's stories is that this was a critique not from the outside, from a distant and, as it were, foreign European point of view, but from within, from the point of view of a Bulgarian European. I am stressing "Bulgarian European," and not "Europeanized Bulgarian," because Aleko's Europeanness came not as a result of a direct sojourn in any Western European country (his education was entirely in Bulgarian and Russian institutions) but from partaking in a shared European culture that did not have national labels and was the common nurture of any educated and cultivated person on the continent.

One of the first commentators of Bay Ganyo, Ivan Shishmanov, indicated that to understand Bay Ganyo, one should begin with Aleko: "Take the opposite of Bay Ganyo, and you get Aleko."[5] In the view of Shishmanov, a historian, literary critic, and prominent cultural and educational figure in Bulgaria at the turn of the century, Bay Ganyo's polar opposite was not an outsider but a product of the same soil: the author and his character were linked in an internal dichotomy. The composition of the book itself prompts such conclusion: the stories are told by a merry company of young educated men, each of whom shares an episode of his encounters with Bay Ganyo. In the case of the Bulgarian compatriots who expose Bay Ganyo, there is no sweet romantic reminiscing about a peasant arcadia. It is the story of a Bulgarian, told by other Bulgarians.[6] Thus, the standard against which Bay Ganyo is measured, although called European, is not an outside one: it is the standard held by a group of his own countrymen. Rather than explaining this simply in terms of Westernized or Europeanized elites who approach their own reality with alienated eyes and disdain as a result of having internalized the hegemonic discourse of the center, one may consider it in the light of Edward Shils's treatment of center and periphery. In his classic essay, he argued that center is not merely a spatial location but a central zone of symbols, values, and beliefs that govern society:

> The existence of a central value system rests, in a fundamental way, on the need which human beings have for incorporating into something which transcends and

transfigures their concrete individual existence. They have a need to be in contact with symbols of an order which is larger in its dimensions than their own bodies and more central in the ultimate structure of reality than is their routine everyday life.[7]

Within such a perspective, the sharing of so-called European values would be seen not as a mechanistic appropriation on the part of belated peripheral elites of values intrinsically emanating only from a circumscribed geographic-historical entity (Western Europe) but would demand the treatment of culture as an autonomous phenomenon within a universal human context. It is in this light, and not as an admission of non-Europeanness, that one should approach Aleko's popular dictum: "We are Europeans but not quite." It is not a minor coincidence, and critics have not failed to emphasize it, that Bay Ganyo was conceived in the literary imagination of Aleko Konstantinov in America, at the time of his visit to the Chicago World's Fair in 1893. On the one hand, he was depicted as the antithesis of Western culture and civilization; on the other hand, he was drawn up as a character organically related to the rapacious and selfish mechanisms of a society whose central motivation was predatory accumulation. In the words of Igov, Bay Ganyo is "the Balkan-Oriental embryo of this same mechanism but in the end he too is 'a wheel in the money-making machine'."[8]

In his own way, Herbert Vivian caught this process when summarizing his view of Serb peasants at the beginning of the century as "sturdy, good-looking, hospitable and merry, . . . rich in everything but money; simple, superstitious, thoroughly mediaeval." He mused that if one could go back four or five hundred years and live among one's forefathers, they would probably tax one's forbearance as the contemporary Serbs did, and that, in fact, if one could only shed off the arrogance of civilization, their many virtues could be appreciated:

> It is only when they go abroad for their education, don black coats and a thin veneer of progress, that they invite criticism. They are not ripe for the blessings of democracy (such as they are), and much painful experience will be necessary to prepare them. I do not say they cannot undergo the preparation, but I do not wish to see them in the process. I prefer to remember them as I have known them—admirable survivors of the age of chivalry.[9]

In a similar vein, A. Goff and Hugh Fawcett described the Macedonian as "picturesque in appearance and, amongst the peasantry, earnest and hard-working. He is, however, easily contaminated by the vicious life of a town, where he prefers to earn the best possible livelihood, without discrimination as to the means, in the easiest possible way."[10] Thus, in the Western balkanist discourse, the disdain for the Balkans did not originate in its medieval, underdeveloped, primitive nature. This was even titillating, and it was the reason for the quasi-romantic appeal they exerted. What the West loathed to see was not its self-image from the dawn of humanity, but its image of only a few generations ago. The distasteful character deplored equally by Vivian as by Aleko Konstantinov was from an age of chivalry closer by: Bay Ganyo with his Belgian mantle has been aptly called the "knight of the primitive accumulation of capital."[11]

Nor has Bay Ganyo been a solitary figure, and Aleko's an uncommon pathos in the Balkans. Other Balkan literatures of this period were also concerned with the genesis of the same phenomenon, the bourgeois upstart. "The Lost Letter" of Ion Luca

Caragiale (1852–1912) is simply the most eloquent and popular piece in a rich opus dealing with an identical issue in Romania. Just as Aleko's Bay Ganyo has entered Bulgarian as a byword, so many expressions from Caragiale's work have entered Romanian everyday speech.[12] Writers at the turn of the century were not looking for essentialist explanations in the realm of the murky category of culture, but were devastatingly specific. The targets of Caragiale's satire was not a Romanian ethnic archetype, but the new oligarchy. Despite the critics' attempts to blunt Caragiale's claws by maintaining he was attacking merely "the thin paint of western civilization that had too hastily crept down to the lower layers of society," his message was more than explicit:

> I hate them, man. In the Romanian country, this is called with the greatest serious-ness a democratic system. . . . And this semi-cultivated or, at best, falsely cultivated oligarchy, as incapable of useful production or thought as it is greedy of profits and honors, has monopolized the state power; with cruel and revolting brazenness, it denies to the peasants (a huge submissive mass and a steady producer of natural wealth), alleging their ignorance and lack of political maturity, any right to intervene. . . .[13]

On the Yugoslav scene, it was Branislav Nušić (1864–1938) who observed the transformation of a small agricultural country into a bureaucratic society of the Western type. His comedies depicted the petty bourgeoisie in this "break-neck process, [where] conscience was pushed aside, lives were destroyed, resisting up-right individuals ruined, and unscrupulous upstarts dominated the scene."[14] The excesses of vulgar class analyses that attempted to situate the case of Bay Ganyo as a particular *homo balkanicus* only at the time of his genesis should not blind us to his historical specificity. In Igov's attempt to steer a middle course between the extreme articulations of Bay Ganyo's interpretations (to see him as "an idiosyncratic national and historic version of a definite social type"), he demonstrates not only the concrete sociohistorical nature of the literary character but comments on his deep roots in Bulgarian realities of a *longue durée* nature, something that makes the problem of Bay Ganyo's grandchildren particularly acute. He almost resignedly remarks that "this type has rather strong roots in reality, or else, this reality changes rather slowly if we see his resilient presence, modernized as his appearance and even his manners are."[15] From a historical point of view, of course, the changes in reality are hardly slow: after all, the provenance of this reality, in which the Balkans have been integrated as the periphery of a West European core, its economic and social laggards, is hardly more than two centuries old. This is not the same as saying that the relative backwardness of the Balkans began only two centuries ago but that the technological gap between the regions of Europe became meaningful only in the framework of new structural relations with the creation of what Wallerstein has designated as a world-economy.[16] More importantly, this is a continuing reality.

How is this reality reflected in contemporary self-identities? It has been asserted that notions like "the European" or "the Balkanite" as collective designations are absent from the Balkan vernaculars. The explanation offered has been that self-designations are usually less abundant than designations of the other.[17] It is more likely that this particular preoccupation is a typically intellectual one and, as such, is confined to the literary languages. What did exist in the Balkan vernaculars of the nineteenth century and throughout the first half of the twentieth, and may still be encountered among a certain generation, was the phrase "to go to Europe." At the end of the nineteenth century, William Miller wrote that "[w]hen the inhabitants of the Balkan Peninsula are meditating a journey to any of the countries which lie west of them, they speak of 'going to Europe,' thereby avowedly considering themselves as quite apart from the European system."[18] At the beginning of the next century, Allen Upward spoke of the Balkans as the east end of Europe or the least known corner of Europe:

> The Europe which plays the part of Providence for the Balkan world leaves off at the Adriatic Sea. The land which cradled European civilization, the isle to which Europa came borne by the sacred bull, are no part of this Europe. It may include Russia for political purposes, but otherwise the term European means, in a Balkan ear, much what Frank meant in a Byzantine one. Europe, in short, is Latin Christendom; Paris is its capital, and French its language.[19]

As an Englishman, Upward lamented the centrality of France in this image of Europe, but he was incorrect in confining it to Latin Christendom. "Europe," when used as a distinction from their own Balkans, was not a synonym for Western Christianity in general, let alone for Latin Christianity; it was a synonym for progress, order, prosperity, radical ideas, that is, an image and an ideal, a Europe belonging to Time (understood as development), not Europe as a geographic entity. After World War II, the phrase faded and practically disappeared from the portion of the Balkans that became part of Eastern Europe. There, it was replaced by West: when still used, "going to Europe" was tantamount to "going to Western Europe." While in 1904 Herbert Vivian could still write that "all over the Balkans it is customary to speak of passing north of the Danube and Sava as 'going to Europe'," fifty years later it would never have occurred to anyone in Bulgaria or Romania to say they were going to Europe when referring to a trip to Hungary, Czechoslovakia, Poland, or East Germany, just as nobody in Greece would use *tha pame stin Evropi* when visiting Spain, Portugal, and even Italy, all bulwarks of Latin Christendom.[20]

How is the link to Europe and the Balkans expressed nowadays? To some extent, the examination of how the word "Balkan" is used in the separate Balkan languages shows the range of assessments and the degree of tolerance about one's presumed Balkanness. Still, it merits to take a closer look at how this is articulated in literary or political discussions.

"Greece—the European's European vacation" was the tourist slogan of 1988, interpreted by some as an attempt to lure more Americans who like to emulate the Europeans.[21] What it also displayed was an obsessive emphasis on their Europeanness, about whose denial the Greeks, as the only Balkan and Orthodox member of the European Union, are particularly sensitive. They do not forget to remind the world that even the word Europe is Greek, and while they use the phrase "to go to Europe," it is not a resigned posture of nonbelonging. The exultant celebration of Greece in Spyros Melas's essay, although using the ill-fated notion, attests to the undeniable feeling of being the center of European culture:

When on our return from our trip to Europe—driven away by gray clouds and storms—we saw from the bottom of the valley of the Strymon a piece of blue sky, I heard my traveling companion exclaim, "This is Greece!" And she was not mistaken. It was exactly under that blue patch that our border began. It is the cradle of our spirit, the substance of our history and civilization. The ideas of Plato and the choric odes of Sophocles are imbued with this blue. The marble harmonies of the monuments and the gaps in their ruins are filled with it. It is reflected in our seas, and thus puts our relief-carved land between two endless strips of blue, the liquid (sea) and the airy (sky). . . . it is the triumph of the blue, which permeates not only the water, the ether, the mood, the speech, the laughter, but also the stone, the mountain, the earth, which grows lighter, as if spiritualized.[22]

The "blue theme" appears also in Stratis Myrivilis's paean of Greece, reveling in the exalted place of his country whose history "is written on its waves, which have rocked and are still rocking her fate": "As the blue pages unfold, I see on them the ancient ships that carried the spirit of my race over all the Mediterranean. . . . The blue pages unfold and I see the Byzantine ships pass with their Imperial eagles. . . . On the tall mast waves the banner of the Madonna of Victory who, for a thousand years, guarded the civilization of Europe and spread the law of Christ to the sacred peoples. . . . The blue pages unfold all the time."[23] Nikos Kazantzakis, too, shared in this sentiment when he wrote about his native island, "Crete was the first bridge between Europe, Asia and Africa. And the Cretan land was the first to be enlightened in a wholly dark Europe. . . . Because four or five thousand years ago the blue bird, the Spirit, passed by this place and stayed."[24]

Like all national identities, the Greeks have a hierarchy of multiple identities: a contemporary Greek would describe him or herself first as Greek, then with a local identity (Cretan, Macedonian, Epyrote, and so on), third as European, and only next as Balkan, Southern European, or Mediterranean. While there is no particular enthusiasm about their Balkanness, even a mocking resignation, the pejorative edge of the Greeks is reserved for the "Orient" (more concretely for Turkey), not for the Balkans. There is no denial about belonging to the Balkans. If anything, there has been historically an excess of superiority complex vis-à-vis the rest of the Balkans, tempered in the past few decades. Not only has Greece been historically central for the Balkan cosmos, but its main designs and political imagination until the recent past had been to a great extent focused on the Balkans. In academic life, "Balkan" is a notion that has a neutral and legitimate place: the leading institute for interdisciplinary research on the Balkans is the *Institute for Balkan Studies* in Thessaloniki, its main publication is the journal *Balkan Studies*, and a recent journal comes out under the title *Evrovalkania* (Eurobalkans).

Greece still views itself as playing a central role in the peninsula although nowadays this role is not considered a priority. Official pronouncements are unequivocal: "The Balkans for Greece is not merely a dangerous region somewhere in the world. Greece is part of the Balkans." Defining itself as the only "Balkan member" of the European Union, Greece feels a particular responsibility for the stability of the Balkans and has lately endorsed an initiative to create an "Open Balkan University."[25] While proud of being the only European "Balkanites," Greeks display a concern over the threat to their distinctiveness, and there is a growing tendency "to preserve a static organic notion—a nexus of state, nation, religion, and Greekness—as formulated in the early nineteenth century."[26] Obviously, with the process of European integration getting ahead, Greece will face mounting pressures to reconstruct its identity. Still, what one can observe in the Greek case is that despite ongoing disputes over identity and the Angst in some circles over losing their essence—the Romeiosini—the place of Greece in the institutionalized framework of the European Union has conferred on it a remarkable sense of security, so much so that it can be postulated that in the Greek case one may speak of "the bearable heaviness of being" Balkan.

Likewise, in the country that Edward Gibbon described as "within sight of Italy but less known than the interior of America" there has never been denial that the Albanians are Balkan, which has been used almost exclusively in its neutral geographical meaning. At the beginning of Albanian statehood, their pronounced lobbyist Christo A. Dako asserted that the Albanians were the oldest and most beautiful race of the Balkan Peninsula and had, until the Middle Ages, occupied all Balkan countries, that their national consciousness was stronger than any of their neighbors', that they were "not only an Aryan people, but European in their national instincts," that their sense of family in particular was "European and not Turkish."[27] This was not done to extricate them from some demeaning Balkanness, but to establish their rightful place as a sovereign nation among the other Balkan nations, to argue "to admit the Albanian people, the most ancient people of the Balkans in the circle of the family of nations," to state Albania's desire "to become an element of order and peace in the Balkan peninsula."[28] That in the memoranda sent to President Wilson and to the foreign services of the other great powers Albania's "Aryanness" as well as its "European family values" should figure repeatedly and prominently, comes only to confirm the swiftness with which dominant political clichés were appropriated by the champions of the Albanian cause.

Neither is their belonging to the Balkans disputed nowadays. In a speech in March 1995, President Sali Berisha referred to Albania as one of the Balkan and Eastern European countries, but sought to assert the direct, unmediated relationship with Europe to which Albania aspired: "The program is our word of honor, our contract with the Albanian electorate, democracy, Albania, and Europe."[29] Conversely, writers on Kosovo sought to emphasize its "Balkan vocation," "Balkan dimension," "Balkan perspective," even when warning that it may become a new "Balkan powder keg." The common desire, however, is to make Albania "a beachhead of stability in the turbulent Balkans."[30] Despite the fact that there has been no tradition of pejorative use of "Balkan" in Albanian, the new cliches of the postcommunist period are beginning to introduce it. An Albanian article on Christianity explains that "exploiting the Balkan and Albanian paternalistic tradition, fifty years of hardline communism totally devastated the moral and spiritual values of man." This paternalism "is a socio-psychological model typical of the Balkan peoples, reinforced by the Islamization of life there and primitiveness of our social and economic development." The only hope for Albania is its young generation "which has loved European civilization and Christian values."[31] This frank appeal to Christian values from a country that before it became atheist was 70 percent Muslim bespeaks the naïveté and straightforwardness of the new Albanian political discourse that has not yet mastered the ennobling façade of the pluralist vocabulary. It is, however, also a tribute to the sound political instincts of the new Albanian political elites who have not been duped by the pretense of suprareligious, nonracial, and nonethnic universalism and pluralism of the European or Western discourse. The Albanian professor was doing simply what others before him had practiced: externalizing undesired qualities on some imputed Balkanness.

Romanians have usually insisted on their direct connections to the Western world (not even via Central Europe) and on their missionary role as outposts of Latinism and civilization among a sea of (Slavic and Turkic) barbarians. While covering the Eastern front during World War I, John Reed reported from Bucharest: "If you want to infuriate a Romanian, you need only to speak of his country as a Balkan state. 'Balkan!' he cries. 'Balkan! Romania is not a Balkan state. How dare you confuse us with half-savage Greeks or Slavs! We are Latins.'"[32] This had not always been the case. Even throughout the nineteenth century, with the rise of "Romanianism" and its emancipation from Hellenism, as well as the purification of its strongly Slavic vocabulary, apartness was not the obsession of the Romanian idea. Reading the travelers' accounts of a dozen Romanians, such as Teodor Codrescu, Ion Ionescu de la Brad, Dimitrie Bolintineanu, A. Pelimon, D. Rallet, Maior Pappazoglu, Cezar Boliac, Stefan Georgescu, and Bishop Melchisedec, one is struck by how much at home they feel when they cross the Danube; their travelogues were written by insiders with an intuitive grasp for situations, behavior, and words.[33]

The idea of uniqueness and complete separateness, the "cultural Narcissism — often encountered within 'small cultures' — [which] is the counterpart to the officially entertained isolationism" was a later phenomenon, intensified to its extremes after World War I.[34] Yet, there was a tension in this self-identity, present even in the writings of Nicolae Iorga, Romania's greatest historian (at least in terms of the size of his opus and influence at home and abroad). The opening to his 1919 "History of Romania" placed his country "between the center of Europe and the Russian steppe, the sombre lands of the north and the sunny Balkan peninsula in the south," clearly putting the northern boundary of the Balkan peninsula at the Danube River.[35] Yet, Iorga recognized the central place the peninsula had for the evolution of the Romanian state and nation, and used South-Eastern Europe as a unit of analysis. In Iorga's vision, *L'Europe du sud-est* or *L'Europe sud-orientale* was the Balkans plus Romania, just as in German historiography *Südosteuropa* was the Balkans (including Romania) plus Hungary. In his inauguration speech at the opening of the Institute for the Study of South-Eastern Europe in Bucarest in 1914, Iorga spoke of the common Thracian and Illyrian foundations of the peoples of this region, whose traces were living in the subsequent legacies of Greeks, Bulgarians, Serbs, Romanians, Turks, and of the common character on these peoples of occidental, oriental, and septentrional influences.[36] The idea of a Southeast European continuity was further developed by B. P. Haşdeu and especially Victor Papacostea, one of the few to prefer the term Balkan.[37] It was under the distinguished leadership of Papacostea that an Institute of Balkan Studies functioned in Bucharest between 1937 and 1948, which published a scholarly journal *Balcania*.

During the interwar period, Romania weakened its political hypersensitiveness to the tainted geographical term, and put its signature under the "Balkan Pact."[38]

Yet, what was maybe the most brilliant cluster of Romanian intellectuals, "Romania's mystical revolutionaries," firmly refused to be associated with the Balkans: their measuring rod was Western, not even Central Europe. This generation, described as the Balkan counterpart to the revolutionary aristocratism of Ernst Jünger, was antibourgeois, antimercantile, antidemocratic, and anti-Semitic. Three men of this generation shared the prestigious prize of the Young Romanian Writers Association in the 1930s: Emil Cioran, Constantin Noica, and Eugène Ionesco. A fourth, Mircea Eliade, was the "recognized spiritual leader of the Young Generation." Between them, they dominate the intellectual horizon of today's post-Ceausescu Romania, "where many within the new generation of students and intellectuals identify themselves with the spirit of the rebellious radicals of the thirties."[39]

Of the four, only one, the least Romanian, who produced a single book (his first) in Romanian, did not succumb to the affliction of "rhinoceritis," as he described the seduction of his closest friends by the ideology and activities of the Iron Guard in his surrealist masterpiece *Rhinoceros*.[40] In a piece written in 1940 and published in 1968, Ionesco attributed the phenomenon of the Iron Guard to some imputed Balkanness:

> An original and authentic Balkan "culture" cannot be really European. The Balkan spirit is neither European nor Asiatic. It has nothing to do with western humanism. . . . Passion can exist, but not love. A nameless nostalgia can exist, but without a face, not individualized. And rather than humor, rather even than irony, there is merely the coarse and ruthless bantering of the peasant. . . . Most of all [the Balkanites (les Balkaniques)] are devoid of charity. Their religion might not be even considered religion, so fundamentally different is it from the emotional, psychological and intellectual religion of the Catholics and the Protestants. The priests are materialist, practical, atheists in the western sense; they are brigands, satraps, cunning with their black beards, without mercy, telluric: real "Thracians." . . . The Iron Guard phenomenon is not something transitory, it is profoundly Balkan, it is truly the expression of the cruelty of the Balkan spirit without refinement.[41]

Despite Ionesco's repudiation of Balkan irony, it is indeed ironic that the only mass grassroots fascist and anti-Semitic movement in the Balkans, the truly original, idiosyncratic, genuinely and exceptionally Romanian doctrine of Codreanu and company, was attributed to the Balkans by the group that was most vociferous about its un-Balkanness. But already here one can grasp some of the central characteristics of the general balkanist discourse: the ambiguity ("ni européene, ni asiatique"), the externalization of evil on an abstract Balkanness, the dark side within. The undisguised revulsion with the peasantry, on the other hand, is so exclusively Romanian and unheard of in the other Balkan discourses as to render indeed the Romanian claims of un-Balkanness authentic. A phrase like Emil Cioran's: "hating my people, my country, its timeless peasants enamored of their own torpor and almost bursting with hebetude, I blushed to be descended from them, repudiated them, rejected their sub-eternity, their larval certainties, their geologic reverie" would be impossible in any other Balkan context where a very conscious propeasant discourse has been traditionally cultivated.[42]

There was a definite ambiguity also in Cioran's image of the Balkans that came from his consistent rejection of bourgeois society both in the interwar period, when he produced *Schimbarea la faţa României* (*România's Transfiguration*) in 1937, and after the war, in *History and Utopia* in 1960. He was still expecting an anticapitalist revolution but, disappointed with the failure of the Russian revolution, witnessed with disgust the stabilization of the decadent West, though with the mellow tiredness of old age. Still, even in his later book, the Nietzschean fire was present in the "cult of force, of instinct, of vitality and will to power, which are represented — the West being so exhausted — by Russia and even by the Balkan peoples."[43] The latter, with their "taste for devastation, for internal clutter, for a universe like a brothel on fire" were the "last 'primitives' in Europe [who] may give her a new energy, which she will not fail to regard as her last humiliation."[44]

Even with due credit to Cioran's famous posture as gadfly, his love of paradox for the sake of the aesthetics of the exercise, there was something more to his thought. He distinguished between major, aggressive, and messianic cultures (like the French, German, and Russian), and small or minor cultures that were weak because they lacked a mission in the world. Cioran expressed uncompromising aversion for the Romanian peasantry's unredeeming backwardness, passivity, and fatalism, but still thought that Romania's culture could reach an intermediary status between the major and the minor ones (like the culture of Spain) and dominate the Balkans.[45] Both Cioran and Eliade subsequently denied links to the Iron Guard, in Cioran's case with vehemence and contempt for the movement. Yet Cioran contributed in the 1930s to ultranationalist and Guardist newspapers eulogizing Hitler and the Nazis and "urging Romanians to . . . enjoy the politics of delirium." Eliade, too, had published in 1937 an article entitled "Why I believe in the Triumph of the Legionary Movement" in the Guardist newspaper *Buna Vestire* in which he declared: "I believe in the destiny of the Romanian people. That is why I believe in the victory of the Legionary movement. A nation that has demonstrated huge powers of creation at all levels of reality cannot be ship-wrecked at the periphery of history in a Balkanized democracy, in a civil catastrophe."[46] Even the repudiation of democracy had to carry the Balkan stigma. Finally, Constantin Noica, the only one not to leave Romania, who did not and could not deny his brief ties with the Guardists, for which he was persecuted until 1964, was destined to become the cultural guru to Romania's young intellectuals in the 1980s.[47]

The theme of Romania's uniqueness was continued in the postwar period and reached its frenetic culmination under Ceausescu, as a compensatory mechanism for the self-conscious and troublesome feeling of being trapped in an ambiguous status, the in-betweenness of East and West. One would have thought that the performance of Romania in the last decade of Ceausescu's rule would have sobered somewhat the exclusiveness of Romanian intellectuals, at least in their rapport to the other Balkan nations, at least for some time. There are some indications for that; there are others against. Today, one can hear different signals from a chorus of voices striving to get out of isolation. Some are mediocre reiterations on the theme of Latin island in a Slavic or Asiatic sea. A member of *Vatra Româneasca* speaks of the tolerant Romanians who welcome Hungarians and Jews and who are different from the easy-to-manipulate Slavs, with their mass mentality, and from the cruel, brutal, and heartless Asiatic Hungarians.[48] Lucian Pintilie, the acclaimed film director of *Unforgettable Summer*, stated: "If there is one regime with which I identify, it's the bourgeois regime up to the arrival of the Communists. And I'm proud to belong to a people known for their tolerance."[49]

More thoughtful contemplations indicate an identity that vacillates nervously over the reopened borderline between the Balkans and Central Europe, and more generally between West and East, a country embodying the "transition between Occident and the great Asian Orient," "some kind of no-man's land, not European at all, but not Asiatic at all."[50] As a whole, Balkanness is a deprecatory category to which Romanians rarely allude. While having made and continuing to make major contributions to Balkan studies, the Romanian academic community is the only one in the Balkans that does not employ the term Balkan studies, but has organized its research in the *Institut des études sud-est européennes*, with its main publication *Revue des études sud-est européennes*.

In 1975, Niyazi Berkes, an eminent Turkish sociologist and historian, wrote that "Turkey today is neither a Western nor a Moslem nation; it does not belong to a Christian, socialist, or capitalist community. . . . It is neither Asian nor European. . . . The dominant direction of Ottoman history has tilted more toward the west than toward the east. But its adherence to an eastern cultural reference has prevented Turkey's inclusion in the Western world."[51] This sounds like the perpetual Balkan refrain of in-betweenness, except that in the Turkish case the Balkans are not remotely a decisive vector. In the long list of dichotomies—Asian or European; Muslim or secular; settled or nomadic; grandchildren of Mehmet the Conqueror or children of Atatürk; "the sword of Islam or a Christian punishment"; Ottoman orphans or Turkish citizens; conquerors or conquered; warriors or civilians; part of the West or defenders of the West; army, community, or nation; contemporary society or historical bridge; "Eastern, Anatolian, or Western"—the Balkans are not even considered as an alternative.[52]

The reason for this has been suggested to be a particular case of repression. On the one hand, some Turkish historians have emphasized that the Ottoman state began as a Balkan empire, that the Balkans remained the priority of the Ottoman Empire throughout its existence, and that through its historical continuity modern Turkey is a Balkan state. This view found its culmination in the passionate plea of Turkey's late president Turgut Özal for acceptance of his country into the European Economic Community. His book *Turkey in Europe and Europe in Turkey* was dedicated to "the peoples of Europe and to the Turkish people who belong among them."[53] He questioned the usual East-West dichotomy: "Do the categories 'Asia' for the barbarians, and 'Europe' for the civilized and civilizing Indo-Europeans, correspond to reality?" He further claimed that the Ottoman conquest of Anatolia saved and preserved the Orthodox church which, had it been captured by Western Europe and the papacy, would have perished.[54] Finally, he took considerable pride in the Ottoman Empire's Byzantine-Balkan heritage:

> If the Roman Empire represented the extent of the spread of Western culture, it also played a no less important part in the structure of the Ottoman Empire. In addition to the contributions of the Greeks, whether converted to Islam or not, the Ottomans received from the East Roman Empire the entire Balkan heritage, including Greece herself.[55]

On the other hand, the Balkans were the first geographic region where the Ottomans began to loose territory, and this shaped a feeling of resentment and betrayal: "[T]he loss of Balkan territories has functioned as a major trauma leading to a deeper preoccupation with the survival of the state among both the members of the Ottoman ruling class and the adherents of the Young Ottoman and Young Turk movements." The response to this trauma seems to have been an "official tendency to forget about the Balkans," a tendency grafted on the official republican ideology that rejected any continuity between the Ottoman Empire and Republican Turkey.[56]

The attitude toward the Balkans, however, is much more complex, and reflects ideological tendencies, group interests, and individual preferences. There is, for example, a meeting ground between the official republican nationalist ideology and the radical Turkist-Turanist nationalism in their preference to forget about the Balkans not simply as the attribute of an undesirable imperial past but also as the most troublesome region of Modern Europe. The stress on Anatolia in the construction of the territorial aspect of Turkish nationalism has led to the widespread idea that the Balkans diverted precious attention and energy from "the pure Turkishness" of Anatolia, and in the end "betrayed" the Turks. This feeling informed the popular 1960s series of newspaper articles and interviews by Yılmaz Çetinler in *Cumhuriyet* under the title "This Rumelia of Ours," published later under separate cover and in a revised edition.[57] In the case of the Turkists, it has fueled a "revengeful, hostile and humiliating" attitude toward the Balkan nations without necessarily presupposing revanchist or irredentist designs.[58]

It is chiefly among conservative intellectuals opposed to the republican ideology that the memory of the Balkans is kept alive. This is not, however, the almost benevolent and romantic nostalgia of descendants of or even first-generation Turkish immigrants from the Balkans. On the contrary, it exhibits a hostile and haughty posture toward "those hastily founded states [which] cannot even be as noble as a former slave who sits at the doorsteps of her master who has lost his fortune."[59] At the same time, there is a matching rise of interest toward the Balkans among leftist and Westernist liberals, often from a neo-Ottoman perspective. The popular writer Nedim Gürsel published impressions of his 1993 and 1994 visits to Bosnia, Macedonia, Greece, and Bulgaria in a charming volume "Return to the Balkans," dedicated to all the dead in the Balkan soil and to all friends living in the Balkans. It is a warm, human description calling on friendship and cooperation between all Balkan peoples, which nevertheless falls into the trap of idealizing the Ottoman Empire as a real *pax ottomana* for the Balkan nations and ascribes their cessession and particularly the Balkan wars to the instigation of imperialist states.[60] Many advocate a geopolitical approach as a means of securing Turkey's European integration. In the words of Cengiz Çandar: "The Balkans once again make Turkey into an European and world power just like the Ottomans started becoming a world power by expanding into Rumelia. . . . Therefore Turkey has to become a Balkan power in the course of her journey into the twenty-first century. . . . Anatolia is a region that quenches the Turkish spirit. The Balkans introduce Turkey to the world dimensions."[61] While there is no doubt that after seven decades of official amnesia, the Balkans have reentered the public discourse about Turkish identity, the attitude toward the Balkans, multifarious as it may be, has remained a sideline in this discourse.

The East-West dichotomy, on the other hand, is central, especially in the present passionate search for group identity between Islam and a secular statist Turkishness. While it prominently figures among the other Balkan nations, not a single one among them accepts even a minor redeeming quality about "Easternness." The Turks, while certainly feeling the tension between East and West, seem to have reached a certain synthesis, not the incompatible talking at cross-purposes Kipling described in his "Oh, East is East, and West is West, and never the twain shall meet." For Ziya Gökalp, this was the organic blend of the Turkish people, the Islamic community and Western civilization; in the words of the Turkish author and critic Peyami Safa, it is a synthesis between East and West, between Turkishness and Islam.[62] A poet like Fazîl Hüsnü Dağlarca gives a splendid articulation of this feeling in "The Epic of the Conquest of Istanbul":

> East or West cannot be told apart.
> The mind heralds the funeral whose images abound.
> Your feet, your feet
> Are swept off the ground.[63]

A new wave in the quest for Turkish identity was unleashed by the dissolution of the Soviet Union, particularly with the possibilities it opened in Muslim and Turkic Central Asia. The disintegration of Yugoslavia, and especially the war in Bosnia, inflamed Islamic passions in Turkey, stronger even than the ones triggered by Cyprus two decades earlier. The overriding slogan that Andalusia would not be repeated was an allusion to the Spanish *reconquista* and the expulsion of Muslims from Spain. The lively interest toward Bosnia and to the fate of Turkish minorities in the Balkan countries, the activization of Turkish diplomacy, even the existing nostalgia in some circles about "bizim Rumeli" ("our Rumelia") should not mislead one in overestimating the place of the Balkans in Turkish political and cultural priorities. The Balkans are significant primarily as the "western" hypostasis of the Ottoman historical legacy, and their importance is elevated or rejected in a complex and indirect correlation to the rejection or acceptance of the Ottoman past, especially today with the passionate reexamination of Atatürk's republican legacy by practically all the Turkish ideological and political spectrum. Most important, the category Balkan is devoid of any pejorative meaning. While Balkan studies as such do not figure prominently in Turkish scholarship, they have managed to create a respectable niche for themselves: a new journal, *Balkanlar*, is published by the *Ortadoğu ve Balkanlar Incemeleri Vakfı*, and there is a commission for Balkan Studies (*Balkan araştırmaları komisyonu*) at the Turkish Historical Society. Alongside Bulgaria, Turkey is the only other country where "Balkan" is employed as a proper name. Although in Turkish "Balkan" can appear both as a personal and family name, this is rare compared to the frequently used Bulgarian family name "Balkanski." Whenever the concept "Balkan" is evoked at all, it vacillates between the neutral and the nostalgically positive, maybe because it has never been seriously considered a central category of identity.

In times of extreme crisis, identities may become vague or else, perhaps more often, they are starkly defined. In a short masterpiece written in the fall of 1991, the Yugoslav (Croat) writer Dubravka Ugrešić conveyed the feeling of being lost, identity-less, yet with the sharply outlined spheres of belonging or exclusion that come to the fore under intense stress.[64] With the Yugoslav problem in the limelight today, one would have expected the obvious fault lines in her case to be the ones between Croatianness and Yugoslavness. In fact, Ugrešić's subtle description leaves the impression of a fault line in the making, of a tissue torn in unexpected and painful places, not a clear and neat cut. Two years later, this process was still unfinished for Ugrešić when she refused to be circumscribed by an ethnic category and defined herself as "anational," in the rubric "others."[65] More interesting for our purpose here is the broader framework of identification, not the painful ambiguities within. Sitting in an Amsterdam café, Ugrešić needs a larger frame of reference to define her place (or lack of) than the borders of Yugoslavia. So she sips her coffee and jots down opposition pairs on a piece of paper: organized-disorganized, tolerance-intolerance, civility-primitiveness, rational consciousness–mythic consciousness, predictability-unpredictability, citizen-nationality, and so on; the first column she calls Western Europe, the second Eastern Europe:

> And at once it seems that I clearly see this Eastern Europe. It sits at my table and we look at each other as if in a mirror. I see twisted old shoes, neglected skin, cheap makeup, an expression of servility and impudence on its face. It wipes its mouth with its hand, it speaks too loud, it gestures as it speaks, it talks with its eyes. I see a glow of despair and cunning in them at the same time; I see the desperate desire to be "someone." . . . My sister, my sad Eastern Europe.[66]

This is an important identification given that Yugoslavs throughout the cold-war period proudly refused to identify with Eastern Europe and looked down on it. Ugrešić herself describes how, in the better days of Yugoslavia, when confronted with questions about life behind the "iron curtain," she would explain "that we are not 'like them,' like Romania, Bulgaria, or Czechoslovakia. We are something else." Only at a moment when Eastern Europe is disintegrating, and part of it, claiming not to be even Eastern but Central European, looks with aversion and a feigned incomprehension at the Yugoslav quandary as if it belongs to an entirely different species, does it become possible for Yugoslavs to refer to Eastern Europe, and in a moment of despair to recognize it as an equal, a mirror image.

This goes even more so about the relation of Yugoslavia to the Balkans. Twice, Ugrešić mentions them by name. Once, when among the different positive qualities of her Yugoslavia—what she calls her "trump card"—she speaks of "the beauty of Dubrovnik, the diversity of cultures in a small Balkan country, the beauty of our coast, the advantages of our self-management, our relative democracy, our free passport, our absence of censorship, our variant of soft communism."[67] These are all, of course, the staple advertising lures of a tourist agent, tailored for the Western customer. They all relate to the whole spectrum of the West's professed beliefs and preferences, and would serve different, even opposing tastes: here some sunny Adriatic with a touch of cultivated Renaissance Italy in Dubrovnik for either curious and adventurous westerners or for second-class ones who cannot afford Venice or the Riviera; there a bit of multiculturalism *à la balkanique* and some soft communism for university professors and other politically correct intellectuals who are curious about the dawn of humanity; elsewhere an almost-market and an almost-democracy for the ones who have an aversion to communists.

The other reference of the Balkans occurs when Ugrešić alludes to the war in Yugoslavia: it is "the mounds of deaths 'down there' in the Balkans." Later, while not mentioning Balkan by name, she utilizes the "down there" as a label. Before the war, the Yugoslavs are different from "them"; despite today's emphasis on civilizational divisions along Catholic, Orthodox, and Muslims lines, the Yugoslavs had in toto rejected their belonging to the Balkans. The only exception had been the world of scholarship where Balkan has had a legitimate place and is used as the name of institutes and journals. Already between 1934 and 1941, a Balkan institute in Belgrade was issuing the *Revue internationale des études balkaniques*; today's *Balkanološki institut* at the Serbian Academy of Sciences publishes *Balcanica*; and a new journal, *Balkan Forum*, is published in the former Macedonian Republic. Outside of academia, the Yugoslavs had preferred to be seen as a Danubian or Adriatic presence, or even better, in nongeographical terms, as the elite of the nonaligned world. Now, they are becoming the "we down there," "the excrement of Europe, its problem, its moronic relative," "we guys down there."[68] In a way, this is exactly how they are perceived by the West, as the dark side within a collective Europe. For the former Yugoslavs, too, Balkanness serves to sustain their Croatianness, Serbianness, Macedonianness, and so on pure and innocent, or at least salvageable, while enabling them to externalize their darker side.

Apprehending the horror of the future war, in September 1990, the Sarajevan daily *Oslobođenje* published a piece with one of the first mentions of "Balkan," a notion that had faded during the past few decades from the Yugoslav vocabulary and self-perception: "Thus, instead of being an integral part of Europe," read the article, "we are again becoming the Balkans, we are sinking into it equally in Ljubljana as well as in Zagreb, in Belgrade, Stara Pazova and Fcoča, in Velika Kladuša, Priština and Skopje."[69] "Balkanization," the author pointed out, has entered the political vocabulary as a synonym of "lebanonization," that is, divisions accompanied by internecine conflicts. Imbued with liberal and democratic ideas, the piece accused all Yugoslav political leaders of the moment—Milošević, Tudjman, Izetbegović, Rašković, and so forth—of leading the country, instead to democratic liberties, "into the gloom of the Balkan call for 'soil and blood.'" It takes, indeed, some significant historical ignorance to ascribe to the Balkans the "Blut und Boden" ideology and practice, something that makes this statement the unconscious, and therefore pardonable, predecessor of Robert Kaplan's infamous and very conscious statement about the Balkan origins of Nazism. It also takes the arrogance and innocence of someone who really has never felt Balkan and who has internalized the anti-Balkan stereotype to heap on the Balkans all the burden of her own Yugoslav frustrations. Apart from that, this is a well-known mechanism in psychology where stigmas have a distinct relief function and serve as the externalization and projection of repressed preoccupations.[70]

Four years into the Yugoslav war, with all due exemptions one may feel for scholars under stress and in isolation, one marvels at the nerve and hubris of declarations about Yugoslavia epitomizing an evolution between the "Balkan paradigm" and the

"European type of development"; even today's rump Yugoslavia is assigned a position "between the East and West as Switzerland has between the Latins and the Germanics."[71] It may be pardonable for people under duress to think they are the center of the world, but it is unacceptable to think they are the center of the Balkans. In an otherwise admirable piece, for its advocation of tolerance and Christian love, the Croatian American theologian Miroslav Volf constantly described the war between Serbs, Croats, and Muslims as Balkan: "[N]ew demons had possessed the Balkan house and were preparing their vandalistic and bloody feast, first in Croatia and then in Bosnia," the new Europe is vanishing "into the thick smoke of the stubborn Balkan fire," "today, Balkan is aflame in the name of Serbia's identity with itself," "the Balkan conflict," "the Balkan war," "Balkan hate," and so on, ad nauseam.[72] Slavenka Drakulić, too, writes about "the war in the Balkans," about *the Balkan Express*, although she never would refer to herself as Balkan. Even the so-called "Croatia syndrome," coined to describe posttraumatic stress in patients who "have committed or witnessed ghastly acts" has to be reported under the heading of "Balkan violence."[73] On the other hand, a cosmopolitan Yugoslav author, the Croat playwright Slobodan Snajder, who lives in Germany, has voiced a spirited defense of the Balkans:

> The Balkans are a mythical territory. . . . Just as the Mediterranean can be described as the cradle of human history, this is true of the Balkans. I would like to stress that this is not only a region of misfortunes but also a space in which the strong traditions that have shaped European culture are oscillating. One should not connect the Balkans necessarily with something negative, even as the word "balkanization" makes us think about a suicidal war.[74]

The other Balkan countries, in the meantime, are not at war and have no intention to go to war, despite the constant apocalyptic scenarios that the Yugoslav crisis is impossible to contain within Yugoslav borders. They are also amused by the newly (and unwillingly) discovered Balkanness of some of the former Yugoslavs, but they understand: it is the need for solidarity in the abyss. To quote the Bulgarian poet Boris Khristov, it is an abyss with a maze at the bottom.[75] Among the Balkan nations, the Bulgarians share in all the frustrations of being Balkan, and yet they are the only ones who seriously consider their Balkanness, probably because of the fact that the Balkan range lies entirely on their territory. There is no other Balkan literature that has dedicated such eulogies to the Balkans as the Bulgarian; in fact, there is no other where it even figures as an object.

The Balkans appear in many folk songs as the abode and shelter of the *haiduts*, the venerated resistance-fighters; they were the symbol of Bulgaria's urge for national liberty in the poetry of Dobri Chintulov (1822–1886), Khristo Botev (1848–1876), Ivan Vazov (1850–1921). Lyuben Karavelov's 1867 declaration of love to his country began with: "I love you, my dear fatherland! I love your balkans, forests, creeks, cliffs and their crystal-clear and cold springs! I love you, my dear native land!"[76] The "Balkan lion" as the epitome of Bulgaria's victorious spirit appeared in the first national hymn of the country, composed by Nikola Zhivkov, until 1944:

> Lion of the Balkans, thy winged spirit glorious,
> Leads and inspires us, over all victorious![77]

The Balkan Mountains are also a central image in the present national hymn. The most passionate troubadour of the Balkans was the poet Pencho Slaveikov, maybe the most intellectual among a brilliant group of modernist poets at the turn of the century, who had immortalized the mountain in his epic poem *Kîrvava pesen* (The Song of the Blood):

Hither and thither was I carried by Fate,
Hither and thither in the labor of my days,
But always there stood before me and always there will stand
The shape of the proud, the wonderful Balkan,
For I hold it in my soul's sacred place
. . . .
Balkan, our father Balkan, have eyes of grace,
Harshly dost thou look from the judgment place.
What of our mothers now, of the tears they brought
To blot away the sins which the fathers wrought?
Look on those who look upon thee from the graves —
Did they live no life save the life of slaves?
Had their children naught save the milk of slaves?
Had their souls no thought save the thoughts of slaves?
Behold the wounds that out of our bosom stream!
Count the numberless heroes who fell for a dream!
In thy crevasses, there on the rugged heights
We, thy sons, have died in a hundred fights —
But yet we awakened Time and we urged him on,
We drew the curtain of night and the daylight shone.
Now turn thy glance to the queen of the mountain throng,
Hear thou the music of swords, hear thou of songs the song!
Thither thy people fly, for liberty lies in chain,
Thither we fly, the dead, to the glorious place again.
Ah! we have risen, we ride from a shadowy shore
To see the fate that our country shall have in store.
And softly then as the stars to the twilight sing
So slept the voice that spoke to the mountain-king.
And as he looked to the gloom of the woodland glades
The chin of the Balkan drooped and his lips were dumb
And he was sunk in a dream of the days to come.[78]

The popular story "Balkan" by Iordan Iovkov, possibly the greatest Bulgarian short-story writer, recalls the second Balkan war of 1913 when Romania invaded Bulgaria. In the story, Balkan is the name of a military dog that guards the frontier and becomes the allegory for patriotism and human dignity.[79] In 1904, Pencho Slaveikov wrote an extended preface to a collection of Bulgarian folk songs, published in London and appropriately called "In the Shadow of the Balkans." He stressed the close alliance between the Balkan and the Bulgarians, for whom "Father Balkan" appeared as a synonym for Fatherland. There is not even an inkling of awareness that Balkan might mean something ignoble, although less than a decade later the name was already saturated with a pejorative meaning:

The word "Balkan" should not in this case be narrowly applied, that is, not merely to the glorious troop of mountains which from the north-west set out on their mysterious journey, which proceed through the center of Bulgaria and hasten towards the east, where in magnificence they tower above the Black Sea, listening to the sleepless waves and their unconquerable song. "Balkan" is the name of all the mountains that are scattered over the peninsula which lies to the south of the "white and silent Danube"—and despite the fact that every mountain has its own name, fair, melodious and intertwined with memories and poetic legends.[80]

The Balkan range as a pillar of Bulgarian independence and symbol of its nationhood continued to be a central theme in the works of contemporary writers like Emiliyan Stanev, Iordan Radichkov, and Georgi Dzhagarov. It was taken up also by philosophers and historians who emphasized the crucial role of mountains in general, and of the Balkan range in particular, in Bulgarian history: "Without the Balkans, and then also without the mountains on our soil, here in the European southeast what has existed now for so many centuries under the name of Bulgarians would hardly have survived and might not have appeared." "The Balkan in our history" was Petîr Mutafchiev's popular historical essay that illustrated the role of the mountain in supporting and defending the Bulgarian state in its centuries-old struggles with Byzantium. Himself a medievalist, Mutafchiev drew on numerous examples from Byzantine sources to show the decisive strategic significance of the mountain range for preserving Bulgarian statehood. His essay ended at the time of the Ottoman conquest: "As a veritable warrior on guard, the Balkan did not betray its duty to protect the Bulgarian state from its mighty neighbor. And if several centuries later it did not succeed in defending it from the hordes of Bayezid, this was because medieval Bulgaria, having exhausted its life-force in an existence filled with insoluble contradictions, was stepping into its own grave.[81]

What is remarkable about this essay, despite its occasional romantic affectations, typical for the interwar period, is the fact that "Balkan" was the name employed unreservedly by Mutafchiev. For a first-class medievalist, conversant with his sources and faithfully reporting from them the only existing name "Haemus," to utilize "Balkan" (the designation brought by "Bayezid's hordes") indicated merely the extent to which the name was deeply and firmly rooted in the Bulgarian language and imagination. These literary examples can be continued ad infinitum but there are more than literary proofs for the special place that "Balkan" has among the Bulgarians. Geography is an important element of the school curriculum, and the 1994 seventh-grade textbook features three parts: Europe, the Balkan Peninsula, and Bulgaria. Bulgaria is a country whose airlines are called "Balkan," whose tourist agencies are "Balkantourist" and "Balkan holidays," whose record-making industry is "Balkanton," whose best export to the COMECON was an electrocar called "Balkancar," whose most fashionable hotel in the center of Sofia is "Sheraton-Balkan," whose third largest bank is "Balkanbank," and which has thousands of citizens with the family name "Balkanski."

Yet, in the Bulgarian case there is also strongly present the standard pejorative attitude toward Balkanness. In his work on the Balkan Union of the 1930s, in all other aspects a solid work of factological research, Geshkov had accepted the Western stereotype to such extent that he would even slip into shoddy psychological pronouncements about "the proverbial Balkan mentality—the inability to give and take."[82] A recent journalistic essay lamented "the late, partial and unequal incorporation of the Balkans into the genuine Europe." The Balkans are the crossroads between two different worlds—the West and the East: "different cultures, languages, traditions and even civilizations. The demarcation line, which during the cold war was called 'the iron curtain,' is the same where several centuries ago the Turkish conquering whirlpool had stooped and which had saved the West from violence and assimilation." The unsystematic, improvised, provincial Europeanization of the Balkan countries makes qualities like generosity, tolerance, goodwill, respect for the individual alien to the Balkan mores. As a result, "'uncorrupted politician' sounds in our Balkan vocabulary as 'virtuous criminal.'"[83] Pieces like this attest to the fact that the rhetoric of Balkanism, created and imported from the West, has been completely internalized.

Thus, a Balkan name and a Balkan identity is seriously considered only by the Bulgarians, but even among them it is ambiguous and subordinated to their claim of Europeanness. In the words of a former UDF deputy foreign minister: "We live in Europe and in the Balkans, which are part of Europe and have their own peculiar historical aspects."[84] In the Bulgarian case, the Balkan is intimately known; therefore, the name is a Bulgarian predicament, from which Bulgarians not only cannot escape but have found a way to aestheticize. Balkan studies have had a particularly strong development in Bulgaria where they serve, among others, to overcome the usual parochialism of the nation-state approach so typical for all Balkan countries.[85]

Despite the fact that some accept, although reluctantly, their Balkanness while others actively renounce any connection with it, what is common for all Balkan nations is the clear consensus that the Balkans exist, that there is something that can be defined as Balkan, although it may be an undesired predicament and region. What they would like to prove is that they do not belong to the repellent image that has been constructed of it. The problem of identifying with the Balkans is a subspecies of the larger identity problem of small peripheral nations. To borrow Paul Valéry's rhetorical question: "Comment peut-on être ce que l'on est?" has a different meaning depending on the distance from what is or what is perceived as the core. While someone from the "center" can ask oneself "How can one be what one is?" and arrive at abstract philosophical conclusions, the same question for someone outside of the "center" is "likely to be less abstract and less serene," as Matei Calinescu has aptly remarked. It more likely would evoke feelings of envy, insecurity, inferiority, "frustration or distress at the marginality or belatedness of his culture." It can also trigger a mood of self-abuse; finally it could provoke resentment that could, in some cases, be transmuted, by way of compensation, into a superiority complex.[86]

In all Balkan cases, we are clearly dealing not only with different ways to cope with stigma but also with self-stigmatization. Although the psychological mechanism of self-stigmatization has not yet been exhaustively researched, there is a plausible correlation between self-stigmatization and destigmatization (*Selbststigmatisierung als Entstigmatisierung*). In the hypothesis of Wolfgang Lipp, self-stigmatization becomes a reflective process that is relocated and directed not against the stigmatized but against the "controlling authorities."[87] Another feature common to all Balkan nations is the self-perception of being at the crossroads of civilizational contacts, of having the character of a bridge between cultures. In this respect the Balkans are not unique or even original in their awareness; it is common to most other East European nations. Within this context, the frustrations of the Balkan intelligentsia are an indelible part of the frustrations of the Eastern European intelligentsia that "was almost without exception infused with the residues of material lack and the fact of technological backwardness."[88] The strong insistence of the Visegrád group that they indisputably belong to the West is delivered in a firm voice usually meant for export. With the possible exception of the Czechs, everywhere else the metaphor of the bridge, the quality of in-betweenness, is evoked in internal discussions. As recently as the spring of 1994, the Museum of Ethnography in Budapest had staged an excellent exhibition on "Hungarians Between 'East' and 'West'" which explored this salient ambiguity in Hungarian identity.[89] Elisaveta Bagryana's verse about the Bulgarian spirit being between East and West is not much different from György Konrád's musings on the "transitory, provisional" nature of Central Europe, its being "neither east nor west; it is both east and west."[90] This tension is, of course, a permanent feature of Russian identity and it exists also, with more subdued overtones, among Poles.

East is a relational category, depending on the point of observation: East Germans are "eastern" for the West Germans, Poles are "eastern" to the East Germans, Russians are "eastern" to the Poles. The same applies to the Balkans with their propensity to construct their internal orientalisms, aptly called by Milica Bakić-Hayden the process of "nesting orientalisms." A Serb is an "easterner" to a Slovene, but a Bosnian would be an "easterner" to the Serb although geographically situated to the west; the same applies to the Albanians who, situated in the western Balkans, are perceived as easternmost by the rest of the Balkan nations. Greece, because of its unique status within the European Union, is not considered "eastern" by its neighbors in the Balkans although it occupies the role of the "easterner" within the European institutional framework. For all Balkan peoples, the common "easterner" is the Turk, although the Turk perceives himself as Western compared to real "easterners," such as Arabs. This practice of internal orientalisms within the Balkans corresponds to what Erving Goffman has defined as the tendency of the stigmatized individual "to stratify his 'own' according to the degree to which their stigma is apparent and obtrusive. He then can take up in regard to those who are more evidently stigmatized than himself the attitudes the normals take to him. . . . It is in his affiliation with, or separation from, his more evidently stigmatized fellows, that the individual's oscillation of identification is most sharply marked."[91] With the exception of the Turks, in whose self-identity the East occupies a definite, although intensely discussed, place, all other Balkan nations have renounced what they perceive as East and think of themselves as, if incompletely Western, certainly not Eastern. They would allow to have been marked by the East, but this is a stain, not a sign in any fruitful way. Although competing in their pretense to be more "European" than the rest, and creating their internal hierarchies of less and more "orientalized" members, the only constituents who are brandished by an ultimate and absolute "orientalness" are the Turks.

What is symptomatic and, admittedly, disquieting is the perception that the state of transition, complexity, mixture, ambiguity is an abnormal condition. In-betweenness is rejected not only by Western observers and hurled on the Balkans as stigma, but is considered an intolerable state of existence by a majority among the observed:

"It is well known that one cannot live on a bridge or on a crossroads. . . . The bridge is only part of the road, a windy and dangerous part at that, not a human abode."[92] The metaphor of bridge or crossroads has acquired a mantralike quality that most writers on the region like to evoke as its central attribute: "[T]he Balkans have always signified fragmentation and adversity. The junction of western and oriental cultures and a threshing floor of different peoples (Greeks, Latins, Slavs, Bulgars and Turks) and religions (Catholics, Orthodox and Muslim), Southeastern Europe appears in every sense to be a crossroads of continents."[93] The metaphor is evidently premised on the endorsement of an East-West dichotomy, an essentialized opposition, an accepted fundamental difference between Orient and Occident: "The Balkan peninsula is a region of transition between Asia and Europe—between 'East' and 'West'—with their incompatible political, religious and social ideals."[94] Yet, with all the ambiguity of the transitional position, the central pathos of all separate Balkan discourses (with the sole exception of the Turkish) is that they are not only indubitably European, but have sacrificed themselves to save Europe from the incursions of Asia; a sacrifice that has left them superficially tainted but has not contaminated their essence.

In the face of a persistent hegemonic discourse from the West, continuously disparaging about the Balkans, which sends out messages about the politicization of essentialized cultural differences (like in the Huntingtonian debate), it is hardly realistic to expect the Balkans to create a liberal, tolerant, all-embracing identity celebrating ambiguity and a negation of essentialism. And yet there are some heartening symptoms of resistance to the dominant stereotype. Eva Hoffman noted in her journey through the new Eastern Europe a remarkable "acceptance of ambiguity," which struck her as typical for the Bulgarians, Romanians, and Hungarians. Of course, the interesting twist is her added Polish/American perspective when she writes: "Perhaps such acceptance is characteristic of these regions, which are closer to the Oriental East, after all." This neologism "the Oriental East" can come only from an insider or someone who has acquired the insider's eye, someone intimately conversant with the internal orientalisms of the region.[95] An early case of reaction against the presumed abnormality of life on the bridge has been registered in a short ethnological piece. Reflecting on the well-known phenomenon of symbiosis between Christianity and Islam, a Bulgarian scholar concludes:

> Humans and gods *meet and pass each other* on a bridge and on a cross-roads. In the Balkans they *join* in a complex process of contact-conflict, which makes them different from the ideal types of religious or ideological doctrines. In the evolution of human civilization, the Balkans are not a transitionary zone, but a space, in which *humans* overcome the contradictions of *God* and *gods*. This is the high price of life paid by numerous generations, which requires to revise the ideologemes disclosed through the metaphorical labels of the bridge and the cross-roads and the strategies resulting from them.[96]

One might add that it would be helpful for the self-confidence of Balkan intellectuals to repeat occasionally Nietzsche's dictum from *Also Sprach Zaratustra* that "What is great in man is that he is a bridge and not a goal." This is, in fact, what informs a recent piece about "our Europe," that is, the Balkans, and the "other Europe," that is, the West, by another Bulgarian scholar who concludes proudly: "What drama does this transitional position bring, but also what power! Ours!"[97]

Finally, despite professions to the contrary, all Balkan nations are intensely conscious of their outside image. This is not reduced merely to politics but is vividly present in the cultural sphere where it can be illustrated, for example, by the craze for Balkan and particularly for Bulgarian folklore. The interest toward Bulgarian folk songs and dance has been sustained in the past two decades by a number of highly professional and amateur groups—American, Japanese, Dutch, Danish, and so on—and surely culminated in the success of the Swiss recording of "Le mystère des voix bulgares," followed by a worldwide tour of the Bulgarian vocal ensemble. This interest has little to do with Bulgarian folklore per se, that is, with the phenomenon in its organic Bulgarian context where it is essentially a rural art; the crave for Bulgarian folklore in the West is a basically urban phenomenon.[98] It also displays a specific preference for a particular type of folklore—mostly from the Pirin and the Shop region—that is, the polyphonic zones. Foreign interpretations of Bulgarian folklore followed two models defined by Timothy Rice: emulating the original and attempting its exact reproduction; and assimilation of the music, often in the so-called musical collage, like in one of the Parisian attempts to collate Bulgarian music with music from Zaire.

What is interesting here is not the problem of reception of art in a different cultural context or milieu, but the reception of the adaptation of Bulgarian folklore by Bulgarian musical critics, that is, in a broader sense the problem of the sensibility of the observed being aware of being observed. In an article called "The Others in the 'Mystère': Observations on Foreign Interpretations of Bulgarian Musical Folklore," two Bulgarian critics asked the question of whether the collage secured the proper environment for Bulgarian folk music:

> Losing their singularity, the original Bulgarian folk songs are transformed into an abstract component which, when superimposed upon the real image of the foreigner's musical thinking, becomes the springboard which launches the listener into the unknown, beyond the familiar, but also bouncing over the springboard itself—the unique musical text of the Bulgarian folklore. But maybe this is the goal—the combination of two "primitives" (such are from an eurocentric viewpoint both the African and the Bulgarian folk music) creates the vital and exotic musical cocktail which serves as a dope for the bored contemporary listener.[99]

The authors pointed out the reception of Ivo Papazov (incidentally a Rom) in the English press, and later in the United States, where he is compared to Benny Goodman and Charlie Parker but what was accentuated was his crude masculinity. The tones of his clarinet were characterized as "the depressed violence of spirits which have been kept for centuries in the bottle," his music was "frightening, exhilarating, arousing." He was described physically as something "in between a third-rate boxer and a tavern-keeper, his orchestra as an impressive team of bearded fellows in ugly shirts, and the public falls to the ground from the 'savage' sight from [Papazov's] quick flute solo through his right nostril." The article ended on a broad-minded note:

> Unique or 'savage', Bulgarian musical folklore is sought by foreigners in their quest for individual harmony. . . . For the foreigners, the representations of our folklore music (somebody called it the sound icon of the Bulgarians) are not an anachro-

nistic restoration of Balkan exoticism, but new chronotopes of their own vitality which they have achieved through the vitality of our own Bulgarian voices. Even if they do not perceive these voices as Bulgarian, it is enough that they need them.

Even while wording their opinion quite generously, the authors were acutely conscious of and actually evoked what Tsvetan Todorov has called Western xenophilia, characterized by the benign perception of foreign culture as having a lower value: "for the Westerner, our traditions . . . are exciting with their primitiveness, the elemental quality, the backwardness, the exoticism of the wild."[100] Unlike Western observers who, in constructing and replicating the Balkanist discourse, were (and are) little aware and even less interested in the thoughts and sensibilities of their objects, the Balkan architects of the different self-images have been involved from the very outset in a complex and creative dynamic relationship with this discourse: some were (and are) excessively self-conscious, others defiant, still others paranoic, a great many arrogant and even aggressive, but all without exception were and continue to be conscious of it. This is not something unique to the Balkans. Chakrabarty has shown how non-Western scholars study their own history in conjunction and in reference to the history of the West, whereas Western academia does not reciprocate with the same approach.[101]

Becker and Arnold have convincingly demonstrated that "stigma is not only a cultural universal but has universal importance cross-culturally." The stigmatization originating in one society can have a rippling effect through others, and the responsibility for conflicts both within and between societies is not to be underestimated. It is the belief of these authors that "social scientists have a role in these sometimes subtle, sometimes cataclysmic forces—to tease out the critical factors in understanding stigma, both cross-culturally and intraculturally, and to develop tools with which to better understand our own and other cultures."[102] Multidisciplinary studies of stigma have revealed its three most important aspects: fear, stereotyping, and social control, which are its primary affective, cognitive, and behavioral components. These studies also assert that, alongside the usually invoked restrictive effect undesired differences have on social realization and opportunities, the imposition of social control is decisive in stigmatization. Such an approach to stigma brings forth its complex relational framework and allows it to be understood as "not primarily a property of individuals as many have conceptualized it to be but a humanly constructed perception, constantly in flux and legitimizing our negative responses to human differences."[103]

Musing on the formal symmetry of the process of definition by opposition, James Carrier has concluded that, in practice, we are confronted with an asymmetrical model that "privileges the West as the standard against which all Others are defined" because of its historical, political, and economic power. Westerners possess a relative autonomy to construct the images of alien societies as they see fit because of the existing political imbalance: "Western anthropologists, describing societies that they may have studied closely and sympathetically, are likely to confront only their own honor as a check on the representation they produce. Even if those being described come to read and reject the representation, their rejection is unlikely to be voiced in the academic and social contexts that matter most to anthropologists."[104] It is hardly reassuring to face the stark reality that one has to wait for the West to confront its "own honor" as a check on the representation it produces.

The Discovery of the Balkans

Un voyageur dois se garder de l'enthousiasme
s'il en a et surtout s'il n'en a pas.[1]

Helmuth von Moltke

The Balkans per se, that is, as a distinct geographic, social, and cultural entity,
were "discovered" by European travelers only from the late eighteenth century
on, with the beginning of an awareness that the European possessions of the Ottoman
Empire had a distinct physiognomy of their own that merited separate attention apart
from their treatment as mere provinces of the Ottomans or simply as
archeological sites. Until then, the Ottoman Empire was treated as a unity in Europe
and Asia. The change that set in "shattered the unitary character of the oriental world."[2]
This was part of a manifold process, the result of the deep structural changes that took
place in the political, social, and cultural life of Europe: the technological advances
and change in modes of industrial production, growing internal and foreign trade,
improved means of communications, the transformation of the traditional social order,
the spread and fulfillment of the main ideas of the Enlightenment, the realization to
its full potential of the revolution in printing and education that enormously enlarged
the reading public as well as the production of literary material.

At the same time, the intensifying activities of the Balkan populations for political sovereignty during the eighteenth and nineteenth centuries drew the attention of
outside observers to populations that had been hitherto subsumed under the undifferentiated title of Ottoman or Turkish Christians. The specific admixture of nineteenth
century romanticism and *Realpolitik* on the part of the observers created a polarized
approach of lobbying for or demonizing these populations. Particularly evocative
was the vogue of philhellenism that swept over Europe in the 1820s and the subsequent disillusionment with realities. The same trend can be observed in the peculiar
brand of Turkophilia and Slavophobia, together with their mirror-
image phenomena of Turkophobia (or rather Islamophobia) and Slavophilism, as
direct functions of great power politics, and specifically nineteenth century attitudes
toward Russia.

By the eighteenth century, British and French commercial activities in the Near
East had managed to supplant the Italian city-states. After the middle of the century,
there was a gradual shift of travelers' interests to the east: in the case of the English

Grand Tour, Greece replaced Italy, especially with the closure of Western Europe during the revolutionary period and the Napoleonic wars. There was continuing interest in the literature and monuments of classical antiquity, particularly fervent during the Enlightenment period. In the words of the young Gibbon: "A philosophical genius consists in the capacity of recurring to the most simple ideas, in discovering and combining the first principles of things. . . . What study can form such a genius? . . . the study of literature, the habit of becoming by turns, a Greek, a Roman, a disciple of Zeno or of Epicurus."[3]

Literature, however, was becoming insufficient in the great romance with antiquity, as were monuments. The Enlightenment added a new desire stemming from the concept of stages of evolution: the clue to determining one's place in the history of civilization was their reconstruction, and the urge to reach the roots of human history was accomplished both through historical research and ethnological observation. In the year IX of the *Révolution*, Louis-François Jauffret, permanent secretary of the Société des observateurs de l'homme, founded in 1799 in Paris, argued that the best way to shed light "on the most obscure problems of our primitive history" was to compare the customs, languages, practices, and work of different peoples, "especially the ones who are not yet civilized."[4] Joseph-Marie, baron de Gérando, a harbinger of anthropology and the later *géographie humaine*, argued against the superficial approach of travelers in the past with their attention focused on minerals, flora, and fauna, and instead encouraged the description and study of man in his natural and social environment in view of "reestablishing in such a way the august ties of universal society" and reconstructing the various degrees of civilization: "Here . . . we shall in a way be taken back to the first periods of our own history. . . . The philosophical traveller, sailing to the ends of the earth, is in fact travelling in time. . . . These unknown islands that he reaches are to him the cradle of human society. . . . Those peoples . . . recreate for us the state of our own ancestors, and the earliest history of the world."[5]

A generation earlier, in "A Voyage Round the World," George Foster, sailing as assistant naturalist on Captain Cook's second voyage, found many points of comparison between the habits, physique, even the politics of ancient Greeks and Tahitians.[6] The next step was to turn to the soil of the ancient Greeks themselves, and Robert Wood, traveler and politician, who went on his eastern voyages to read "the Iliad and Odyssey in the countries where Achilles fought, where Ulysses travelled, and where Homer sung," argued finally that Homer was a representative of a primitive society.[7] The effort to study the ancient world through the lives of the contemporary inhabitants of the classic lands brought an awareness of the present Greeks and their problems. This was soon extended to the different Slavs and other ethnic groups inhabiting the peninsula who became the live figures of what came increasingly to be seen as the Volksmuseum of Europe.

The evaluation of travelers' accounts and other descriptions as historical sources has vacillated between complete enchantment and overreliance, especially for periods where other information is scanty, and (less often) an absolute rejection on the grounds that this literature has been superficial and can only serve to illustrate national prejudices. Both extreme views have been inspired by a desire to overgeneralize and an inattentiveness to the merits and weaknesses of each concrete case. Nowadays, travelers' accounts are receiving not only due attention in the best critical tradition but are used as indispensable materials in the study of otherness. Postulating the "discovery" of the Balkans at such a relatively late historical moment does not mean that travelers' accounts or other descriptions were only a post-eighteenth-century phenomenon. Many of the earliest reports, especially the ones compiled by political observers, intelligence officers, and diplomats, were often the product of keener eyes and better informed than some of the later travelers' accounts. Nor is "discovery" a precise term to describe the earlier accounts, implying that areas well known in antiquity and the Middle Ages were subsequently obliterated from the memory of the West and had to be "rediscovered" anew. Byzantine and Balkan themes had always been present to some degree in West European historiography and literature, but after the fifteenth century there was growing individualization and concreteness rather than a literal "rediscovery."[8]

Several circumstances make the later accounts significant and the object of immediate interest. First, one can trace in them the beginnings and gradual formation of a perception of the Balkans as a distinct geographic and cultural entity, rather than just the site of classical history or the provinces to be traversed on the way to the Ottoman capital. Second, they were produced and published for a comparatively broad-reading but enthusiastic public; thus, these travelers functioned as latter-day journalists: they shaped public opinion, expressing themselves the dominant tastes and prejudices of their time. Almost none of the earlier descriptions were specifically written for publication: with a few notable and influential exceptions, most were published either in very limited editions, which turned them immediately into bibliographical rarities, or only later in the nineteenth or twentieth centuries, which confined them mostly to a scholarly clientele. Some, popularized at a later stage, introduced perceptions or earlier prejudices in the formation of a comprehensive image. Third, it is precisely among the later accounts that one can trace the combination of almost all elements that have shaped the existing stereotype of the Balkans. Of course, some elements can be observed already in the travelogues and descriptions of the sixteenth and seventeenth centuries: after all and *pace* Troeltsch who saw the commencement of moderity only in the eighteenth century, they were written at the beginning of the same period of history in which we are still partaking, the declared advent of the postmodern predicament notwithstanding.

Many have accepted with Henri Pirenne that with the arrival of Islam, the "Mediterranean world" was irretrievably split into two irreconcilable camps of Christianity and Islam, which cut medieval Christendom from its sources in the Near East. The establishment of the Ottomans in the southeastern corner of Europe was the final blow to the crusading urge of the West to reestablish this connection. The successful Ottoman expansion toward Central Europe until the end of the sixteenth century kept the idea of crusade alive, at least several decades after the Battle of Lepanto in 1571 and even in the wars of the Holy Leagues until the end of the seventeenth century when the recession of the Ottoman Empire in Europe finally became definite and irrevocable. It would be a simplification to maintain that there was a homogeneous and monolithic response of the "West" to the "Ottoman peril," although there was an overriding common fear before a powerful enemy, the embodiment of the quintessential alien. The fascination with Ottoman power was so great that historical and literary works dealing with the Ottomans far outnumbered those dedicated to the discovery of the New World.[9] However, what came to prevail in the dealings with the new European power were considerations of balance of power (directly inspiring the famous Franco-Ottoman alliance) as well as the desire to better know and accommodate the new masters of important trade routes and lands.[10]

There had always been travelers traversing the peninsula, but most were in a hurry to cross and reach the two focal points of attraction: the Holy Land and Constantinople. Among European writings from the first centuries of Ottoman rule, the narrative accounts of travelers par excellence occupy a relatively modest place, the bulk being works of anti-Ottoman polemic and propaganda, descriptions of military campaigns, and political treatises.[11] No doubt, the best knowledge of the Ottomans and the Balkans in the early period was generated by the Venetians who had traditionally strong commercial, political, and cultural ties to the late Byzantine empire. The creation of a vigorous Greek intellectual diaspora after the fall of Constantinople in 1453 secured a continuous and fruitful exchange that became a fundamental element of the humanistic spirit of the Renaissance. Vitally dependent on the preservation of its elaborate and sophisticated trade mechanism, Venice managed, by vacillating with skillful diplomacy between appeasement, collaboration, neutrality, and war, to maintain its privileged position in the Ottoman realm until the end of the sixteenth century, in the face of the increasing competition from the emerging continental European powers. Long after its eclipse, Venice continued to be present even physically in parts of the Balkans (the eastern Adriatic and the Peloponnesus until the beginning of the eighteenth century) and the reports of the Venetian ambassadors are of unrivaled quality.

The Venetian *relationi* were an indicator of the evolution of Venetian political discourse and perceptions of the Ottoman Empire. There was a drastic change of assessment around 1560. Before, the ambassadors' dispatches, while never completely free from the traditional Christian view of Islam, showed an inquisitive and rational curiosity in the reasons for Ottoman success. This led them to informed fascination and openly pronounced respect for the internal order of the empire, which was linked to the absolute power of the sultan, views that also informed the attitude of the Ragusan patriciate. What set in after that was a complete and abrupt reversal: the discreet admiration for the sultan's absolute rule was transformed into a harsh verdict of his tyrannical practices; the Ottoman Empire began to be painted as the epitome of despotism. This was due to a shift in the Venetian understanding of the nature of tyranny, prompted by political changes taking place in Italy, especially the rivalry between the Medici principate of Florence and the Venetian republic: "Once the dichotomy between the state of liberty and the state of tyranny was conceptually formed, it was then applied to the Ottoman empire as a tyranny par excellence, for what could be predicated of the Florentine Principate largely, it could be said of the Ottoman empire absolutely."[12]

Ironically, the Renaissance value of liberty entered Venetian political discourse as its central tenet at the height of the Counter-Reformation. Its anti-Ottoman aspect, moreover, explains the further paradox that the militant post-Tridentine Catholicism of the papacy "appropriated many Renaissance values for its own unmistakably anti-Renaissance as well as anti-Reformation purposes." The seventeenth century saw the peak of Catholic propaganda in the Balkans, through the activities of the Congregation for the Propagation of Faith, founded in Rome in 1622. In its special missionary policy toward the Balkan Slavs, the Counter-Reformation was both "an ideologically motivated force as well as a product of a system of Western alliances directed against the Turks."[13] In 1637, Francesco Bracciolini, former secretary to Antonio Barberini, cardinal and head of the Propaganda Fide, dedicated a poem devoted to the Christianization of Bulgaria to the cardinal. This came at a time when Protestantism viewed Greek Orthodoxy as closer to the evangelical tradition and had made several attempts to promote closer ties with it. An openly polemical and propagandist piece, "La Bulgheria Convertita" was also a baroque morality tale structured around the dichotomy of Good and Evil, Evil being represented by the triple force of schismatic Orthodoxy, Islam, and Protestantism.[14] Papal propaganda, disseminated in the vernaculars of the region, made a sustained and successful effort to acquire immediate and detailed knowledge of the different Slavic peoples. In this respect, it continued the Venetian diplomatic legacy of keen and concrete observations. The intimacy of Venice's, and later Italy's, relations with the Balkans was promoted also by the continued presence of Balkan emigrés, particularly the prosperous and influential Greek diaspora, but also representatives of the different Slavic ethnic groups.

In the second half of the eighteenth century, when the activation of Russian policy in the Mediterranean stirred parts of the Balkans in open revolt against the Porte, Italy acted as intermediary between east and west in a complicated relationship defined as "Italo-Greco-Russian symbiosis." Italy's traditional ties to the Balkan world nourished "Hellenic enthusiasm, solidarity with the Greek exiles, neo-classical visions, discovery of the Russian world" as elements strongly affecting the culture of Venice, Tuscany, Naples, and even Piedmont.[15] Italy, alongside France, became the most important cultural channel for the transmission of enlightenment ideas to Greece, and from thence to the rest of the Balkans.[16] At the same time, maybe because of its physical proximity or because it did not become organically afflicted with a *mission civilisatrice*, Italy on the whole did not develop an abstract and hectoring pose toward the Balkans and never lost sight of their concreteness.

Like the Italians, the German-speaking world came in direct contact with the Ottomans, and the Habsburgs became the main bulwark against further Ottoman expansion into Europe, which coincided with the exhausting Reformation struggles in the German lands. The enormous output of anti-Turkish propaganda created a stereotyped image of the Ottoman as savage, bloody, and inhuman, and produced a demonized antagonist epitomizing the hereditary enemy of Christendom. This propaganda was utilized for internal political problems, closely linked to the issues of absolutism and the "social disciplining" of the population.[17] At the same time, the popular mind was deeply marked by what has become known as "Türkennot und Türkenfurcht" (Turkish troubles and Turkish fright) attested for by numerous folk songs, sermons, and specific customs.[18]

On the other hand, the image of the Ottoman Empire in the travel literature of the same period was remarkably different from the abstract stereotypes of the propaganda materials. The perceptive observations typical for the Venetian *relationi* have been matched probably only by the Habsburgs, and in general by the German-language travel literature, which has left the most numerous, detailed, and informed accounts of the Balkans from the sixteenth to the eighteenth centuries.[19] These were mostly descriptions of regions coming from journals compiled during official diplomatic missions to the Porte, but also diaries of merchants, pilgrims, or war prisoners. Their writers were usually high-ranking officials of the Habsburg Empire with excellent education, often leading humanist scholars. Some of them were of Slavic (Croatian, Slovenian, Czech, and so on) descent, which gave them an additional immediacy of observation.

The intimate knowledge and detailed interests of the Habsburg emissaries made them also much more sensitive to the ethnic differences in the peninsula, and many of the sixteenth-century travelers—Kuripešić, Vrančić, Dernschwamm, Busbecq, Gerlach, Schweigger, Lubenau—differentiated correctly between Slavic groups and left valuable descriptions of costumes, dances, and customs among Serbs, Bulgarians, Dalmatians, and so forth. There was a wealth of concrete knowledge often missing from the later observation of travelers from lands farther away from the Ottoman Empire. Anton Vrančić has given one of the first and most detailed descriptions of the hairstyle and headgear of Bulgarian women, a favorite topic among European writers and readers of the period. The inexpensive decorations seemed "strange and simple" and "light and funny" to the tastes of the Habsburg mission, conditioned to court jewels and ceremonial dress. Vrančić, however, magnanimously brushed aside the aristocratic hauteur of his fellow travelers with such an explanation, that only its well-meaning innocence matches the extent of its prejudice: "If the plainness [of their ornaments] was not among an oppressed and mostly rural people, we would hardly have believed that these were sensible individuals. Their clothing hardly deserves to be called that. It is shaggy, coarse and cheap, made of hairy furs, like the ones worn probably by the primitive people." Yet, this was followed by an elaborate full-page description of the unique headgear of Bulgarian women of the Pirot district, their rings and bracelets, and ends with a good-natured philosophical digression on fashion:

> Once, when we had many women around, and they were marveling at us, and we were marveling at them and their ornaments, one of them asked us whether our women adorned themselves as well. How happy were these women, who did not know our extravagance, and theirs was confined to objects which cost nothing. They were no less content in their poverty than our women were in their wealth.[20]

Ever the gallant gentlemen, almost all Habsburg aristocratic observers focused on the beauty of the country women they encountered, and emphasized their hospitality and industry. Unlike their later French and English counterparts, who also extolled the beauty of Balkan women but contrasted it to the wild and beastly appearance of their men, the Germans preferred to pass the males in silence. An exception were the few travelers of nonaristocratic provenance, like Hans Dernschwamm or Reinhold Lubenau, who were equally and nonjudgmentally interested in the male costume of the natives. Reinhold Lubenau traversed the Balkans in 1587 as pharmacist to the imperial mission bringing the annual tribute to the Porte. Born to an old burgher family in Königsberg, the Protestant Lubenau received a good education and, eager to see foreign lands, agreed to serve in the Habsburg mission despite his aversion to Catholicism. Once entering Bulgaria, he gave detailed descriptions of the language and dress of its inhabitants. Far from being surprised, let alone shocked, by their clothing, Lubenau sensibly remarked that "the men go around with long hair like our Kurlanders and Lithuanians, dressed in gray coarse cloth, usually without a hat, and remind me of the Kurlandish and Estonian peasants." The women, with their colorful shirts, and ornaments, adorned themselves just like "the Prussian, Estonian, Kurlandish, Russian and Lithuanian women do in our parts, so that there is no difference. When I reached the Danube, I thought that the Lithuanian women had moved there from their lands." This is a world apart from the mockingly shocked description of Vrančić. Here was someone who had been used to the sight of peasants and who, moreover, had keenly observed them. Since he knew Polish and had learned some Czech, Lubenau wrote that he found it easy to communicate with the local inhabitants who were speaking Croatian or Slavic. (He maintained that the Slavs over the whole huge territory of Poland, Lithuania, Russia, the Czech lands, Moravia, Hungary, Serbia, Bulgaria, Thrace, Macedonia, Dalmatia, Albania, Illyria, and so on were speaking the same language which he called Slav or Dalmatian.) Lubenau was told that the women with the strange decorated hats were descendants of the old Bulgarian noble houses that had disappeared, and found this the proper moment to add some of his own philosophical reflections on aristocracy, using Bulgaria as the scene for a morality tale:

> In this country Bulgaria there is no nobility whatsoever, just as in all the Turkish lands. . . . Many coming from the families of ancient rulers, even the ones from the house of the Paleologues, are marrying sheperds' daughters, so that the aristocracy is completely uprooted. Such among our nobility who become too arrogant and despise the ones around should better ponder over the fact that here delicate young women of noble lineage are marrying peasants.[21]

Ogier Ghiselin de Busbecq, the Flemish aristocrat, scholar, polyglot, and distinguished diplomat of the Habsburg court, wrote perhaps the most popular account of the Ottoman Empire, one of the few published in the lifetime of its author. Known as "Legationis Turcicae epistolae quatuor," Busbecq's account saw over twenty editions in many European languages throughout the sixteenth and seventeenth centuries. Commenting on the headgear of the Bulgarian women at the same time and in the same region as Vrančić's observations, Busbecq thought that they looked like some Trojan Clytemnestra or Hecuba entering the scene.[22] The classical education and obsession with antiquity paid off handsomely in his case. The scores of materials that he assembled and sent back to the emperor's library in Vienna laid the foundation of the rich collection of Greek manuscripts: "I am carrying a countless number of coins. . . . I filled numerous carriages and ships with Greek manuscripts that I collected. I sent about 240 volumes by sea to Venice."[23] Busbecq was no exception: all visitors to the Balkans were well educated, almost all were intimately acquainted with classical learning, and many were accomplished humanist scholars and passionate antiquarians.

Still, the bulk of information in their accounts, indeed, the reason they compiled them in the first place, was to give a detailed idea of the system of government of the Ottomans. While informed with a strong pro-Christian bias, and while the overall impression of the Muslim empire was one of tyranny, plunder, disorder, and oppression, the descriptions they left are surprisingly rich and matter of fact. Often, when going into detailed description of institutions and events, the writers were favorably impressed by the efficiency of Ottoman bureaucracy and the organization of its military force, by the sobriety of the society in contrast to the alcohol problem in the German lands, even by their friendly disposition. It was in this period of harsh interdenominational struggles and wars in most of Europe, that the toleration, albeit with a subordinate status, of Christians and Jews in the Ottoman Empire made a great impression on the observers, especially on Protestants. The despotism of the sultans, in particular, was the object of a somewhat ambiguous admiration where considerations of efficiency often took the upper hand in overall evaluations.[24]

The Habsburg accounts of the sixteenth century were unique in their quality compared to later descriptions, and especially in the attention given the ordinary population.[25] This comes as no surprise, since the seventeenth century was a period of intensive ideological and political struggle around the Reformation, the Thirty Years War, and a strenuous power equilibrium between Habsburgs and Ottomans, all of which accounts for the cultural stagnation in the German-speaking world. As late as 1743, a book appeared in Jena with a title advertising the minute description of newly discovered peoples, mixing up ethnic and local names, social and professional groups, and sobriquets: "Hussaren, Heydukken, Tolpatchen, Insurgenten, Sclavoniern, Panduren, Varasdinern, Lycanern, Croaten, Morlaken, Raitzen, Walachen, Dalmatinern, Uskoken," that is, hussars, robbers, Butterfingers, insurgents, Slavs, Albanian guards, inhabitants of Varasdin and Lika, Croats, Morlachs, Serbs, Wallachians, Dalmatians, bandits.[26]

An early eighteenth-century oil painting from Styria shows the reigning perceptions of ethnic hierarchies and the place of Germans in the family of European nations.[27] This "Brief description of the European nations and their characteristics" shows ten male figures portraying different nations and obviously ranged from positive to negative: Spaniard, Frenchman, Dutchman, German, Englishman, Swede, Pole, Hungarian, Moskovite, Turk, or Greek. While the ranging comes as no surprise, it is remarkable that Turk and Greek are represented together by a turbaned male to fill in the negative extreme of the picture. The tableau compares these figures in seventeen categories: temperament, nature, intellect, vices, passions, knowledge, costume, diseases, military prowess, religion, political form, and so on. It is an amusing illustration not merely of stereotypes but of the powerful and unexpected shifts of stereotype. In terms of qualities of mind, the Spaniard is categorized as intelligent and wise, the Frenchman as cautious, the German as witty, and the Englishman as ill humored.

In the same category, the intellect of ridiculed nations is described as "limited" for the Pole, "even less" for the Hungarian, "nothing" for the Russian, and "less than that" for the Turco-Greek. The painting was obviously executed by and for Catholics, because the church service was given highest scores in Spain, good in France, and fair in Germany. The English were "changing as the moon," the Poles believed in everything, and the Russians were dissenters. The Turco-Greek was described as "the same" as the Moscovite, thus conflating the Orthodox deviation with the Islamic aberration. Their clothing ranged from the Spanish "honorable," the French "changeable," the German "imitating," the English "following the French ways," to the long dress of the

Poles, the many colors of the Hungarians, the furs of the Russians, and the womanly dress ("auf Weiber art") of the Turks and Greeks. While Spaniards, French, Germans, and English were compared to elephants, foxes, lions, and horses, Poles, Hungarians, Russians, and Turco-Greeks were matched with bears, wolves, donkeys, and rats. More significantly, however, they were all "European nations." For our purposes, of course, the most interesting aspect was the monolithic vision of the inhabitants of the Otto- man Empire, a vision that was very different from the usual dichotomy between Christians (albeit Orthodox) and Muslims, something that can be explained with the deteriorating stage of knowledge of the European southeast in this period.

It was only after the end of the seventeenth century that a substantive shift in the perception of the Ottomans set in with the Enlightenment. The reassessment of the image of Islam in general and the creation of a positive Ottoman image in particular was pioneered in France but gradually also influenced the Germans.[28] Gerard Cornelius Driesch served as "secretary and historiographer" to the *magna legatio* sent to Constantinople by the Habsburg emperor in the wake of the Peace of Passarowitz in 1718. He published his bulky Latin journal in 1721 in Vienna, and two German edi- tions followed in Augsburg and Nürnberg. Not only was Driesch's account extremely well informed, a virtual treasury about everyday life in the Ottoman Empire; he openly admired certain aspects of the Ottoman social and political system, particularly the absence of hereditary aristocracy, which he contrasted positively to the behavior of the Habsburg nobility.[29]

Captain Schad, traveling through the Balkans in 1740 and 1741, shared these views but prefaced the first part of his notes with a phrase from Voltaire: "Able conquerors among tyrants and bad rulers exist, but even they are closer to the latter." He offered extremely detailed and lively descriptions of everyday life in the Balkans and remarked that the Christians in Europe were greater thieves than the Muslims. Instead of the conventional pictures of grim Janissaries, Schad commiserated with them at the out- rageous price (1.2 florins against their daily pay of only 6 florins) that they had to pay for the services of Gypsy prostitutes near Razgrad.[30] While Schad's journal was not published during his lifetime, similar travel accounts increasingly influenced the read- ing public: until the 1780s, the German readers were the main consumers of travel literature in Europe.[31] By the end of the eighteenth century, even the good Turk, "le Turc genereux," had made his entry into the German-speaking world and was popu- larized with Mozart's "Entführung aus den Serail," to mention only the most popular among numerous examples.[32]

During the nineteenth century, the Christian-Muslim dichotomy was dropped from the political and cultural vocabulary, at least in the terms known before. Now, the opposition was phrased as nations eager to develop along the path of European progress against a backward traditionalist polity. Philhellenism has been defined as "an international movement of protest in which nationalism, religion, radicalism and commercial greed all played a part, as well as romantic sentiment and pure heroism."[33] The German kind was almost exclusively of the latter two varieties. Despite the fact that Byron's stature and the voluminous literature on English philhellenes has created the impression that they were the most ardent and selfless lovers of Greece, the Germans who actually fought for Greece far outnumbered any other European nation: among the 940 known European philhellenes fighting in Greece, the majority (one-third) were Germans, followed by French, Italians, and only after them British and Americans.[34] For comparison, the volunteers from the other Balkan nations were much more numerous. The Bulgarians alone who fought on the Greek side during the war were reported by a contemporary Greek writer to be over 14,000. The names of at least 704 of them have been preserved in Greek and Russian archives, more than any of the western philhellenes.[35] That the participation of other Balkan volunteers may not be technically subsumed under the narrow heading of philhellenism does not justify the silence over this expression of Balkan solidarity, especially in the face of so much emphasis on incurable Balkan enmities.

Moltke's "Briefe aus der Türkei" have been praised as surpassing even Goethe's "Italienische Reise" in the objectivity of detail and beauty of description.[36] The future military genius served in his youth as instructor in the Ottoman army, which the Ottoman government, after the radical destruction of the Janissaries, was determined to reform on the European model. Moltke had no qualms to attribute the sad state of Wallachia to the "Turkish yoke which has thrown this nation in complete servitude." Whatever progress he encountered in the country—liberation of the peasants, easing of their tax burden, training of a local militia, organization of an efficient antiplague system—he attributed to the Russian occupational forces under General Kisselev. Yet he did not dismiss the reform attempts of the Porte as mere political hoax to accommodate the powers, something other Europeans did. In 1837, he accompanied the sultan on his tour of the Balkans. Listening to his speeches delivered two years before the official proclamation of the Tanzimat, in which the sultan proclaimed equal treatment before the law for all his subjects irrespective of religious affiliation, Moltke conveyed his moderate optimism that this was the right path that would lead to success.[37] Moltke proved to be the ideal executor to his own maxim that the perfect traveler should run the middle road between an excess and a lack of enthusiasm, but in his time there were also others who produced perceptive accounts of high quality and nonjudgmental lucidity. During the second half of the nineteenth century, the breadth of vision, diversity of interest, and quality of information of the scholars from the German-speaking world surpassed even the accomplishment of the German humanists.[38] An exquisite example in this respect was the work of Felix Philipp Kanitz, the result of travels in the course of two decades and a veritable mine of rich and scholarly information on Bulgarian and Balkan geography, ethnography, demography, archeology, linguistics, folklore, art, and so forth; no attempt at summarizing this achievement can do it credit. It was also a work of great literary merit and until World War I the unrivaled source of serious information on the Bulgarians who were, no doubt, Kanitz's "pet" folk.[39]

The great archaeologist and philologist Karl Krumbacher, founder of German Byzantine studies, visited the new state of Greece and the Greek-inhabited regions of the Ottoman Empire in his late twenties. The account of his journey was dedicated to the "great philhellene Ludwig I, the King of Bavaria." Krumbacher opposed the injustice of harsh judgments passed on Greece, stemming from the disappointment of high expectations when employing the criteria of European states or applying a totally idealized viewpoint. Instead, he demonstrated a real and intimate understanding of the problems besieging Greece and of the progress achieved so far. He made subtle

comments on the identity transformations among the Greeks when they were gradually shedding off their self-designation as "Romaioi" and "Graikoi," and adopting an
identifications as "Hellenes." He was extremely critical of the mechanistic methodology of contemporary European (especially German) ethnography that, by "statisti-
cally calculating the percentage of blond and dark hair, counting blue and brown
eyes, and taking detailed measures of the skull," passed authoritative judgments on
whole nations. Of course, there was a self-congratulatory element in his comparison
of Greek tenacity, sharpness, and steady forward-looking ways to the manners of the
Prussian state but, in general, he judged the Greeks on their own merit. For
Krumbacher, the Balkans definitely existed as a separate entity and he saw its originality in the ethnic diversity, different costumes, and specific social relations, rather than
in some kind of deeply imprinted cultural attitudes or value system. Once in Corfu,
he remarked on its Italian character where only occasional Albanian street sweepers,
Vlach spinners, and Greeks dressed in fustanellas reminded one of the proximity of
the Balkan peninsula.[40]

The newly emerged Bulgaria also attracted attention and in the 1880s inspired
even a literary/theatrical attempt. After the abdication of Alexander Battenberg in
1886, the Bulgarians were desperately looking for a new prince to satisfy the demands
of the great powers, primarily Russia. By August 1887, the new prince was found—
Ferdinand von Saxe-Coburg-Gotha—who ruled the country for the next thirty-one
years. The same year, a short book was published in Leipzig under the title "Would
You Care for a Bulgarian Crown? To All Those Who Would Like to Say 'Yes,' Dedicated as a Warning." Written by Julius Stettenheim, a popular Berliner satirist, it
consisted of four parts: an opera in fifteen minutes with piano accompaniment ("The
trumpeter of Säkkingen or the solution of the Bulgarian question"); a series of bur-
lesque letters written in Berliner dialect to Prince Ferdinand ("Muckenich and
Bulgaria"); and two short pieces ("To the solution of the burning question" and "Bulgarian miscellanea"). The advice given to Ferdinand was concise: "Take to Bulgaria
only the most essential. Deposit all your valuables at the Coburg bank. Pack, at the
very most, three suits, underwear, your shaving things, several loaded guns, a cook-
book, several pounds of insecticide, and a used scepter. Once you arrive, make them
pay you the advance for the first quarter."[41] While Stettenheim's ridicule was directed at the pretensions of German princelings whose megalomania was in reverse
proportion to their significance at home, he documented well the current view of
the Balkans: the southeast was a backward and disorderly place manipulated by Russians, and German princelings had better watch out. Indeed, the new values of
Ordnung und Gesetz were already so deeply internalized that, at the turn of the century, a student of Johann Gustav Droysen working on a dissertation about the Turkish fright during the Reformation ended with a criticism of the present policy of the
great powers for upholding an unreformable state based on conquest and power instead of law and order.[42]

The Balkans, although as part of the Near East, were also the object of a very
different muse: this time of a romantic incarnate, Karl May (1842–1912), whose books
by the 1960s had reached a circulation of over forty-five million and have brought
him the often derisively used title of the "most read German author." Karl May had
the bad luck of having been liked by Hitler, and for a period of time this stained his
reputation. He has since been rehabilitated, his pacifism and even anti-imperialist

stance emphasized, and has secured a prominent place in this peculiar black-and-white genre of adventure literature whose knightly heroes do not fail to inspire the young. Although his popularity rested on his Red Indian novels, and generations of European adolescents have been weaned on his stories about Old Shatterhand and Winnetou, Karl May also published a series of novels on the Near East. His *orientalische Reiseromane*, whose fourth volume was "In the Balkan mountain gorges," immortalized the romantic protagonist Kara Ben Nemsi. Karl May had not visited the Balkans and the Near East, just as he had never set foot in North America, but his Near Eastern novels were so well researched, mostly from travelers' accounts and geographical works, that it is possible to verify his travel routes.[43] Karl May may be said to be the first practitioner in the new genre of invention-tourism describing the relationship between tourism and staying at home, and aptly termed as *écritour* in distinction to *écriture*.[44] As late as 1980, a German linguist visiting Kosovo and Albania admitted he had rather nebulous ideas of these lands that "amounted to little more than an image of a predominantly rural, patriarchal, conservative society, unfamiliar in its Oriental tendencies and with pronounced martial characteristics. Certainly the image reflects childhood readings of Karl May's works."[45]

What Karl May also inspired, although he did not invent the genre, was a host of less talented experts on imaginary adventures, chivalric contests, and less chivalric battles, many of which took place in the Balkans. There was a proliferation of so many "Karl Mays" specializing in imaginary combat that Stettenheim took them to task. Writing for the satirical journals "Mephistopheles," "Kladderadatsch," and "Die Wespen," he contributed immensely popular fictitious war communiqués from the site of the Russo-Turkish war in the Balkans signed with the name of the invented war correspondent "Wippchen." "Wippchen" has entered the German vocabulary as yet another word for fairy tales.[46] What is remarkable is how the nearby Balkans, together with the distant North American prairies, could tickle the popular imagination as fanciful sites for the setting of morality plays, romantic or antiromantic.

The Enlightenment brought a reassessment of the Turk image and nowhere was it stronger exemplified than by the French case. With the French, however, it was the energizing of a continuity rather than an abrupt shift. Where Venice and the Habsburgs had to go through a direct clash with the victorious Ottomans from the outset, France was not involved in an immediate relationship because of lack of proximity and its absorption in the almost continuous Hundred Years War with the English. The only exception was the active policy of Burgundy under the rule of Philippe II le Bon. The few accounts from this period were informed by the traditions and pathos of the crusades, in which the Ottomans were referred to as Saracens, although on occasion an intelligent observer would surmount some of the dominant clichés. Bertrandon de la Broquière, who traveled on a secret mission in 1432–1433, praised the military prowess of the Turks and their greater friendliness compared to the Greeks. He preferred them in general to the Greeks who showed open hostility toward a representative of the Catholic nobility, no doubt sustained by fresh memories of the dubious activities of the crusaders in Byzantium.[47]

The sixteenth century, which saw the intensive rivalry between France and the Holy Roman Empire, brought about the "sacrilegious union of the Lily and the Crescent" in their struggle against the Habsburgs. This "impious alliance" was fated to persist with ups and downs until Napoleon's days. Between the urges of humanism dictating a rational and empirical approach, and the political considerations of French interests, the French travel literature of the sixteenth century created a rather positive image of the Ottoman Empire.[48] It was the sense of order and tranquility that most impressed the observers. Jean Chesneau spoke with admiration about the excellent organization of police and the security at night, and Pierre Belon cited a Greek from Lemnos who extolled the beneficial effects a long-term peace had for the prospering of the countryside.[49] Although this travel literature was the result of firsthand impressions, practically all sixteenth-century accounts, with minor exceptions, were written by members of diplomatic missions: Jean Chesneau, Jacques Gassot, and Pierre Belon, all in 1547, Nicolas de Nicolay (1551), Philippe du Fresne-Canay (1572), Pierre Lescalopier (1574). Their views of the institutions of the Ottoman Empire were important not only for the formation of French foreign policy but greatly influenced French essayism, drama, prose, and verse, as well as the general development of ideas about culture and religion.[50] The image of the despotic but well functioning Ottoman Empire exerted an important influence in shaping the European, particularly French, ideology of absolutism.[51]

A problem that intimately interested foreign observers was the religious institutions of the empire and the modus vivendi of the rich variety of religions and denominations. Pierre Belon, the prominent natural scientist, clearly impressed that the different Christian denominations, as well as the Jews, who had found refuge in the Ottoman Empire after their expulsion from Spain and Portugal, had their own houses of worship, attributed the strength of the Ottomans to the circumstance that "the Turks force nobody to live according to the Turkish way, but all Christians are allowed to follow their own law. This is precisely what has supported the power of the Turk: because, when he conquers a country, he is satisfied if it obeys, and once he receives the taxes, he doesn't care about the souls."[52] While such impressions have been instrumental in creating the widespread notion of Muslim tolerance, it needs to be emphasized that they were conceived at the peak of religious intolerance in Europe, particularly France, and should therefore be properly contextualized.

At the same time, the effect of these positive images of the Ottomans on public perceptions cannot be overestimated. Rabelais's *Gargantua and Pantagruel*, written between the 1530s and 1550s, for all its humor and humanistic breakthrough, was informed by the popular spirit of crusade and prejudice when it came to the Turks. When Picrochole was assured that his army had won him everything from Brittany, Normandy, Flanders through Lubeck, Norway, Swedenland, had overcome Russia, Wallachia, Transylvania, Hungary, Bulgaria, Turquieland, and was now at Constantinople, his fiery exclamation was: "Come . . . let us join with them quickly, for I will be Emperor of Trebizonde also. Shall we not kill all these dogs, Turks and Mahometans?" Panurge, on the other hand, having fallen in the hands of cannibalistic "rascally Turks," would have been most surely roasted on a spit larded like a rabbit, were it not for the mercy of divine will.[53]

By the end of the sixteenth century, there was an increasing ambiguity toward the Ottoman Empire, manifest throughout the next century. While the line of active alliance against the Habsburgs together with intensive commercial links was continuously pursued, there was also strong support for the Catholics of the empire and even diplomatic actions to foster resistance movements among the Christian

Balkan populations. This was partly a result of the overall activization of Catholic propaganda during the Counter-Reformation, partly an attempt on the part of France to counterbalance the adverse impression its alliance with the Ottomans had left.[54] Accordingly, both lines were represented in the travelers' accounts of the seventeenth century, which were written, as in the previous one, almost exclusively by diplomats. Louis Gédoyn, "le Turc," was first secretary to the French embassy in Constantinople between 1605 and 1609 and served as French consul in Aleppo in 1623–1625, where he witnessed the conspiracy of Charles Gonsague, Duc de Nevers, a French nobleman of Greek descent, who had enlisted the support of the pope, the Holy Roman emperor, Spain, Poland, and even the Druze in Syria in a holy Christian league against the Ottomans, and who had sent emissaries to Serbia and Bosnia. In a letter from Belgrade in January 1624, Gédoyn exclaimed: "God grant that all this can be achieved and that this first attempt succeeds in awaking the Christians, who today are asleep." Only a month later, this time from Sofia, he concluded: "The Levantine Christians are awakening everywhere and long for the support of Christian princes."[55]

After the Thirty Years War, the Habsburg Empire was so enfeebled that Louis XIV even sent a military unit to join the victorious coalition against the Turks at the battle of St. Gotthard in 1664. The French also sent help to Crete in the 1660s, jeopardizing but never completely severing their relations with the Porte. At a time when the Ottoman Empire was clearly on the defense and its structural defects came to the fore, there appeared in France the first plans for its future partition.[56] In the 1670s, Delacroix, son of the famous orientalist and official royal translator from Turkish and Arabic, was sent with a mission to collect oriental manuscripts, an activity that had become a unique feature of France's policy in the Levant. After ten years in the Near East, Delacroix became head of the chair of Arabic at the University of Paris and inherited his father's post at the court. A prolific writer and translator from Turkish, Arabic, and Persian, he published his memoirs in 1684, exposing the corruption of the main Ottoman institutions and concluded that "the Ottoman empire is much stronger in the imagination of the foreigners than it is in actuality, and that Christian rulers need not unite in order to vanquish this might. The French kingdom would suffice, and it seems that heaven is reserving this victory for His Majesty."[57]

The former line of favorable depictions continued but lost much of its convincing argumentation. In 1657, A. Poullet passed through Sofia and was impressed by the beauty of Bulgarian women in the adjacent villages. They did not cover their faces like other women in the Orient and struck him as "gentle, almost identical to our French women," polite and possessing a French temperament. He was even more deeply impressed with their dress and necklaces made of copper, silver, or gold coins: "On their breasts they wear kerchiefs covered with some of these coins so that they hide everything beneath, arranged and attached quite deep down on the cloth like tiles on a roof; all this makes one suppose that the oppression is not such as our writers would make us believe."[58] Poullet was certainly a connoisseur, having previously expressed his scorn for the ladies' toilette in Dubrovnik, which made them look like "a pair of buttocks without any body."[59] Still, using decolletage covers was a most uncommon but certainly imaginative evidence against exaggerated accusations of tyranny. But even among the accounts committed to encourage the development of relations, particularly commercial, between France and the Ottoman Empire, critical notes were creeping in, and illustrations of weakness, venality, and overall decline were increasingly accompanying the general descriptions.

This dichotomy of judgment continued during the eighteenth century. Charles de Peyssonnel, diplomat and writer, left valuable descriptions of the Ottoman Empire and the Crimea from the 1750s to the 1770s, in which he explored their commercial potential. He was a staunch supporter of the Ottoman Empire, particularly in view of its role as counterbalance to the rising power of Russia. No less devoted advocate of the official French line, Esprit-Mary Cousinéry provided his government with detailed and useful information about the territories in which he served as consul until the 1790s. His chief and passionate interest was the ancient world and, besides collecting several tens of thousands of ancient coins and medals, which now adorn the museum collections of Paris, Munich, and Vienna, he left one of the most valuable and impartial descriptions of Macedonia, despite the characteristic classical affectations of his prose. Baron François de Tott, diplomat and general, who was instrumental in the efforts to modernize the Ottoman army, could not hide his disdain at the persistence of erroneous ideas about the courage, splendor, dignity, and even justice among the Turks. So harsh was his verdict that he was criticized for overstating his case.[60]

Where there were only Greeks and Turks, after the middle of the century French travelers began to discover or distinguish also the other Christian Balkan nations.[61] Toward the end of the century, the skeptical and critical opinions expressed in regard to the future of the Ottoman Empire turned into open rejection, especially among the ones imbued with the views and tastes of the Enlightenment and shaped by the events of the French Revolution. The romance with efficient despotism was over; already in the seventeenth century the Ottoman Empire began to be identified as the seat of Oriental despotism, while the French monarchy was spared this affliction: "Not all monarchies are *despotiques*; only the Turkish is of that kind." Still, it was only with the enormous popularity of Montesquieu's *De l'esprit des lois* that the term became central to eighteenth-century political thought and, with the exception of Voltaire, was maintained as a distinct type of government qualitatively different from monarchy and typical for all the great empires of Asia and Africa, notably by Rousseau, Mably, Holbach, Boulanger, and Turgot.[62] The pronounced anticlericalism of the Enlightenment, its onslaught on religion as the sanctuary of conservatism, prejudice, and backwardness, also produced a twist in the assessment of Islam. The view of the Ottoman Empire as the epitome of despotism was coupled with the conviction of the unreformability of Muslim religion, afflicted with fanaticism and bigotry, a far cry from the previous views about Muslim tolerance. Count Ferrières de Sauveboeuf, a passionate Jacobin, wrote in 1790:

> If only the Turks could enlighten themselves one day! Vain dreams! Fed with ignorance, fanaticism restricts their horizon and they aspire to nothing else but entertainment. . . . The Ottomans may be driven out of Europe but they will never change. Their fanaticism will follow them everywhere and the veil of religion will always cause this lack of consciousness which makes them despise all that, being close to our habits, could have distanced them from their prejudices.[63]

Similar was the verdict of François Pouqueville, doctor and member of the French scientific expedition sent to Egypt in 1798, who was captured by the Ottomans and spent three years in the Ottoman Empire: "The Turks, sunk in profound barbarity, think only how to devastate, something which they relish, and this misfortune is linked to their religious beliefs." Pouqeville, who in 1805 became French consul at the court of Ali pasha of Ioannina and later in Patras, published memoirs abounding in valuable statistical data and geographic detail. He was one of the first to use the notion of Europe in an allegorical rather than purely geographic sense and to disassociate the Ottomans from the family of civilized European nations. Constantinople had become "a city inhabited by a people who belong to Europe merely on account of the place they are inhabiting." Likewise, the famous traveler and entomologist Guillaume-Antoine Olivier attributed the decline of the Ottoman Empire to the fanaticism of "an oppressive religion" and to the moral degeneration of society.[64]

In 1829, when Count Louis-Auguste Félix de Beaujour published memoirs summarizing his impressions of his stay in the Ottoman Empire in the 1790s, he shared Pouqeville's judgment and wrote that "estranged from the big family of European nations by its customs and beliefs, as well as by the despotism of its rule, Turkey cannot encounter any support or sympathy for its political existence and is sustained solely by the rivalry of the other governments who fear that it might be conquered by one of them, to the detriment of all the rest." On the other hand, whenever instances of religious tolerance were encountered, they were attributed to the ignorance of a populace untouched by the graces of civilization, another category elaborated during the Enlightenment. When Alexandre-Maurice, Count d'Hauterive visited the empire in 1785, he admired the "religious skepticism, so quiet and good-natured" among the Bulgarians, which he deemed "quite pardonable." But while he thought that the peculiar symbiosis between Christianity and Islam, which Lady Mary Montagu before him had noticed among the Albanians, was preferable to the religious wars in Hungary and Transylvania that had left more than a million dead Hussites, Jacobites, and Catholics, he nevertheless attributed it not to any innate nobility of character but to the "ignorance and simplicity of a people without education and enlightenment." This "blindness" as he defined it was due to the fact that "these unfortunates are so far from civilization, because they possess none of the passions which prejudice renders so common and incurable elsewhere."[65]

The passion of their enlightenment ideas and revolutionary fervor did not entirely break the practical streak of these men. Count Marie-Gabriel de Choiseul-Gouffier published the extremely popular "Voyage pittoresque de la Grèce" in 1782, six years after his visit to Greece. The illustrations to his book depicted the Maineotes in a pastoral idyll, but Choiseul was calling on France and the other European countries to join forces with Catherine II and liberate Hellas. Two years after the publication of his book, Choiseul was appointed Louis XVI's ambassador to the Porte. The British ambassador, Sir Robert Ainslie, duly informed the sultan of his French rival's subversive ideas and showed him the book with a raised eyebrow and the comment: "This is the man France is sending you!" Not losing face, Choiseul had a pro-Turkish version privately printed, and pronounced the original to be a forgery.[66]

Still, the new ideas of the eighteenth century had introduced a fundamental transformation in the attitudes toward the non-Turkish populations of the Balkan Peninsula. The abasement of the modern Greeks compared to their illustrious forefathers was treated at length in sixteenth- and seventeenth-century accounts, but whenever they would muse on its etiology they would attribute it "to inner forces of decay and to the stray ways of the Greeks." Not only were expressions of sympathy rare but there was practically no desire to see the Greeks independent. Christian as they were, they were schismatics, and although different from their rulers, were placed "in a twilight zone illuminated neither by the radiance of the West nor by the exotic glow of the East." With the elevation of the natural and civil rights of men, and the powerful critique against absolute authority, the decline of the modern Greeks was viewed as a result of loss of freedom first under the Byzantines, but especially under the Turks. The political emancipation of the Greeks began to be seen as the sole guarantee for reviving the classical past with its rejuvenating influence. It was the linking of politics and culture that brought about this reassessment.[67]

François-René Chateaubriand is the most famous example of the first attitude, who only later fell under the sway of French political philhellenism. His "Itinéraire," inspired by his passage to Greece in 1806 and 1807, was the first truly literary travel account in French literature and paved the way for Alphonse de Lamartine, Gustave Flaubert, Gérard de Nerval, and Maurice Barrès. It was a new type of travel account, focused not on external reality but on the subjective world of the author. Completely engrossed in his own romantic persona, Chateaubriand became the foremost poet of Greek landscape. The modern Greeks, just like the Albanians and the Turks, annoyed him with their uncivilized manners. Asked by a Turk about the reasons for his journey, Chateaubriand retorted he had come to see people and "especially the Greeks who were dead." The ones alive he disdained and rendered in distorted caricaturesque descriptions. Only in 1825, at the height of the Greek struggle for independence, did he endorse the Greek Revolution and call on Europe to assist it in the name of Hellenism, Christianity, and the natural rights of men. Merely a flashing exception to his previous and subsequent views about modern Greece, this secured Chateaubriand's immortality in the heart of grateful Hellas. And yet, even when they embraced the ideal of Greek liberty, the French could not shed the air of *mission civilisatrice* of culturally superior Europeans, "who sought to bring about the rehabilitation of the modern Greeks on their own terms, namely, through the efficacious imitation of Western-derived classical models. Ironically, although it proposed the reunification of Greek culture, in actuality it fostered its bifurcation because it pitted its more recent Christian-Byzantine-Ottoman legacy against its ancient past."[68]

During the eighteenth and nineteenth centuries, diplomats were outnumbered for the first time by travelers per se: antiquarians, merchants, scholars, or simply adventurers. For many of them, the attractions of the Balkans were linked to their relationship with the classical world. Marie-Louis-Jean-André-Charles, Viscount de Marcellus, a Restoration politician, philhellene, and passionate admirer of antiquity, who left a description of his voyages between 1816 and 1820, remembered Homer, Strabon, and comic verses from Menander about polygamy while barefooted women, young and old, served him meals in a small village in the foot of the Balkans. The propensity to dream in ancient Greek did not deprive him of practical acumen and to him we owe the presence of the splendid Venus of Milo in the Louvre.[69] One is so conditioned to stories about the venality of Ottoman officials or the greed of ignorant Balkan peasants who were selling off their classical and medieval heritage for which they cared but little that it is worth citing the complaint of an earlier traveler, Paul Lucas, who was desperate that he could not acquire manuscripts from the libraries of Mt. Athos because the monks would become "furious even if one offers to buy." Female beauty left almost none of the French travelers indifferent. The same Paul Lucas was amazed that the peasant women in the Maritsa valley had the manners of gentlewomen, and he compared them to the bacchantes of Nicolas Poussin.[70] Beaujour wrote about the freshness of young girls picking roses in the Rose Valley near the town of Sliven who reminded him of pastoral scenes described by the ancient authors.[71]

Males fared worse. While Pouqueville opined that the lecherous Oriental monarchs should look for their roses of love among Bulgarian women endowed by great beauty, high stature, and noble gait, their male counterparts were portrayed as having "a pleasant appearance, without possessing a noble stature; their open face, small eyes and protruding forehead describe them better than their crude character."[72] This was a comparatively mild verdict over the male part of populations that were usually characterized as "wild" or "semi-wild." An earlier traveler and female admirer, Poullet, was repulsed by the boisterous dances of the Catholic Slavs along the Dalmatian coast, but especially by the religious ceremonies of these men "wild like animals," who sang prayers "in their half-Latin, half-Slavic tongue."[73] Even as an aside, the theme of the mongrel nature becomes increasingly present among the travelers.

The rise of the Napoleonic Empire saw direct French presence in the Balkans, with the creation of the French province of Illyria in Slovenia, Croatia, and Dalmatia, the reestablishment of French rule in the Ionian islands, and the activization of French diplomacy in Serbia, Wallachia, and Moldavia, as well as among the semi-independent rulers of Northern Greece and Western Bulgaria—Ali pasha Tepedelenli and Osman Pazvantoğlu. A new type of traveler appeared: the military (J.-C. Marguerite, Compte de Charbonnel in 1801, Louis de Zamagna in 1807, Compte Armand-Charles Guilleminot in 1826, J.-J.-M.-F. Boudin, Compte de Trommelin in 1828, Félix de Favier in 1830), the military engineer (Antoine-François, Comte de Andreossy in 1812, François-Daniel Thomassin in 1814, Jean-Jacques Germain, Baron de Pelet in 1826, J.-B. Richard in 1828), and the geographer (J.-G. Barbié de Bocage in 1828) joined the diplomat in important intelligence missions. This also produced a new genre: itineraries with detailed information on topography, the state of the roads, villages, and towns, fortifications, and so forth, but where the local population was the last priority, and the ethnographic and other types of data often yielded in quality to earlier descriptions. There is no doubt, however, that these descriptions, many of which appeared in scholarly journals or remained unpublished, served to immensely advance the concrete knowledge of the peninsula.[74]

The great French poet, diplomat, and politician Alphonse-Marie-Louis de Lamartine passed through the Balkans in the early 1830s as part of a long-cherished dream to visit the eastern Mediterranean. The realization of an essentially romantic fantasy, the journey also was motivated by politics and publicity. In 1835, he published his impressions, known from later editions as "Voyage en Orient," which sold well despite the mixed critical reception. Lamartine's arresting and emotional prose, his views on the Eastern question, and especially his enormous popularity as a poet had a powerful influence in shaping public opinion against the official foreign policy line of upholding the integrity of the Ottoman Empire. He employed all popular keywords of the period—liberty, reason, civilization, progress—and was in the forefront of propagating the struggle for national independence. Yet his parliamentary speeches immediately after his return were more concerned with the issues of European balance of power disturbed by the decline of the Ottoman Empire. Lamartine's solution was an European protectorate over the Middle East to the exclusion of unilateral intervention by any single power.[75] Having come down with serious fever in a Bulgarian village, Lamartine came to know and appreciate the peasants, and was one of the first to profess they were completely mature for independence and would, together with their Serbian neighbors, lay the foundations of future states in Europe. Despite his favorable opinion of Mahmud II and his reforms, he thought the empire was doomed and called on Europe not to hasten its demise but also to not actively prevent it: "Do not help barbarity and Islamism against civilization, reason and the more advanced religions they oppress. Do not participate in the yoke and devastation of the most beautiful parts of the world."[76]

The Bulgarian peasants reminded Lamartine of the Alpine population of Savoy, their costumes of German peasants, their dances of French. Writing at the height of the folklore craze, when uniqueness was the yardstick, he displayed in his penchant for similarities the work of another attitude, that of class: "The customs of the Bulgarians are the customs of our Swiss and Savoyard peasants: these people are simple, subdued, industrious, full of respect toward their priests." His only objection was that, like the Savoyards, they had an expression of resignation, a remnant of their slave condition. The Serbs, on the other hand, impressed him with their devotion to liberty and reminded him of the Swiss in the small cantons. He dedicated several moving paragraphs to the monument of human skulls the Ottomans had erected in the vicinity of Nish after having quelled a Serbian uprising. This notwithstanding, Lamartine considered the Turks "as a human race, as a nation, still the first and most dignified among the nations of their vast empire," because he thought that liberty left an indelible imprint on one's appearance; it was the degeneration of their rule and customs, their ignorance and lawlessness that had turned them into inept masters.[77] Full of inaccuracies, a typical romantic piece, Lamartine's work fostered a sustained interest in the peoples of the Ottoman Empire.

Despite professed and internalized reservations about objectivity, reading some nineteenth-century products of the great descriptive effort aimed at the collection and accumulation of positive knowledge cannot fail to fill one with enormous respect for the broad endeavor, immense erudition, and tireless labor that went into these works. This is not to say that there are not the occasional flashes of preconceived ideas or outright prejudice but the amount of disciplined and critical observation vastly superseded the minor faults one is always bound to discover. Von Moltke was of this kind; so was Kanitz. Maybe the crowning achievement was the multivolume work of Ami Boué, a truly encyclopedic mind, who left important scholarly works in geology, mineralogy, orography, geography, topography, botany, and cartography, as well as valuable observations about the ethnography, toponymy, history, folklore, demography, linguistics, and literature of the nations inhabiting the Ottoman Empire.[78] Boué set himself the task to correct the "inborn or acquired European prejudices against the Ottomans and their subjects." He knew that by following the middle road he would disappoint both the excessive enthusiasts of the sultan's reforms as well as his opponents. While he hailed the liberation of Greece, he also drew attention to the other nations of the empire, particularly the Slavs who were bound "to join the development of European civilization and the balance of power." Although operating with the hazy categories of East and West, Boué was a precursor of conversion theory and hoped that "in the merging of East and West, the latter, after grafting the useful aspects of its civilization onto the ancient Asian customs, will find in the East as many ideas to correct its overly artificial and complicated life, as the changes triggered in Europe by the Crusades."[79]

"The manner of travel in Turkey," the appendix to his last volume, is an exquisite introduction to everyday life and displays the sensitivities of an accomplished anthropologist. Boué's advice on how to listen and extract information from the locals is worth circulating today. He apparently was successful in "conversing frankly with the serious and good-natured Ottoman, as well as with the witty Albanian, the refined Greek or the shrewd Vlach; with the industrious Bulgarian, as well as with the militant Serb, the rough Bosnian and the cheerful Hercegovinian."[80] It is the enormous body of systematic knowledge assembled, organized, and analyzed by Boué that not only gave an immense impetus to different branches of social and natural science dealing with the region but continues to be one of the richest sources for the nineteenth-century Balkans. With Ami Boué, one is forced to believe that it is possible to reach, or at least approach, the precarious point of balance where one has grown over one's "enthousiasme" but has not yet lost it completely. The same may be said of his illustrious compatriots, Emile de Laveleye, Cyprien Robert, and Louis Léger. Laveleye held strong opinions on the Eastern question and was an exponent of the idea of Balkan federation, all of which did not prevent him from writing an informative and impartial account of the Balkan Peninsula. Cyprien Robert authored numerous works on the Slavs, some of which dealt in particular with Balkan Slavs or "the Slavs of Turkey." Writing with great sympathy, Robert saw the chief role of Slavdom in history as the perpetual mediators between "Asia and Europe, between immobility and progress, between the past and the future, between preservation and revolution," a channel between the Greeks and the Latins, between East and West. This mediating, undefined role was acclaimed by Robert, something quite in reversal with the soon-to-follow unflattering assessment of the in-betweenness of the Balkans. Louis Léger left among his numerous works a valuable description of Slovenes, Croats, Serbs, and Bulgarians from the early 1880s, although in his case the occasional affectations of the civilized visitor who lauds the return of these nations into the European family, bringing into a "regenerated Orient the precious elements of power, order and civilization" serve as an anticlimax, or reminder of the preoccupations of European discourse at the end of the century.[81]

Compared to the Italian, French, and German, Russian descriptions of the peninsula came from a later period. This was only natural as, following the "gathering of Russian lands" under Ivan III in the fifteenth century, Russia expanded to the east and incorporated Siberia throughout the seventeenth and only during the eighteenth century did it turn southwest, clashing with the Ottomans. Beginning with Peter's reign, the Russians gained a foothold on the Black Sea but it was only with Catherine the Great that they finally became a Black Sea power. There were three types of Russian travelers: clergymen en route to the Holy Land or to the monasteries of Mount Athos; the military visiting on a reconnaissance mission; and scholars or writers pursuing a specific project. There was also a variety of diplomatic and journalistic accounts which, although not strictly belonging to the travelogue genre, had a comparable significance for shaping contemporary opinions.

Although the few seventeenth-century accounts distinguished between Slavic and non-Slavic Christians, and between the different Slavs, there is no sign of the later pathos of solidarity either for Slavs or for Orthodox in general.[82] Even the detailed and professional account of the finances, military state, and diplomacy of the Ottomans by the ambassador, Count Peter Tolstoy, in 1703 was an evenhanded treatment of the Turks as a "proud, mighty and ambitious nation," remarkable for their sobriety, who were not only cruel to the Christians and members of other religions, but had a strong propensity for internecine struggle and antistate rebellions. While Tolstoy pointed out the oppression of the Greeks, he did not single them out but enumerated them alongside Serbs, Vlachs, Arabs, and others as suffering from the inexorable tax burden and constant humiliation. Even the idea of Christian coreligionists was used not to legitimize Russia's policy, but to illustrate the feeling of threat the Turks felt from Russia and the hopes arising among Greeks and other oppressed peoples that their liberation would arrive from Russia.[83]

Several decades into the nineteenth century and the Eastern question, when Russia emerged as the main Ottoman opponent, Russian accounts became informed with real passion and undisguised championship for the oppressed Christians; to F. P. Fonton in 1829, "The coexistence of Muslims and Christians is the epidemic sin of the present situation. Until it is put to an end with the emigration of the Turks, there can be no prospect for an acceptable arrangement."[84] All Balkan nations at one time or other have served as pet nations for the great European powers. The Greeks, due to the magnetism of their ancient history and the influence of Enlightenment ideas, have been the chosen ones. Because of their geographic position, lack of a glorious ancient period, and their relatively later (several decades after the Greeks) national mobilization, the Bulgarians were not only "discovered" last but, with few exceptions, inspired only scarce degrees of compassion in an otherwise typical tradition of neglect or indifference. Part of the explanation lies in the fact that the time when the Bulgarians came to the attention of west Europeans coincided with growing apprehensions toward Russia and panslavism. The real deviation from this rule were, of course, the Russians. Not only did they, because of linguistic closeness, recognize quite early the distinctiveness of Bulgarians, but they singled them out as the nation mostly oppressed by the Turks.

Almost at the same time as Fonton, in 1830, Yuri Ivanovich Venelin, an accomplished philologist and historian, went on a mission to study the Bulgarians in the northeastern regions of the Ottoman Empire. Born Georgii Khutsa, the 28-year-old Ukrainian had completed his studies at the University of Moscow and became interested in the Bulgarian colonies in southern Russia. His seminal two volume study of Bulgarian history, language, and ethnography, as well as his subsequent publications, were of unparalleled importance in spurring national consciousness among the Bulgarians.[85] Venelin's summary of the position Bulgarians were occupying in the Ottoman Empire, compared to the other Balkan peoples, has dominated Bulgarian self-perceptions ever since:

> For the Turks this unhappy people is like a sheep for man, i.e., the most useful and necessary animal. From it they get milk, butter, cheese, meat, fur, wool, i.e., food and clothing. . . . It serves the Bulgarians bad that they are the best builders and craftsmen in Turkey. In a word, Turkish domination and existence in Europe is based mostly and perhaps exclusively on the Bulgarians. The Moldavians and Wallachians have always been half free. Some of the Serbs have intermingled with the Turks, others have totally converted, yet others have maintained their independence, and all of them have profited from the protection of the mountainous terrain. The Albanians have always been semi-independent, being by nature proud warriors who have served the Turks only for profit and for payment. Their enormous mountains have shielded them in their little corner. The same can be said of the Greek mountaineers in the Morea. The Greeks of the islands have had different advantages and have breathed more freely. . . . Among the Slavs, the Bulgarians have suffered the worst. . . .[86]

Heart-rending and detailed stories of the Bulgarians' plight were present in practically all Russian descriptions of the region, something unique among the travel literature in general: Fonton (1829), E. Kovalevskii (1840), V. Grigorovich (1844–1845), E. Yuzhakov (1859), O. M. Lerner (1873). Because of the linguistic link and their concerns over Orthodoxy, they were the first to pay close attention to the Bulgarian-Greek church conflict.[87] Contrary to Friedrich Engels's disparaging remark that the Russians, coming themselves from a country "semi-Asiatic in her condition, manners, traditions and institutions," best understood the true situation of Turkey, the most interesting circumstance about the Russian travelers was their self-identity as Europeans.[88] Fonton spoke of the selfless policies of Russia and referred to the unjustified suspicions of "Europe" (as a generic name for the other great powers) without implying Russian non-Europeanness. The poet Viktor Grigor'evich Teplyakov had been imprisoned as Mason and Decembrist, but was pardoned and sent as war correspondent to the front in 1828–1829. Well-educated and a connoisseur of antiquities, Teplyakov managed to gather a collection of thirty-six marble bas-reliefs and inscriptions, two statues, eighty-three coins, and so forth and shipped them to Russia: Lord Elgin's Russian version on a modest scale. He was charmed and thrilled with the oriental appearance of Varna, the bustle, noise, and colors of its streets: "Among this Asian crowd, one could encounter many sons of Israel and a lot of Europeans: Russians, French, Italians, Germans, English."[89] In the same vein, M. F. Karlova, probably the first Russian woman to travel to Macedonia and Albania, exclaimed: "Men stop, examine the travellers, and with utter amazement scrutinize me, the unseen miracle: an European woman!"[90] For Vsevolod Vladimirovich Krestovskii, the famous Russian writer who accompanied the Russian troops in 1877–1878 as war correspondent of the *Government Newspaper*, the Danube was the veritable frontier between the Romanian "Europe" and the Bulgarian "Asia":

> Unattractive as it may be, Zimnitsa is still 'Europe.' On its streets one might suffocate from the dust, but the streets themselves are broad enough and follow a regu-

lar plan in the quarter. Here, on the other hand, there is no dust, and there is enough water in the reservoirs, but these stone wall fences and these impossibly narrow streets are such a labyrinth that, unused to it, even the devil might break his foot. . . . In a word, there it is Europe, and here—Asia, but its appearance and all of its primitive and naively open earthly street order are so new and peculiar to us, that they instinctively invoke curiosity and sympathy precisely with their novelty and originality.

Not only was Krestovskii partial to the charm of the Orient, he preferred it in its untainted purity. His description of the home and family costums of the wealthy Bulgarian merchant Vîlko Pavurdzhiev is a valuable ethnographic portrait both of urban Bulgaria in the 1870s and of the patronizing affectations of the educated Russian middle class caught in the middle of the European romantic vogue:

> The embroidered tablecloths, the covers on the divans, the low tables are part and parcel of the refinement and luxury of the eastern furnishing. And how unpleasant to the eye when, side by side with these objects, one sees sometimes in the same room winding Viennese chairs, a table for cards and similar objects of the all-European, so to say, civilized banal quality. They fit the original atmosphere as much as European clothes fit the Bulgarian man and woman.[91]

Russian attitudes toward the Bulgarians were often reminiscent of the general European philhellenic stance: just as Europeans were discovering *their* Greeks as the source of their civilization, Russians were discovering *their* Bulgarians as the roots of Slavic culture. Although some Russians were fascinated with ancient marbles and texts, the real counterpart to the West European craze was the Russian craze over Slavic manuscripts. Yuzhakov, a journalist at *Sovremennik*, traveled in 1859 and described how the Bulgarians in Kukush asked to hear the service in the Slavic tongue:

> My God! This people, from whom we have received the Church Slavonic books, who has taught us to read and write in the Slavic language, this people was asking us now to read the service in Slavic—they are asking us to make them happy by hearing Slavic sounds in their church. . . . One feels the urge to apologize for, to absolve the ones who have brought them to this condition. . . . But how can one forgive them?[92]

"Discovering" the Bulgarians at the height of the slavophile sentiment after the middle of the nineteenth century—when both the cultural slavism of the Czechs and the Russian slavism of Mikhail P. Pogodin, Aleksei S. Khomiakov, Aleksandr S. Danilevskii, Timofei N. Granovskii, Jurii F. Samarin, and the brothers Ivan S. and Konstantin S. Aksakov, despite creeping overtones of imperial power politics, still inspired an all-encompassing solidarity and affinity with the Slavic world at large— brought an additional air in the dominant melody of commiseration:

> It is sad and painful to see how, at a time when so many Slavs enjoy the fruits of peace and liberty, proudly and knowingly look into their future, benefiting from their untroubled present, and are hurriedly marching on the road of progress, something which made the Europeans watch them with respect, the Bulgarians—this strong and healthy nation yearning with all its power to go ahead—with hearts filled with despair, look at the heavy chains which restrain them and do not allow them to reach their coveted goal.[93]

During the Eastern crisis of 1875–1878, the grassroots feelings for solidarity with the southern Slavs surpassed any of the manifestations of Western philhellenism, which was usually confined to the educated strata. The Russian intelligentsia was unanimous in passionately opposing the oppression of the Balkan Slavs; many supported also their political efforts to achieve independence from the Porte. Among the well-known Russian writers, Ivan Turgenev, Feodor M. Dostoevskii, Leo N. Tolstoy, M. E. Saltykov-Shchedrin, Vladimir G. Korolenko, Gleb I. Uspenskii, Vsevolod M. Garshin, Vasilii I. Nemirovich-Danchenko, and many others contributed immensely to the formation of a public opinion that forced Russia to enter the war against the Ottoman Empire. Tolstoy himself, feeling that "All Russia is there, and I should go myself," was dissuaded only with great difficulty from joining as a volunteer.[94]

Yet, one should not overestimate the intensity of slavophile feelings and their influence on Russian foreign policy, characterized by Barbara Jelavich as defensive and peaceful rather than expansionist, paternal rather than messianic.[95] The real interests and attention of Russia during the nineteenth century—economic, strategic, military, and even cultural—although involving the Balkans, were not intractably fixated on them; they were almost exclusively concentrated on Central Asia and subsequently on the Far East. Knowledge of things Slavic, especially South Slavic, was by no means a widespread phenomenon. As late as the beginning of the twentieth century, there were complaints that not merely the ordinary Russian but educated high-ranking officials and a great number of intellectuals were better informed about Germany, France, Italy, Spain, England, and Sweden than about the neighboring Slavic nations. Cadets at the military academy were guessing as to the Romanian or Hungarian origins of the Serbs who were supposed to be a Protestant nation, and newspapers erred on the generous side, enumerating as separate Slavic languages Czech, Bohemian, Serbian, Montenegrin, Dalmatian, "Horvatski," and "Kroatski."[96]

Even among "Balkan specialists," apologies were not the only genre. Konstantin Nikolaevich Leont'ev had been embassy secretary, vice-consul, and consul of Russia on the island of Crete and in Ioannina and Tulcea during the 1860s and 1870s. Born of an old noble family, he was an open, vocal, and unrepentant exponent of aristocratic superiority, and focused his mortifying disdain on the mediocrity of bourgeois standards. Completely alien to the moral pathos of nineteenth-century Russian literature with its acute social criticism, he pronounced that "a magnificent, century-old tree is more precious than twenty common peasants and I will not cut it down in order to buy them medication against cholera."[97] A devout Orthodox Christian, but only of its rigorous monastic Byzantine version, Leont'ev admired the Catholic hierarchy and saw in Catholicism the mightiest weapon against egalitarianism. A Nietzschean before Nietzsche, a precursor of Ibsen and the French aestheticists, this "philosopher of reactionary romanticism" and self-professed "friend of the reaction" stood closest to Joseph Marie de Maistre in his desire for a revolution on the right that would exonerate beauty, religion, and art from bourgeois drabness. His most piercing condemnation was reserved for "the tumor of progress," this fetish of positivism. In Leont'ev's philosophy, society passed through three developmental stages: a primitive, prestate condition; the mature complex organism of the Middle Ages which was the zenith of human evolution with its intricate hierarchies, knighthood, and well-defined estate distinctions; and, finally, a secondary simplification of society accompanied by the decay and death of individualism, the bourgeois era. Only diversity and despotism could secure a vigorous and dynamic society. Western Europe was seized by a pathological affliction, whose main symptoms were equality, liberty, and universal happiness, which were beginning to endanger also the Slavic world. Not a slavophile, Leont'ev despised the worship of the people. Despite his sympathies with Catholicism as the epitome of discipline, he was neither a westernizer nor an exponent of the Eurasian idea. In his system of thought, the state had precedence over any other principle, and byzantinism was a universal idea threatened by nationalism. These were the basic philosophical ideas informing Leont'ev's attitude to the Slavic and Balkan nations that were articulated in many of his writings.[98]

In Leont'ev's view, a fundamental difference distinguished Russians and Poles from the rest of the Slavs: only those two nations had a long-term state evolution and their own nobility, which had secured "the education of the nation along estate principles — something which has left almost no trace among the Austrian Slavs and which is totally absent from the mores of the Slavs in Turkey." Of the other Slavs, the Czechs were Germans with Slavic blood, the Slovaks Magyars speaking a Slavic language, and the Bulgarians Greeks speaking a Slavic tongue. The Serbs, on the other hand, were the most fragmented nation, divided between four state formations, three religions, two dynasties, and a variety of profound foreign influences, so that they not only did not manage to work out a unique judicial, religious, and artistic system, but were beginning to lose their inmost Slavic characteristics. Leont'ev's jeremiad was reserved, however, specifically for the Bulgarians:

> The Bulgarian nation is simple (not unpretentious or good-natured as many here believe, nor stupid, as the Greeks mistakenly think, but precisely simple, i.e., underdeveloped). Besides, the Bulgarian is not so fervently and glowingly religious like the ordinary Russian, who is much more sensitive than the Bulgarian. And so, the Bulgarian nation is simple, especially in the villages. On the other hand, the small Bulgarian intelligentsia is cunning, determined and, it seems, quite united; the training that it has received from the Greeks, the Russians, the Europeans and partly from the Turks is just sufficient to enable it to launch a successful national-diplomatic struggle.[99]

A pronounced opponent of nationalism, Leont'ev considered it the expression of liberal democracy, the illusionary quest for equality among people, estates, provinces, nations, indeed the universal equality that was jeopardizing the "great western cultures" ever since the rabble in 1789 raised these ideas.[100] He compared the rebellions of the "minor and secondary nations" during the nineteenth century and concluded that none among them, that is, Poles, Czechs, Greeks, and Hungarians, was waving to such extent "the banner of progressivism" as were the "backward, and seemingly innocent and modest Bulgarians." He was deeply perturbed by the implications of the church dispute between Greeks and Bulgarians culminating in 1870, the ultimate challenge to the spirit of byzantinism:

> The most backward, the last among the rising Slavic nations — the Bulgarians — are beginning their historic life in war with the traditions and authority of byzantinism, which is at the basis of our Great Russian statehood. . . . Dangerous is not the for-

eign enemy, whom we have always kept in sight. . . . Not the German, not the French, nor the Pole—our half brother and rival. The most dangerous is the close, younger, and seemingly indefensible brother, if he is sick with a disease that, with the slightest negligence, can be lethal also to us. . . . Neither in the history of the learned Czech revival, nor in the movement of the militant Serbs or in the rebellions of the Poles against us can we encounter this mysterious and dangerous phenomenon which we can observe in the peaceful and quasi-devout movement of the Bulgarians. Only with the Bulgarian question have the two powers that brought about Russian statehood—the consciousness of belonging to the Slavic race and church byzantinism—for the first time in our history clashed in the Russian heart.[101]

The Bulgarian disease was democracy. The ones who pitied them for their weakness, poverty, subjection, and youth, Leont'ev warned with Sulla's words about the young Caesar: "Beware, there are ten Mariuses [democrats] in this young man!" There was nothing "aristocratic and monarchical" about them; everything was in the hands of doctors, merchants, Paris-trained attorneys, and teachers; even the clergy was under their control: "It is quite clear that this bourgeoisie, linked by its origins partly with the urban, partly with the rural population of Danube Bulgaria, Thrace and Macedonia, enjoys the complete trust of the people." The stubborn, somber, and shrewd Bulgarian couldn't be a greater contrast to the generous and frivolous Russian; they differed from each other like the German from the Italian, the mechanic from the poet, Adam Smith from Byron. So strong was the Bulgarian affliction with democracy, so firmly were they following France and the United States in their delusion that "nobody and nothing should be above the people," that their only salvation lay in the sovereignty of the sultan. Leont'ev actually went so far as to declare that "here, in the East, genuine Orthodoxy and the Slavic spirit are preserved solely thanks to the Turks." The reason Bulgarians as well as Greeks were possessed of the spirit of constitutionalism and demagogy was that there was no estate principle in the empire, and because "excessive love of freedom [is] unhealthily developed amidst people who have been subjugated but not entirely assimilated by their conquerors."[102] In his best novel, the unfinished *Egyptian Dove*, published in 1881–1882 in *Russkii vestnik*, Leont'ev described the Christian beau monde of Constantinople and the diplomatic rivalries between the great powers. In a telling episode in the house of the Austrian consul, Österreicher, after the Russian consul, Ladnev, gives a fiery speech against the boring German "social revolution" of 1848 and in defense of the Prussian military genius, the Bulgarian dragoman, Boyadzhiev, remarks that it is only natural for a Russian to sympathize with militarism and the aristocracy. Ladnev bursts out:

> Listen, Mister Boyadzhiev. . . . If for example someone like Mister Österreicher reflects on Russia, even without knowing the country well, that's not so serious. I can argue with him: he is a son of the great German civilization, to which we Russians are indebted. But you? What are your rights? . . . I entreat you not to intrude in our conversation and not to speak to me about anything and ever.[103]

It is an episode that many subsequent Russian diplomats learned, instead of learning from. Not only Bulgarians but Turkish Christians in general easily changed their "patriarchal habits with bourgeois-liberal customs" and turned from protagonists of Homer and Cooper into characters of Thackeray and Gogol. To them, Leont'ev preferred the Turks who were "honest, artless, pleasant in conversation, good and mild, until their religious feeling is inflamed." He was convinced Turks admired the administrative system of the Russians, their submissiveness and deference: "I am sure that if tomorrow the Turkish government left the Bosphorus and not all Turks followed but remained in the Balkan Peninsula, they will always hope that we would defend them against the inevitable troubles and humiliations inflicted on them by the formerly enslaved Balkan nations, who in general are far too cruel and coarse."[104]

In an article written a few years later on national psychology, Leont'ev described all Balkan nations as more practical, shrewder, more diplomatic, and more cautious than the Russians, which had to do with the commercial spirit prevailing over idealism; the Bulgarian intellectual in particular was the "bourgeois par excellence." The whole "Eastern Christian intelligentsia—Greek, Serbian and Bulgarian" was marked by its "greater proclivity to work in order to make its living compared to our upper class," by its crudity, lack of creativity, deficient refinement of the feelings, and little sophistication of thought. Additionally, they had taken up the role of parvenu vis-à-vis Europe and progress. Indeed, it takes an aristocrat with the panache of a Leont'ev to describe labor as disgrace.[105]

Leont'ev's verdict was opposite to Krestovskii's romantic enchantment with Bulgarian patriarchal mores. For Krestovskii, "Balkan, and especially Bulgarian Slavdom, is probably the only corner of Europe, where family morals have retained their inviolable purity. And this is so, because European civilization has not been able to import here its worldly goods and its debauchery." To Leont'ev, this was rather a testimony to the feeble imagination and boredom reigning in the Balkans. Even murders in the Balkans had nothing to do with poetry: the Bulgarian, Serb, and Greek could kill out of jealousy, greed, or vengeance but not out of disappointment, despair, yearning for fame, or even boredom as in Russia. Bourgeois simplification and European radicalism were replacing the former primitiveness or simplicity of the Eastern Christians. What they were skipping was the middle stage, the authentic flourish, the continuity that alone was instrumental in the preservation of a nation and that was most distinctly expressed in the development of "aristocratic England, less so in continental Europe and even weaker, but still noticeably so in Russia."[106] The southwestern Slavs, as Leont'ev called them, that is, Czechs, Croats, Serbs, and Bulgarians, were, due to their youth and without exception, democrats and constitutionalists: "their common feature, despite all their differences, is their predisposition toward equality and liberty, i.e., towards ideals American and French, but not Byzantine and British."[107] The pairing of Great Britain and Byzantium evokes a striking fault line that invites the comment of thinkers in the Huntingtonian mode. What is even more striking is that Leont'ev's pure and sincere aristocratic scorn was only seldom surpassed by the most arrogant among descriptions by the English whom he so strongly admired; ironically, however, one can find similar overtones, despite the different value given to the word democracy, in recent diatribes against the Balkans.

Patterns of Perception until 1900

While travel literature became a fashionable genre and produced a significant body of writings all over Europe, its widest and most welcome market was Britain, which had the strongest opportunity to disseminate particular attitudes to a comparatively large audience. It is impossible to compare the travel literature of different countries fairly, but there is no doubt that in Britain travelers' accounts were the preferred reading after novels in the course of several centuries, and "although the literature of travel is not the highest kind, . . . yet a history of English literature rightly assigns a space apart to such books, because this kind of writing, perhaps more than any other, both expresses and influences national predilections and national character."[1] In the eighteenth century, there was hardly an important English writer who did not produce some kind of travel writing, and the third Earl of Shaftesbury, who considered travelogues "the chief materials to furnish out a library," compared them to the books of chivalry in the days of his forefathers.[2]

If approached strictly as historical sources containing useful information, the British accounts before the end of the eighteenth century do not compare favorably to the earlier, detailed, and sustained interest of Germans and French. This is easily explained by the discreet presence of the British in continental affairs and by the much later activation of their relations with the Ottoman Empire. During the nineteenth century, on the other hand, British accounts became informative and knowledgeable, rising high on the comparative scale of European travelogues. It is not, however, their quality and significance as historical sources that warrants the special attention they are given. For one thing, they represented the travel literature of the most important global colonial power. More significant, it is primarily through these works that the transmission of perceptions was accomplished within the English-speaking realm (what came to be known in Europe as the Anglo-Saxon tradition).

As already pointed out, the bulk of European writings on the Ottoman Empire during the fifteenth and sixteenth centuries consisted of political treatises, usually compiled by scholars and diplomats with little or no firsthand knowledge. Born as a genre in Italy, this type of writing quickly took root in England, enhanced by the

establishment of the Turkey Company in 1581 and the opening of permanent diplomatic relations in 1583, which "marked the real entry into the English mind of a consciousness of things Ottoman."³ Richard Knolles' "General History of the Turkes" (1603),
which went through seven editions during the seventeenth century, was compiled by
someone who had never set foot in the country but nevertheless became "the most
enduring monument to Elizabethan interest in the Ottoman empire."⁴ A few decades
earlier, the arrival of Greek emigrés to England could not arouse any interest, and
while their literature was liked, the Greeks themselves were treated as conniving pre-
tenders. "In Shakespeare's day *Greek* was a household word for 'crook'."⁵

English images of the Turk during the sixteenth and much of the seventeenth
centuries were ones of tyranny, arbitrariness, extortions, slavery, piracy, savage punishments, and Christian ordeals; they were also images of strangeness and diatribe against
Islam. At the same time, they were images of strength, the picture of an empire in its
zenith. Gone were the days after Lepanto, when Europe briefly rejoiced in its triumph
and imagined that the Ottomans were on their way to irreversible retreat. The seventeenth century began with revolts and anarchy in the Ottoman realm and ended with
the beginning of their retreat from Europe. The century was, however, even more
exacting on the western and central parts of Europe, which were ravaged by revolutions, religious clashes, and bloody wars, not to speak of what has entered the historical vocabulary as the "crisis of the seventeenth century." This produced an equilibrium of power between the Ottomans and the continental states that was upset only at
the end of the century.

Remarkable in the English accounts of the time was the conscious attempt to
reach an "objective" verdict for the differences in civilization. The corollary of this
approach was Henry Blount's "Voyage into the Levant," published in 1636 and characterized as setting "a new standard for fairness and impartiality in English travel literature."⁶ Describing his travel of two years earlier, Blount, the son of a founder of
Oxford's Trinity College and himself a highly educated lawyer, was in many ways the
practical embodiment of Bacon's empiricist philosophy which postulated that knowledge could be reached only through experience and that generalizations could be
based only on observation. True to this commitment, Blount decided "to observe the
Religion, Manners, and Policie of the Turkes," so as to ascertain whether "the Turkish
way appear absolutely barbarous, as we are given to understand, or rather an other
kinde of civilitie, different from ours, but no lesse pretending."⁷

This was one of the first attempts to depict the Ottoman ways in their own context without the usual Christian prejudice against Islam; Blount's is "an account which
merges into the history of Deism in England."⁸ There was an undisguised admiration
for the Ottomans, because they were "the only moderne people, great in action, and
whose Empire hath so suddenly invaded the World, and fixt it selfe such firme foundations as no other ever did." According to Blount:

> if ever any race of men were borne with Spirits able to beare downe the world
> before them, I thinke it to be the Turke. . . . The magnanimous are apt to be cor-
> rupt with an haughty insolency, though in some sort generous: this is the Turkish
> way, remorcelesse to those who beare up, and therefore mistaken for beastly; but
> such it is not; for it constantly receives humiliation with much sweetnesse: This to
> their honor, and my satisfaction, I ever found.⁹

Despite his criticism and constant fear that the Turks might sell him as a slave for the sake of ransom, he concluded that "this excepted, the Turkish disposition is generous, loving, and honest; so farre from falsefying his promise, as if he doe but lay his hand on his breast, beard, or head, as they use, or chiefly breake bread with me, if I had an hundred lives, I durst venture them upon his word, especially if he be a naturall Turke, no More, Arab, or Egyptian."[10] It is attractive to explain this magnanimous attitude with Blount's overall philosophy. Indeed, he saw as his first task the unprejudiced observation of "Turkes." However, when this statement is compared to others, it is clear that behind the favorable assessments of the Ottomans (whom Blount like most other travelers called Turks), there were other motivations at work. His second great task, Blount wrote in his introduction, was "to acquaint my selfe with those other sects which live under the Turkes, as Greekes, Armenians, Freinks, and Zinganes, but especially the Iewes; a race from all others so averse both in nature and institution, as glorifying to single it selfe out of the rest of mankinde, remains obstinate, contemptible, and famous."[11]

What actually transpires from Blount's account is the almost unconscious reverence to political success. In the Ottoman he described the character of a master nation. Blount could empathize with it. A master nation in the making was recognizing an established one. This trend is displayed in much of the travel literature and was certainly present among the English ambassadors to the Porte whose "general attitude . . . towards the Ottoman ruling class was one of favor, of approval even." For Sir Richard Bulstrode, a Stuart diplomat, Constantinople was "a post of more honour, and more profit, than Paris," and William, Lord Paget, ambassador between 1693 and 1703, found the Turks "grave and proud, yet hitherto they have received and used me upon all occasions very civilely," so that he could accomplish "reasonable fair dealings in common business."[12]

Some three decades after Blount, Paul Rycaut produced his major literary work, a firsthand account of *The Present State of the Ottoman Empire* (1668) in which he echoed Blount's misgivings about how things were termed "barbarous, as all things are, which are differenced from us by diversity of Manners and Custom, and are not dressed in the mode and fashion of our times and Countries; for we contract prejudice from ignorance and want of familiarity." Better acquainted with Ottoman society, for the next forty years Rycaut's prolific voice was moving "forward from the context of 'crusade' to the context of a peaceable intercourse through trade." Indeed, he wrote in a period when both Islam and the West were folding the "tattered banners of Crusade and *Jihad*."[13]

During the eighteenth century, "the peaceable trade intercourse" was intensified and, without effecting any drastic change of opinion, the accounts became more detailed and concrete. Lady Mary Wortley Montagu's letters from the East were published in 1763, the year of her death; before that, they seem to have been handed around in manuscript. Lady Mary was one of the first to savor the ancient authors in the authenticity of their country of birth. Her great fame, however, derived from the introduction of inoculation against smallpox in England, a practice she encountered among the Greeks in Constantinople. Other than that, as wife of the British ambassador, she preferred to mix with the noble society of the Turks. Her description of the Turkish baths in Sofia, "the women's coffee house, where all the news of the town is told, scandal invented," served as the inspiration to the famous 1862 painting of Ingres, "Le bain turc." In the baths of Sofia, Lady Mary admired Turkish women with skins "shineingly bright," whereas the Bulgarian peasant women on the road were "not ugly but of tawny complexion," a striking example of the aesthetic preference for class rather than race.[14]

The encounter with the subject races produced ambiguous responses. There was a tension between the natural empathy with the rulers and the traditional opposition to the Muslims but quite often the first feeling took the upper hand. Steeped as they were in classical learning, many visitors looked for living illustrations of ancient museum archetypes. This was especially true for the ones on their Grand Tour, which by the latter half of the century was increasingly shifting from France and Italy to Greece.[15] In the words of Eisner, "the great age of travel to Greece—to paint it, to loot it, write about it—had begun."[16] The travelers, or *tourists*, a word coined in this period, were usually disappointed, particularly in the case of the Greeks, partly by the lack of striking physical resemblance but mostly by the absence of classical manners. The lack of continuity between ancient Greeks and the degenerate situation of their modern heirs or else the abyss between ballroom expectations and stark reality can be traced in many works, which can be described as frustrated philhellenism even before the advent of the phenomenon. Nowhere was the outcry of disappointed classical taste more desperate than in John Morritt who, on observing laughing, dancing, and wrestling Greeks in the Peloponnesus in 1796, exclaimed: "Good God! if a free ancient Greek could for one moment be brought to such a scene, unless his fate was very hard in the other world I am sure he would beg to go back again."[17]

Only young women were graciously spared these inclement verdicts. Instead, they were, as a rule, described as astoundingly beautiful, a tradition that was faithfully observed and created quite a reputation for Greek women. Describing Greek women around Smyrna in 1794, Morritt, who otherwise had despaired of the Greek race, wrote:

> You will, of course, ask me if the praise travellers generally favour Greek beauties with are deserved. Indeed they are; and if you had been present with us, you would, I think, have allowed that the faces of our village belles exceeded by far any collection in any ball-room you had ever seen. They have all good eyes and teeth, but their chief beauty is that of countenance. . . . It is an expression of sweetness and of intelligence that I hardly ever saw, and varies with a delicacy and quickness that no painter can give. . . . Besides this, their appearance in their elegant dress did not give us the least ideas of peasants, and joined to the gracefulness of their attitudes and manners, we began to think ourselves among gentlewomen in disguise.[18]

These statements were more revealing about the phantasms of young, healthy English aristocrats of classical education in the transitional age between enlightenment and romanticism than about the merits of Greek female physique at the end of the eighteenth century. They were, however, a very clear illustration of a distinct class attitude that was unfailingly present in the majority of accounts although with different degrees of intensity. "Gentlewomen in disguise" was the qualifying feature for the Greek females. The absence of gentlemanhood was the primary complaint against Greek men and its presence, the highest praise for the Ottoman overlords. It led to the popular slogan: "Johnny Turk was a gentleman." In Athens, Morritt first lodged with the British consul "who is poor and Greek, two circumstances which together always make a man a scoundrel." The Greeks were invariably described as cheaters and crooks, although the only actual mention of theft was the indulgent report on how the British party was acquiring ancient marbles: "Some we steal, some we buy, and our court is much adorned with them."[19]

Without entering into the great Elgin Marbles controversy, one may remember how the archeologist Edward Dodwell described the reaction of the locals: "the Athenians in general, nay, even the Turks themselves, did lament the ruin that was committed: and loudly and openly blamed their sovereign for the permission he had granted!"[20] The sovereign was unjustly, or too severely, blamed: the *firman* he had issued to Lord Elgin authorized a group of painters to fix scaffolding around the ancient Temple, model ornaments and figures in plaster and gypsum, measure the remains of other ruined buildings, excavate the foundations in order to discover inscriptions, and only at the end of this lengthy list was there a broadly stated mention that some pieces of stone with old inscriptions or sculptures could be taken away. The measuring and drawing expedition was quickly reorganized into a demounting one. Another traveler, Edward Clarke of Cambridge, reported how the *disdar*, on observing the removal of a particularly beautiful Parthenon *metope* "letting fall a tear, said in the most emphatic tone of voice, 'Telos!' positively declaring that nothing should induce him to consent to any further dilapidation of the building."[21] Dodwell himself was not particularly sentimental about the Greeks or prudish about the ways in which he acquired his rich collection of bronzes, marbles, ceramics, and coins. Known for his bribes as "the Frank of many 'paras,'" most of his collection was sold to wealthier or more enthusiastic collectors: his vases (143 of them, including the famous "Dodwell vase") were purchased by the Munich Glyptothek, other objects were sold to the crown prince of Bavaria.[22]

In stark contrast to the description of the Greeks was that of the magnanimous behavior of their Turkish masters. While in Lesbos, tired of their poor Greek quarters, Morritt's party managed to invite themselves to the local aga, who treated them handsomely. A sumptuous dinner with excellent Cyprus wine relaxed Morritt's repugnance of the Levant: "I begin to think there are gentlemen in all nations. These Agas live very comfortably. Their houses are large, good, and well adapted to the climate. . . . They have many horses, are fond of shooting and hawking, and have often, with their agricultural servants, not less than three or four hundred attendants." In Thessaly and Boeotia, Morritt was revolted by the few miserable villages entirely inhabited by Greeks and Jews. The Greeks exercised their self-rule in a such a rascally manner that "we inquired after Turks as eagerly as we should elsewhere after Englishmen. . . . I assure you the Turks are so much more honourable a race that I believe, if ever this country was in the hands of the Greeks and Russians, it would hardly be livable." He reiterated this in another elaborate letter of 1795:

> We are very well with the Turks here, and particularly with the governor of the town, who has called on us, sent us game, made coursing parties for us, offered us dogs, horses, etc., and is a very jolly, hearty fellow. We often go and smoke a pipe there, and are on the best of terms. I shall really grow a Mussulman. If they are

ignorant it is the fault of their government and religion, but I shall always say I never saw a better disposed and manlier people. Their air, from the highest to the lowest, is that of lords and masters, as they are, and their civility has something dignified and hearty in it, as from man to man; while I really have English blood enough in me almost to kick a Greek for the fawning servility he thinks politeness.[23]

What in Blount's case seemed the unconscious recognition of a master race by one in the making here was consciously and openly asserted. The only difference was the slight change of roles: the master nation of the world was recognizing one that was beginning to pass away. Morritt's attitudes were shared by a number of English observers although his conscious bluntness, stemming from aristocratic arrogance and young age, was more subdued in the descriptions of his countrymen. They generally preferred Turks to Greeks, and not only deplored the Greeks' lack of classical scholarship and affinities but also found their degenerate religion totally repulsive. The Greeks were factious, unfriendly, obsequious, ignorant, superstitious, lazy, greedy, venal, intriguing, dirty, ungrateful, and liars.[24] Still, the nineteenth century brought more intensive and more regular contacts with the Balkan populations through commerce and increased political, military, religious, and educational activities. Accordingly, the travelers' accounts displayed a more competent knowledge and were occasionally marked by deep insights and genuine human empathy.

The great romance of the English in the second decade of the century was Greece. "We are all Greeks," said Shelley in the preface to his poem "Hellas," written shortly after the outbreak of the Greek revolt. Shelley had never set foot in Greece. The ones who did often remembered Chateaubriand's maxim: "Never see Greece, Monsieur, except in Homer. It is the best way." C. M. Woodhouse summarized English philhellenism as a brief caesura in a continuity of "prejudice and indifference": "Before the flame was lit by Byron and again after it was extinguished, although there was some interest in Greece, there was no philhellenism." This interest was the product of classicism, the Grand Tour, and strategic interests in the eastern Mediterranean, apprehensive first of France and later, mostly of Russia; it was never, however, an interest in the Greeks per se. The love for Greece has been brilliantly characyterized by Woodhouse: "They loved the Greece of their dreams: the land, the language, the antiquities, but not the people. If only, they thought, the people could be more like the British scholars and gentlemen; or failing that, as too much to be hoped, if only they were more like their own ancestors; or better still, if only they were not there at all."[25]

Before the outbreak of the revolt, the prevailing opinion was that until the Greeks got better educated, independence was premature. This opinion was voiced not only by Europeans but also by some of the leaders of the Greek enlightenment, notably Adamandios Korais. During the war itself, sympathy for the Greeks was on the rise, nourished by pro-Greek journals and pamphlets: "The Greeks thus joined the Spaniards, the Italians and the Latin Americans (but not the Irish) among the oppressed nationalities for whom British hearts should bleed and British pockets be touched." The romance was brief. Few of the philhellenes persisted throughout the whole war effort and even fewer committed to the building of an independent Greece stayed behind. The epithets that had been used about the Greeks before, and that had all but disappeared during the philhellenic thrill, resurfaced in full order. The new complaint was that the Greeks were incapable of governing themselves, especially when observing the clumsy way modern Greek institutions and policies were taking place. Several decades into independence philhellenism had become incomprehensible and Constantinople and the provinces were more popular with travelers. There was, however, a fundamental difference in that there was no question of reestablishing Ottoman rule; Greek independence was a *fait accompli*.[26]

Without entering into the question of the reciprocity of foreign policy and public discourse, suffice it to say that a correlation between the tone of the majority of British travelers' accounts and the main trends in foreign policy is clearly discernible. The 1830s were a dividing line in both British Near Eastern policy and the character of travel literature. Until the middle of the eighteenth century, relations between England and the Ottoman Empire were mainly commercial, and only during the eighteenth century did diplomatic duties gradually take precedence.[27] By the end of the eighteenth century, Great Britain had become the leading industrial and commercial nation on the globe, and after Napoleon's defeat and the expansion of its overseas territories, it was also the greatest colonial power whose policy was directed at increasing the predominance of "Pax Britannica." In Europe, this policy was implemented in maintaining the system of "balance of power," one of whose decisive links the Ottoman Empire had become. Up to the 1830s, however, Britain had not formulated a specific foreign policy line toward the Ottoman Empire. Only with the emergence of Russia as a central figure on the European scene, and its territorial successes against the Ottomans, was a definite line of action shaped. British foreign policy after 1830 was not completely new but it assumed the form of a definite program of preserving the integrity and inviolability of the Ottoman Empire.[28] The extraordinary assertion of British power led, by the middle of the nineteenth century, to the attempt by Palmerston "to overturn the world power balance of power, in hopes of ushering in a period of British global hegemony and shoring up a pseudoliberal status quo at home."[29]

One can observe also the politicizing of many of the travelers' accounts during this period. A majority were tainted strongly with the authors' political views, which almost never dissented from the official government line except when they were zealous enough to overdo it, as in the case of the prominent Turkophile and possessed Russophobe David Urquhart. With minor exceptions, the political implication of the travelers' books in the nineteenth century was that, as Barbara Jelavich has aptly put it, "what they described was what was generally accepted as true."[30] In this lengthy panorama of Western verdicts of the Ottoman Empire and the Balkans, it would be refreshing to hear a voice and an opinion from the other side. At the turn of the century, Allen Upward reported about his encounter with a Turkish statesman, renowned for his sagacity, who had told him: "I have noticed that your ruling class can always make the people think what it wants them to think." Upward tended to agree: "In spite of Parliament and the Press, there is probably no country at the present time in which the bureaucracy exercises such unchecked power as in England, and in which the influence of the public is so slight."[31]

With his subsequent career, Urquhart was the most eloquent example of thwarted philhellenism. Having almost sacrificed his life for the Greek cause (his brother actually did), he subsequently discovered the Ottomans and bestowed them with his excessive and obsessive passions. In Urquhart's masterpiece, *The Spirit of the East*, the whole stereotype was reversed. It was no longer Turkish tyranny that was to blame for the servility of the Greeks, but Greek servility that had corrupted the simplicity of Turkish pastoral habits.[32] It seems that Urquhart thought himself personally responsible for having contributed to the disruption of the Ottoman Empire.[33] He went on to make up for it with the same zeal by championing the cause of the Ottoman Empire against Russia. Urquhart's activities in the East not only enjoyed the tacit connivance of the British government, but his flamboyant anti-Russian journalism tremendously swayed public opinion and exerted some influence on policy making, an early example of the leverage of the press.[34] Benjamin Disraeli, on the other hand, never suffered the contagion of philhellenism: his disdain for national movements was permanent and consistent. During his Grand Tour of 1830, he even volunteered to join the Ottoman army in its campaign to crush a revolt in Albania. In Ioannina, he had an audience with the grand vizier and wrote down in his journal "the delight of being made much of by a man who was daily decapitating half the province." Ever the aesthete of imperial excesses, Disraeli not only approved of them as a young traveler but later presided over them at the helm of the British Empire.[35]

Politics, however, did not leave its mark on what came to be known as the model travel book of the English speaking world: Alexander Kinglake's *Eothen*. Having been liberated by the East from the "stale civilisation of Europe," Kinglake set out to describe his journey of 1834–1835 through Serbia, Bulgaria, Greece, Turkey, Cyprus, the Lebanon, Palestine, Egypt, Jordan, and Syria. Of the well over 200 pages of his work, a mere ten were spent on the route through the Balkans to Constantinople. Although Kinglake and his companion gloried in their "own delightful escape" from the "Europeanised countries" and relished their travel in the East, which became a "mode of life," they nevertheless, while covering the stretch from Semlin to Constantinople, "often forgot Stamboul, forgot all the Ottoman Empire, and only remembered old times. . . . We bullied Keate, and scoffed at Larrey Miller, and Okes; we rode along loudly laughing, and talked to the grave Servian forest, as though it were the 'Brocas clump'."[36] As a later critic of "the race of Kinglakes" was to observe, Kinglake was an outsider in regard to the culture he traversed, but "it was this egotistical outsideness that so pleased his readers" and it won him numerous "dinner invitations for having so suavely caressed the cultural prejudices of his audience."[37] Serbia and Bulgaria were simply the setting for the beginning exotic adventure; they had not much of interest to offer and one felt "not called upon to 'drop a tear' over the tomb of 'the once brilliant' any body, or to pay your 'tribute of respect' to any thing dead, or alive; there are no Servian or Bulgarian Litterateurs with whom it would be positively disgraceful not to form an acquaintance." Nor did the country around abound in worthy classical monuments:

> the only public building of any interest that lies on the road is of modern date, but
> is said to be a good specimen of oriental architecture; it is of a pyramidal shape, and

is made up of thirty thousand skulls, contributed by the rebellious Servians in the early part (I believe) of this century; I am not at all sure of my date, but I fancy it was in the year 1806 that the first skull was laid. I am ashamed to say, that in the darkness of the early morning, we unknowingly went by the neighbourhood of this triumph of art, and so basely got off from admiring "the simple grandeur of the architect's conception," and "the exquisite beauty of the fretwork."[38]

All this was delivered with irony and the proverbial aristocratic stiff upper lip but it is a far cry from the denunciations of Balkan barbarity that followed after the turn of the next century; it is also far removed from any outburst of moral outrage against the Ottoman perpetrators of the crime, a line followed by some of Kinglake's country-men a couple of decades later. Ten years after Kinglake, William Makepeace Thackeray cruised the Mediterranean on board the *Iberia*, and arrived on the Greek mainland at Athens. While reputed to be the only distinguished novelist of the nine-teenth century to have experienced the traditional classical education, he did not show much interest in the monuments of classical antiquity. Rather, the present pal-ace of the king of Greece attracted his attention: "The shabbiness of the place actually beats Ireland, and that is a strong word. The palace of the Basileus is an enormous edifice of plaster, in a square containing six houses, three donkeys, no roads, no foun-tains (except in a picture of an inn)." Neither was Thackeray much interested in the rest of the Mediterranean; he "behaved like a bourgeois solipsist."[39]

Edward Lear became famous as a talented landscape artist (although he had made a name for himself with ornithological drawings, and is remembered mostly among children because of his "Book of Nonsense"). His landscapes were acclaimed for their boldness of conception and accuracy of detail. Most of his exquisite draw-ings, watercolors, and oil paintings came from journeys through Albania and Greece in the 1840s and 1850s.[40] Lear was less enamored with humans whom he rarely depicted. He liked them only when they matched the picturesqueness (a favorite word) of the landscape: "Let a painter visit Acroceraunia — until he does so he will not be aware of the grandest phases of savage, yet classic, picturesque-ness — whether Illyrian or Epirote — men or mountains; but let him go with a good guide or he may not come back again." Accordingly, Lear employed an Albanian servant, Giorgio Kokali, a "semi-civilised Suliot, much like wild Rob Roy" who was fiercely devoted to him. In regions that looked more subdued and civilized, however, Lear loathed "the mongrel appearance of every person and thing," a theme that becomes a discreet refrain in many descriptions.[41]

In the complex interplay between foreign policy, travelers' discourse, and public opinion, different sides of the triangle at different times played the role of *agent* (the source of influence) and *target* (its recipient).[42] Where travelers' accounts were instru-mental in shaping public opinion, this was not always in only reproducing and dis-seminating the official foreign policy line. In fact, there was always a plurality of British sympathies in the East and there is hardly a single group or nation that had not at-tracted the support of *some* group in English society at *some* time, although, in general (and with all the due exceptions to a gross generalization), there was a Turkophile aristocratic bias and a pro-Christian bias among the liberal middle class.[43] An important example of dissenting voices as the forerunners of an important though temporary shift in Britain's traditional foreign policy was the series of public lectures of two women travelers, Georgina Mackenzie and Adelina Irby, following their extensive tours of the Balkans, and especially Bulgaria, Serbia, Bosnia, and Macedonia between 1861 and 1863. The subsequent publication in 1867 of their popular and influential *Travels in the Slavonic Provinces of Turkey-in-Europe*, adorned with the drawings of Felix Kanitz, introduced the British public to a virtually unknown subject: the plight of the subject Slavs.

It would not be exaggerated to say that the two travelers discovered the South Slavs for the English public, which in 1860 still "vaguely supposed all the lands [of the Balkans] to be inhabited by Turks or Greeks," in which latter category were classed all non-Muslims.[44] In August 1862, while visiting the famous Rila monastery, Mackenzie and Irby were received by Abbot Neophyt Rilski, a renowned educator and linguist, prolific writer, and author of the first Bulgarian grammar. He was concerned by news that the Montenegrin Cetigne monastery was burned by Muslims. Reassured by his visitors that France would not allow this to happen, he exclaimed: "France, perhaps; but England!" The ladies' response was that "the want of interest displayed by England in the Slavonic Christians arose in great part from her ignorance respecting them—that one really never heard their name." Neophyt's reaction revealed his awareness of the intricacies of great power politics: "It is, however, a pity that so great a country, whose children are free to travel where they please, and publish what they please, should remain in such profound ignorance of the *Christians* in a country where she is on such intimate terms with the *Turks*."[45]

Mackenzie and Irby not only discovered the South Slavs, but became their staunch supporters; "they penetrated the country more deeply, saw beyond the sullenness, the poverty and the squalor of the Christian Slavs, and were less contented by the mannered courtesies and the facile explanations of the Turkish officials." One the daughter of a baronet, the other the granddaughter of a peer, "they were ladies of the Victorian era: they had great faith in their religion, great belief in progress, great confidence in their nationality and their background; and they were possessed of a passionate call that drove them on." The result was not only an attempt to enlighten the English public but also to enlighten the objects of their championship. In 1869, a school for Orthodox girls began operating in Sarajevo and, after Mackenzie's death in 1874, it became the lifelong passion of Irby, who presided over the establishment until her death and burial in Sarajevo in 1911. In the Bosnian people, Irby had found a purpose for dedication and was their unswerving champion although she never forgot her class and country and was "proudly conscious of her superiority of birth, breeding, and civilisation." The Bosnians always remained "semi-barbarians," and despite the efforts to produce "a better class of peasant woman," "the dishonest outweigh the honest," and their lasting weakness was "their inability to work hard."[46]

Within a decade, public opinion had changed so substantially that William Gladstone, in his preface to the second edition of *Travels* in 1877, wrote that "very nearly all, whether freely or reluctantly, now confess that in treating the question of the Ottoman Empire we cannot refuse to look at the condition of the subject races."[47] Before, even her closest friends, Florence Nightingale included, looked on Adelina Irby's ardor and her involvement in Bosnian and Serbian politics with uneasiness and suspicion. Yet, even here there was a change: "in the summer of 1876 it was no longer indiscreet to have friends among the 'semi-barbarians', nor eccentric to have a knowledge of the Turkish provinces, the Serbian language."[48] New books on the Southern Slavs were published, which added new information and openly criticized the British government for paying little attention to the future dominant nations of the peninsula.[49]

Exposing the press that "systematically suppresses the copious evidence of continuing Turkish outrages in Bulgaria," especially the bloody suppression of the April uprising of 1876, Gladstone concluded that it has "become generally known that the reign of terror is still prolonged in that unhappy Province." He disclosed the desolate state of Bosnia and Hercegovina where "more than a third of the population are exiled or homeless" and where "the cruel outrages . . . are more and more fastening themselves, as if inseparable adjuncts, upon the Turkish name."[50]

Following the gruesome Bulgarian massacres, Viscountess Emily Strangford set up a fund for the relief of Bulgarian peasants which, with the help of the American Missionary Establishment in Samokov and its head, James Franklin Clarke, distributed clothing and gave other help to the needy. The youngest daughter of Admiral Sir Francis Beaufort, Emily Anne had, before her marriage, traveled and written extensively about the East and, as a descendent of the Beauforts of the Crusades, was given the order of the Holy Sepulchre by the Patriarch of Jerusalem. Her husband, Percy Ellen Frederick William Smythe, was the eighth Viscount Strangford and son of the famous British ambassador to Constantinople and St. Petersburg in the 1820s, and was himself one of the most accomplished philologists and ethnologists of the day. With a thorough knowledge of Persian, Turkish, Arabic, Afghan, Hindi, and modern Greek, and some acquaintance with Slavic languages, he had been attaché and secretary at the British embassy in Constantinople in the 1840s and 1850s. After his accession to the peerage, he continued to live "the life of a dervish" in Constantinople until his marriage in the early 1860s. His views on the Eastern question were published in numerous contributions to the *Pall Mall Gazette* and the *Saturday Review*. Considering himself an antiphilhellene but a prophiloromaios, a revealing differentiation between an abstract affectation with an imaginary past and the active involvement with the present problems of the Greek nation, he nevertheless believed that the future of southeastern Europe belonged to the Bulgarians, "the most numerous and promising body of Christians in Turkey."[51]

Sharing her deceased husband's views, Viscountess Strangford engaged in charitable work, one of the great virtues as well as great fashions of Victorian society. Although her mission was "wholly and solely one of charity and practical benevolence to suffering fellow-creatures," she was "determined to avoid everything that could be open to the reproach of Westernizing them, or of advancing them in an artificial manner beyond the level to which they had brought themselves." Had the Bulgarians been "a stupid people, apathetic and dull," she would have seized the opportunity to urge them on; but since they were burning with the desire for progress, all they needed was encouragement in self-improvement. She was mostly impressed by their thirst for education which she found "the most remarkable feature in the Bulgarian character. . . . They begged for a school-house before they asked for shelter for themselves."[52]

To Lady Strangford, the Bulgarian was "a curious mixture of industry and thrift with laziness and apathy; at one time he appears so Oriental, at another so Western." A firm believer in progress, she thought that with freedom and independence, "all their faults—the hardness of character, poorness of sentiment, and apathy of heart, even the love of drink, will pass away like morning clouds; and the nation will shine out." All faults described good-naturedly by Viscountess Strangford are the perennial and international "faults" of poor and overworked peasants all over the globe. While even the slightest reservation about the high-mindedness of Lady Strangford's personal charity would be more than reprehensible (she later established hospitals for Turkish soldiers during the Russo-Turkish war, opened hospitals in Cairo and Beirut, and originated the National Society for Providing Trained Nurses for the Poor), her *Report* illustrated some of the discrepancies that have earned Victorian charity a reputation for hypocrisy. Describing a scene when on a Sunday, forty-six Bulgarian boys "of a class above peasants, whose parents had been well off before the destruction of their property," came to thank her for the clothes she had given them and sang grateful songs, she felt ashamed for their appearance in "long black cloaks, looking like penguins, while singing so nicely and gravely. But I did wish the kind English who gave the things had sent me more appropriate garments" rather than bales full of "faded, torn, old muslin gowns; children's socks without heels or toes, and shoes without soles; cheap frippery, bits of soiled finery, and odd gloves."[53]

The coincidence between the discovery of the oppressed Christian nationalities and the discovery of the Victorian poor with their respective discourses after the middle of the century was especially remarkable. Just as, "for most of the nineteenth century, Englishmen looked at poverty and found it morally tolerable because their eyes were trained by evangelical religion and political economy," so the political status quo in the Near East was considered tolerable. The passionate debate about the two nations in English society found its analogy in the awareness of the "other nations" in the Balkans, although in both cases the intellectual climate saw "little that could be done about it beyond the humanitarian charity frowned on by Malthus."[54] Not only charity presented a useful method for ideological self-preservation among the English. The East offered easy possibilities of translating in simple terms the complex issues that the English colonial metropolis was facing at the time: the uneasiness about Ireland was translated into uneasiness about Macedonia; the vogue about the poor was transformed into a vogue for suppressed nationalities; the feminist movement focused on life in the harems; the remorse about India or the Boer war was translated at the turn of the century into guilt about Turkish atrocities.[55] When Harry Thomson lamented in his journey through Bosnia, Hercegovina, and Macedonia that "England has been justly looked upon all through the Balkan States as the friend of the Turks and the enemy of their Christian subjects," he concluded that because of the obsession with its Indian possessions and its jealousy of Russia, "England, more than any other of the European powers, is responsible for the desolation and misery of those portions of the Balkan peninsula which have not yet shaken off the Turkish yoke."[56] Or, as another Englishman summarized England's emotional engagement with different Balkan groups:

[T]he minority staff was invariably a winner. It appealed to two instincts in the English character, one quite worthy, the other not so worthy. The first was our quite genuine, if unduly sentimental, desire to help the underdog, without first enquiring if he were a nice dog. The other was the capacity of some of us to salve our consciences for neglecting the unpicturesque poor of the East End of London by taking an interest in the picturesque poor of the East End of Europe.[57]

While public outrage, Gladstone's in particular, did not bring an involvement of British policy in Bulgarian or Bosnian affairs, it did bring to power his Liberal Party in 1880, following the Midlothian election campaign that recognized the importance of the new mass electorate and the power of newspaper reported political speeches. Deftly exploiting the Balkan question (while genuinely and even obsessively empathizing with the remote populations), Gladstone focused on the necessity for a moral foreign policy.[58] The savageness of the diatribes of Gladstone's supporters against Disraeli perfectly matched the equally savage accusations of the Turcophile public and press (Gladstone was even accused of being a Russian agent). If there is any lesson to be drawn from the Bosnian crisis of 120 years ago, it is more about the domestic imperatives in great power foreign policy than about "ancient enmities."

Aside from political expediency, there existed an evolution in the perceptions of the Balkans, and often observers espoused opposing views. Yet, despite the presence of such influential figures as Mackenzie and Irby, Gladstone, Viscount and Viscountess Strangford, and a few others on the political scene, theirs was not the dominant discourse. As a British journalist summarized his attitude before his pro-Bulgarian conversion: "I went out to Bulgaria prejudiced—if at all—in favour of the Turks, and that is the leaning of the average Englishman."[59] Even fewer were actually converted: "Indeed, the conviction of the English that all the South Slavs were inferior and semibarbarous was a stumbling block for any solution of the problem of Turkey and her European provinces."[60]

Two years after Mackenzie and Irby's book, a passionate counteraccount appeared, authored by Captain Stanislas St. Clair and Charles Brophy. Its purpose was to show the falseness of accusations of Turkish misrule and to appeal to Europe to first study Turkey, and only "then judge it, but not on the evidence of Philhellenic tourists and newspapers." American missionaries were added as perpetrators of disinformation in the revised edition published some twelve years later.[61] Christian discontent was represented as the sole result of Russian machinations. Russian emissaries were ubiquitous, and even the Bulgarian-Greek schism, strongly opposed by Russia, was seen as a Russian manipulation. Christianity in the East had degenerated from a religion into a secret society comparable to Fenianism. But even the Fenians fared better than the Balkan Christians, who were denied any history: "the aspirations of the Irish are certainly more legitimate than those of the Rayah, who has no history and therefore no fatherland."[62] The Bulgarians, "the immaculate pets of Russia," became the object of particular hatred:

> Strongly but heavily built, with broad shoulders and round back, a walk like that of a bear, coarse and blunted-looking features, a heavy moustache covering the sensual lips, a beard shaven once a week, and little twinkling eyes, which, whilst always avoiding to meet your own, give a general appearance of animal cunning to the

face—you will hardly say, notwithstanding the prejudices in favour of the interesting Christians of the East which you have brought with you from Europe, that this long exiled off-shoot is a prepossessing type of the great Slavonic Nationality which All-Mother Russia is so fondly eager to receive into her bosom and mould into one mighty and harmonious whole."[63]

The chief defect of the Bulgarians was that they had preserved no aristocracy and thus were deprived of history, literature, and even a perfectly formed language: "The Armenians, the Greeks, and the Servians, have a history, the Bulgarians have none." Even worse, they were supposed to be entirely deprived of educated men: "Rich Bulgarians there certainly are, . . . but perhaps the most eminent literary man of the nationality is a Choban [Turkish for shepherd] of our acquaintance who has composed and set to music (to the gaida, of course) a threnodia on the death of one of his herd of pigs."[64] Ethnic abuse is by no means an exception but it is surprising that it was heaped on the Bulgarians precisely during the 1860s and 1870s, the two decades that were marked by feverish journalistic and literary activities, when the Bulgarians made spectacular advances in their education.

Most unpardonable to St. Clair and Brophy was the fact that it was these Bulgarians, "brutish, obstinate, idle, superstitious, dirty, *sans foi ni loi*," that Europe thought could be civilized. The Turks were actually the ones who were "already in a great measure civilized by nature, by instinct, and even by taste" and even "the most sensitive Rayahphile, after a year's residence amongst the professors of the Greek rite, will hardly be able to deny that in all points, even that of Christianity, the Eastern Christian is far inferior to the follower of Mahomet." In an appeal that has the unmistakable quality of a retrospective déjà vu, they implored England to "adopt at Constantinople not the policy of non-intervention fashionable in the West, but a policy of action, such action as, while it serves Turkey, will benefit the true interests of civilization throughout the world."[65]

Even the most fiery philhellenic and pro-Christian treatises confined themselves to strictly ideological arguments, characterizing Ottoman rule as arbitrary, despotic, uncivilized, fanatical, and so forth, but never resorted to racial slurs against Muslims or Turks. Most of the pro-Turkish ones, on the contrary, even if not reaching the histrionic tones of St. Clair and Brophy, depicted the Christian *reaya* as piteous underlings. At the same time, the predominant opinion, even among staunch liberals and Turkophobes, was that the South Slavs were incapable of efficient and independent development and that Russia would inevitably manipulate them. Thus, the dissenting discourse was also not the one whose images have been perpetuated in lasting stereotypes, although at times (especially around the turn of the century) it seemed to control public opinion, if not foreign policy. Having established the dominant discourse, the question of how deeply it was diffused into the public, although important and interesting, is not central to this argument. What is important is that this discourse, with its distinct political and class bias, was further transmitted and perpetuated and can be understood within the framework of the disposition of power.

During the nineteenth century, a new travel literature in the English language began to be formed: the American. American descriptions from the beginning of the century are rare but become more numerous toward the end of the century. Many were the products of the American version of the Grand Tour; in fact, it can be argued that the share of real tourists among the Americans was greatest. They also included missionaries or other clergymen, educators, diplomats, and journalists.[66] The first account left of a journey to Greece was written in the spring of 1806 by Nicholas Biddle, the second American to visit the country.[67] The future scholar, politician, and prominent financier was only twenty at the time of his visit, but had a solid classical education, having graduated from Princeton at the age of fifteen. Coming from a wealthy Quaker family, Biddle, with his education, upbringing, appearance, and personal tastes, was as close to an American aristocrat as one could be: "Biddle on Chestnut Street was more than a match for any aristocratic Roman parading the Forum in a carefully arranged toga."[68] Much as his vision was shaped by his classical ideas, prominent in his judgments was the blazing Puritan disdain for Catholicism and Orthodoxy alike.

Biddle felt he had first touched the soil of Greece when he reached the mainland of Morea after a boat ride from Zante: "I now felt that I was in Greece. I felt that I was alone in a foreign country distant from all that was dear to me & surrounded by barbarians who yet occupied a soil interesting from its former virtues & its present ruin." The descriptions of the Greeks vacillated between commiseration, disappointment, and scorn, the latter solidly predominating. Biddle did not refute the possibility that the "descendants of a free nation who inherit their talents without their fortunes . . . may one day rival the brightest glory of their ancestors," but for the time being their fate was simply an illustration for the "passage from a civilized nation to its barbarous posterity." Biddle specified that their condition has to be defined as "half barbarous. They are connected with civilization; but in dress, in manners, in society they approach very near the level of the Mahometan nations." This characterization of in-betweenness is important, given the scorn Biddle heaped on the Greeks compared to his greater degree of toleration for Muslims and in the light of the "mongrel" theme in the whole travel literature. The reason for the deplorable condition of the Greeks was that they were slaves and "like other slaves, they are vile & abject in their submission, haughty & cruel when they can be so with impunity. Unable to act, they scarcely dare to think freely; and every thing, even down to their music and the miserable nasal noise of a slave afraid to speak out aloud, tells us that they have a master."[69] In Athens, Biddle exclaimed: "Are these few wretches, scarcely superior to the beasts whom they drive heedlessly over the ruins, are these men Athenians?" In Livadia, he witnessed an incident where a Turkish dragoon humiliated the chancellor of the town whose blush on the cheek "was a tribute to manhood which like his country's freedom passed in a moment." Biddle was appalled at the reaction of his countrymen:

> Did they rise in arms & massacre every thing that bore the name of a Turk? Did they demand the punishment of the wretch who had dared thus to insult their friend & their countryman? By heavens they laughed. Their wretched debasement was matter of jest to them. Yet Livadia is an hour from Cheronea, four hours from Platea, ten from Thermopylae![70]

Biddle, for whom slavery was a central notion in his enlightenment vocabulary, not once in his journals or letters reflected on its central position in his own society of which he was tremendously proud, and found it easier to comprehend the masters rather than the slaves. Although the Turks were described as indolent, receiving without any strain the fruits of labor of their inferiors, still "being the masters, [they were] in fact the gentlemen of the country." Biddle was evidently pleased with his visit to the aga of Mistra, an "old gentleman [who] is in general very civil; they know that Francs come only to amuse themselves, & spend their money, & they like the English," and he commented on the patriarchal character of the Turkish government. He was impressed by the shortness and effectiveness of the Ottoman judicial proceedings and not only concluded that "the people cannot be called litigious" but even asked himself whether the Turkish form of justice was not preferable to the lawsuits of Europe and America. His many examples of tyranny served him mainly to illustrate the slavish character of the Greeks. The Turks in Greece, on the other hand, impressed him with their tolerance: "There they do not mingle with the Christians but they are on a very good footing with them. They are tolerant." He found the Turks much more humane to animals than the Christians and also liked their language, which sounded softer than the European languages, but thought it not worth the trouble of studying. He described a Turkish wedding and, immediately following, a Greek wedding that he found "much meaner in every respect. The ceremony disgusting and ridiculously unmeaning."[71]

The most noticeable trait of Biddle's journals is the striking parallel to Morritt, and his editor admits as much, although he finds him less arrogant and with a notion of society that "was apt to be wider than the aristocratic Morritt."[72] Biddle's was a Grand Tour in the best English tradition. Not only was the new elite of the United States "still under the impress of British culture,"[73] the wealthy young Americans were usually taken for British, especially as they most often traveled in the company of Englishmen: Biddle himself joined the Scottish artist H. W. Williams in Athens. Another young American, Edward Everett, the future president of Harvard, governor of Massachusetts, minister plenipotentiary in London, and secretary of state, was the first American to visit Ali pasha of Ioannina. When he reached the pasha's court at Tyrnavo, he was greeted with "God Save the King," played by a band of German musicians.[74] It is a pity that, in *Innocents Abroad*, Mark Twain spent only two short chapters on Greece and Turkey. He sneaked out for a night to the Parthenon while his ship was kept in the port of Piraeus, and reserved his more scathing and well-deserved irony for the mores of Constantinople. Even when occasional and inevitable stereotypes creep in (like when he flirts with the lovely Smyrniotes, whose beauty averages a shade better than American girls but who speak only "Greek, or Armenian, or some such barbarous tongue"), they are conveyed with a charming and disarming unpretentiousness, although not with the resplendent hilarity of his Italian journey.[75]

Tourism was not the only channel for contacts. Much more serious was the American missionary enterprise, the effort to evangelize the world. It began in the early decades of the nineteenth century with an enormous outpouring of religious feeling which has been compared to the English religious zeal of the seventeenth century and even the Reformation. It had many positive side effects, although in practical terms it failed in its prime task of conversion. Although it was initially designed to convert the Muslims, the American mission in the Ottoman Empire became confined to the minority Christian populations, principally Armenians and to a lesser extent Greeks.[76] Beginning in 1819, a missionary station was established in Smyrna, followed by Constantinople in 1831; by 1869 there were twenty-one stations with forty-six American missionaries, mostly assisted by Armenian workers, and 185 schools. Being the most important project of the American Board of Commissioners for Foreign Missions, in less than a century the mission to Turkey had reached seventeen principal stations and 256 substations with 174 American missionaries. It stimulated the founding of schools, which after the turn of the century numbered 426 attended by 25,000 students.[77] The emphasis on Bible religion served as a powerful incentive to translate the Scripture in the vernacular and publication of the first Gospels in modern Bulgarian was accomplished under the auspices of the American Board in Smyrna.[78] The most spectacular achievement was the founding of the overseas colleges in Constantinople and Beirut. The famous Robert College, which opened in 1863, although connected to the American Board, became an independent institution and the most important foreign school in the Ottoman Empire. While hardly any Turks attended it, its role in the formation of minority elites, particularly Bulgaria's educated elites immediately after its secession in 1878, was quite considerable, although not so exclusive as Samuel Cox, the American minister plenipotentiary to the Ottoman Empire in the 1880s, would have it. According to Cox, "the dormant intellect" of Bulgaria was aroused in Robert College, where its leaders' minds "have been developed, permeated, disciplined and elevated by American teaching and tenets."[79] The phrase "Robert College made Bulgaria," popular among English and Americans, and which William Miller considered a "pardonable exaggeration," was a bragging overstatement.[80] American philhellenism in Greece was a romantic and disinterested affair, and Americans followed the British in number of enthusiasts participating in the war of independence.[81] It was also a private affair. George Jarvis, "the first and best American philhellene in action," who later became general in the Greek army, did not even merit an entry in the *Dictionary of American Biography*. The U.S. government was never involved in an official action against the Porte, and American naval constructors even rebuilt the Ottoman navy after the battle of Navarino, the "untoward event" of 1827, in which the joint fleet of Britain, France, and Russia had inflicted a devastating blow on the Ottoman-Egyptian fleet. At the time of the Greek revolution, diplomatic relations between the two countries had not been established yet, although negotiations for a commercial treaty were under way.[82]

An American legation opened in Constantinople on 2 March 1831 with Commodore David Porter as chargé d'affaires and minister resident as of 1839. The beginning was not auspicious. The Porte was dissatisfied that the Americans gave their representative only a minor rank that was evidence for the lack of proper esteem. Besides, the giving of presents in the East, a tradition of thousands of years with an elaborate symbolic ceremonial side, was not understood by a young nation exalted by its Puritan righteousness; inevitably, it was seen as mere corruption. When Commodore Porter sent presents for the treaty to the Porte, he made sure that the value of each present was well marked on it. The Reis Effendi wrote Porter a note to the effect that if so much had been paid for the presents as the notation indicated, he had paid too much. Porter interpreted this as an attempt at additional extortion and replied that he was well aware of the value.[83] The Reis Effendi threatened to return all gifts, but in the end the matter was luckily closed and, subsequently, David Porter left an admirable and balanced description of Constantinople in the reign of Mahmud II in which, far from being "the apologist of Turkish prejudices," he ascribed the enmity between Christian and Turk to bigotry and fanaticism on both sides.[84] One of the best informed, intelligent, and unbiased descriptions left of Greece in the first decade after its independence also belongs to an American, the U.S. consul in Athens G. A. Perdicaris, maybe because he himself was of Greek origins.[85] Throughout the nineteenth century, the traditional policy toward the Ottoman Empire was simply to protect the rights of American citizens. Only in the first decade of the twentieth century was an attempt made to receive shares in the mining projects, the irrigation and railroad concessions, but the European powers were too entrenched and this effort in "dollar diplomacy failed in Turkey."[86]

There were also the token dissenters from the official foreign policy line. Two of them were instrumental not in changing their own government's position, which was not important at that time anyway, but in rousing public opinion in Britain to the extent that it caused a sharp turn in its hitherto unyielding stand. In January 1876, Eugene Schuyler, the scion of a wealthy New York family of Dutch descent, was appointed secretary and consul-general of the American legation in Constantinople. This was a transfer from Russia, where Schuyler had occupied diplomatic posts since 1867. He had been so fascinated and involved in Russian culture, language, and literature, that his was the first English translation of Turgenev's *Fathers and Sons*. In St. Petersburg in 1873, Schuyler made the acquaintance of an adventurous American newspaperman, Januarius MacGahan, a second generation Irish immigrant from Ohio. A prolific writer with quick intellect and a gift for languages, MacGahan managed to become foreign correspondent for the *New York Herald*. His personal courage made him the ideal war correspondent. He covered the Franco-Prussian war as well as the Paris Commune when he befriended Jaroslaw Dombrowski, the Polish general, and nearly perished with the communards. In Russia, MacGahan was present at the Russian conquest of Khiva, won the respect and friendship of many Russian officers, most notably Mikhail Skobelev, the future general of the Russo-Turkish war of 1877–1878, and was married to the daughter of an old noble Russian family. When the Eastern Crisis broke out, he requested to be sent to the Balkans, but a conflict with his editor terminated his appointment. Instead, he associated himself with the liberal *London Daily News* and set out to cover the Serbo-Turkish war. En route to Constantinople, he learned about the atrocities committed against the Bulgarians a couple of months prior, and reached the Ottoman capital determined to pursue the issue.[87]

Schuyler had arrived in Constantinople a fortnight earlier to find the American community, especially the faculty of Robert College, where a number of young Bulgarians were studying, highly agitated by the news of the Bulgarian massacres. The American educators approached the British ambassador Sir Henry Elliot but the information fell on deaf ears. Only after it was published by the *Daily News* and produced a moral outrage in Britain was Disraeli compelled to order an investigation to be headed by a member of the staunchly Turkophile British embassy in Constantinople who had no knowledge of the requisite languages. Since the British investigation was expected to be a whitewash, the Americans decided to launch a separate one, without prior authorization from the State Department. The group consisted of Schuyler; Petîr Dimitrov, a Bulgarian instructor at Robert College; MacGahan; Karl Schneider, the correspondent of the *Kölnische Zeitung*; and Prince Tseretelev, secretary at the Russian embassy in Constantinople. The revelations about the Bulgarian horrors published in the *Daily News* brought about an explosion of public opinion in Britain and made the unconditional support of the status quo untenable.[88] There was much grisly sensationalism in MacGahan's writings although there was no question about the authenticity of his facts. This was especially true about the plight of women raped and killed: "[O]n matters relating to outrages on women, the Victorian conscience, which was at one and the same time excessively puritanical about sex and excessively sentimental about women, was shocked, yet morbidly fascinated."[89] MacGahan got himself an accreditation as war correspondent in the Russian army and covered the war of 1877–1878. While preparing to leave for Berlin to cover the proceedings of the congress, he died of typhus in the summer of 1878 in Constantinople.

Nor was MacGahan the only American journalist to cover the war. Edward Smith King, a reporter for *Scribner's Monthly* and for the *Boston Morning Journal*, was also sent to the Balkans in 1877–1878 after he had made a name for himself with reports of the American Civil War and the Carlist war in Spain. A liberal who cast a sympathetic eye on the Paris Commune, King was persuaded that Ottoman rule in the Balkans was unfit for modern civilization.[90] The result of his sojourn in the Balkans was stimulating also in another way: in 1880, he published his first book of verse prompted, as he said, "by a journey in Turkey in Europe,—that strange border land of the East,—a land literally filled with 'Echoes from the Orient.'"[91] It was a collection of romantic poems, mostly inspired by Balkan legends and folk songs. King's next venture in belles lettres came some three years later, obviously permeated by the same sentiment but prompted already by local exoticism: his first novel, *The Gentle Savage*, was about an Oklahoma Indian against the background of European sophistication. King constantly ruminated about the similarity between the picturesque Balkan mountaineers and "the splendid types of the fading Cherokee and Choktaw races" and his Hercegovinian guide, Tomo, reminded him mostly of the "stalwart bronze-colored men who I had seen in the Indian Territory."[92] The Balkans as Europe's Indian territory was only an implicit metaphor that took someone like Hitler to bring from metaphor to reality by also enlarging its geographical space to all of Eastern Europe.

In the meantime, displeased with Schuyler, the Porte protested his action and succeeded in having him recalled. *Blackwood's Magazine* published a scathing article against Schuyler accusing him of violating the rules of his profession: "If Mr. Schuyler wished to continue as public champion of a certain class of Ottoman subjects, he has a perfect right to do his hobby, but he is bound to resign his appointment." Schuyler was accused of many sins, among others being a secret Russian agent. Although he was cleared of the most extravagant ones, the investigation of the State Department found that his views "aided greatly to alienate British sympathy from Turkey in her struggle with Russia" and he was demoted. Soon, however, he was summoned back to the Balkans, to serve first as chargé d'affaires in Romania, and from 1882 as the first American minister to Romania, Serbia, and Greece. In 1884, in an economy move, Congress altogether abolished the post of minister in the Balkans. In Romania, Schuyler had begun studying Romanian literature and mythology and this earned him election as corresponding member of the Romanian academy of sciences; in Bulgaria, he was held in enormous esteem by the "certain class of Ottoman subjects."[93] This episode might merit more attention with its implications for the rationale of diplomatic appointments, that is, the issue of whether one should select people who are knowledgeable but can become too emotionally involved with the country or whether officials should be sent whose ignorance would make them impermeable to any sentiment that could swerve them from the official line (or lack of it). With minor exceptions, Americans seem to have followed the safer option, at least in the Balkans.[94] In fact, until the turn of the century, they were not even used to the notion of the Balkans but were speaking still in terms of "the Turk and his lost provinces."

William Curtis, the correspondent of the *Chicago Record*, was a real globetrotter and had covered everything from Japan, India, Burma, Central Asia, Turkey, Egypt, and the Eastern Mediterranean to Latin America. His book on Greece, Bulgaria, Serbia, and Bosnia, *The Turk and His Lost Provinces*, was a good-natured account although, as is almost inevitable with quick and prolific writers, full of superficial observations and historical errors. Both Serbia and Bulgaria were described as peasant states and, in a refreshing respite from the usual contempt for the peasantry, Curtis found them "industrious, ingenious and intelligent," and Bulgaria in particular struck him with its physical resemblance to Pennsylvania, the Quaker state. Both countries were favorably contrasted to Romania for their lack of anti-Semitism.[95] Curtis's sole, although not malevolent, disappointment was reserved for Greece, most likely because of his greater expectations. In a paragraph that reminds one of the present laments over the insensibility of Indians over the Amazonian forests, he wrote how "unconscious of their artistic and archeological advantages, which students travel four thousand miles to enjoy, Grecian peasants continue to plow the adjacent fields" of Corinth. His conclusion that Greece was a true democracy was not laudable: the democratic spirit was often revealed in ways that he found disagreeable. Curtis was especially taken aback by the general "feeling of equality" which he deemed to be one of the great obstacles to progress, a theme with a striking continuity in later American criticism of the communist Balkans. He was also a sui generis forerunner in that absolute belief in the operative and beneficial role of western public opinion that one has encountered especially at the end of the cold war. Describing the appalling practice of Ottoman sultans to execute their brothers, he remarked that "public sentiment in Europe has forbidden the application of that heroic precaution during the last fifty or sixty years."[96] Curtis was at fault with some two and a half centuries: the slaughter of royal princes was terminated by the end of the sixteenth century for reasons very different from public sentiment in Europe.

For our purposes, however, what follows from the above survey is the close connection, indeed convergence, between American and British attitudes until the end of the nineteenth century. Not only is this seen in the accounts of tourists who were still willingly and consciously part of the cultural empire of England, but it is especially obvious in the foreign policy line and diplomacy of the United States, which was closely coordinated with Great Britain, and dictated to a large extent by apprehensions of Russia.

By the close of the nineteenth century, among the rich, diverse, and not always harmonic chorus of impressions in different languages and different voices, one can discern the contours of at least two patterns of perception that can be termed loosely the aristocratic and the bourgeois. Clumsy as this definition may sound, especially with the fashionable dismissal of "modes-of-production narrative," "historicism," and class analysis, I am using it not simply for lack of a better one but because, first, I would like to convey that these were patterns informed by attitudes of class, and second, because the two concepts, bourgeois and aristocratic, have their legitimate place and authentic cognitive value especially during the nineteenth century. Until at least the middle of the century, the aristocratic was the dominant discourse, and even after that it was not entirely displaced. The commonality of this pattern is partly explained by the fact that the articulate observers of the Balkans who left written accounts of their impressions until well into the nineteenth century were, in their great majority, aristocrats or individuals closely connected with them and who emulated their tastes and attitudes. Nowhere is this more striking than in the contemporary account of an American, the diplomat Samuel Cox, who extolled the principles of constitutionalism, republicanism, and democracy. Yet he shared Gibbon's admiration for the Turks, their patience, discipline, sobriety, bravery, honesty, and modesty: "It is because of these solid characteristics, and in spite of the harem, in spite of autocratic power, in spite of the Janizary and seraglio, that this race and rule remain potential in the Orient."

The Bulgarians he described as a body of peasants, a "rural democracy" as in Norway, Kansas, Switzerland, and Texas, with good qualities as honesty, sincerity, and economy, but rather slow, domestic, sober, and uninviting. Bulgaria's "elder glory" was in the Middle Ages, when she had a refinement of civilization comparable to Germany, Hungary, France, and England. Cox's Romanian description, on the other hand, is amazing for anyone who is familiar with its social disparities and profound problems at the time. The Romanians, he said, deserved special attention because they had the touch of Western civilization, "strictly speaking, Romania is not a Balkan province." Romanians traveled a lot, loved music and shows, had fine horses, were "unexampled for the gaiety of their equipages," had shapely and elegant houses, and also chivalry, gallantry, and pride.[97]

The aristocratic lens through which developments in the Ottoman Empire and the Balkans were evaluated can be seen clearly in the respect shown for Ottoman might in the earlier centuries. One can find it even behind the display of later contempt for the downfall of the empire, which was more regret and even helpless rage at the betrayal of greatness. It was also a deep-seated acceptance of empire and authority. Despite the overall anti-Islamic, often righteous fundamentalist Christian rhetoric, for the vast majority of the ruling elites in Europe, even quite apart from considerations of balance of power, it was easier to identify (and they, in fact, did) with the Ottoman rulers, rather than with the Balkan upstarts. It was not only empathy with the rulers but also the sympathetic, yet condescending attitude toward the subjects that was revealed in this approach. It was the essentially prejudicial but also protective patronizing of the aristocrat toward the peasant. In this respect, there was much in common with the general attitude of the Ottoman government toward the peasantry as the basis and centerpiece of society, a class to be protected and preserved.

The second pattern derived from a completely different set of values, essentially opposed to the aristocratic, but curiously superimposing its idiosyncratic stereotypes on the previously developed prejudicial configuration. It was an entirely nineteenth-century phenomenon, based on enlightened linear evolutionary thinking and dichotomies like progressive-reactionary, advanced-backward, industrialized-agricultural, urban-rural, rational-irrational, historic-nonhistoric, and so on. This was summarized by Rebecca West:

The nineteenth-century English traveller tended to form an unfavourable opinion of the Christian subjects of the Ottoman Empire on the grounds that they were dirty and illiterate and grasping (as poor people, oddly enough, often are) and cringing and inhospitable and ill-mannered (as frightened people, oddly enough, often are). He condemned them as he condemned the inhabitants of the new industrial hells in Lankashire and Yorkshire, who insisted on smelling offensively, drinking gin to excess, and being rough and rude. Even as he felt glad when these unfortunate fellow-countrymen of his were the objects of missionary efforts by philanthropists drawn from the upper and middle classes, he felt glad because the Christian Slavs were in the custody of the Turks, who were exquisite in their personal habits, cultivated, generous, dignified, hospitable, and extremely polite.[98]

However, where this new approach differed from the aristocratic was in the gradual but finally complete rejection of the Ottomans as a basic hindrance to progress. Indeed, progress had became the key word at the close of the nineteenth century much like democracy has become one at the close of the twentieth century. For William Miller, one of the more perceptive English historians and a critic of British foreign policy in the 1890s, Great Britain "ought to seek the friendship of those Christian states which, in spite of their obvious faults, contain at least what Turkey does not contain, the germs of progress." Despite being hitched on progress, Miller was still the patronizing conservative who was convinced that "the only government suited to an Oriental people, lately emancipated from centuries of Turkish misrule, is a benevolent autocracy. Of all forms of political folly the worst is to bestow full representative government upon an Eastern nation before it had had any chance of obtaining a training in public affairs." He sincerely deplored the disastrous results of parliamentary rule and the "unlimited," "absolute" democracy in Greece, Serbia, and Bulgaria.[99] Democracy in those days was a singular threat to the cherished hierarchies of class internalized by the British. Another English writer at the beginning of the century also thought the Greeks to be the most democratic people in the world: "The absence of class distinctions is apt to astonish the Western traveller, who finds his muleteer a fellow-guest at the table of his host, the doctor or the demarch of the village. The familiarity of waiters and domestics is rather trying to the new-comer, but he soon grows accustomed to it, and, indeed, it is not offensive."[100] Many others were thinking in terms of a general rejection of empire and autocracy: "I became newly doubtful of empires. Since childhood I had been consciously and unconsciously debating their value, because I was born a citizen of one of the greatest empires the world has ever seen, and grew up as its exasperated critic."[101] It was much easier for an American to repudiate empire. Edward King was convinced that "in the future, European majorities will be democratic, non-Imperial, progressive." With typical Yankee optimism, King foresaw a bright future for the Balkans linked to the ideas of progress through industry and commerce. He exulted at the "release from barbarous despotism of all South-Eastern Europe, soon to be seamed with through lines of rail, and by the opening up of its vast resources to exercise new influence on European commerce."[102] What this view shared with the aristocratic approach was the general contempt for the peasantry, but it was not coupled with the almost benign patronage of the aristocrat. It looked at the peasantry as a social group still to be reckoned with but essentially belonging to a past economic and social order. In the best case, it considered it a class retreating from center stage, a curio and repository for archaic customs and beliefs. In its most extreme form, as among nineteenth century socialists, it flatly predicted its disappearance. Ironic as it may sound, the *Communist Manifesto* became the epitome of the bourgeois outlook, understood in its broadest and global meaning of urban, rational, industrialized, and progressive:

> The bourgeoisie has subjected the country to the rule of the towns. It has created enormous cities, has greatly increased the urban population as compared with the rural, and has thus rescued a considerable part of the population form the idiocy of rural life. Just as it has made the country dependent on the towns, so it has made barbarian and semi-barbarian countries dependent on the civilised ones, the East on the West.[103]

The aristocratic bias against egalitarian peasant societies was translated into the bias of the urban bourgeois rational culture against what was perceived as the superstitious, irrational, and backward rural tradition of the Balkans, whose sole value lay in providing the open-air *Volksmuseum* of Europe. There was also a noticeable shift in the aesthetics of perception: "As aristocratic culture slowly gave way to bourgeois attack on corruption and sensuality, the cosmopolitan, hedonistic appreciation of the exotic and oriental was supplanted by a preoccupation with 'propriety,' accompanied by intolerance."[104] These patterns of perception were also shaped by what was increasingly becoming a common outlook of the educated European, sharing in the beliefs and prejudices of the intellectual currents and fashions dominant at different periods: renaissance values, humanism, empiricism, enlightenment ideas, classicism, romanticism, occasionally even socialism, but almost inevitably tainted with what Aijaz Ahmad has called "the usual banalities of nineteenth-century Eurocentrism."[105] They were transmitted throughout the following periods and perpetuated, sometimes literally, sometimes in a modified form, often intertwined, by consecutive generations.

These legacies are most obvious in discussions in which the Balkans are marginal to the main problems and the perspective on them is completely unself-conscious. On 21 April 1894, the Avenue Theatre in London presented the first of George Bernard Shaw's *Plays: Pleasant and Unpleasant*. On its initial program, *Arms and the Man* was subtitled "A Romantic Comedy." Probably because the audience took the subtitle too literally, the subsequent publications carried the subtitle "An Anti-Romantic Comedy." Shaw wrote *Arms and the Man* "to explode the conventions of military romance and replace them with a much more common-sensical view of war and women."[106] According to his own testimony, Shaw had first written a piece in which the characters were simply called The Father, The Daughter, The Stranger, The Heroic Lover, and so on. He then asked Sidney Webb to find out a good war for his purpose. Webb "spent about two minutes in a rapid survey of every war that has ever been waged, and then told me that the Servo-Bulgarian was what I wanted." Shaw had decided first that the action take place in Serbia, in a Serbian family. Then he changed the characters form Serbians to Bulgarians because he read the play to the admiral who had commanded the Bulgarian fleet during the war and was residing in London, and the latter supplied him with descriptions of Bulgarian life and ideas.[107] The admiral turned out to be the Russian admiral Serebryakov, who had been in charge of the Bulgarian Danube fleet but, after having been suspected of nihilist sympathies, escaped to England.[108]

A week before the premier, Shaw advertised his play by a witty interview with himself that he drafted for *The Star* on 14 April 1894. Responding to the imaginary question whether *Arms and the Man* was a skit on Adelphi melodrama, he explained: "Bulgaria is like the Adelphi Theatre in one respect. Romantic dreams and Quixotic ideals flourish luxuriantly in the rose valleys of that country. They play their due part in 'Arms and the Man'; and I have not represented them as standing the test of reality any better or any worse than they do in actual life." He heaped lavish praise on the cast and vowed to take all the blame should the play fail. To the question "Who is to be the hero?" he responded:

> Everybody is a hero in Bulgaria. Mr. Gould will embody the chivalry of the Balkans;—you know what Mr.Gould can do with parts which have a touch of the fantastic. The audience can choose, for their pet hero, between him and Mr. Yorke Stephens, who will be the incarnation of the comparative coolness, good sense, efficiency, and social training of the higher civilisation of Western Europe. Then there is Mr. Welch. . . . On him will fall the duty of expounding the ethnology of Bulgaria, the peculiar customs and prejudices of the native races, and the eccentricities of their military system. He will thus supply a grave scientific background for the lighter scenes in which the other characters participate.[109]

One such scientific scene produced frowns by the critics. It was a soliloquy of Mr. Welch alias Major Petkoff in which he remarked on the mixed blessings of personal hygiene:

> PETKOFF *over his coffee and cigaret:* I don't believe in going too far with these modern customs. All this washing can't be good for the health: it's not natural. There was an Englishman at Philippopolis who used to wet himself all over with cold water every morning when he got up. Disgusting! It all comes from the English: their climate makes them so dirty that they have to be perpetually washing themselves. Look at my father! he never had a bath in his life; and he lived to be ninety-eight, the healthiest man in Bulgaria. I don't mind a good wash once a week to keep my position; but once a day is carrying the thing to a ridiculous extreme.[110]

Dismissive as Shaw was of his critics, he went to great lengths to rebuff the accusations of cynicism and vulgarity because of "certain references to soap and water in Bulgaria." What he wanted to achieve, he said, was to "bring home to the audience the stage of civilisation in which the Bulgarians were in 1885, when, having clean air and clean clothes, which made them much cleaner than any frequency of ablution can make us in the dirty air of London, they were adopting the washing habits of big western cities as pure ceremonies of culture and civilisation, and not on hygienic grounds." He regretted that this "piece of realism should have been construed as an insult to the Bulgarian nation."[111] The misunderstanding between what Shaw called "my real world" and "the stage world of the critics" was inherent in the play itself. In order to lay out this point, Shaw introduced a brief summary of the historical moment of 1885 when the Bulgarians, after having achieved the union of their country, fought an unexpectedly victorious war against the invading Serbs. This "made the Bulgarians for six months a nation of heroes."

> But as they had only just been redeemed from centuries of miserable bondage to the Turks, and were, therefore, but beginning to work out their redemption from

barbarism — or, if you prefer it, beginning to contract the disease of civilisation — they were very ignorant heroes. . . . And their attempts at Western civilisation were mush the same as their attempts at war — instructive, romantic, ignorant.[112]

In this world of romantic and patriotic heroes is introduced the experienced and skeptical westerner, "a professional soldier from the high democratic civilisation of Switzerland." This juxtaposition is the crux of the play: "[T]he comedy arises, of course, from the collision of the knowledge of the Swiss with the illusions of the Bulgarians." The allegory of romanticism versus reality was steeped in a further one: realism versus theatrical preconceptions: "In this dramatic scheme Bulgaria may be taken as symbolic of the stalls on the first night of a play. The Bulgarians are dramatic critics; the Swiss is the realist playwright invading their realm; and the comedy is the comedy of the collision of the realities represented by the realist playwright with the preconceptions of stageland."[113]

There is no doubt that Shaw was little concerned with the Bulgarian issue per se but with the broad philosophical questions of the encounter between romantic follies and bare reality. He never intended, indeed, to specifically offend Bulgarian sensitivities, although four years later, in the preface to the first publication of his plays in 1898, he could not resist evoking the particularly gruesome assassination of the Bulgarian premier Stambolov as "a sufficiently sensational confirmation of the accuracy of my sketch of the theatrical nature of the first apings of western civilisation by spirited races just emerging from slavery." And yet, none of the vituperative disdain toward the Balkans that is to be found among authors of some decades later is to be discovered in Shaw's writings: there was present a, no doubt, dismissive but also good-humored and patient condescension, the condescension of an adult toward a child.

What he was really involved in was the allegation that the general onslaught on idealism implicit and explicit in *Arms and the Man* would cast a blow on the type of political and religious idealism "which had inspired Gladstone to call for the rescue of these Balkan principalities from the despotism of the Turk, and converted miserably enslaved provinces into hopeful and gallant little States." As far as Shaw was concerned, the sooner this blow would happen, the better: "for idealism, which is only a flattering name for romance in politics and morals, is as obnoxious to me as romance in ethics and religion." In a scathing diatribe against the hypocrisy of "a Liberal Revolution or two," Shaw declared:

> I can no longer be satisfied with fictitious morals and fictitious good conduct, shedding fictitious glory on robbery, starvation, disease, crime, drink, war, cruelty, cupidity, and all the other commonplaces of civilisation which drive men to the theatre to make foolish pretenses that such things are progress, science, morals, religion, patriotism, imperial supremacy, national greatness and all the other names the newspapers call them.[114]

While Shaw might have been misunderstood by some of his critics, he was very literally and correctly understood in the Balkans, and particularly in Bulgaria. *Arms and the Man* was never a favored item of the Shaw repertoire in the country. In the 1920s, a performance of the play was even disrupted in the town of Petrich by members of the Macedonian revolutionary organization.[115] Neither was it a staple item of the Serbian theater, and John Reed reported that Serbs were sensitive about the play when he visited the country in 1915.[116] Shaw's play, under the title "The Heroes" was staged by the Viennese Burgtheater and played in Schönbrunn on 11 June 1921. It incurred the noisy disapproval of the sizeable Bulgarian student community in Vienna, and Pancho Dorev, head of the Bulgarian legation, protested to the police and the board of state theaters about the impropriety of the performance. The next performances censored the sharpest anti-Bulgarian barbs, but the Bulgarian students still booed and demonstrated against it. The Austrian press unanimously ostracized the Burgtheater for its tactlessness in damaging the dignity of former allies. The scandal reached the attention of the federal chancellor and on 15 June, after only four performances, the play was banned and taken off the theatre's repertory.[117] It was not, however, trifles over soap and water that upset his Balkan audience. Shaw was right when he derided the irrational courage and the ignorance of Bulgarian soldiers, but it was also true that only their reckless determination and intense devotion turned a hopeless cause into a brilliant victory. In fact, the nineteenth-century Balkan states were all products of a passionate and reckless nationalism, this quintessentially romantic ideology, for which Shaw's rationalism had no patience. Shaw's "anti-romantic comedy" was a frontal attack on the very essence of the Balkans.

Although most clearly crystallized in the British tradition, these attitudes can be traced in different degrees in many of the separate European traditions. That there were distinct national traditions was remarked in jest as early as the 1890s by one of the first scholars of travelers' accounts, the Bulgarian Ivan Shishmanov:

> It is curious how the manner of narration often reflects the national characteristics of the travellers. The German notes first and foremost what he has eaten and drunk on his way, where he has found good wine, where bad, where his companions have fallen sick from consuming too many vegetables, etc. The Frenchman— toujours galant—carves his name on silver coins and distributes then among the young women as souvenirs; the Englishman, loyal son of Albion that he is and a pupil of the sentimental Richardson, does not miss to record in his notebook the price of goods but, at the same time, shows sincere delight with the beauties of Balkan nature.[118]

This verdict is in many ways simply a witty riposte of conferring national stereotypes on the observers, yet differences are clearly noticeable. Indeed, before the twentieth century, despite the commonality of outlook of the educated European, it is more appropriate to speak of separate national traditions, rather than a common European or Western one. It is only with the increasing globalism of the twentieth century, especially after World War II, that European or Western identities have come to be operative, and even they are fragmented along ethnic, political, class, professional, ideological, and other lines. The crusading spirit had been the last manifestation of an ecumenical Christian approach toward Islam, and the five centuries of Ottoman rule coincided with an increasing particularism, and later nationalism, of the separate European state formations. No doubt, this was reflected also in what can be termed as national schools of travel. These stemmed partly from the fact that at different intervals one or another European power conducted the most active relations with the Ottomans and consequently produced the bulk of descriptions for a given period: the Venetians dominating the fifteenth and, together with the Habsburgs, the sixteenth century; the German language literature being the preponderant for the sixteenth and seventeenth centuries, to be gradually supplanted first by French and finally English accounts in the next two centuries. It was also due to the fact that a majority of the travelers and other observers of the Balkans were official agents or perceived themselves as representatives of their respective states. Finally, despite translations and increased mutual knowledge, they tended to work within the continuity of their own linguistic literary tradition. These considerations, despite the presence of truly cosmopolitan observers, such as Ogier Busbecq or Luigi Marsigli, among the travelers have been the chief justification for the choice of presenting the travelers' views in a quasi-national fashion (following the criteria of language and state) rather than in a common chronological one.

Another reason why the "national" approach of presenting the represcenters has been favored was that it better illustrates my deep reservations about using totalizing concepts like "Western" views, "Western" perceptions, and "Western" politics, implicitly postulating a homogeneous and monolithic outlook that I believe did not exist at the time. Despite the presence of the aforementioned common patterns, an equally important conclusion is that there was no common Western stereotype of the Balkans. To declare this is not to say that there were no common stereotypes but that there was no common West. And even within the different national stereotypes, informed as they were by their respective political realities and political and intellectual discourses, there was a great diversity of opinion and an even greater variety of nuance. Moreover, within the whole natural spectrum of positive and negative assessments, one could rarely, if ever, encounter entirely disparaging or scornful judgments addressed to the region as a whole, let alone attempts to exclude it from the fold of civilization. This was attempted under a different effort, with the organization and utilization of the knowledge of the Balkans in grand classificatory systems.

From Discovery to Invention, from Invention to Classification

Si les Balcans n'existaient pas, il faudrait les inventer.[1]

Hermann Keyserling

By the beginning of the twentieth century, an image of the Balkans had already been shaped in European literature; moreover, it was almost exclusively under the name Balkan that it was further elaborated. Although far from being unanimous, it held many features in common. The geographic discovery was going hand in hand with a simultaneous invention of the region; the two processes are, in fact, inseparable. A travel narrative, like any other, "simultaneously presents and represents a world, that is, simultaneously creates or makes up a reality and asserts that it stands independent of that same reality."[2] The discovery of the Balkans falls within the general rubric of how people deal with difference. The human attempt to give meaning and order to the world has been called a "nomos-building activity" involving the process of typification which confers knowability and predictability.[3] What exactly impels humans to develop formal categories has not been answered in a formal categorical fashion, but it is clear this is a deep-seated craving and "the categories in terms of which we group the events of the world around us are constructions or inventions. . . . They do not 'exist' in the environment." Among the different achievements of categorizing, the primary ones reduce complexity and the necessity of constant learning; the two main goals of perception are stability and clarity or definiteness.[4] In perceiving, we fit our impressions into what has been called "schemata" by Frederic C. Bartlett, "recipes" by Alfred Schutz, or "forms" by Maurice Merleau-Ponty: "Perceiving is not a matter of passively allowing an organ—say of sight or hearing—to receive a ready-made impression from without, like a palette receiving a spot of paint. . . . It is generally agreed that all our impressions are schematically determined from the start." We organize the information we receive into "patterns for which we, the perceivers, are largely responsible."[5]

While postulating the inseparable nature of the processes of discovery and invention, it has to be emphasized that during the nineteenth century, when the Balkans were discovered and described, the process of accumulating knowledge did not yet rigidly compartmentalize it in prearranged schemata. We are all aware that there is no such category as "essentially descriptive," that to describe is "to specify a locus of meaning, to construct an object of knowledge, and to produce a knowledge that will be bound by that act of descriptive construction."[6] And yet, it was the process of acquiring and accumulating knowledge that gave the image of the Balkans in this period a more floating character, generally devoid of categorical and excruciating judgments. Indeed, "where there is no differentiation there is no defilement." Yet it seems that the "yearning for rigidity is in all of us," the longing for "hard lines and clear concepts" is part of the human condition. In the course of piling up and arranging more information, one invests deeper in a system of labels: "So a conservative bias is built in. It gives us confidence. At any time we may have to modify our structure of assumptions to accommodate new experience, but the more consistent experience is with the past, the more confidence we can have in our assumptions."[7] The essence of the patterning tendency—the schema—although certainly dynamic in terms of *longue durée*, has a certain fixity over a short-term period.

Already, brigandage in Greece had strongly contributed to the decline of philhellenism and, after the Dilessi murders of several English tourists in 1870, to its death. The return of Macedonia to the direct rule of the Porte after the Treaty of Berlin in 1878 opened the way for revolutionary action against the Ottoman Empire and, at the same time, guerrilla warfare between the contending factions of the neighboring countries. The birth of the Macedonian question enhanced the reputation of the peninsula as a turbulent region and of Macedonia as the "land of terror, fire, and sword." The hatred and atrocities committed by rival Christian bands prompted a well-informed and well-meaning writer like Fraser to label the peninsula "a confused kettle of fish," and the Macedonian question "the Balkan problem."[8]

For a tradition boasting about its empiricism, the English of the period were surprisingly prone to facile generalizations. Harry De Windt recounted his journey through the Balkans and European Russia as a trip "through savage Europe," traversing the "wild and lawless countries between the Adriatic and the Black-Seas" which were "hotbeds of outlawry and brigandage."[9] Describing Macedonia in a book with the significant subtitle *A Plea for the Primitive*, two British authors mused on the "immature, unenlightened intellect" of the Macedonian peasant. In a short passage about the character of the Macedonians, they achieved a virtual synthesis of the nature-nurture debate: "Oppression and an entire lack of education . . . have joined forces and evolved a crafty disposition and a natural tendency towards savagery."[10] In the United States, nothing advanced this opinion more than the famous Miss Stone affair when a long-time American missionary and educator was kidnapped in 1901 by one of Yane Sandanski's bands. Although the affair ended happily and Miss Stone was released against a handsome ransom and later became a sympathizer of the Macedonian cause, it sealed to the region the epithet "terrorist."[11] The Macedonian question was so much at the center of Balkan affairs that it was difficult for observers to remember its fairly recent origins. The reason Berkovici, an otherwise informed writer, declared in the early 1930s that "the affairs of Macedonia have kept the whole of Europe agog for the last hundred years," may have been to confer additional weight to his statement.[12]

A singularly grisly act of violence outraged Western public opinion in 1903: the murder and defenestration of Alexander and Draga in Belgrade, a regicide particularly distasteful to royalists in Austria-Hungary and Great Britain. *The New York Times* explained that defenestration was "a racial characteristic" attributed to "a primitive Slavic strain": "As the bold Briton knocks his enemy down with his fists, as the southern Frenchmen lays his foe prostrate with a scientific kick of the savante, as the Italian uses his knife and the German the handy beermug, so the Bohemian and Servian 'chucks' his enemy out of the window."[13] The violence led a respected historian as late as 1988 to maintain that "the turning point in the relations between Austria and Serbia was not so much the annexation of Bosnia-Hercegovina in 1908, as the brutal military coup in Belgrade five years earlier."[14] It seemed that it was the particular repulsiveness of the deed that the civilized Austrians could not stomach, and not some esoteric economic frictions, nationalism, and raison d'etat. H. N. Brailsford, active in the British Relief Fund after the suppression of the 1903 revolt in Macedonia, was one of the first to spell out in disgust his belief in a fundamental difference between the moral standards of London or Paris and those of the Balkans. Without second thoughts about English performance in South Africa, the Indian continent, or Ireland, he wrote:

> I have tried, so far as a European can, to judge both Christians and Turks as tolerantly as possible, remembering the divergence which exists between the standards of the Balkans and of Europe. In a land where the peasant ploughs with a rifle on his back, where the rulers govern by virtue of their ability to massacre upon occasion, where Christian bishops are commonly supposed to organise political murders, life has but a relative value, and assassination no more than a relative guilt. There is little to choose in bloody-mindedness between any of the Balkan races— they are all what centuries of Asiatic rule have made them.[15]

Robert W. Seton-Watson, the redoubtable historian of the Habsburgs and the Balkans, took the dual monarchy to task for not being consistent in its political and cultural mission in the Balkans. He maintained that the triumph of the Pan-Serb idea would mean "the triumph of Eastern over Western culture, and would be a fatal blow to progress and modern development throughout the Balkans." There is no doubt that aggressive Serbian expansionism was not the most desirable development in the Balkans, yet to ascribe the phenomenon of nationalism, of all things, to "Eastern culture" sounds strange from a specialist on the rise of nationality in the Balkans.[16]

It was always with reference to the East that Balkan cruelty was explained. Harry De Windt, describing a scene of vendetta in Montenegro, concluded that "life is valued here almost as cheaply as in China and Japan."[17] Comparison with the East enforced the feeling of alienness and emphasized the oriental nature of the Balkans. For all the growing criticism of Balkan performance, it was not until the second Balkan war that the existing, if only moderate, expectations of betterment were substituted for almost total disappointment: according to Seton-Watson, "excessive enthusiasm for the triumphs of Balkan unity has been replaced in Western Europe by excessive disgust at the fratricidal strife between the former allies, and by an inclination to ignore its underlying causes."[18] The great crime of the Balkans, however, indeed their original sin, were the shots of Gavrilo Princip, which signaled the outbreak of World War I. This left an indelible mark on all assessments of the region. While even after the Macedonian rising of 1903, the British correspondent to the *Graphic* could speak good-naturedly of "the good old Balkans, where there's always something going," 1914 wiped off any ambivalence.[19] The immensely popular *Inside Europe* of John Gunther thus summarized the feelings on this side of the Atlantic:

> It is an intolerable affront to human and political nature that these wretched and unhappy little countries in the Balkan peninsula can, and do, have quarrels that cause world wars. Some hundred and fifty thousand young Americans died because of an event in 1914 in a mud-caked primitive village, Sarajevo. Loathsome and almost obscene snarls in Balkan politics, hardly intelligible to a Western reader, are still vital to the peace of Europe, and perhaps the world.[20]

Understandable as the bitter feelings might be, it is symptomatic that this section was preserved even in the war edition of 1940. The snarls of Hitler were, obviously, more intelligible to Western readers, because they were Western. It is only one step from here to the flat assertion that even World War II can be blamed on the Balkans. Admittedly, it is a difficult step to take, and over fifty years were needed for someone to take it. Robert Kaplan, who openly aspires to become the Dame Rebecca West of the 1990s, maintained, in *Balkan Ghosts*, that "Nazism, for instance, can claim Balkan origins. Among the flophouses of Vienna, a breeding ground of ethnic resentments close to the southern Slavic world, Hitler learned how to hate so infectiously."[21] It is ironic to read the paragraph about "the mud-caked primitive village" in the light of today's eulogies about the multicultural paradise of the beautiful cosmopolitan city of Sarajevo destroyed in the 1990s. Following Gunther's logic, it must have become this wonderful city under the barbarous rule first of the independent South Slav monarchy and especially under the Yugoslav communists, while it had been a loathsome village under the Western enlightened rule of the Habsburgs.

Even during the course of the war, the Balkan stereotype was not immutable. Mechthild Golczewski's analysis of German and Austrian war accounts between 1912 and 1918 shows a differentiated treatment of the separate Balkan nations in the absence of a clear-cut notion of what Balkan actually represented. Insofar as the category was utilized to denote general regional characteristics (e.g., hospitality, clichés about peasants and mountaineers, people close to nature, backwardness, uncleanliness, and so on), it was so vague and unspecified that it could be applied to people outside the Balkan region. Whenever employed, its persuasive power was based on its haziness in combination with an emotive component. Moreover, it was used alongside other generalizing catchwords, of which "Oriental" was most often employed, to stand for filth, passivity, unreliability, misogyny, propensity for intrigue, insincerity, opportunism, laziness, superstitiousness, lethargy, sluggishness, inefficiency, incompetent bureaucracy. "Balkan," while overlapping with "Oriental," had additional characteristics as cruelty, boorishness, instability, and unpredictability. Both categories were used against the concept of Europe symbolizing cleanliness, order, self-control, strength of character, sense of law, justice, efficient administration, in a word, "the culturally higher stage of development which also ennobles human behavior."[22] Yet, although one can readily agree that the notion "Balkan" was fuzzy enough to denote a specific regional characterization, there was no doubt that the emotive component to which writers were resorting or appealing intuitively rested on a by-then internalized but not yet clearly articulated stereotype. Only the completely ignorant could plead complete innocence, like the American woman who, when referring to Dalmatia, called it "the place where the dogs come from."[23]

There were also sober voices that tried to look into the real causes of the war, and some came from outside the usual social-democratic critiques. Charles J. Vopicka had spent seven years between 1913 and 1920 in Romania, Serbia, and Bulgaria as extraordinary envoy and minister plenipotentiary of the United States. His detailed memoirs, although sometimes imperfect on historical particulars and informed with typical American Wilsonian optimism and naïveté, were nevertheless adamant in their verdict: "The World War began in the Balkans, yet its origin was in the hearts of the unscrupulous autocrats whose ruthless ambition knew neither justice nor limit."[24] He refuted the insinuation that the Balkan peoples were natural troublemakers but instead depicted them as pawns in a great power game.

The prevailing spirit of the time, however, blamed the war on the Balkans in general, and on the Serbs in particular. Mary Edith Durham, confident she would be taken as seriously as she took herself, returned the order of St. Sava to King Peter with an accompanying letter saying she "considered him and his people guilty of the greatest crime in history." Serbia was a "hornet's nest" and the nation, both in Montenegro and Serbia, knew only how to love or hate; there was no medium.[25] The episode reprovingly illustrating the Serbs' incapacity for moderation was the opening to a book Durham had written some fifteen years earlier. In it, the informer who told her "One must either like or hate" was unspecified, simply a Balkan man, "and he is but one example of many, for thus it is with the Balkan man, be he Greek, Serb, Bulgar, or Albanian, Christian or Moslem." When Durham first started her expeditions, she stepped into the Balkan world with the same notions and emotions with which today's children step into a dinosaur museum: "Its raw, primitive ideas, which date from the world's well-springs, its passionate strivings, its disastrous failures, grip the mind; its blaze of colour, its wildly magnificent scenery hold the eye." Yet, at this point she was still enchanted with the region and admonished the hectoring propensities of the ones who posed as a kind of Salvation Army to the different Balkan nationalities:

> None of the Balkan people are so black as they have often been painted. They all possess fine qualities which only require opportunity to develop, and their faults in most cases are but those of extreme youth. The atrocities which they will all commit upon occasion are a mere survival of mediaeval customs once common to all Europe. 'Humanity' was not invented even in England till the beginning of the nineteenth century; up till then punishments of the most brutal description were inflicted for comparatively trivial offenses. In dealing with the Balkan Peninsula, far too much 'copy' has been made out of 'atrocities' for party purposes.[26]

Durham's account of this period is particularly important because it offers a rare glimpse into the reaction of Balkanites who were apparently well aware of how they were judged by the West. One of her acquaintances, most likely an Albanian, told her passionately:

You think in England you are civilized, and can teach us. I tell you there is no one here that would commit crimes as are found in London. . . . Our brigands are poor men. By working hard in the fields they can only just live. They are quite ignorant, and have never been to any school. They rob to live, and do so at the risk of their lives. But your brigands have often been to a university, and rob to obtain luxuries by lies and false promises. You have had all the advantages of education and civilization for years, and this is what you do. But you call us savages because we shoot people.[27]

Some of Durham's statements read like the introspective diary of a modern anthropologist: she wrote about the dilemma of not being able to see the Balkans with Eastern eyes; yet, at the same time "you never again see it with Western ones." She lamented that even after you learn to eat, drink, and sleep with the natives, indeed, live as they do, and just as you think you are beginning to understand them, something happens and you realize "you were as far as ever from seeing things from their point of view. To do this you must leap across the centuries, wipe the West and all its ideas from out of you, let loose all that there is in you of primitive man, and learn six languages, all quite useless in other parts of the world."[28] In about a decade, Durham had realized the Balkans were too complex to fathom as a whole. At about the same time, Paul Scott Mowrer, the author of the book introducing the concept of "balkanization," shared the same exasperation: "To the schoolboy, certainly, the collapse of Turkey and Austria-Hungary is a severe blow; instead of learning two countries, he must now learn ten; and no wonder that elderly persons, brought up in the simplicity of the older geography, should feel rather impatient at the complexity of the new."[29]

One had to specialize only in some aspects of this complexity, and Durham accordingly followed the pattern of all Westerners dealing with the Balkans: she found her pet nation. Durham has secured a richly deserved place in Balkan historiography for the high quality of her ethnographic descriptions of tribal life in Northern Albania and Montenegro, particularly for paying attention to one of the least known nations in the Balkans, Albania, but she herself knew not the medium of affections. Her dislike for the Serbs, and by extension for the Balkan Slavs, was so bitter that she in all seriousness ascribed the venom of the Janissaries to their Balkan origins, "a singular fact, and one which should be emphasized." To her, "it was largely to the fanaticism of the Orthodox Church that the Balkan people owed their conquest by the Turks." Although not a particular friend of the Turks, she fell for and reproduced the myth of their tolerance. Her commendable love for the Albanians blinded her to indiscriminately allot religious and racial slurs instead of coolly analyze geopolitical configurations. Her Albanians, who had "resisted denationalization for a thousand years" and were only begging to "take their place in the Balkans and live in freedom and harmony," were now facing a far worse foe than the Turk, "and that was the Slav: Russia with her fanatical Church and her savage Serb and Bulgar cohorts ready to destroy Albania and wipe out Catholic and Moslem alike."[30]

The term "balkanization" came into being as a result of the Balkan wars and World War I, and a thoroughly negative value was conclusively sealed to the Balkans. Yet this was not an abrupt occurrence and even during the Balkan wars the Western press was more ironic than contemptuous.[31] The image of the Balkans brought to the fore violence as their central, and heretofore not dominant, feature. Violence in Balkan history was nothing new. Europeans appeared to be horrified by some of the specifically "Eastern" barbarities, especially impaling, which struck the imagination of all travelers. It was its exoticism that turned the historical Vlad Ţepeş into the immortal figure of Dracula, but the latter is less an illustration of Balkan violence than an attribute of morose Gothic imagination. Yet these punishments were usually taken as idiosyncrasies of the rulers and were not attributed to the region as inherently biological qualities. Violence as the leitmotiv of the Balkans was, strictly speaking, a post–Balkan wars phenomenon. To quote Rebecca West:

> Violence was, indeed, all I knew of the Balkans: all I knew of the South Slavs. I derived the knowledge from memories of my earliest interest in Liberalism, of leaves fallen from this jungle of pamphlets, tied up with string in the dustiest corners of junk-shops, and later from the prejudices of the French, who use the word "Balkan" as a term of abuse, meaning a *rastaquouère* type of barbarian.[32]

The image of specifically Balkan violence inspired Agatha Christie in 1925 to write a mystery of the kind aptly described as "romances dealing with imaginary Balkanoid principalities of homicidal atmosphere."[33] Christie created a sinister character, Boris Anchoukoff, with Slavic features (although not the typical features of the South Slavs): "a tall fair man with high cheekbones, and very deep-set blue eyes, and an impassivity of countenance." Naturally, the man spoke English with a harsh foreign accent. He was the valet to the freshly murdered Prince Michael and, as befitted Balkan characters, was burning with desire to avenge his master:

> "I say this to you, English policeman, I would have died for him! And since he is dead, and I still live, my eyes shall not know sleep, or my heart rest, until I have avenged him. Like a dog will I nose out his murderer and when I have discovered him—Ah!" His eyes lit up. Suddenly he drew an immense knife from beneath his coat and brandished it aloft. "Not all at once will I kill him—oh, no!—first I will slit his nose, and cut off his ears, and put out his eyes, and then—then, into his black heart I will thrust this knife."[34]

The shocked Englishman muttered in response: "Pure bred Herzoslovakian, of course. Most uncivilized people. A race of brigands." Herzoslovakia was the invention of Agatha Christie: "It's one of the Balkan states. . . . Principal rivers, unknown. Principal mountains, also unknown, but fairly numerous. Capital, Ekarest. Population, chiefly brigands. Hobby, assassinating kings and having revolutions."[35] What is charming about this geographic invention is that it nicely illustrates two points: one is that Christie reproduced a crystallized collective image of the Balkans, not the previous differentiated treatment of separate Balkan nations; the other is the lack of differentiation between the Balkans and the newly created states of Central Europe. Herzoslovakia is obviously a rhyming parody of Czechoslovakia, a combination between Herzegovina and Slovakia. Written in 1925, much before appeasement times, it looked at Czechoslovakia as the distant and unknown land of Neville Chamberlain's celebrated mot. There was no inkling of the future guilt feeling that would inform British and American writing about "the most civilized Slavic outpost." Even though *The Secret of Chimneys* is not Agatha Christie's most popular novel, it underwent several editions in the next decades and, given the omnivorous obsession of Christie devotees, it is a good illustration of the popular channels through which the balkanist discourse was disseminated and introduced to the broad public. During this period, one can tentatively speak of the gradual formation of a common Western attitude that supplanted the different national approaches, the internationalization of the stereotype.

The interwar period added yet another view, racism, which had already seasoned an integral part of nineteenth-century European thinking. While racism in its modern sense can be traced already in sixteenth-century Spain, as a European phenomenon it "was grounded in those intellectual currents which made their mark in the eighteenth century in both western and central Europe, namely, the new sciences of the Enlightenment and the Pietistic revival of Christianity." The geographic discoveries fostered curiosity in distant cultures and gradually gave birth to the new science of anthropology, concerned with humanity's place in nature and specifically with the classification of the human races. There was exultation in nature as opposed to the artificiality of human society, but the early idealization of the noble savage soon gave way to a feeling of superiority. Natives were assigned a lower stage in the great chain of being and were quickly stigmatized as barbarians who had to be dominated and educated. When the Balkans became the focus of attention, the myth of the noble savage was long passé.

A distinctive feature of modern racism was the "continuous transition from science to aesthetics," accomplished by the fusion of the main techniques of the new sciences—observation, measurement, and comparison—with valuative statements based on the aesthetic criteria attributed to ancient Greece: "All racists held to a certain concept of beauty—white and classical—to middle-class virtues of work, of moderation and honor, and thought that these were exemplified through outward appearance." Even after the retreat of the pseudosciences of phrenology and physiognomy, the highly subjective categories of beauty and ugliness remained important principles of human classification alongside measurement, climate, and environment. Beauty, based on an immutable classical ideal, became "synonymous with a settled, happy, and healthy middle-class world without violent upheavals—and a world attainable solely by white Europeans."[36] As a rule, it was based on racial purity. In very few circumstances did racial mixture allow for even some positive counterbalancing quality: "The Balkan Slavs represent the most remarkable blending, and it was this blend of various Indo-European and Asiatic tribes, that imprinted upon the Balkan Slavs many unsympathetic as well as many admirable traits."[37]

The racial verdict over the Balkans began with a more open rendering of the formerly subdued and nonjudgmental motif of racial mixture. At the beginning of the century, Thessaloniki was still only an uncouth Tower of Babel with a sprinkling of civilization from the West: "Bulgarians, Servians, Albanians, Vlachs, Armenians, Anatolians, Circassians, Greeks, Turks, Jews, infidels and heretics of every land and language. Between and among these are sprinkled the races of civilized Europe."[38] "Infidels and heretics" to denote Muslim and Orthodox Christians had apparently become a catchphrase and was used by another British author in his description of Mostar where one was "jostled in the dark, narrow streets by the same Jews, infidels and heretics as in the bazaars of Stamboul." Sarajevo "swarmed with strange nationalities": Bosnians, Croatians, Serbians, Dalmatians, Greeks, Turks, Gypsies.[39] Some two decades later, these almost neutral renderings of the ethnic and religious complexity of the Balkans, which evoked only an occasional characterization as "strange nationalities," produced feelings of revulsion and impurity. In 1921, two Englishmen contemplated the inevitably "hybrid race" of the inhabitants of Macedonia:

> Being essentially cross-bred, the Macedonian is hardly distinguished for his physique. . . . The Turks are perhaps the best physical specimens of the various Macedonian types, probably because they have indulged in less cross-breeding. . . . Turkish women, when not interbred to any pronounced extent, are generally attractive, but those of Bulgar or Greek extraction usually have broad and very coarse features of the Slav type. Such features, comprising thick lips, broad flat noses and high cheek-bones, scarcely conduce to beauty in a woman. Darkish hair with yellowish brown complexions cause them to resemble the Greek type, which is invariably sallow, with jet black hair and luminous eyes.[40]

It is disputable whether the "coarse features of the Slav type" were typically delineated or common among Greeks, but the description of the unprepossessing physique reminds too much of Negroid characteristics usually held at the bottom of the referential scale. Racial impurity went hand in hand with "an immature, unenlightened intellect, . . . a crafty disposition and a natural tendency towards savagery."[41] Although the Germans were only apprentices of Joseph-Arthur de Gobineau and H. S. Chamberlain, they overdid the masters. Hermann, Graf von Keyserling, married to a granddaughter of Bismarck, was an influential figure in the philosophy of self-knowledge, and had created a school of wisdom in the 1920s that aimed at bringing people through creative knowledge to self-attainment. In 1928, he published *Das Spektrum Europa*, produced in a simultaneous translation in the United States. Of his twelve chapters, one was devoted to the Balkans:

> What is the significance of the Balkans to us who live in other lands? . . . Why is it that the word 'Balkanization' is almost always rightly understood and rightly applied? . . . Its symbolic sense may best be apprehended from two starting-points; the first is the generally accepted statement that the Balkans are the powder-magazine of Europe. The second is the fact of a peculiarly elemental and irreconcilable racial enmity.[42]

Having provided lengthy characteristics of Greeks, Romanians, and Turks (Serbs, Bulgarians, and Albanians he deemed "primitive warrior and robber races" not worthy of attention), Keyserling summarized the essence of the Balkans:

> The Balkans of today are nothing but a caricature of the Balkans of ancient times. The spirit of the Balkans as such is the spirit of eternal strife. Inhabited as they are by primitive races, they present the primal picture of the primal struggle between the one and the all. In the case of the highly gifted and highly educated nations and individuals, this picture emerges as the spirit of the agon. But the earth-spirit of the Balkans as such is the primal formative power.[43]

The same year saw the American translation of a Swedish book that appeared in Stockholm in 1927. It clearly articulated a motif only discreetly present in the previous century. Its author, Marcus Ehrenpreis, had traversed the Balkans, Egypt, and the Holy Land in quest of "the soul of the East." He spoke with disgust about his copassengers who have brought back only "their precious possessions, photographs and big hotel bills": "This is not the way to visit the Orient! If you would win something of the soul of the east do not approach it as you would a strange country but as if you were returning home—to yourself. . . . Do not go condescending as a bringer of civilization, but as a disciple, humbly and receptively."[44] This spirit was conspicuously absent from his first chapter, "Across the New Balkans." Already, his opening words made the crucial distinction between the Balkans and the authentic Orient:

> The Orient is already in evidence at the Masaryk railway station in Prague. Not the real Orient of the Azhar at Cairo or the one of Haifa's street cafes, but that variant of the East known as Levantinism; a something, elusive of definition—the body of the East but without its spirit. It is a crumbling Orient, a traitorous deserter from itself, without fez, without veil, without Koran: it is an artificial, trumpery New Orient which has deliberately broken with its past and renounced its ancient heritage.

The description of the inhabitants of this Levant (as contrasted to the true East) illustrated their racial degeneration:

> There is something eccentric in their conduct, they are overloud, too sudden, too eager. . . . Oddish, incredible individuals appear on all sides—low foreheads, sodden eyes, protruding ears, thick underlips. . . . The Levantine type in the areas between the Balkans and the Mediterranean is, psychologically and socially, truly a "wavering form", a composite of Easterner and Westerner, multilingual, cunning, superficial, unreliable, materialistic and, above all, without tradition. This absence of tradition seems to account for the low intellectual and, to a certain extent moral, quality of the Levantines. . . . In a spiritual sense these creatures are homeless; they are no longer Orientals nor yet Europeans. They have not freed themselves from the vices of the East nor acquired any of the virtues of the West.[45]

In both Keyserling's and Ehrenpreis's ideas one can distinguish unmistakably overtones that were present previously but that are immeasurably more intense. The former dichotomy between gentlemanly overlords and cringing subjects had found a theoretical rationalization: it was the cultural expression of a fault line, and the racial and cultural crossbreed was worse than the purebred oriental Other. Long forgotten was the brief flirtation with the Greeks, but then even the Philhellenic support was in some sense racist, "bestowed not merely in libertarian support for yet one more European revolution but in the conviction that the modern Greeks were lineal descendants of the ancient Greeks and the Turks were barbarians."[46] Already in 1830, in *Geschichte der Halbinsel Morea während des Mittelalters*, Jakob Fallmerayer shattered this prevailing belief with his theory that the ancient Greeks were submerged into the subsequent waves of Slavs who actually constituted the racial basis of contemporary Greeks, and that "not a drop of genuine and unmixed Hellenic blood flows in the veins of the Christian population of modern Greece."[47] This theory made him a persona non grata in Greece until recently. Fallmerayer's fervid dismissal of the Greeks was intended as an antidote to the prevailing philhellenism in Bavaria at the time, and was motivated by a paranoid fear of Russian political ascendancy.[48] While highly exaggerated, his theory nevertheless had some valid components, particularly the onslaught against the idea of racial purity. In Nazi Germany, however, Fallmerayer's theory was revived during the occupation of Greece "for the benefit of classically educated officers, so they could excuse their atrocities against the Greeks as done to an inferior, not a noble, race."[49]

It was no sheer coincidence that both Keyserling's and Ehrenpreis's books appeared in successful simultaneous translations on the other side of the Atlantic. The 1920s were the culmination of the activities of the Immigration Restrictive League, the most important pressure group for protectionist laws. Imbued with the Anglo-Saxonism of the latter half of the nineteenth century, the league, whose backbone as the Boston Brahmins, advocated restriction of influx from Central and Eastern Europe "or else the American 'race' would be committing suicide."[50] The 1920s was also a time of hectic activities of the American Eugenics Society, which espoused a theory of natural genetic superiority of races and social groups. Many of its members believed that racial mixture would bring about social deterioration and advocated that assimilation with cultural inferiors, particularly Slavs, should be avoided as much as overbreeding of social inferiors. The Balkan Slavs, in particular, were shunned, treated as outlaws, and called Hunkies (Huns) in the industrial cities. Even the ones who pleaded for their active inclusion in American society warned that "we must bear in mind that the Balkan Slavs, in spite of their continual gravitation toward European and, particularly, Western civilisation, are intrinsically Oriental."[51] Theoretically at odds with social Darwinism, the society nevertheless attracted considerable numbers of social Darwinists on the basis of a commonly espoused nativism.[52] These ideas have reverberated and occasionally reappeared although never with the mantle of propriety and official support as in the early decades of the century.

Echoes of these views can be discerned even in the best intentioned enterprises. Although his monumental project "Slovanská epopej" fell on the last three decades of his life, Alphonse Mucha, the great Czech master of art nouveau, was inspired by the romantic aspects of cultural slavism. In fact, this was the reason for the mixed response he received after he donated "The Slav Epic" to the city of Prague in 1928, while still continuing to work on it. Many critics deemed it more appropriate of 1848 and imbued by a romanticism that was considered passé in the nervous interwar period. In a direct paraphrase of Herder, Mucha believed that "each nation has its own art, as it has its own language."[53] He had conceived of his idea while still in the United States and in 1910, after intensive consultations with slavicists, he set out on a trip to Russia, Poland, Serbia, Montenegro, and Bulgaria to get a firsthand feel for the culture of the different Slavs.

What Mucha saw was what he wanted to see: he was inspired by his own expectations and visions of Slavdom. The culmination of his trip was Russia where he believed to have found his own origins. He wrote in ecstasy to his wife: "Music and singing, all profoundly Byzantine and Slavic. It's like living in the ninth century. . . . Nothing has changed for two thousand years."[54] Mucha was moved not only by a sentimental romanticism, although this is what mostly animated his iconography. His observations were informed by other notions that dominated the ideological horizon of his time. One was the belief that the eastern fringes of Europe presented a unique view of the dawn of humanity, the premodern stage of Europe, the historical museum of Europe's own past. Only with this in mind can one explain that he was blissfully ignorant of the profound changes taking place in Russia, especially the intense and very modern cultural life in prerevolutionary Russia, and instead was enchanted by the fantasy of two millennia frozen in a picture that he would capture.

More interesting was Mucha's reaction to the Balkan Slavs. Although full of sympathy for Serbs, Montenegrins, and Bulgarians, they hardly aroused in him the lofty praise he heaped on Mother Russia. With their curved Turkish sabers, oriental slippers and costume, they seemed to him mere curiosities, worthy only of a wax museum. Only during his second visit, when confined to the medieval monasteries of Mt. Athos, was he really stimulated. It was not only that they did not conform to his own image of what was supposed to be Slav. One can perceive in Mucha also a subdued version of the longing for cultural and racial purity, the ideology that dominated the civilized world of Europe at the time, with no foreboding yet for its disastrous consequences. The Balkan Slavs lacked the purity of a single breed (or of how the breed was imagined); in their case the mongrel nature was more than visible—it was their essence. It is true that in Mucha this tension is very delicate and barely discernible under the thick and rich slavophile layer; there is nothing of the crude and frank aversion articulated by his contemporaries, Keyserling and Ehrenpreis. For Mucha, the Balkan Slavs simply did not conform to his purebred ideal abstraction of Slavdom; for Keyserling and Ehrenpreis, the Balkans were a contemptuous deviation from the less than flattering abstraction of the Orient.

It would be dogmatic and simplistic to insist that there were no exceptions to this discourse of rigid and harsh qualifications: not everyone subscribed to the temptation of orderly classification that permitted one to make sense of the Balkan chaos, but nonconformists are always the minority and they did not challenge or change the dominant stereotypes that finally crystallized in this period. Rarely would someone exclaim with the Englishman Archibald Lyall: "I knew enough of South-eastern Europe never to believe anything anybody told one if it was humanly possible to look into the matter for oneself." Lyall himself left witty and spirited descriptions of late 1920s' Romania (with Bucharest as a sort of Balkan Hollywood), Istanbul, Greece, Albania, Montenegro, and Dalmatia in *The Balkan Road.* An acute and epigrammatic observer, he managed to articulate the reasons for the uneasiness a westerner would feel in the Balkans in a matter-of-fact manner not only devoid of venom but with mocking sympathy. One of the chief reasons was the lack of bourgeois comforts and behavior:

> Amost everywhere east of the lands of solid German and Italian speech there is a thin whiff of the Balkans in the air, hardly perceptible in Bohemia, but growing stronger with every eastward mile—a certain lack of comfort, a certain indifference to rules and timetables, a certain *je-m'en-fichisme* with regard to the ordinary machinery of existence, maddening or luminously sane according to temperament and circumstance.[55]

Punctuality was never a Balkan virtue, although even there progress has been made in the half-century after Lyall. Greek steamers, he complained, were always late an hour and a half but this was nothing compared to the annoying propensity of Yugoslav trains to leave ten minutes ahead of schedule. The most unsettling characteristic of the "pays balkaniques, pays volcaniques," however, was "the cult of the gun" that had led to the barbarity of the Skupština murders in Belgrade, the Sveta Nedelya bomb outrage in Sofia, and the shooting of Greek ministers. And yet, Lyall would earnestly insist that the Balkans were no more unsafe for the foreigner than anywhere else:

> The natives only shoot their friends and acquaintances, and they seldom interfere with strangers. In Paris or Chicago you kill a man because you think he may have the price of a drink in his pockets, but in the Balkans you only kill a man for some good cause, as that you disagree with his political views, or that his great-uncle once shot a second cousin of yours, or for some equally sound reason of that kind. If you are seized with a desire to go for a walk in a Balkan town at three in the morning, the risk of being knocked on the head is so small that it is not worth while not doing it.[56]

Lyall wrote this in the section on Albania, where he thoroughly enjoyed himself despite warnings about the "horrible country" by a Persian Presbytarian with whom he spent some time in Athens. It is curious to listen to the funny incantations of the Persian, that is, to a prejudice from the east, rather than the usual one from the west. The standard offense to the Balkans in a Western rendition is that they are too Eastern; in the hierarchies of a civilized easterner the pejorative referral was Africa:

> Why do you want to go to Albahnia, my dear sir? Zere is nothing to see zere, only black stones. And no houses, only little forts wiz cracks and holes in zem, wiz rifles peeping out of zem; and ze Albahnians, zey sit zere and zey go pop-pop-pop. It is worse zan ze Wild West. Kentucky! Tennessee! Zey are orphans to Albahnia! Orphans! Children! It is Timbuctoo, my dear sir, ze very middle of Timbuctoo. Promise me you will not go to Albahnia. It is a pity. You are so young. . . . I tell you zis, my dear sir, God 'e made ze Albahnians after he'd just had a fight wiz his muzzer-in-law.[57]

It was the ethnic complexity of the Balkans that proved the most frustrating characteristic. Unlike Western Europe where nations lived in more or less homogeneous blocks, in the East they were jumbled in a way that added the word *macédoine* to the vocabulary of menu writers. This complexity that has continued to defy easy categorizations and upsets neat recipes invoked, instead of condemnation, a simple and fair remark by Lyall: "Everywhere east of the Adriatic there are at least ten sides to every question, and it is in my mind that one thing is as good as another."[58] The complex ethnic mixture was held responsible for the instability and disorder of the peninsula, which was diagnosed as afflicted by "the handicap of heterogeneity."[59] Indeed, minority issues have been an endemic part of the development of the nation state particularly in Eastern Europe. Practically nobody, however, emphasized the fact that it was not ethnic complexity per se but ethnic complexity in the framework of the idealized nation-state that leads to ethnic homogeneity, inducing ethnic conflicts. Not only was racial mixture conducive to disorder, racial impurity was disorder. "The confused experiences and training of the races and states of the Balkans" was explained with their particular "stage of civilization." In the words of a British diplomat: "Nationalism in Eastern Europe is naturally more prone to warlike expression than in Western Europe, for it is in an earlier stage of development."[60]

The end of the nineteenth century and the beginning of the twentieth saw the culmination of theories of evolutionism, particularly its version of progressionism, the continuous movement of history toward a desirable goal. This idea originated in the seventeenth century, matured in the eighteenth, and modified the dominant static medieval "chain of being." This modification, which first appeared in Leibniz, regarded the stages of the hierarchy as coming into existence successively in time, moving from lower to higher. In this way, the understanding of a static chain of being was transformed into the idea of a unilinear process of ascent to greater perfection. The assumption of continuous improvement made the very notion of development culture-impregnated; "it has assumed the status of an absolute, a universal value, a symbol of modernity and, as such, a conscious goal or ideal in a growing number of social cultures."[61] One of the central categories employed in the progressivist assessment of the historical process was that of civilization which, alongside culture, gained currency in European thought during the eighteenth century.

Shaped in the nineteenth century, research on the Balkans was influenced heavily both by the traditions of romanticism and evolutionism. The first resulted in an extreme fascination with, coupled with a methodical study of, folklore and language, in search of the specific Balkan *Volksgeist(s)*; the second, in the framework of the taxonomical obsessions of nineteenth century academics, grounded the Balkans firmly in the dawn of humanity. The elevation of folklore and language as the essence of peoples' identities and as the legitimation of their existence revolutionized social thought through the work of Johann Gottfried von Herder. The breakthrough of Herder's ideas can be genuinely appreciated only if juxtaposed to the assessment advanced by his former teacher and intellectual adversary, Immanuel Kant, who in his *Anthropology* reasoned that the "sketching" of the "nationals of European Turkey," as well as those of Poland and Russia, could be passed over because "they have never been and never will be up to what is requisite for the acquisition of a definite folk character."

Herder's revolution was sustained in the east of Europe principally because it triggered the passionate self-interest among the nations of Eastern Europe and gave them their raison d'être. It delineated the main spheres of research until today: language, history, ethnography, folklore. In the West, on the other hand, it did little to elevate their status within the hierarchy of nations but at least it put them on the map, even if only as folkloric groups. Hegel accepted Herderian categories and even conceded that Eastern Europeans played a role as advance guards in "the struggle between Christian Europe and non-Christian Asia," but was indifferent to Herder's obsession with folklore. His criterion for historical value was whether a group had "stepped forward as an independent force in the array of the forms of reason," and the state was paramount in this array of forms. The Slavs, much as they had become part of the political history of Europe, were not worth a historical survey, even though part of them had been conquered by Western reason, since they still were merely "intermediaries between the European and the Asiatic spirit."[62] Ironically, "Herder, in formulating the Slavs as above all an object of folkloric study, helped to establish the philosophical perspective according to which Hegel would exclude them from historical consideration."[63] The legacy is so strong that, despite the general demise of evolutionary thinking in Western historiography, the Balkans still come out as the *Volksmuseum* of Europe even in most sophisticated discourses. Even though in the interwar period there was widespread disappointment with the idea of progress, it was preserved as a valid criterion in the assessment of the Balkans. It took two mutually exclusive forms. One was premised on the conviction that the Orient (into which the Balkans were often subsumed) was immobile. Therefore, the study of the present inhabitants would throw adequate light on the past. The opening to Brailsford's *Macedonia* stated:

> That nothing changes in the East is a commonplace which threatens to become tyrannical. Assuredly there is something in the spirit of the East which is singularly kindly to survivals and anachronisms. The centuries do not follow one another. They coexist. There is no lopping of withered customs, no burial of dead ideas. Nor is it the Turks alone who betray this genial conservatism. The typical Slav village, isolated without teacher or priest in some narrow and lofty glen, leads its own imperturbable life, guided by the piety of traditions which date from pagan times.[64]

The other approach accepted that the Balkans were also subject to the universal laws of evolution but theirs was a backward culture and civilization. Even the most benevolent assessments stressed their "inexhaustible but underdeveloped powers"; one should not expect from them "the principles and point of view peculiar to the more advanced civilization of the West."[65] This is a most rigidly persisting view. Even at the end of World War II, Bernard Newman could not resist from noting that "despite their great advance during this last generation, Balkan codes of conduct do not yet approximate to Western standards."[66] Because of their intermediary state somewhere between barbarity and civilization, the Balkans were considered to be "a marvelous training school for political scientists and diplomats" of the First World preparing to perform in the Third; they were utilized as a "testing ground": "In the nonacademic world, for example, a significant proportion of American governmental and semigovernmental personnel at present attempting to cope with the problems of the Afro-Asian countries received its training, so to speak, for such work in the Balkans, which have thus retrospectively become the original underdeveloped area."[67]

Likewise, although civilization and culture as central categories of the developmental process, and the elevation of Western civilization as the apex of human achievement, were increasingly considered problematic in the wake of World War II, they remained operative notions in the public mind. True, there are sophisticated treatments of culture and civilization in the specialized academic literature and, as a whole, social sciences have been averse to utilizing "civilization," either in the singular or in the plural: "Civilization has thrived only in the bastard field of Orientalism, which came to be defined precisely as the study of other 'civilizations.'"[68] These conclusions, however, have rarely been popularized outside the graduate level of education. On the contrary, *pace* all passionate academic debates, criticisms of ethnocentrism and pledges toward multiculturalism, the general thrust of American and West European humanistic undergraduate education revolves around the subject of "Western civilization."

The recent discussions around Samuel Huntington's latest article and book conferred to the category a new legitimacy. Huntington claimed the fundamental source of conflict in the future will be cultural rather than economic or ideological. Defining civilization as the highest cultural grouping of people, he postulated that "the principal conflicts of global politics will occur between nations and groups of different civilizations." Stepping openly on the debatable legacy of Toynbee, Huntington identified seven or eight major civilizations in the present world: Western, Confucian, Japanese, Islamic, Hindu, Slavic-Orthodox, Latin American, and possibly African. For anyone sensitive to the dynamics and subtleties of the historical process, Huntington's piece cannot fail to strike as overly mechanistic, designed to engineer a prescription rather than a vision. Huntington has encountered devastating criticism from very different quarters, but his name, stature, and the appealing simplicity of his ideas have assured that the phrase "clash of civilizations" is abundantly thrown around, especially by academics and journalists who have read neither Huntington nor his critics.[69] Huntington first proclaimed that the conflict between communism, fascism-Nazism, and liberal democracy, as well as the struggle between the two superpowers during the cold war, were conflicts within Western civilization, "Western civil wars." This implicitly embraced all of Eastern Europe and Russia within the category of Western civilization. Yet, he declared that with the disappearance of the ideological, "the cultural division of Europe between Western Christianity, on the one hand, and Orthodox Christianity and Islam, on the other, has reemerged." The logical conclusion is that while atheistic communism, despite the cold war, placed the lands of traditional Orthodox Christianity within the sphere of Western civilization, liberal democracy and the end of the "Evil Empire" returned them to where they belonged.

The fault line was pronounced to be the eastern border of Western Christianity around 1500. It came to supplant the previously fashionable cold-war line of Leningrad-Trieste, which ran a little more to the west and subsumed all of the former communist Europe. Now, Poland, the Czech Republic, Hungary, Slovenia, Croatia, as well as the two parts with Hungarian minorities (Transylvania and the Vojvodina) were pronounced Western. Naming the civilization east of the fault line "Slavic-Orthodox" instead of simply Orthodox, apparently tried to account for Greece, "the cradle of Western civilization" and a NATO and European Union member, but at the same time crammed into it non-Slavs (Romanians, Gagaouz, Georgians, Albanians, and so on) and left out many Slavs (Poles, Czechs, Croats, and so on) whose Catholicism apparently saved them from the cumbersome "Slavic" quality. But the map that was supplied in the article to make sure that the fault line was not imaginary but that stressed its physicality had Greece on the wrong side of the fault line. Of course, it can be argued that exceptions prove the rule, but this did not reassure the Greeks, who reacted strongly against their implicit marginalization.[70]

Huntington would have us believe that the fault line he proposed between "Western civilization" and the Slavic-Orthodox world (incidentally the only land border of "Western civilization") was one shaped not of economy or politics but one of culture. Yet when defining the two civilizations, economic characteristics were paramount:

> The peoples to the north and west of this line are Protestant and Catholic; they shared the common experiences of European history—feudalism, the Renaissance, the Reformation, the Industrial Revolution; they are generally economically better off than the peoples to the east; and they may now look forward to increasing involvement in a common European economy and to the consolidation of democratic political systems. The peoples to the east and south of this line are Orthodox or Muslim; they historically belonged to the Ottoman or Tsarist empires and were

only lightly touched by the shaping events in the rest of Europe; they are generally less advanced economically; they seem much less likely to develop stable democratic political systems."[71]

Naturally, Huntington was speaking only in general terms, thus leaving room for geographical variations. Still, the inescapable conclusion was that the cultural divide was there to mask the *real* divide: between rich and poor. After all, the same criterion was applied to South America where, while "Huntington lumps together Christian Catholics and Protestants in Western Europe and North America, he excludes Catholics in Spanish- and Portuguese-settled Latin America, delegating the latter (for economic reasons?) to a separate culture area/civilization."[72] The inclusion of Poles, Hungarians, Czechs, Slovaks, Croats, and Slovenes in the fold of "Western civilization," albeit at this point merely verbal, left the benevolent impression that the new "Eastern wall" was not one to protect a rich man's club but one of longstanding and fundamental historical differences.

It is not an overstatement that the popular image of the Balkans has been inscribed in a similarly popular, and often vulgar, interpretation of several families of ideas, revolving around the notions of race, progress, evolution, culture, and civilization. The British diplomat who wrote the Balkan survey for the Carnegie Endowment concluded that one "may boldly assert that the only basis of European culture and the only bias towards European civilization to be found in the Balkans, after centuries of subjection to Asiatic Byzantinism, is the consciousness of nationality." Therefore, "wherever and whenever in the Balkans national feeling became conscious, then, to that extent, does civilization begin; and as such consciousness could best come through war, war in the Balkans was the only road to peace." In his line of reasoning, "the Bulgar komitadji hiding dynamite bombs in a Messageries mailboat in Salonika harbour was an emissary of European civilization, while Hilmi Pasha, that courteous, cultivated gentleman, administering 'Macedonian reforms' and 'Mürzsteg programs' from his study in Salonika Konak, was not."[73] This was written a few months before the outbreak of World War I, yet it is ironic that Balkan nationalism, which later was described as intrinsically alien to Western civic and supposedly civilized nationalism, was considered to be the only Balkan feature on which the mantle of Europeanness was conferred. Soon enough, the same Bulgarian *komitadji* was transformed by the high priests of European peace and civilization from emissary of European civilization into originator of international terrorism.

These reflections came, of course, as no surprise at the time, when it was not considered a breach of bon ton to announce that "Mohammedanism is of as much less social value than Christianity as the Koran is of less spiritual value than the Gospels." They would come as no surprise today when the post–cold war rhetoric devotes similar paeans to the two big Cs of the free world, Christian faith and Capitalism: "Our western civilization has both a moral and a material basis: it is both an ethical and an economic system: its strength of accumulated civic experience equivalent in some respects to Christianity, and of accumulated prosperity expressed in some of its forms as Capital." Aside from the saving grace of nationalism, there was nothing European in the Balkans, because "civilization cannot exist without both such ethical and economic components, and both of them were impossible under the unholy alliance between Orthodox obscurantism and Asiatic autocracy." It was, however, against Or thodoxy that the real scorn of the anonymous British diplomat was directed. In a masterpiece of diplomatic language, he attributed even the failure of the Turks to "Byzantinism, that daughter of the horse leech."[74]

European civilization was held responsible for even the tiny improvements in Balkan civilization. Building on the widespread belief that it was rampant among Muslims, Harry De Windt asserted that "polygamy is now greatly (and voluntarily) restricted in the Austrian Balkans, where even rich men are generally content with four or five wives at the most."[75] He could not have known that demographers have ascertained that polygamy had always been a very rare phenomenon among Balkan Muslims. What he should have known, at least, was that four was the legitimate number of Muslim wives. Other authors minimized the influence of European civilization on the Balkans: it "has never been one percent of what the influence of the Balkans is on Europe," which was "the rule of violence, murder, intrigue, spoliation, bluff and denial of contract." In a true illustration to Keyserling's "If the Balkans did not exist, they had to be invented," all that did not conform to the idealized notion of Europe had to have been imported, like a contagious disease, from the Balkans.[76] Corresponding to the kitschy, postcard culture of the period, one cannot resist seeing the picture of an innocent Europa with Nordic features being seduced by a boorish Balkan serpent.

A new feature in the image of the Balkans was added first between the wars but especially after World War II when a new demon, a new other—communism—was grafted on it. The Balkans were proclaimed "lost to the Western world" and "written off by proponents of Western civilization," as long as Russia remained strong in the peninsula, because Russian communism was "the end of Europe."[77] The paradox was the neat exemption of two of the most important representatives of the Balkan *Kulturraum* of their membership: Greece and Turkey. As far as Greece was concerned, there had always been the special attitude stemming from the classical heritage of the country appropriated by the enlightened West but this attitude was uneven, and only rarely was Greece entirely disassociated from the Balkans. During World War II, just as Fallmerayer's theory served the Germans in their treatment of the Greeks as *Untermenschen*, the allies' attitude was informed by a revived memory of the Greeks' contribution to Western civilization; the national heroes and events of Serbs and Albanians could not reverberate in the souls of Englishmen, but not so the Greek:

> In turning from the Balkans proper to Greece—really not a Balkan state at all, but part of the great Mediterranean civilization—we find ourselves spiritually on friendly ground. Instead of struggling with the outlandish names of battles, rulers, and law-givers that decided the fate of some unfamiliar land—Kossovo, George Kastriota, Lek—we recognize those that helped to form the destinies of all civilization—Marathon, Pericles, Solon. To this tiny land we owe the greater part of our own culture, our arts and sciences, the form our religion has taken, our tradition of sport—and the ideals for which we are fighting today.[78]

Joseph Roucek, an American professor who diagnosed the Balkan affliction as "the handicap of heterogeneity," worked in the framework of racial clichés, but the Greeks were ennobled: "The Bulgar is Alpine Slav, whose blood has Asiatic, Finnish, and Turkish components. The Greek is Hellenic mixed with Nordic, mellowed by

Mediterranean strains. Though the Romanian will never acknowledge that he is anything else but a Latin, he is Slav grafted to Mediterranean and overgrown with Asiatic."[79] Henry Miller's *Colossus of Maroussi*, an almost fictionalized depiction of his romantic flight from European civilization, was another occasional burst of hellenophile sentiment. It is fascinating to compare Miller's account with the *Balkan Journal* of an American diplomat, Laird Archer, written at the same time but over a longer period. Archer's absorbing narrative gives a detailed impression of how the Balkans were sucked into the war. It should be a companion countertext to the discovery about the Balkan origins of Nazism produced by yet another American, Robert Kaplan. Moving from Tirana to Athens, Sofia, and Belgrade, Archer commented in 1938 on how Hitler's demonstrations of hate were regarded in the Balkans: "The average adherent of the Orthodox Church in the Balkans is outraged and a little alarmed at the newest result of the raw-meat diet fed the younger generation in the Greater Reich—the looting of Catholic churches and the burning of synagogues."[80]

Archer shared Miller's deep attachment to Greece, but there was a crucial difference. Archer was enamored with a concrete political Greece. Miller's story, on the other hand, was informed by a concrete abhorrence for his own American culture, but his infatuation with Greece was an escapist idealization of a most abstract kind. The sincerity and beauty of Miller's feelings for the Greeks he met and loved are beyond any doubt; it is also equally beyond doubt that his Greece was the embodiment of all that was absent in the West. Once he arrived in Greece, he felt "completely detached from Europe." Miller, then, would replicate the fundamental difference between this putative Europe and Greece, although with a reverse sign: to him Greece was infinitely superior to the spiritless and mechanistic Europe. One of the most caring and beautiful perceptions of Greece, Miller's would occasionally overdo his case when, for example, he insisted the deforestation of Greece was brought about by the Turks in their fervid desire to desolate Greece. As a result, the Greeks, according to Miller, had been struggling since their emancipation to reforest their land and had made the goat their national enemy. Despite the pleasure in reading Miller, one cannot help thinking that with a bit of classical education he would not have committed the same mistake, although then, of course, he might have slipped into disliking the modern Greeks for their failure to resemble their idealized forefathers.[81]

Miller's close friend Lawrence Durrell began his two-decades-long diplomatic career with a post at the British Legation in Athens in 1940. He put his affection for Greece in strong and somewhat melodramatic terms: "I am so happy that England and Greece are in this together; with all their faults they both stand for something great. It is a cosmic trio really—Greece, China, England." His ardent hopes for an appointment in Rhodes after the war were defeated when he was sent as press officer to Belgrade, a place he termed "this centre of barbarism comparable only to the darkest of the dark ages."[82] In his literary works, Durrell displayed his aversion to communism, but its articulation was mellowed by his talent and his unfailing sense of the comic. In 1952, he had produced a farcical anticommunist pantomime *Little Red Riding Hood*, which was to be performed at the British Embassy in Belgrade. Five years later came the hilarious *Esprit de Corps*, immortalizing the travails of the corps diplomatique in Yugoslavia from its trip on the "Liberation-Celebration Machine" between Belgrade and Zagreb, through the dinner party for the Communist People's Serbian Trade and Timber Guild, to the repertoire of communist medals: the Order of the Sava, the Order of Mercy and Plenty with crossed Haystacks, and the Titotalitarian Medal of Honour with froggings.[83]

His letters to Henry Miller, however, were not tempered by the same sense of humor. His loathing for communism rivaled Churchill's: "What a madhouse Communism is. And how grateful we are to the USA for taking it seriously. Europe is a sheepfold full of bleating woolly Socialists who simply *cannot* see that Socialism prepares the ground for these fanatics." There was no word about the devastation of Yugoslavia during the war but plenty about how "the government frantically depressing the standard of living in order to buy capital equipment which is broken as soon as they try to use it." Unlike Miller, Durrell praised the United States for its stand in defense "of every value we stand for": "the USA witch-hunting and all is taking a far more sensible line than anyone else. . . . Even a great war would be justified to prevent THIS, and liberate the millions under the yoke of this tyranny, this moral prison. That is why my heart leaps when I see that the USA has really tumbled to Communism and has bounded into Korea. Hurrah."[84]

At least in his rhetoric, Churchill had not discriminated against the other Balkan capitals and had included Sofia, Bucharest, and Belgrade alongside Athens, Warsaw, Prague, and Budapest in his Fulton speech. His portrait of a raped European civilization has been used to demarcate the symbolic beginnings of the cold war. Yet, when it came to fighting for this civilization, only Greece was deemed worthy of it; the rest had been neatly handed to the Soviet Union, in the famous percentage deal of Moscow, in October 1944. When Fitzroy Macleen, the head of the British mission to Tito's partisans, had dared compare the Yugoslav and Greek communists and warned about Tito's open allegiance to communism and his pro-Soviet orientation, Churchill had calmed him down with the infallible argument:

> "Do you intend," he asked, "to make Jugoslavia your home after the war?"
> "No, Sir," I replied.
> "Neither do I, " he said. "And, that being so, the less you and I worry about the form of Government they set up, the better. . . . "[85]

When it came to the Greeks, the accommodating attitude was all but gone. The staunchest anti-German fighters in Greece were depicted as "gangsters," "brigands," and "a gang of bandits from the mountains," and Churchill secured Britain's position only after the bloody quenching of the Left in Greece. Thus, Greece was rescued from the ignoble company of the other Balkan states, from which, at least in British eyes, it differed significantly. Turkey, Greece's main adversary and NATO ally, had never been considered, *stricto senso*, Balkan. In the postwar era, however, it was gradually exempt from a much older and persistent characterization: being oriental. Regarded as an important forepost of defense (or aggression) vis-à-vis the Soviet Union, it was later seen as the secular alternative to the increasing activization of Islam. In the imagination of Western political propaganda Greece was constructed as the stronghold of democracy, and received green light for its internal policies. This was carried on in the post–cold war period, and the military campaign of the Turkish army against the Kurds in their own and in Iraqi territory in 1995 was clumsily justified by President Clinton over West European verbal protestations.

Yugoslavia, despite the lack of initial Western commitment, and although it was the first genuinely communist dictatorship without Soviet prodding, was exempt because of its early conflict with Moscow. To paraphrase Churchill's earlier criterion—"What interests us is, which of them is doing most harm to the Germans"—the postwar criterion was which of them was doing most harm to the Soviets. This attitude saw that Nicolae Ceauşescu, the most heinous dictator of Eastern Europe, compared to whom the Moscow geriatric regime seemed like the most benign rule, was invited by the queen to London, and George Bush returning from Bucharest declared that Romania was more civilized than any other part of Eastern Europe.[86] Neither Yugoslavia nor Romania (nor Albania, which was not referred to at all) in this period was referred to as Balkan. This attitude can be easily explained as a function of their general stand toward the Soviets, were it not for the only exception: Bulgaria. Even while the country was derided for its servile attitude toward the Soviet Empire and for its irreparable Russophilia, the charge of "Balkanness" was on the whole not hurled on it. In fact, the Balkans as a geopolitical notion and "Balkan" as a derogation were conspicuously absent from the vocabulary of Western journalists and politicians. Even in the Western academic world, despite the fruitful growth of Balkan studies after the mid-1960s, the dominant category with few exceptions was Eastern Europe, and until recently there were seldom attempts to differentiate between its Balkan and non-Balkan parts.

The new wave of utilizing "Balkan" and "balkanization" as derogative terms came only with the end of the cold war and the eclipse of state communism in Eastern Europe. Even Greece was not spared the brandishing label by Adam Nicolson: "Greece, from being one of us since the War, has become one of them (Balkans). With the collapse of the Soviet empire in eastern and central Europe, Greece's usefulness as an eastern bulwark of NATO has disappeared."[87] The immediate result was "the strategic downgrading of the Balkans in East-West relations" and the accompanying competing attempts of separate Eastern European nations to enter the privileged economic or security clubs of the West.[88] The unfolding of this process coincided with the violent destruction of Yugoslavia. While it adversely affected the neighboring countries, it did not plunge them into the much prophesied Balkan war. On the other hand, the persistent use of "Balkan" for the Yugoslav war has by now rekindled old stereotypes and licensed indiscriminate generalizations about the region. History and anthropology, in particular, have been harnessed to provide a scholarly interpretation for the events in Yugoslavia in a Balkan context and give a credible explanation for the violence, particularly the one exhibited by the warring Serb side.

The argument goes like this: during the seventeenth and eighteenth centuries, the Habsburgs settled Serb migrants from the Ottoman Empire in the borderlands between the two empires, the Military Frontier (Vojna Krajina). These colonists were offered, in exchange for military service as border guards, self-rule (including religious tolerance) and land. The military ethos of these Serbs was fueled not only by their profession but by the messianic awareness as defenders of Christianity against Islam. A further explanation was the anarchic state of the medieval and Ottoman periods, when plundering and brigandage were endemic. Especially in the mountainous regions of the Balkans (Montenegro, Bosnia, Albania) that discouraged agricultural activities and fostered pastoralism, extended families practicing transhumance were organized as clans and tribes, and indulged in the plunder of passing merchants and constant feuds over pastureland and routes: "the warrior ethos became deeply ingrained in many of the pastoralists, particularly among those of Eastern Hercegovina. . . . They are today playing an active part in the violence that is marking the end of Yugoslavia. As relatively uneducated armed hillsmen, with a hostility toward urban culture and the state institutions . . . they have proved susceptible to Serbian chauvinistic propaganda."[89]

It seems as if the mountaineers of the seventeenth century have reentered the political stage of the late twentieth unmarked by any change. What is at stake is the specific character of the perpetrated violence. With all professed and sincerely felt aversion against the atrocities of World War II, especially the Holocaust, these are seen as extreme aberrations and not typical consequences of the otherwise rational, liberal, and predictable polity of the West. The present Yugoslav atrocities, and in general Balkan atrocities, on the contrary, are the expected natural outcomes of a warrior ethos, deeply ingrained in the psyche of Balkan populations. Balkan violence thus is more violent because it is archaic, born of clan societies, whose archaic forms reveal the "disharmonic clash between prehistory and the modern age."[90] This argument seemingly takes into account environmental factors (mountainous terrain), economy (sheep and horse raising), social arrangements (extended families, clans, tribes) to explain the creation of a cultural pattern. Its flaw, however, is that once the cultural pattern is created, it begins an autonomous life as an unchangeable structure and no account is taken of the drastic changes that have occurred in the social environment of the Balkans in the past century, although there are corners and pockets less influenced by these transformations. There is an additional aspect to the comparisons of atrocities. The jump from medieval brigands to contemporary armed hillsmen involves a comparison of medieval violence (of which both are representative) with highly technological contemporary warfare, in which backwardness is attributed not only to the weapons of destruction but also to the perpetrators. Primitive technology and primitive warfare, then, goes parallel with human primitiveness. This is obviously, though unconsciously, premised on the by-now demolished idea that human nature has positively metamorphosed through technology.

All this is founded on the apparent conviction in unconscious motors of behavior: it is cultural tradition that is driving them. Yet one can approach the phenomenon from a different standpoint, acknowledging rational calculations and behavior on the part of the agents and not explaining them only in terms of driving passions and mentalities formed throughout centuries and millennia. Then the terror will be seen not simply, or not only, as externalization of the warrior side, but as adopting rational tactics of terror. The differences between the tactics employed by the warring parties in Yugoslavia and the Germans in World War II have been pointed out, thus implicitly disputing parallels between "ethnic cleansing" and the Holocaust. The Nazis organized the systematic killing of populations aimed at their total extermination but without creating public furor; in fact not creating public furor was an element for the successful implementing of the operation. The ethnic cleansers in Bosnia, on the other hand, have consciously induced public furor, not with total extermination as their final goal, but in order to create an impossible psychological atmosphere that would drive out the undesirables from their territories. The point here is not to make absurd speculations as to whose policy is less barbarous, but to argue that in both cases there is an underlying logic explicable in terms of rationally set aims, rather than irrational (or subconscious) urges.

Similarly, the reporting of incidents of rape in the Yugoslav war has coincided with a heightened sensitivity to the fate of women in general. It has led to a view of the Serbs as particularly heinous rapists, indeed as originators of a rationally conceived and systematically executed policy as a tool of war. It has further proclaimed that the use of rape in the former Yugoslavia can be understood only in the framework of the cultural values unique to the region. To question all this does not mean in any way to trivialize the abhorrent deeds committed on the territory of the former Yugoslavia. As Eugene Hammel beautifully put it within a slightly different context: "I have no personal problems with the idea of tracking down proven rapists in Bosnia and hanging them from the nearest cottonwood (or the relativistic cultural equivalent thereof), with due apologies to those who abhor the death penalty. Vengeance in the name of the degraded would be my aim. I have no problems as a vigilante, just as an anthropologist."[91]

What is in question is two tendencies: to elevate (or descend) the Yugoslav event to a unique occurrence without precedent in history; and to explain it by means of pseudoscientific interpretations. In the case of rapes, anthropologists stepped in to offer opinions on their specific character in Yugoslavia. In their view, they could be understood only in the context of the heroic tradition and the specific code of shame in Yugoslavia and the Balkans, stemming from patterns of patriarchal, pastoral, rural, and communal life, particularly the acculturation of individuals in the values of extended and multiple families held to be predominant (or hegemonic) in the region:

> The rape is meant to collectively humiliate the enemy. What do the raped women think of first? Of something different than the Austrian, American or English women. The latter would ask themselves: Why precisely me? They would receive support from their families, but they would think primarily in individual terms. *These* [the raped Yugoslav women] women think first of their husband, of the children, of the parents, of the relatives—of shame. This is how the many rapes can be explained. They are symbolic acts, which are supposed to reach the opponent in his political entirety.[92]

This categorical statement written by men about what raped women think is not based on sociological surveys or interviews. Quite apart from the fact that it does not differentiate between groups of women, based on education, occupation, and other criteria, it lumps together all Yugoslav women and constructs them as a cultural species quite apart from the similarly constructed group of Austrian, American, or English, that is, Western women. This is typical of the ease and irresponsibility with which overgeneralized categories are used in academic discourse, despite numerous evidence to the dubious repercussions in extra-academic settings.

Scholarship has had a less direct relationship to the balkanist discourse but has contributed to it, even if unwillingly, in providing the framework for sweeping generalizations that appear to be substantiated by scientific research. This is especially true at the crossroads of disciplines where models created in one field of study have been utilized by induction to reach conclusions in different domains, as the utilization of family history in grand sociological and ideological classifications. The distinction between two marriage patterns in historical Europe—one defined by high marriage ages for both sexes and high degrees of celibacy, the other typical for its low age at marriage and universal marriages—which were seemingly innocently labeled "European" and "non-European," has had unforseen repercussions outside historical demography. In his opening speech to a recent conference on family history entitled "Where Does Europe End?" Rudolf Andorka, the rector of the Budapest University of Economics and a renowned historical demographer, declared that the structure of families in the Middle Ages may be of some, though marginal, interest to some people, but whether Hungary belonged to Europe was of paramount importance. It has become a pathetic compulsion for demographic historians of or from the regions on the margins of the "European marriage pattern" to demonstrate that their areas bear if not all, at least a majority of characteristics that allow them to be squeezed into the "European" rubric.[93]

Clearly, though not explicitly, family history (and any other discipline) has strong ideological connotations, quite apart from the intentions of its practitioners. Given the use of "Europe" in any present analytical discourse in the human and social sciences, the epistemological value of European family models, and particularly the posited divide between so called "European" and "non-European" societies within the geographical entity Europe, becomes extremely problematic. In the ambiguous relation between geography and politics within the concept of geopolitics, the latter seems to have the upper hand. "Europe" ends where politicians want it to end, and scholars should be at least aware of this and of how one's research can and is being used.

Between Classification and Politics

The Balkans and the Myth of Central Europe

Beyond and below what was once Czechoslovakia lie the deep Balkans. They are, it has been said, a sort of hell paved with the bad intentions of the powers.

John Gunther[1]

The right question is not "Is it true?" but "What is it intended to do?"

S. H. Hooke[2]

In the geographical and political classifications after World War II, a portion of the Balkans had secured an unobtrusive place as part of a common Eastern Europe perceived as a homogeneous appendix of the USSR by the West; another portion had been willingly included into Western Europe, something inconceivable but for the prevailing anticommunist paranoia. In the Balkans themselves, the feeling of Balkan commonality was pushed aside, and the self-designation followed an East-West axis. The vanishing of the bipolar world after 1989 saw a nervous search for more appropriate categories for the organization of academic and journalistic knowledge, principally in the United States. The study of Russia and the Soviet world was euphemistically renamed "Eurasian studies." Eastern Europe also received attention, in an effort to emancipate it not only from the former superpower but also from the tutelage of Russian studies. A reassessment of East European studies in the United States argued that "the trajectory of Russian history is substantially different, particularly from that of East-Central Europe [which] retained more religious, cultural, and economic linkages with the West than did the Russians." The Balkans, too, were contrasted to the "the Orthodox lands that eventually fell under the sway of Moscow." Accepting the three-region division of Europe of the Hungarian historian Jenö Szücs as "fundamentally correct," the study argued for a further elaboration, namely that "Eastern Europe should be divided into two sections, East-Central and Southeast Europe."[3]

Thus the Balkans began to reemerge as a separate entity, albeit under what was apparently considered a more neutral title: Southeast Europe. While this particular study was undoubtedly motivated by the lofty goal of stressing the diversity of Eastern Europe through reclassification, it should be clear by now that the treatment of classification as "an outcome of an ordering process as if the organisation of thoughts comes first, and a more or less fixed classification follows as the outcome" is highly problematic. Rather, "the ordering process is itself embedded in prior and subsequent social action."[4] The study in question implicitly accepted the notion of a homogeneous Western Europe to which different Eastern European entities were juxtaposed. It was simply a version of the West European syndrome "to conceive of the entire Euro-Asian land mass as four Easts (Near, Middle, Far, and Eastern Europe) and only one West, itself."[5] It explicitly grounded itself in the conception of Szücs, one of the pillars of the Central European ideology, thus elevating the whole Central European discourse to an important heuristic device.

The restructuring was not confined to academe. In 1994, the State Department decided to banish "Eastern Europe" from the lexicon of the department's Europe bureau: "Eastern Europe would now revert to what it was before the start of World War Two in 1939—Central Europe." While it was unclear how an entity was to have a center flanked only by a west, this episode is a testimony that the claims of the Central European champions were taken seriously, at least for the sake of diplomatic nomenclature. Later, by speaking about the "two large nations on the flanks of Central Europe," Richard Holbrooke intimated that Russia was assuming the role of Eastern Europe but never spelled it out explicitly, because "at the State Department, nomenclature is an expression of foreign policy."[6]

The newscast tried to reform, too. As of 1 January 1995, the daily report "Central and Eastern Europe" of Radio Free Europe/Radio Liberty (RFE/RL) split in two daily digests of the Open Media Research Institute (OMRI): "East-Central Europe" (the Visegrád four [Poland, Hungary, the Czech Republic, and Slovakia], the three Baltic republics, Ukraine, and Belarus) and "Southeastern Europe" (the former Yugoslavia, Albania, Bulgaria, Romania, and Moldova). In this classification the unarticulated "Eastern Europe" seemed to be reserved for Russia. While one need not envisage a conspiracy with macabre consequences, in general, structures can become self-generating, and the apportioning of knowledge is geared to a subsequent validating of the structure. OMRI's classification may be attributed to a genuine effort to overcome the legacy of cold-war divisions, but its "Southeastern Europe" was castrated exactly along the former cold-war line: Greece and Turkey continued to be subsumed under "Western Europe" and the "Middle East."

The great vogue over Central Europe began in the early 1980s with the almost simultaneous publication of three works by well-known authors representing the voices of the three countries claiming partnership in the idea: Jenö Szücs, Czeslaw Milosz, and Milan Kundera. The most erudite of the three pieces was written by the Hungarian historian Jenö Szücs, and had enormous influence in Hungary but remained virtually unknown in the West and in Eastern Europe outside the narrow circle of professional historians. This was due not only to its length and dense professional prose but also to the fact that it did not offer an easy polemical argument. In a kaleidoscopic summary of several centuries of European development from the fall of the Western Roman Empire to the end of the eighteenth century, Szücs argued that the notion of the West had been born already in the ninth century, and by expanding to the north and east *Europa Occidens* enlarged its bounds to include East-Central Europe. In the meantime, "a 'truncated' Eastern Europe and South-Eastern Europe . . . took shape under the sphere of influence of Byzantium." The modern period witnessed the second expansion of the West over the Atlantic and the almost simultaneous expansion of "truncated" Eastern Europe, which assumed its "complete" character by annexing Siberia. "East-Central Europe became squeezed between those two regions, and at the dawn of the Modern Times . . . it no longer knew whether it still belonged within the framework of *Europa Occidens* or whether it remained outside it."

Szücs's piece was not a loner; there was a whole genre of works dealing with the dilemma of Hungarian identity crucified between "East" and "West," and especially for the roots of its backwardness. According to Szücs, Hungary carried the predicament of a border region between two opposing centers. These two poles developed divergent trends: urban sovereignty and intensive commodity exchange growing up in the interstices between the sovereignties of rival powers in the West versus centralized bureaucratic state structures holding in their grip the traditional urban civilization of the East; Western corporate freedoms and the system of estates against the East's "ruling power with an enormous preponderance over the fairly amorphous society"; "the internal principles of organizing society" dominating over those of the Western state, and the reverse in the Eastern case; the different development of serfdom with the Western absolutist state compensating for its disappearance of serfdom, and the Eastern consolidating it; Western mercantilism with the capitalist company at its center versus state dominance of the industry in the East; Western evolution toward national absolutism against Eastern development toward imperial autocracy; Latin Christianity versus caesaropapist Orthodoxy; and so on.[7]

His doubtless erudition notwithstanding, Szücs can be criticized on his own turf. Sometimes he resorted to reductionism, as with Russian absolutism, which he reduced to Byzantine autocratic mysticism, disregarding the legal and political discussions over absolutism that led to a short-lived but nevertheless constitutional change in the nature of the Russian polity; despite his considerable historical culture in medieval and early modern history, he conveniently preferred to ignore the — by-now enormous — literature exposing the simplified treatment of the Byzantine tradition as caesaropapism; more seriously and surprisingly for a historian, he assumed a homogeneity of the West almost out of a political science textbook. Most importantly, Szücs built his case on the notion of Europe unfolding around two poles that seemed to have evolved independently of each other; he went so far as to describe "the organic western process of changes in forms," implicitly suggesting an "inorganic" process for the East.[8] Within a different methodological approach, this polarized view would have been much more shaded, and the sharp spacial borders delineated by Szücs, in which he conveniently established his East-Central Europe, would have been transformed into more transparent and gradual temporal transitions. But Szücs made this conscious methodological choice in order to wrap up an indirect political message.

In a way, Szücs wrote in what has been aptly called the East European periphrastic where the political case was not readily transparent but followed from the overall argument. Although not drawing explicit political conclusions, Szücs utilized all the proper terms of the current political science vocabulary. He abundantly employed the problematic notion of "civil society," "the new *cause célèbre*, the new analytic key that will unlock the mysteries of the social order,"[9] although the idea of civil society was developed theoretically only during the Scottish Enlightenment. Szücs utilized it to show that a *societas civilis* had appeared in the West already in the mid-thirteenth century "as a synonym for the autonomous society," where the "organizing principles of law and freedom" had managed to carve out a "plurality of small spheres of freedom." Even the feudal categories of medieval *honor* and *fidelitas* were reinterpreted in terms of "human dignity" as a constitutive element of the West, not to speak of the fortuitous combination of *virtus* and *temperantia* in European behavior.[10]

Actually, there was a direct political message, although Szücs chose to present it from the viewpoint of István Bibó: "the search for the deepest roots of a 'democratic way of organizing society.'" Always careful to hide behind Bibó, Szücs outlined his view of the structural preconditions for democracy and presented Hungary as fitting the objective preconditions. His grand finale was an undisguised appeal for action, again legitimized by Bibó: "His basic concept, which he put down several times and meant to serve as a long trend, is also valid and opportune: chances inherent in reality are not necessarily realized—their realization depends on effort and goodwill." Szücs's vision, as indeed all the Central European debate, was informed with "the grand history . . . of human progress towards freedom."[11] Within this majestic framework, the Balkans were not even deemed relevant to be analyzed; already at the beginning of his argument, Szücs had disposed of what he called South-Eastern Europe: "Since this last area was to secede from the European structure along with the gradual decline of Byzantium by the end of the Middle Ages, I shall disregard it."[12]

The second founding father of the Central European idea was the author of a "much more culturally argued definition, in which he makes the point of Central Europe's liminality to Europe as a whole."[13] In *The Witness of Poetry*, Milosz did not specifically use the term Central Europe let alone define it. His 1983 essays are a contemplation on the world of poetics by a refined and nuanced intellectual who was well aware that "the twentieth century, perhaps more protean and multifaceted than any other, changes according to the point from which we view it." Milosz spoke from what he defined as "my corner of Europe," but this was not the Central Europe ascribed to him. It was both broader and more confined than Central Europe. In the narrow sense, his "corner" was his Poland, more specifically his even smaller corner in the Lithuanian periphery, revolving around three axes: the North-South axis, the opposition but also synthesis between Latin and Polish, between Roman classicism and its ancient poets and the poetry produced by his Polish predecessors; the West-East axis, between home and the new capital of the world, Paris; the Past-Future axis, the quality of poetry as "a palimpsest that, when properly decoded, provides testimony to its epoch."[14]

These three axes should not be associated with another opposition delineated by Milosz which, decontextualized, has been taken to represent his definition of Central Europe. "I was born and grew up on the very borderline between Rome and Byzantium" was the introduction to his birthplace, which was taken to mean that "thus only from the outer edge of Europe, which is Central Europe or, in this case,

Wilno, can one properly understand the true qualities of Europeanness." Although George Schöpflin was aware that such an interpretation raises "the more or less geographical and semantic question that if Central Europe constitutes the outer edge of Europe, where is Eastern Europe to be found?" he still persisted in it.[15]

Milosz had an ambivalent attitude toward Russia: he spoke of the centuries-long division of Europe between Roman Catholicism and Eastern Christianity but at the same time hastened to specify that the sense of menace he felt came "not from Eastern Christianity, of course, but from what has arisen as a result of its defeat."[16] In order to illustrate Russian isolation, he went so far as to quote the absurd statement by Russian historian Georgii Fedotov that all of Russia's misfortunes had stemmed from having substituted the universality of Greek for the Slavic idiom. And yet, he never entirely purged Russia from Europe; what he did was to oppose Russian messianism to the body of Western ideas.

Milosz was also much more political than his interpreters allowed him to be. He not only raised his voice for the emancipation of all of Eastern Europe but he was doubly political: directly, by documenting the cynicism of the cold-war division of Europe, and more subtly, by recognizing the political significance of cultural images:

> The literary map of Europe, as it presented itself to the West, contained until recently numerous blank spots. England, France, Germany, and Italy had a definite place ... ; while to the east of Germany the white space could have easily borne the inscription *Ubi leones* (Where the lions are), and that domain of wild beasts included such cities as Prague (mentioned sometimes because of Kafka), Warsaw, Budapest, and Belgrade. Only farther to the east does Moscow appear on the map. The images preserved by a cultural elite undoubtedly also have political significance as they influence the decisions of the groups that govern, and it is no wonder that the statesmen who signed the Yalta agreement so easily wrote off a hundred million Europeans from these blank areas in the loss column.[17]

Once the discussion over the fate of Central Europe was in the air, Milosz rejoined it with an essay that at first glance left the impression that he was becoming much more explicit about his Central Europeanness: "I assume there is such a thing as Central Europe, even though many people deny its existence."[18] Although he set himself the task to define specific Central European attitudes, it is a tribute to the humbleness and intellectual integrity of Milosz that whenever he would venture into broader generalizations, he was careful to do so within the confines of the world he knew best: the domain of literature.

To Milosz, the most striking feature in Central European literature was its awareness of history. The other characteristic trait was that "a Central European writer receives training in irony." Here Milosz made a rare lapse into reductionism by stating that, in contrast to the Central European realm of irony, "Russian contemporary art and literature, obstinately clinging to cliches, frozen by censorship, seems sterile and unattractive." This statement is preposterous in the face of a splendid line of authors like Il'ia Il'f and Evgenii Petrov, Isac Babel', Mikhail Bulgakov, Andrei Platonov, Venedikt Erofeev, and Vladimir Orlov, to mention but a few, but was the only breach of bon ton. Although it seemed that Milosz had begun to accept the short formula of Central Europe as "being a Pole or a Czech or a Hungarian," when he elaborated on the different literatures partaking in the Central European literary experiment, he enumerated "Czech or Polish, Hungarian or Estonian, Lithuanian or Serbo-Croatian"; he also referred to the Ukraine, Slovakia, and Romania. Without mentioning the Balkans separately, Milosz clearly embraced them together with the rest of the non-Russian Eastern Europe in his Central Europe which was "an act of faith, a project, let us say, even a utopia."[19] It was the ambiguity toward Russia that came to the fore.

This ambiguity was transformed into prohibitive certainty in the best known and most widely read of the three pieces, the essay on Central Europe by "the man who more than anyone else has given it currency in the West . . . a Czech, Milan Kundera."[20] Now, rereading Kundera after more than ten years is disappointing in terms of logical consistency and moral integrity: the essay sounds melodramatic and, at times, outright racist but, given the historical context of the time, its emancipatory pathos was genuine; thus, the sincere emotional appeal, alongside its excessive reductionism, explains the attention that it received. Kundera's essay became the focus of an intensive intellectual turnover, and it has become impossible to approach the original text without taking into account the ensuing powerful but less numerous critiques and the more numerous but less powerful endorsements. It is as if the initial text has lost its autonomy; one cannot revisit it with innocence.

This forces me to resort to a different strategy: presenting Kundera's view through the eyes of people familiar with the debates and who share in his belief about the distinctiveness of Central Europe—the editors of *In Search of Central Europe*. This "postmodernist" technique is justified by the fact that Kundera himself did not allow the publication of his essay in their volume "for reasons of his own," and Schöpflin and Nancy Wood supplied a summary of his argument. Iver Neumann throws some light on the reasons for Kundera's refusal by evoking the postscript to the Czech version of *A Joke* where he insisted that "the essay falls into that part of his production which he disowns, because it was tailormade for Western consumption."[21] According to Schöpflin and Wood, Kundera recast the upheavals in Hungary (1956), Czechoslovakia (1968), and Poland (1956, 1968, 1970, and 1981) not as East European dramas but as quintessentially dramas of the West. "In Kundera's schema, it is not politics, but *culture* which must be seen as the decisive force by which nations constitute their identity, express that identity and give it its own distinctive mould." Within this cultural approach, Kundera argued that the Central European identity as the identity of a family of small nations was an inextricable part of the larger European experience, while at the same time having its own distinctive profile. In the case of Russia, on the other hand:

> Kundera asserts . . . both the continuity of Russian traditions and their profound *difference* from the European ones. This explains why in his view Central Europe's adherence to the West is a natural disposition, arising as it does from a constant and intimate intermingling of cultural traditions, whereas Russia represents an 'other' civilization, a fundamentally different culture, despite its periods of cultural reapprochement with Europe.[22]

Kundera's essay produced a torrent of reactions revolving around the complete banishment of Russia from Europe as an essentialized alien. The strongest voice to object against assigning "a demonic power to the Russians" was Milan Šimečka's. Responding to Kundera's allegation that "when the Russians occupied Czechoslovakia, they did everything possible to destroy Czech culture,"Šimečka pointed out that "we are not too distant from the events, however, to forget that it was not the Russians who put paid to Czech culture . . . It was our lot: Central Europeans born and bred. . . . Our spiritual Biafra bore an indelible local trademark." Kundera ascribed much weight to the pan-Slavic idea for the fate of Central Europe: "I feel that the error made by Central Europe was owing to what I call the 'ideology of the Slavic world.'" He did not go so far as to assert that Czechs were not Slavs (like Joseph Conrad in 1916 for the Poles) but he affirmed that apart from their linguistic kinship, neither Czechs nor Poles had anything in common with the Russians.[23]

There is a detail in Kundera's argumentation that stands out because it was replicated later in an almost symmetrical way by his compatriot Václav Havel. Kundera evoked Kazimierz Brandys meeting Anna Akhmatova, who responded to his complaint about his banned works that he had not encountered the real horror: being imprisoned, expelled, and so on. To Brandys these were typically Russian consolations, the fate of Russia was foreign to him, Russian literature scared, indeed horrified him; he preferred "not to have known their world, not to have known it even existed." Kundera added: "I don't know if it is worse than ours, but I do know it is different: Russia knows another (greater) dimension of disaster, another image of space (a space so immense entire nations are swallowed up in it), another sense of time (slow and patient), another way of laughing, living, and dying."[24] In 1994, Joseph Brodsky wrote an open letter in response to Havel's speech on the nightmare of postcommunism. This was a philosophical manifesto of a kind and, without necessarily agreeing with it, one has to respect it for its profound intellectual effort and honesty. It addressed problems of human nature and society, the role and responsibility of intellectuals, particularly philosopher-kings. Havel's polite response was essentially a rebuttal; he refused to discuss the crucial problems raised by Brodsky (about the legacy of the Enlightenment, Rousseau, and Burke, compromise and saintness, survival and conformism, mass society and individualism, bureaucracy and culture, and so on), on the ground that these matters were too complex and it would require "an essay at least as long." Instead, he wrote an essay about one-third of Brodsky's in length whose only idea was that there was an essential difference between their experiences:

> For ordinary people in your country of birth, any change aiming at a freer system, at freedom of thought and action, was a step into the unknown. . . . By contrast, Czechs and Slovaks enjoyed a considerable degree of freedom and democracy in the late nineteenth century under the Austro-Hungarian constitutional monarchy. . . . The traditions of those times live on in family life and books. Thus, although the renewal of freedom is difficult and inconvenient in our country too, freedom was never a completely unknown aspect of time, space and thought.[25]

Thus, while the Russian was raising existential problems of universal significance, the civilized Central European was responding in a patronizing manner evoking, in a typically provincial way, a relatively less significant issue about differences of degree in historic experiences of two countries (of which one is a continent and thus even less subject to sweeping generalizations). Maybe the issue does not deserve more than the verdict about the Czechs who, "like other nations at the fringes of the West, were particularly susceptible to the siren song of this elitist snobbery," the convenient presumption of the unbridgeable cultural gap between West and East.[26] In this, Russia was becoming "Central Europe's constituting other." What was remarkable in Kundera is that there was no mention of the Balkans whatsoever; the only opposition was Russia.

Thus, at the beginning round of its articulation, there was an attempt to define the Central European idea both in cultural (Kundera and Milosz) and in historical terms (Szücs) while always describing it in opposition to Russia. At this stage, the Balkans simply did not exist as a separate entity: they were either ignored or subsumed in a general Eastern Europe or sometimes, although rarely, in Central Europe itself. The Central European idea of the 1980s was an emancipatory idea, "a metaphor of protest," which in itself was a subspecies of a whole genre dealing with "Europeanness," represented in different periods and intensity in all European countries. The main issues were the inclusiveness or exclusiveness of Europe, and since a lot more was at stake than merely intellectual prowess, the discussion was highly impassioned.

During the second round in the development of the Central European idea until 1989—the Eastern European annus mirabilis—many works were published in both mainstream Western editions and publications of the East European intellectual emigration and the *samizdat*: *Cross Currents, East European Reporter, Eastern European Politics and Society, Daedalus, Cadmos, The New York Review of Books, Svcedečtví, La Nouvelle Alternative, Nowa Koalicja*, and so on. A representative part was assembled in the 1989 volume *In Search of Central Europe*. The introductory essay admitted that the discussion over the Central European identity "takes a putative Central Europeanness as its launching pad, seeks to define it in terms most favourable to its unstated though evident goals and insists that the whole concept is apodictic, that it is up to its opponents to prove it false." The "evident goals" were vaguely described in negative terms: the construction of a consciousness emphasizing values "other than those propagated by the existing system" and of an identity "authentic enough to act as an organizing principle for those seeking something other than Soviet-type reality."[27]

Schöpflin followed Szücs in the central attempt to prove the essential contrast between Russia and Western Europe, and then position Central Europe between them but as an organic part of the West because the incompatibility between the two ideal types effectively precluded transitional models. The real differences were cultural, "thereby making a discussion of European values essential." Europe had "developed values specific to itself and these appear to be immanent, as well as ineradicable." How such statements accommodate the spirit of experimentation and innovation in the European cultural tradition "in which no solution is permanent" is difficult to envision logically, but logic is not the most important prerequisite for a political manifesto. And this is how Schöpflin himself conceived of it: "In the late 1980s, all the evidence suggests that the identity of Central Europeanness is attractive enough to a sufficiently wide range of people to give it a good head of steam."[28]

Despite the clear distinction from Russia, this treatment of Central Europe was not explicitly defined in opposition to the Balkans. The rare and indirect references reflected uncertainty about this region. In some statements, the Balkans were subsumed in a broader Eastern Europe that was not clearly distinguishable from Central Europe: "The Polish eastern marches—the Kresy—the Pannonian plain, not to mention the Balkans, were the untamed Wild East of Europe." At the same time, the religious fault line between Latin and Orthodox lands was strictly adhered to: "Croatia and Slovenia see themselves rightly as Central European, whilst the remainder of the country is not."[29] The logic was amazing: the pretensions of the former were justified, while the perceptions of the latter were not even considered; they simply were not part of Central Europe.

In the 1980s, one can trace the progression of the three master narratives, not necessarily in terms of ethnic continuity but in methodology, style, and overall concerns. With one exception, the contributions did not move out of the purported cultural parameters of the idea. The exception was Péter Hának, who followed in the steps of Szücs, attempting to update his narrative for the nineteenth century. Hának's piece, even more than Szücs's, displayed the dominant concern with backwardness and modernization. Hának's definition of Central Europe coincided with the Habsburg realm: "The Monarchy (including Hungary) as a system of state powers and of politics stood in the middle between the fully-fledged parliamentary democracy in the West and autocracy in the East. This is precisely the meaning of Central Europe." While postulating the radical difference between the feudal systems of Central and Eastern Europe, his argumentation revealed only differences of degree: "In Hungary and Poland the nobility was more numerous, better organized and more independent than in Russia," "there were quite considerable differences in the development, legal position and economy of towns."[30] Comparative judgments on difference and similarity are relative, and "variation in both relevance and importance can be enormous," the crucial variable being "who makes the comparison, and when."[31] It comes as no surprise that while Hungarians, Poles, and Czechs focus on the differences between Central and Eastern Europe (exemplified by Russia), their German counterparts stress the differences between *Westmitteleuropa* and *Ostmitteleuropa*.[32]

Czaba Kiss, following in Milosz's footsteps in the attempt to outline a Central European identity through literary works, was remarkably nonexclusive. His literary map of Central Europe was marked by three aspects: "the intermediate and frontier character of the region and interpretations of being between West and East"; "the literary formulation of the fate of small nations"; and "the linguistic and cultural variety of the region, as well as their coexistence."[33] Literary Central Europe was represented by two halves: one German and the other consisting of a series of peoples from small countries—Poles, Czechs, Slovaks, Hungarians, Slovenes, Croats, Serbs, Romanians, and Bulgarians; he also added Finns and the Baltic peoples, Belorussians, Ukrainians, and Greeks. He formulated their difference from the Russian literary scene not in terms of incompatible values but in the fact that Central European writers were obsessed with national ideology and their literature was subordinated to the realization of national goals. Finally, Kundera's argumentation was followed by Mihály Vajda, although Vajda claimed he wrote independently of Kundera. Displaying the same passion and exclusiveness, Vajda went much further in logical inconsistency and in heaping open slurs on "the beast on our borders with . . . its feelings of inferiority."[34]

Thankfully, he epitomized an exception to the otherwise well-mannered, at least in writing, *Középeuropa*.

The only voice that did not come from or on behalf of the trio—Poland, Hungary, Czechoslovakia—was Predrag Matvejević's "Central Europe Seen From the East of Europe." Matvejevíc did not feel threatened by exclusion from the vision of Central Europe although he offered a correction to Kundera's claim that "today, all of Central Europe has been subjugated by Russia with the exception of little Austria." He drew attention to other little countries who were likewise not under Russian domination like "Slovenia, Croatia and other regions of Yugoslavia, where Kundera is one of the most frequently translated authors." His Central Europe was one of the fuzziest: "Central Europe might even be said to extend as far as its styles—the Baroque, Biedermeier and Secession, or a certain distinctive music, painting and sensibility." Matvejević never spoke of the Balkans per se but Belgrade and Bucharest were in, though Bulgaria was not even mentioned. What is really interesting in this piece, which first appeared in 1987, was how much it was informed by an organic view of Yugoslavness despite the realization of divisive identities: "are we just Slovenes, or Yugoslavian Slovenes; are we just Croats or Yugoslavian Croats? By the same token, is a Serb exclusively a Serb or is he also a Yugoslavian Serb and a European, etc.?"[35] This was worlds apart from the ensuing process of "nesting orientalisms," when part of Yugoslavia was unwillingly forced to rediscover a Balkan identity.

Another voice originating from Romania was Eugène Ionesco, who advocated a Central European confederation, encompassing "not only Austria, Hungary and Romania, but also Croatia, Czechoslovakia" and representing "the only European and human defense against the pseudo-ideological barbarity of Russia and its spirit of conquest." The choice of Vienna as center revealed not merely nostalgia for the Habsburg past, but the appeal of the envious niche contemporary Austria had managed to carve for itself in the bipolar world.[36] The only writer before 1989 who articulated the "divide between Catholic Central Europe and the Orthodox Balkans" was Jacques Rupnik. Though he wisely recognized that visions of Central Europe change "from country to country, affording interesting insights into the motives involved and the perception of one's neighbours," Rupnik was amazed at Ionesco's idea: "Poland is conspicuously absent, but then Ionesco is the undisputed master of the absurd." The "absurdity" consisted in Ionesco's crossing civilizational fault lines and including Orthodox Romania while not even mentioning Catholic Poland.[37]

The second round of the Central European idea until 1989 saw its expansion and the elaboration of its cultural aspects. In its attitude to the Balkans, it replicated the perspectives of the founding ideologues. It has been suggested that Central Europe should be interpreted as a case of region-building, "which is itself a subgroup of what may be called identity politics, that is, the struggle to form the social field in the image of one particular political project."[38] Being undoubtedly a search for identity, "Traum oder Trauma,"[39] the debate over Central Europe was hardly a region-building attempt, because it never came up with a particular concrete political project for the region qua region, outside of the general urge for liberation from the Soviets. All it was about was negating a particular political project.

The only piece that considered possible concrete political scenarios belonged to Ferenc Fehér, and its validity was circumscribed by the pre-1989 political reality.

It skeptically warned against the possibility that "[the idea of Central Europe] could degenerate into a triumph of collective self-gratification for the intellectuals of *Café Zentraleuropa*, a group always delighted to escape from history, and always willing to be stoical in the face of other people's misery."[40] Despite their skepticism, both Fehér and Agnes Heller espoused the categorical view of an intrinsic difference between Central and Eastern Europe: while civil society was emerging in the former, this could never happen in the latter.[41] Still, during this period of its development it was the emancipatory pathos that was the focus of the Central European idea.

The Central Europe of the 1980s was by no means a new term but it was a new concept. It was not the resurrection of "Mitteleuropa": that had been a German idea, Central Europe was an East European idea; "Mitteleuropa" had always Germany at its core, Central Europe excluded Germany.[42] Friedrich Naumann, the most famous proponent of "Mitteleuropa," foresaw an enormous political body from the North Sea to the Alps, and down to the Adriatic and the Danube, excluding in his first version Romania, Bulgaria, Serbia, and Greece, but also Switzerland and the Netherlands; a year later, Bulgaria was deemed ripe to be included.[43] Before Naumann, Partsch had conceived of a "Mitteleuropa" with Germany and Austria-Hungary as the nuclei, and consisting of Belgium, the Netherlands, Switzerland, Montenegro, Serbia, Romania, and Bulgaria; Greece and Turkey were excluded from this vision.[44] Yet it would be also farfetched to look for non-German antecedents to the Central European idea of the 1980s back to the interwar period. *Střední Evropa* was an expression of Czech political thought; it was Thomas Masaryk's "peculiar zone of small nations extending from the North Cape to Cape Matapan" and including Laplanders, Swedes, Norwegians, Danes, Finns, Estonians, Letts, Lithuanians, Poles, Lusatians, Czechs, Slovaks, Magyars, Serbo-Croats and Slovenes, Rumanians, Bulgarians, Albanians, Turks and Greeks, but no Germans or Austrians.[45] In this period, Poland was more concerned with Polish matters than with Central European political geography and the Hungarians clung to their "fanatic revisionism; at best they envisioned a Danubian Europe revolving around their own nation."[46]

The passionate writings of the 1980s were not the first attempt at the intellectual emancipation of the region. In 1950, an American of Polish descent, Oscar Halecki, published a small volume, followed, thirteen years later, by an extended study that was an undisguised Christian polemic against the Marxist view of history and offered a vision of a united Christian Europe: "A positive approach, replacing the Marxist, is badly needed. . . . The alternative is indeed of general significance, because . . . it raises the question whether the Christian interpretation of history and the emphasis of the religious, purely spiritual element in the evolution of mankind is not the best answer to the claims of historical materialism."[47]

Halecki's definition of Europe was strictly cultural: "the European community, especially in the period of its greatness, was always primarily a cultural community." He denied the identification of Christianity with Western culture, which he saw as a synthesis of Greco-Roman civilization with Christianity. His verdict on the Europeanness of ancient Greece was unequivocal: it not only gave Europe its name but was "the nucleus of the Europe of the future," "this part of Europe which was already 'historic' two thousand years ago included the Balkan peninsula." Halecki thus synthesized two of the foundation myths of the European idea: one identifying Europe with Christianity in the fifteenth century, the other with "civilization" in the eighteenth. The attitude to Greece extended also to the Byzantine Empire: Halecki cautioned that the so-called caesaropapism had been overrated. Eastern Europe was not only "no less European than Western Europe" but "it participates in both the Greek and the Roman form of Europe's Ancient and Christian heritage." Though acknowledging Asiatic influences on the Byzantines, his final verdict was unquestionably laudatory: "It must never be forgotten that the same Byzantine Empire was from its origin a continuous, frequently heroic, and sometimes successful defender of Europe against Asiatic aggression, exactly as ancient Greece had been."[48]

For Halecki, the Slavs were an important component of European history, and he specifically included Russia, whose Christianization "had made the eastern Slavs an integral part of Europe." There was, of course, an ambiguity in his treatment of Russia, which as a Christian state was part of the European community but had also experienced the effects of Asiatic influences. These influences were not so much due to the impact of Byzantine autocracy but to the Asiatic form of government of the Mongols. Speaking in terms of the now revived Eurasian character of Russia, Halecki nevertheless accepted its European character between Peter I and Nicholas II. Predictably, it was with the ascent of Lenin and the Bolsheviks that Russia became "non-European if not anti-European."[49]

While strongly arguing the unity between Western and Eastern Europe, Halecki posited his great and essential other as "the Asiatic." He first mentioned the term in the period of antiquity where he recognized the political dualism of the European tradition deriving from Greco-Roman origins but not coinciding "with the opposition between western and eastern Europe. . . . It can be correctly understood only against an oriental background which is not Greek, indeed, nor East European, but Asiatic." This undefined Asiatic was "alien to the tradition of both the Roman Republic and free Greece." Halecki attempted to deorientalize Greece, sanitize the ancient Greeks from some of their fundamental formative influences and from their solid roots in Asia Minor, a perfect illustration to what Martin Bernal has described as the cleansing of ancient Greece from its African and Asian influences. But this amorphous "Asiatic" was soon identified with Islam. Christianity and Islam were "two entirely different civilizations. . . . Compared with the basic difference between these two, the internal differences between Latins and Greeks were really insignificant." Having set this axiomatic premise, Halecki's assessment of the Ottoman conquest comes as no surprise: and centuries-long presence is logically portrayed as an intrusion "completely alien to its European subjects in origin, tradition, and religion" which effectively interrupted "for approximately four hundred years their participation in European history." Notwithstanding the geographical continuity between the Byzantine and Ottoman Empires, they had nothing more in common:

> The Eastern Roman Empire, in spite of four centuries of ecclesiastical schism, had always been an integral part of Christian Europe, and never, in spite of all political rivalries with Latin powers, a real threat to the West. The Ottoman Empire, though it moved its capital to Constantinople, remained a non-Christian and non-European conqueror and a growing danger to what remained of Christian Europe.[50]

For Halecki, "the Ottoman conquest of the Balkan peninsula is the obvious reason why that very region where Europe originated seemed so different from the happier parts of the continent when, at last, it was liberated." It was this liberation, "the division of the Balkans among the Christian successor states of the Ottoman Empire [which] reunited that region of Europe during the last period of its history."[51] There was no doubt in Halecki's mind that the rebirth of Greece and of the other Balkan states was an inspiration and encouragement for the nationalities "in the center of Europe." In a remarkable passage Halecki came to the defense of balkanization:

> The national states of the Balkan area, in which the long submerged nations of southeastern Europe regained their freedom and independence, represented an apparent triumph of self-determination—apparent only, because the great powers, after contributing to the liberation of the Christian peoples of the peninsula, continued to interfere with their difficult problems. The troubles which resulted from such a situation were soon used, as an argument against national self-determination. The loose talk about a threatening "Balkanization" of Europe by the creation of "new" small states was and is not only unfair to the Balkan nations—some of the oldest in Europe—but an obstacle to any unprejudiced approach to the claims for self-determination in the region north of the Balkans.[52]

The really interesting question is the difference between Halecki and the exponents of the Central European idea. There was a change in the political climate of the 1980s, which may have been reflected in the timing of the Central European idea. The events in Poland—the rise of Solidarity and the subsequent introduction of martial law without a Soviet invasion—signaled that Moscow was considering alternatives to its direct interference in the satellite countries. By that time, it was also clear that the treatment of the satellites was specific, something that prompted attempts at piecemeal emancipation. Indeed, when Halecki wrote his second book in 1963, he could only bitterly exclaim that "the liberation of the nations of East Central Europe is simply impossible in the present conditions without a war which most certainly would be a nuclear war involving all Europe and probably the world."[53] What a difference from the feelings that informed East European intellectuals in the 1980s which, although with little hope or foreboding that things would be resolved in the very near future, were nevertheless far removed from this apocalyptic vision. Yet it is not merely the political background that ultimately sets apart Halecki from the ideologues of the 1980s. Halecki was an ecumenical Christian thinker and was openly professing his interpretation of history on behalf of a united Christianity. He also had a subtle understanding of the character of Orthodoxy and was unquestionably opposed to polemic reductionism and to the exclusion of the Orthodox nations from Europe. With him, one can still appreciate Anatole France's famous aphorism: "Catholicism is still the most acceptable form of religious indifference."

The 1980s, on the other hand, brought a different attitude toward Islam, or rather toward what was permissible to be said about Islam. The irony is that the completely (or for the most part) secular zealots of the Central European idea, who have no grand visions but function essentially within a framework of national, or at the very most, regional interests, are waving the banner of religious intolerance *within* Christianity and are essentializing religious differences of which they know but little. At the same time, they have excellently internalized the cultural code of politically correct liberalism. What has changed radically from Halecki's days is that one cannot profess without impunity the complete otherness of Islam. Gone are the days when even Russian liberals convincingly "bolstered Russia's claim to 'Europeanness' by contrasting it to the barbarous Turk."[54] This is already unacceptable for the new generation, which has to show it has overcome Christian prejudice and which, in a move to overcome the legacy of anti-Semitism, has added and internalized the new attribute to the roots of Western culture: Judeo-Christian. One wonders how long it will take before we begin speaking about the Judeo-Christian-Muslim tradition and roots of European culture.

Therefore, the Central Europe of the 1980s was not simply the latest incarnation of a debate going back to the 1950s. The debate of the 1980s was a new phenomenon with different motivations and goals. This explains why it was news for Soviet writers at the time: when in May 1988, at the meeting of Central European and Soviet writers in Lisbon, György Konrád challenged his Soviet colleagues with the question: "You have to confront yourself with the role of your country in a part of the world that doesn't want your presence in tanks but as tourists" and triggered a heated debate. Tatyana Tolstaya answered in amazement, "When am I going to take *my* tanks out of Eastern Europe?" and added that "this was the first she had ever heard of Central Europeans speaking of their culture as something separate from that of the Soviet Union."[55] Larry Wolff has remarked that the Enlightenment idea of Eastern Europe, which was perpetuated in the West in the next two centuries, presupposed neither its definitive exclusion nor its unqualified inclusion.[56] In this perception, the Balkans were an integral part, and it is only in the last decades that a real attempt at their exclusion is taking place. By the end of the 1980s, the argument for an intrinsic difference between Eastern and Central Europe had already taken shape and was internalized by a considerable number of intellectuals. The last article in the Schöpflin/Wood collection squarely dealt with the question "Does Central Europe Exist?" Writing in 1986, Timothy Garton Ash chose to analyze three authors as representative of their countries: Havel, Michnik, and Konrád. With his usual brilliancy as essayist, Ash explored the meaning of the concept as it emerged from voices from Prague and Budapest, rather than from Warsaw. He pointed to an important semantic division between the use of "Eastern Europe" and "Central Europe" in Havel and Konrád. The first was used invariably in a negative or neutral context; the second was always "positive, affirmative or downright sentimental." For all his sympathy with the Central European *Zivilisationsliteraten*, Ash's acute analytical pen could not but comment on the mythopoetic tendency of the idea:

> [T]he inclination to attribute to the Central European past what you hope will characterize the Central European future, the confusion of what should be with what was—is rather typical of the new Central Europeanism. We are to understand that what was *truly* 'Central European' was always Western, rational, humanistic, democratic, skeptical and tolerant. The rest was 'East European', Russian, or possibly German. Central Europe takes all the 'Dichter und Denker', Eastern Europe is left with the 'Richter und Henker'.[57]

Still, for Ash: "The myth of the pure Central European past is perhaps a good myth." His most interesting observation was the apartness of Poland: Michnik himself had never talked of Central Europe and Milosz's Central Europeanness was more attributed than professed, "emotionally, culturally, and even geo-politically the view eastward is still at least equally important to most Poles," "Poland is to Central Europe as Russia is to Europe." Exploring some of the similarities between the 'national' contributions to Central Europeanness (the shared belief in antipolitics, the importance assigned to consciousness and moral changes, the power of "civil society," the partiality for nonviolence), Ash found many more differences that made him exclaim in an exasperated manner whether it was "no more than a side product of shared powerlessness." His final verdict on the Central European idea was that "it is just that: an idea. It does not yet exist," and that its program was "a programme for intellectuals." In his evocative ending, Ash refers to the Russian poet Natalya Gorbanevskaya, who had told him that George Orwell was an East European. Having accepted the idea of Eastern Europe *in acta*, Central Europe *in potentia*, Ash added: "Perhaps we would now say that Orwell was a Central European. If this is what we mean by 'Central Europe', I would apply for citizenship."[58]

In the meantime, Eastern Europe *in acta* ceased to exist (while nobody from the West applied for citizenship either before or after), but it inaugurated a third round in the development of the Central European idea after 1990 when it made its entry from the cultural into the political realm. It also marked for the first time the entry of the Balkans as an entity in the argumentation. This period spelled the end of antipolitics; politics was on the agenda. György Konrád had precipitously declared before, "No thinking person should want to drive others from positions of power in order to occupy them for himself. I would not want to be a minister in any government whatever," and Havel had spoken of "anti-political politics" and against the overestimation of the importance of direct political work in the traditional sense, that is, as seeking power in the state.[59] This chapter was over. Now, one could begin exploring the Central European idea not only in thought but also in action.

One of the first to make the pragmatic jump was Ash himself. In his 1986 piece, he never explored the potential exclusiveness of the Central European idea because he accepted it as an intellectual utopia, the realm of "intellectual responsibility, integrity, and courage."[60] However, early on in the years of the painful efforts of East European societies at transformation, he lobbied for the acceptance of *part* of Eastern Europe in the institutional framework of Western Europe, although he was sensitive enough to promote his plea for no more than what it was: a pragmatic answer to a political challenge:

> Yet where would this leave the rest of post-Communist Europe? Bulgaria, Romania, Slovenia, and Croatia, Lithuania, Latvia, and Estonia, to name but a few, all also want to "return to Europe." And by "Europe" they, too, mean first and foremost the EC. The first, pragmatic answer must be that the EC simply cannot do everything at once. It makes plain, practical sense to start with those that are nearest, and work out to those which are farthest. Poland, Hungary, and Czechoslovakia are nearest not only geographically, historically, and culturally, but also in the progress they have already made on the road to democracy, the rule of law, and a market economy.[61]

The post-1989 world gave the Central European idea for the first time the chance to actualize itself as a region-building opportunity. Despite the Visegrád fanfare and the series of summit meetings, concrete cooperation failed to materialize. Kristian

Gerner observed that "the liberation from Pax Sovietica 1989–1990 revealed that there did not exist any 'Central Europe,'" Dušan Třestik wrote that "we rather feel like poor but still respectable Almosteuropeans and only some, for whom begging is unbefitting, are poor but proud Centraleuropeans," Adam Krzemiński added that "every under-dog wants to be at the center," and Péter Hának published a bitter essay about the danger of burying Central Europe prematurely.[62]

In 1993, György Konrád wrote an ardent supplication *Central Europe Redivivus*. The essayistic genre gives ample opportunity for a happy combination of analytical vigor with emotive power. Konrád exhibited only the latter. Central Europe "was, is, and probably will continue to be"; it existed, Konrád maintained, just like the Balkans, the Middle East, and the Commonwealth of Independent States. It was defined as the small nations between two large ones: Germany and Russia; thus expropriating of its Central European nature the country that used to be its embodiment: Germany. But, then, a Central Europe without Germans and Jews had been the dream, and has be-come the achievement of many groups of Central Europeans.[63] Konrád also emerged as a major theoretician on ethnic civil wars and provided their most concise defini-tion, rivaling Stalin's definition of the nation: "An ethnic civil war requires a check-ered array of ethnic groups, a mountainous terrain, a long tradition of guerilla war-fare, and a cult of the armed hero. Such a combination exists only in the Balkans." It is comforting to hear such reassurance for the rest of the world from someone charac-terized by his translator as an "exemplary Central European writer" next to Havel and implicitly as the greatest Hungarian writer, and described unassumingly by himself in a self-introduction in the third person singular as: "K. . . . a fifty-year-old novelist and essayist. . . . His wardrobe is modest, though he has several typewriters."[64]

The ideal of intellectual solidarity in the region all but disappeared: immedi-ately after 1989, intellectuals from the former Soviet block countries had decided to publish a journal called *East-East* to deal with problems of postcommunist East-Central European societies, to come out in all the languages of the region. The names in the editorial board included Adam Michnik, Marcin Krul, Milan Šimečka, Ferenc Fehér, Richard Wagner, Dobroslaw Matejka, Andrej Cornea, Anca Oroveanu, Eva Karadi, Evgeniya Ivanova, Ivan Krîstev, and others, but the journal was published only in Bulgarian. The rest did not want to participate in a dialogue with the East; in fact, they did not want to have anything to do with the East. The denial of over four de-cades of common existence is understandable, but it nevertheless breeds the particu-larism and parochialism of much of today's Central European discourse. No wonder that one of the most exciting postmodernist accounts of the political aesthetic of communism was written recently by a Bulgarian, who was concerned with the ontol-ogy of the modernist impulse that produced the greatest (and failed) social experi-ment of the twentieth century, rather than with the Manichaean implications of the East-West dichotomy.[65]

Iver Neumann has argued that despite the failure of an institutionalized Central European framework, the Central European project "could still be used politically vis-à-vis Western Europe and Russia" as a moral appeal and reproach addressed to Western Europe.[66] Indeed, at this point it has stepped down as an accessory to the Central European intellectual discourse, and is to be found increasingly in political supplications. This is most evident in the drive to enter NATO and the institutional framework of the European Union. The argumentation is usually based on two pillars: the affinity of Central Europe to the European system of values and the exploitation of the ominous threat of a possible takeover in Russia by imperialist, chauvinist, antidemocratic, and antimarket forces. In this context, Central Europeanness became a device entitling its participants to a share of privileges. President Havel argued:

> If . . . NATO is to remain functional, it cannot suddenly open its doors to anyone at all. . . . The Czech Republic, Hungary, Poland and Slovakia—and Austria and Slovenia as well—clearly belong to the western sphere of European civilization. They espouse its values and draw on the same traditions. . . . Moreover, the contiguous and stable Central European belt borders both on the traditionally agitated Balkans and the great Eurasian area, where democracy and market economies are only slowly and painfully breaking away toward their fulfillment. In short, it is a key area for European security.[67]

Again the Balkans were evoked as the constituting other to Central Europe alongside Russia. The reason for this was the annoying proclivity to treat Eastern Europe as an inseparable entity. Scholars who want to trace structural changes in the newly emerging democracies of the former Warsaw Pact prefer to pursue their analysis in the framework of the whole of Eastern Europe: "although it is often useful to distinguish between an East-Central Europe and the Balkans, the main arguments . . . allow a collective reference to Eastern Europe."[68] Scholars' blunders may be annoying, but more painful was the European Union's decision to treat the emerging democracies in a package deal: as of 1 February 1995, the association agreements of the Czech Republic, Slovakia, Romania, and Bulgaria (which joined the earlier admitted Poland and Hungary) with the European Union went into effect. This *en groupe* treatment annoyed the Czechs, who lately want to go it alone. In an interview published in *Der Spiegel* on 13 February 1995, Havel said that for the Czech Republic admission to NATO was more urgent than joining the EU. If the West accepts that certain, particularly Central European, countries belong to the Russian sphere of influence and thus should not be allowed to join NATO, Europe is heading to a "new Yalta," Havel warned. One would suppose that the logical alternative to this is that if these "particular Central European countries" were admitted to NATO, but the rest were relegated to the Russian sphere of influence, a "new Yalta" would be avoided. If the notion of a *limes* between the civilized west and "les nouveau barbares" is accepted as unavoidable, the question is where exactly should the *limes* run. For someone like Ryszard Kapuscinski, there is no hesitation: "the *limes* normally drawn in Eastern Europe is the frontier between the Latin and Cyrillic alphabet."[69] It is a rule that any social perception (of an out-group by an in-group) tends to construct differences along dichotomic lines. But it is only the degree of institutionalization of these perceptions, or their relative importance and strength for the collective whole, which perpetuates them and makes them potentially explosive.

Havel's pronouncement could be approached calmly as simply a rhetorical device in a lobbying effort. After all, he himself had forsaken his purist stance toward practical politics and was arguing that intellectuals had a responsibility to engage in politics. Ironically, this reasoning echoed much of the argumentation of the former communist regimes in their (not unsuccessful) attempts to co-opt intellectuals: "I asked once a friend of mine, a wonderful man and a wonderful writer, to fill a certain political post. He refused, arguing that someone had to remain independent. I replied that if you all said that, it could happen that in the end, no one will be independent, because there won't be anyone around to make that independence possible and stand behind it."[70] On the other hand, Havel's advocacy on the part of Central Europe leaves an aftertaste of innocence lost. One aspect of this concerns his motivation and former stature. Havel is a believer in the power of words: "events in the real world, whether admirable or monstrous, always have their prologue in the realm of words." He himself traced the mystery and perfidy of words as they had been used in Lenin, Marx, Freud, and Christ. One is tempted to apply to his own position his warning about "the consequences that transcend the nonmaterial world and penetrate deeply a world that is all too material," especially as his words nowadays are consecrated by his new prominence. For all his unmatched stature as a dissident writer, Havel's words before 1989 were living and revered almost exclusively among fellow intellectuals in Eastern Europe and a stray intellectual or two in the West. Only now, anointed by his political rank, has he become a favored subject for name-droppers in political circles in the West but, alongside other former East European dissidents, he has lost his exulted stature among disillusioned or simply weary Eastern intellectuals.[71]

Indeed, one can already trace how these words are readily taken up by shapers of public opinion. The *Chicago Tribune*, emulating Churchill's Fulton speech, made the following solemn statement: "A new curtain is falling across eastern Europe, dividing north from south, west from east, rich from poor and the future from the past. As Hungary, Poland and the Czech Republic sprint into the future of democracy and market economics, Romania and Bulgaria slide into Balkan backwardness and second-class citizenship in the new Europe."[72] Ernest Gellner could not resist a wisecrack when speaking of the Balkans as the third time zone of Europe, clearly but safely intimating or prophesying their Third World status in Europe.[73] However, the Central European countries are called Central European only when something positive is meant. When not, there is a reversal to the notion of Eastern Europe. Thus, when Paul Hockenos covered the rise of the Right and anti-Semitism in Germany, Poland, Hungary, the Czech Republic, and Romania, he preferred to subsume them in a larger Eastern Europe, although the rest of this Eastern Europe was not partaking in these developments.[74] Besides, to this day the Czech Republic, as befits a litigious Western democracy, is the only Central European (and, indeed, the only Eastern European country) that has introduced discriminatory legislation aimed against its Gypsy population.[75]

William Safire, in a fresh cold-war piece, decided magnanimously to extend NATO's umbrella to the courageous Baltics and Ukraine "which cannot be consistently excluded." The Balkans, in contrast, appear only as the epitome of Western failure. Even though he made fun of the shifting nomenclature of Eastern and Central Europe, he asked the obvious commonsense question: "if Poland is part of Central Europe, shouldn't it be allowed in NATO sooner than if in Eastern Europe?"[76] Robert Kaplan, after having demonized the Balkans, sought to resew them, together with the Near East, into a post-Ottoman world, and urged the appropriate construction of American foreign policy: "Turkey, the Balkans and the Middle East . . . are reemerging as one region—what historically minded Europeans have always referred to as the greater 'Near East'. The former Ottoman Empire and even the former Byzantine world are fusing back together following the aberration of the cold war."[77] Kaplan is, of course, no European, even less so a historically minded European, otherwise he would be wary of using so categorically the nonhistorical "always." While his vision reflects definite political interests, it is hardly realistic.

Religion as culture is entering increasingly the vocabulary of political journalism. As late as March 1995, the *New York Times* had the nerve to run an editorial claiming that "Washington's best hope is to appeal to predominantly Roman Catholic Croatia's longstanding desire to extricate itself from Balkan conflicts and associate itself more closely to the West"[78] as if it was not precisely in the name of this Roman Catholic Croatia that some of the most gruesome crimes in the Balkans were committed during World War II and whose present leadership, alongside with Slobodan Milošević, and other internal and external politicians besotted with nationalism and the new orthodoxy of self-determination, have singularly contributed to the present Yugoslav, not Balkan, quagmire.

One may have legitimate doubts about the influence of journalistic writing on policy making, but when journalists themselves concede that "lacking any clear strategic vision of their own, governments appear to be at the mercy of the latest press reports" and that "the president of the United States backed away from military action after reading a book called *Balkan Ghosts*,"[79] there is ample reason for concern. The rhetorical device clearly took on political operativeness when former Secretary of State Lawrence Eagleburger made the same political point without the guise of a seemingly sophisticated discussion of Western values. Addressing the responsibilities and credibility of NATO in connection with the Bosnian crisis, he stated that the organization should be very much alive and should include Poland, Hungary, and the Czech Republic "so that there is a clear message who should be in and who out."[80] The operativeness of the poignant discourse on the Balkans when the future of Europe is discussed, with the prospects of the overexpansion of European institutions endangering the exclusiveness of the privileged club, becomes intelligible only in the light of the agency of this "clear message." Eagleburger was joined by Henry Kissinger, who pleaded for an immediate expansion of NATO to extend membership to the Visegrad countries. Later, Kissinger decided that Slovakia was dispensable and appealed to the administration to support the inclusion only of Poland, Hungary, and the Czech Republic.[81]

Richard Holbrooke, on the other hand, was extremely cautious not to overcommit his administration. There were at present three wings of the security architecture in Europe: the West (which more or less coincided with NATO), Central Europe, and Russia. In this architectural vision, Russia was becoming Eastern Europe and the Balkans, although not explicitly stated, were subsumed under "the fifteen countries of Central Europe." However, when it came to the expansion of NATO into Central Europe, the only countries mentioned were the Visegrad four, and a formula was used for the "Partnership for Peace" arrangement that clearly indicated the lines of differentiation: it was defined as comprising 25 countries with individual programs, of which some were to enter NATO, whereas for others the partnership was to be an end in itself.[82] Or, as the British journalist Charles Moore recently stated in *The Spectator*: "Britain is basically English-speaking, Christian, and white. . . . Just as we want to bring

Poles, and Hungarians, and Russians slowly into the EEC, and open markets for their goods, so we should try to open our doors to their people. . . . Muslims and blacks, on the other hand, should be kept out strictly as at present."[83] In the prophetic vision of Sami Nair:

> There are two ways, only two ways: either confessionalism will win and everywhere in Europe community ghettoes will be erected (as would follow from Pope John Paul II's sermon on the conquest of Christian Europe), and in this sense democracy will be the inevitable casualty; or Europe will modernize its democratic alliance, it will enforce its republican model, based this time not on the unconscious emulation of the papist-caesarean model, but guaranteed by a concrete humanistic universalism.[84]

Speaking of the Judeo-Christian-Muslim tradition and roots of European culture is not such a paradoxical notion. It could mean the opening up of Europe and the recognition of its rich and variable roots; on the other hand, it could mean the selective appropriation of traits that are then determined to be part of the European, respectively Western tradition. The first option has had some modest success; the second has had a rich tradition. While the beginnings of Western thought usually lead to Egypt, Mesopotamia, India, and the Hebrew Bible, the social and political bodies in which these traditions have been developed have been neatly relegated to a different, third, world. The part of Europe that was first and exclusively bearing this name (the ancient Greeks called "Europe" the Balkan mainland beyond the islands) has been stripped of it and bequeathed at best with a modifier—southeastern—in a purely geographic context, and at worst with the *Schimpfwört* Balkan and without the modifier European in almost any other discourse. It is not difficult to anticipate how Islamic traditions can become cleansed of their historical reality and elevated to adorn the tiara of European/Western Tolerance in an act of self-crowning.

Back to the Central European idea, Arthur Schnitzler had once remarked that "the things which are most often mentioned do not actually exist."[85] He was speaking of love. But there is no love lost in Central Europe and the competition to be the first to enter Europe dealt a blow on the Central European project itself: "the program of Havel the participant in the debate about 'Central Europe' was thwarted by, among others, Havel the president."[86] Václav Klaus, Václav Havel's less poetic, more realistic, and more successful political counterpart, angrily rejected the institutionalization of cooperation among the Visegrad group as an alternative to Czech membership in the European community and said that "any concept of the group as a poor man's club and buffer zone to keep the Balkans and the former Soviet Union at a safe distance from Western Europe" was unacceptable.[87] The transformation of the Central European concept from an emancipatory idea to a politically expedient tool was accompanied by a parallel transformation of the concept of Europe from a cultural definition identified with liberalism and democracy into "the international solidarity of capital against poverty."[88]

To summarize, the third round in the development of the Central European idea after 1990 witnessed its entry from the politics of culture into political praxis. Far from becoming a region-building notion, it was harnessed as an expedient argument in the drive for entry into the European institutional framework. It is during this stage that the Balkans first appeared as a dichotomical opponent, sometimes alongside with, sometimes indistinguishable from Russia. This internal hierarchization of Eastern Europe was born out of political expediency but in its rhetoric it feeds on the balkanist discourse. After all, it is not symbolic geography that creates politics, but rather the reverse.

There are two strategies that one can pursue. One would entail the analytical critique of the line of division as conceived by the Central European idea: to take up the challenge of the Central European identity as an apodictic concept. For all its attractions as polemic, this is an exercise in disproving and repudiating, but "myth is beyond truth and falsity." It is the pragmatic function of myth that should be the focus of attention and it requires a closer look not only into the motives of its creators but also into the quality of the recipients, because "the effectiveness of myth depends in large measure upon ignorance or unconsciousness of its actual motivation."[89] But it is not enough to expose the Central European myth as insidious, or its attempt to contrast itself to the Balkans as invidious. The other strategy would consider the problem of the nature of the Balkans, its ontology and perception, and compare it to the Central European idea. Juxtaposing the notion of Central Europe as an idea with its short-term cultural/political potential to the concept of the Balkans with its powerful historical and geographic basis, but with an equally limited although much longer historical span, one can argue that the two concepts are methodologically incomparable, and therefore incompatible constructs.

The Balkans
Realia—Qu'est-ce qu'il y a de hors-texte?

And yet, if the Balkans were no more than horror, why is it, when we leave them and make for this part of the world, why is it we feel a kind of fall—an admirable one, it is true—into the abyss?[1]

Emil Cioran

The volume *In Search of Central Europe* ended with Timothy Garton Ash's essay entitled "Does Central Europe Exist?" No such question can be posed for the Balkans. There is no doubt in anybody's mind that the Balkans exist. Even *Cultural Literacy*, the 1988 national best-seller, included among its 5,000 essential names, phrases, dates, and concepts the noun "Balkans" and the verb "to balkanize," neatly flanked by "balance of power, balance of terror, balance sheet, Balboa," and "ballad, ballerina, ballet, ballistic missile."[2] This is telling, given the fact that Professor E. D. Hirsch, Jr., was not overgenerous with geographic notions. All European states were included, among them all Balkan states at the time of writing: Albania, Bulgaria, Greece, Romania, and Yugoslavia. There were some technical omissions: for example, Turkey was missing (instead there was the song "Turkey in the Straw"), but the Ottoman Empire was in, as was Istanbul, the Bosporus, and the Black Sea. Although it was an oversight, one cannot help wondering about a psychological slip in omitting two Central European states: Poland and Austria. It goes without saying that geographical entities like Eastern or Western Europe, let alone Central Europe, were not in the list. The Balkans, however, were in, much before the world even surmised that it would witness the tragedy of Yugoslavia generalized by the West as a Balkan conflict, a Balkan war, a Balkan tragedy.

If for Central Europe, like for the Orient, one can play with the Derridian "il n'y a pas de hors-texte," the appropriate question for the Balkans is "qu'est-ce qu'il y a de hors-texte?" What, then, are the Balkans?

A survey of the different historical legacies that have shaped the southeast European peninsula would usually begin with the period of Greek antiquity when the city-states colonized the littoral and slowly expanded into the hinterland; followed by the short Hellenistic period when part of the Balkans was united under Macedonian rulers; the Roman period when the whole peninsula was incorporated into the

Roman Empire and, for the first time, was politically united. Although during the subsequent period of the Byzantine millennium the peninsula was politically fragmented, it secured a cultural entity if not political unity, with the spread of Christianity in its Greek Orthodox version from Constantinople, the adaptation of Roman law among the Slavs, the influence of Byzantine literature and art, in a word, the emulation of Byzantine cultural and political models. It is during this period that linguists place the beginning of the "Balkan linguistic union."[3] The Ottoman conquest that gave the peninsula its name established the longest period of political unity that the region has experienced. Although the century following the retreat of the Ottomans witnessed the new political fragmentation of the peninsula, its constituents experienced the same waves of economic, social, and cultural integration into Europe, where the Balkans invariably held a peripheral status.[4] During the past half-century the cold-war line effectively divided the Balkans, and its members functioned within the framework of two, and maybe three political frameworks, if the Yugoslav experience is to be granted its neutral state. Forty-five years of isolated common life in a maybe *mésaliance*, but nevertheless marriage, have left their imprint. This is not a commonality historically as long, and arguably not as profound, as the Habsburg, Ottoman, or imperial Russian, and one might expect that its marks will wither sooner; it is, however, a commonality of only yesterday with the generations who lived it still alive.

In this sequence of historical legacies, the most important for our purposes was the one that left its name on the peninsula; it would not be exaggerated to say that the Balkans are the Ottoman legacy. This in no way underestimates the profound effects of the Byzantine legacy and the concomitant discourse of "byzantinism," which not only functions alongside and on the same principles as "balkanism," but is often superimposed on it. This is especially the case with the treatment of Orthodoxy, where long-standing medieval prejudices are revived and combined with cold-war rhetoric and post–cold war rivalries, a problem that deserves separate attention and thoughtful study. Yet it is the Ottoman elements (often including Byzantine ones) or the ones perceived as such that are mostly invoked in the current stereotype of the Balkans.

There are two main interpretations of the Ottoman legacy. One has it that it was a religiously, socially, institutionally, and even racially alien imposition on autochthonous Christian medieval societies (Byzantine, Bulgarian, Serbian, and so on).[5] The central element of this interpretation is based on the belief in the incompatibility between Christianity and Islam, between the essentially nomadic civilization of the newcomers and the old urban and settled agrarian civilizations of the Balkans and the Near East. Most nineteenth-century European assessments and most assessments emanating from within Balkan historiography are based on this belief.[6]

This view in its extremes has been dispelled from serious scholarly works, but is often unconsciously reproduced in what can be described as the mechanical (or separate spheres) approach, that is, the attempts to decompose the legacy into its supposed constituent elements: language, music, food, architecture, art, dress, administrative traditions, political institutions, and so on. Within this approach, no matter whether the research comes from the Balkans, Turkey, or outside the region, Ottoman becomes synonymous with Islamic or Turkish (and to a lesser extent Arabic and Persian) influences in different spheres, usually subsumed under the heading Oriental elements. This mechanistic division in otherwise excellent but usually exclusively empirical works is brought about by methodological constraints and lack of a theoretical framework, rather than deliberate attempts at isolating constituent elements. Within the Balkan historiographical tradition, which insists on the existence of distinct and incompatible local/indigenous and foreign/Ottoman spheres, the danger lies not so much in overemphasizing "the impact of the West" and overlooking continuities and indigenous institutions, but rather in separating artificially "indigenous" from "Ottoman" institutions and influences.

This interpretation of the Ottoman period in the Balkans, however flawed, has a certain rationale behind it. It rests on the not so erroneous perception of segregation of the local Christian population. For all justified objections to romanticized heartbreaking assessments of Christian plight under the "infidel" Turk, the Ottoman Empire was first and foremost an Islamic state with a strict religious hierarchy where non-Muslims occupied the backseats. While this statement can be refined as to degrees of validity in different periods, there hardly seems to be a serious objection to its overall relevance;"the comprehensiveness of Islam—the bedrock of the Ottoman social system" can be interpreted as an idiom whose "operational rules were shared by many Ottomans of both low and high status."[7] Islam formed a vertical self-sufficient space within Ottoman society that was not coterminous with the whole population of the Ottoman Empire. But it is not only the strict division on religious lines that prevented the possible integration, except in cases of conversion.

At no time, but especially in the last two centuries, was the Ottoman Empire a country with strong social cohesiveness or with a high degree of social integration. Not only was there no feeling of belonging to a common society but the population felt it belonged to disparate (religious, social, or other) groups that would not converge. This is not meant as an evaluative statement—in other words, it can be translated simply as meaning that the Ottoman state until well into the nineteenth century was a supranational (or, better, nonnational) empire with strong medieval elements, where the bureaucracy seems to have been the only common institution linking, but not unifying, all the populace. That the Ottoman Empire did not create an integrated society is beyond doubt; what some Balkan historians seem not to want to understand is that this empire did not necessarily strive to achieve such integration, let alone assimilation.

Once embarked on efforts to attain self-identity, the emerging Balkan nations tried to delineate boundaries between themselves and their rulers. This was done in a framework and a rhetoric—the national—inherently incongruous with the imperial principle, but more importantly, the dominant discourse in Europe. It was a national idea based mostly on ethnicity, with a strong linguistic core. In this light, the belated attempt to forge a common Ottoman identity based on citizenship after the middle of the nineteenth century was a utopian experiment doomed at the outset.[8] What is important is that the alienation long predated the disintegration of the empire, and is thus a systemic element of the Ottoman past. The question to be debated is not whether it did exist but how strong it was in different periods, and what parts of the population it encompassed. Whereas for modern Turkey and the Middle East, the Ottoman legacy can be considered organic (despite vehemently negative assessments), in the Balkans the persistent attempt to depict it as alien is based on more than mere emotional or political conjecture. While the Ottoman period has consistently been the ancien régime for Republican Turkey, this is much more complicated in the circumstances of the Balkans from the eighteenth to the twentieth century. Analytically, it is also the ancien régime but, based on the specific position of Christianity in a Muslim empire, it was constructed and perceived almost exclusively as foreign domination or, in the irreformable language of the region, as the Ottoman *yoke*.

This brings in a completely different framework of assessment: that of struggles for national emancipation and the creation of nation-states that are not only complete and radical breaks with the past, but its negation. To some extent this element holds true also for the Turks (and to a greater degree for the Arabs), but in the Balkan case the break was facilitated and made effective by the existing double boundary of language and religion, the two central foci around which Balkan ethnicity and nationalism was constructed. Whereas Islam provided an important link to the Ottoman past in both Turkish and Arabic cases, language served as an important delineator for the Arabs. It took Kemal Atatürk's political genius to realize the centrality of language in the transmission and reproduction of traditions and to strike decisively with his language reform.[9]

The second interpretation treats the Ottoman legacy as the complex symbiosis of Turkish, Islamic, and Byzantine/Balkan traditions. Its logical premise is the circumstance that several centuries of coexistence cannot but have produced a common legacy, and that the history of the Ottoman state is the history of all its constituent populations (notwithstanding religious, social, professional, and other divisions). The facts underlying this interpretation are the early syncretism in the religious, cultural, and institutional spheres, the remarkable absorptive capacity of the conquerors, as well as the high degree of multiligualism until the end of the empire. The Orthodox church that, in the first interpretation, has been depicted as the only genu-ine institution of the conquered and subject peoples of the Balkans, as a preserver of religion, language, and local traditions, can be successfully seen, in the second interpretation, as quintessentially Ottoman. It benefited from the imperial dimensions of the state, and its ecumenical character and policies are comprehensible only in an Ottoman framework. It is symptomatic that the secession of the emerging nations meant also an almost simultaneous secession from the Constantinople patriarchate, that is, from the Orthodox church of the Ottoman Empire.

It is interesting to speculate whether the success of the imperial venture and the power of its bureaucracy in the first centuries of Ottoman expansion did not command to some extent the loyalties of the Balkan population or, at least, hindered their complete alienation. There is good reason to believe this was the case. Even the controversial *devşirme* (the periodic Christian child levy that effectively filled administrative posts and especially the Janissary corps) and the ambiguous attitudes it generated can be seen, aside from questions of motivation, as an integrative mechanism. The emotionally burdened question of conversions to Islam can also be approached in this light. They started immediately after the arrival of the Ottomans and continued until the nineteenth century, but the crucial period fell in the seventeenth century. Although there were obvious cases of enforced conversions, the majority fell in the category of nonenforced ones, euphemistically called voluntary, the result of indirect economic and social, but not administrative, pressure. Stimulated primarily by the desire to achieve a distinct social recategorization, in the end they offered the possibility for some kind of integration. This is certainly more than can be said about the conversions of Orthodox peasants to Protestantism in Transylvania, which offered no social or political advantages. It can be better compared to conversions to Catholicism or the Uniate church, most of which also occurred during the seventeenth century as a result of the missionary zeal of the Vatican.

As with the first, the second organic interpretation also has its caveats. One of them is the approach that focuses exclusively on the continuity from the Byzantine period, thus trivializing the Ottoman phenomenon, as was done in Iorga's famous and influential work.[10] Although Iorga's theory may be today no more than an exotic episode in the development of Balkan historiography, his formulation *Byzance après Byzance* is alive not only because it was a fortunate phrase but because it reflects more than its creator would intimate. It is a good descriptive term, particularly for representing the commonalites of the Orthodox peoples in the Ottoman Empire in religion, private law, music, and the visual arts, but also in emphasizing the continuity of two imperial traditions where the cultural fracture delineated by the advent of nationalism might have been more profound, and in any case intellectually more radical, than the one brought in with the Ottoman conquest. At the same time, both interpretations, when cleansed of their emotional or evaluative overtones, can be articulated in a moderate and convincing fashion. The preference for either is dictated not only by philosophical or political predispositions, but also by methodological considerations.

It seems that in the macrohistorical domain (economics, demography, and social structure, and other phenomena of *longue durée* nature) the organic interpretation is more relevant, but it is not entitled to exclusive validity. Some long-term developments in the religious and cultural sphere, as well as the history of institutions, seem to be more adequately explained within the separate-spheres approach. Likewise, in the microhistorical sphere (political history, biography, art, and literary history), both interpretations can be evoked. Figures like the famous mystic and revolutionary Şeyh Bedreddin Simavi, who preached the union of Islam, Christianity, and Judaism in the early fifteenth century; the conqueror of Constantinople, Sultan Mehmed II Fatih; the Serbian-born grand vizier Mehmed Sokolović, who had risen within the *devşirme* and successfully served three consecutive sultans at the time of the greatest Ottoman expansion; the Moldavian prince Dimitrie Cantemir, an accomplished diplomat, the first modern historian of the Ottoman Empire, and a renowned figure of the Enlightenment; and even figures of the "nationalist" eighteenth and nineteenth centuries like the great Greek patriot and revolutionary Rhigas Velestinlis, who had been in phanariote service in the Danubian principalities and provided an all-Balkan vision for the future of the peninsula; or the prominent Ottoman reformer and father of the first Ottoman constitution, Midhat paşa, can be understood and described only within the organic approach, although it is possible and imperative to distinguish between dominant and less important traditions in the shaping of their outlook and activities, and in the extent of their influence on different groups. Yet other cases warrant a predominantly separate-spheres interpretation like Aşikpaşazade, the fifteenth-century chronicler; Veisî, the brilliant author of the acclaimed *Habname*; Kâtib Celebi, the greatest polyhistor of the Ottomans; Father Paisii, the fiery monk and author of the much influential *Slavo-Bulgarian History*; Dositey Obradović, the remarkable Serb writer and promoter of South Slav unity; Adamandios Korais, the prominent figure of the Greek political and intellectual Enlightenment. These examples can be continued ad infinitum.

The two approaches do not pretend to exhaust or put in a procrustean bed the possible ways of interpreting phenomena and especially individual historical actors in the framework of the Ottoman Empire. Depending on how research problems are formulated, they might even seem irrelevant. Opposed and even incompatible as they seem, they implicitly presuppose a monolithic entity that is either completely severed from the Ottoman legacy or else forming an organic part of it. This is certainly not the case, and concrete studies demonstrate the deep internal divisions within the respective spheres. The Balkan Enlightenment and the Balkan revolutionary traditions, for example, cannot be interpreted exclusively from the point of view of either of these approaches. They bring to the fore an additional, if not entirely new, vector that focuses on the influence of West European intellectual and socioeconomic developments and on the relationship of these developments with indigenous transformations.[11] The close cultural contacts with the West in the centuries following the Ottoman conquest were tangential to the life of the Balkan populations at large, but the movements of the Enlightenment were "linked from the outset with the incipient stirrings of modern nationalism in Southeastern Europe."[12] As formulated above, the two approaches only reflect the dominant lines of reasoning from the perspective of how phenomena and individuals are seen to be linked to or positioned vis-à-vis the Ottoman polity.

Both views have their rationale, and both have produced, within their own confined approach, works of great quality as well as works of ephemeral significance. What is essential is that these two interpretations of the Ottoman legacy are not merely possible scholarly reconstructions; they actually existed side by side throughout the Ottoman period. Although it was obviously the national discourse of the last two centuries that dramatically escalated the feeling of separateness, it by no means invented the separate-spheres approach: the two attitudes are clearly identifiable from the beginnings of the Ottoman Empire in Europe and, to ground them for example in late Byzantine assessments, one could speak of a Sphrantzes-Khalkokondyles-Doukas paradigm on the one hand, and a Kritoboulos paradigm on the other. Of course, given the character and scarcity of material, it is difficult, if not impossible to speculate about the relative weight of these outlooks. Even more difficult is it to hazard how deep, or whether at all, they had been diffused throughout society. With the risk of a simplified generalization, one could hypothesize that, as a whole, the first view was expounded by the outgoing aristocratic and clerical elites of the independent medieval states, and was later picked up in the national discourse by a substantial part of the new commercial and secular intellectual elites of the eighteenth and nineteenth centuries who not only felt alienated from, but severely hindered by, the Ottoman polity; whereas the second was shared by significant numbers of the newly created elites within the non-Muslim millets that were part and parcel of the Ottoman structure or had achieved an acceptable modus vivendi (high clergy, phanariotes, local notables, and so on).

As for the majority of the population, it was equally alienated from the pre-Ottoman as well as from the Ottoman polity and, in general, the socialization of entire populations and their organic integration into overarching state and other administrative structures is a late historical phenomenon, corresponding to the age of nationalism and mass culture. The degree of separateness was directly proportional to the strength and effectiveness with which the institutions embodying it—the Christian churches or the ulema with their religious and legal functions, that is, the millet system—encompassed these populations. At the same time, on the level of everyday life there occured a remarkable coexistence between the different ethnoreligious groups.

The works of the two *Weltanshauungen* (or *Ottomananschauungen*) can be traced even within the national discourse. One was represented by a group within the national movements that took a gradualist approach to the problem of emancipation within the empire. In the early nineteenth century, the Greek society "Filomousos Etaireia" set its priorities on education and believed in the peaceful penetration and subsequent transformation of the Ottoman Empire into a Greek state through the hegemony of the Greek commercial and cultural element. Likewise, in the 1860s and 1870s, significant strata of the Bulgarian commercial and educational elites espoused evolutionist convictions and saw the ideal future of Bulgaria as achieving administrative autonomy within a strong and reformed empire. Others advocated the creation of a dualist Turko-Bulgarian state, inspired by the Austro-Hungarian *Ausgleich*. This position of acquiring autonomy without breaking away from the empire was dominant among the Albanians, who not only became its strongest champions but staunchly supported it to the end. The attempts to explain these positions simply on the grounds of vested economic interests and social conservatism are unsatisfactory. While in the Greek case the strong motive was, among others, the preservation of the territorial unity of the Greek ethnic element and its *Kulturraum* with visions of a resurrected Byzantium, in the Albanian case one can discern, alongside the fear of encroachments of the newly formed neighboring nation-states, also a political affinity based on religion and the special status Albanians had acquired in the empire. Likewise, the creation of a Bulgarian elite in Istanbul, although far from occupying the privileged positions of the former phanariote circles, prompted the search for legalistic and nonradical solutions. This certainly is not an exhaustive analysis of the numerous visions and subtle differences existing within the national movements; the important issue is that there were groups who advocated the organic approach, no matter if prompted by political expedience.

It was, however, the revolutionary alternative of a complete break with the Ottoman Empire that in the long run "made history." This is not the place to take up the philosophical issue of determinism and counterfactual history. Suffice it to say that from the eighteenth and throughout the nineteenth century, "the nation-state was established as the *natural* model of political development and lodged as such in the ideology of both the Versailles Treaty and the League of Nations."[13] Although nationalism and the formation of nation-states in the Balkans can be viewed as contingent phenomena, it is doubtful whether in an atmosphere in which the national was imposed as the hegemonic paradigm in Europe, as the gold standard of "civilized" political organization, the imperial or any other alternative could be viable. Accordingly, the revolutionaries' attitude, although at the time espoused by what were seen as marginal and radical intellectuals, has become, in a period of nationalism, the Whig interpretation of history and, in the Balkan context, the exclusive approach.

There is another pair of opposing interpretations of the Ottoman legacy. One is that of the objectivist outsider whose central observation point is chronologically situated within the Ottoman period (usually at its end), and who takes a linear view following historical time: from the past to the present. This approach has produced the bulk of the historical literature dealing with the problem. When defining this approach as situating its initial observation point in the Ottoman period, this does not mean that the scholars employing it are either apologists for the Ottoman Empire or necessarily identifying with their subject matter. What seems to be common for all writers within this approach is the fact that they are operating on the premises that the Ottoman legacy can be objectively defined and that, even after the disintegration of the Ottoman Empire, there are elements that can be objectively analyzed in the different regions constituting the former Ottoman Empire. Thus, the Ottoman legacy would be the imprint left as a result of the cumulative effect of centuries of Ottoman rule at the end of the empire.

The other is the highly subjective insider's approach, chronologically situated in the present. In the sense of a complex unity and interplay of habits, attitudes, and beliefs that have been established and link a human community with the past, it can be defined as the evaluative and retrospective assessment of the Ottoman legacy from a present viewpoint. For purposes of clarity, a distinction will be made here between Ottoman legacy as continuity and Ottoman legacy as perception. Any legacy can be understood as something handed down and received from the past, that is, as historical continuities. This presupposes a distinct point when and after which a historical process can be rationalized as legacy. It also means that at different points the same unfolding process can be said to have produced different legacies. In this respect, the Ottoman legacy is not simply the bulk of characteristics accumulated from the fourteenth to the twentieth century, but a continuous and complex process, which ended during the nineteenth and early twentieth centuries. The moment at which this process ended and, thus, turned into a legacy bears first and foremost the characteristics of the historical situation of the eighteenth and nineteenth centuries. For all practical purposes, the Ottoman legacy here is treated as the cluster of historical continuities after the secession of the Balkan states from the Ottoman Empire.

Furthermore, the significant regional differences within the Ottoman Empire, not only between the Rumelian, Anatolian, or North African possessions but within the Balkans themselves, precludes attempts to speak of a unitary Ottoman legacy. How can the political legacy of the Ottoman Empire in the Romanian principalities, for example, be compared to the same legacy in Serbia or Bulgaria or Albania? How can the economic situation in the areas of large estates (Bosnia, Thessaly, Albania) be compared to areas of quasi-independent small proprietors in most of the rest of the Balkans? Obviously, when assessing the Ottoman legacy one has to run the delicate line between succumbing to overgeneralizations and reaching the truistic conclusion that one of the main characteristics of Ottoman rule and, thus, a central aspect of the Ottoman legacy was the great interregional variability. It follows that any detailed in-depth study of the Ottoman legacy would be probably best accomplished within a regional framework. On a more general level, the central problem in dealing with the Ottoman legacy is the question of continuity or break. The important subquestions are: (1) Which are the possible "spheres of influence" or continuities? (2) Is there and, if so, what is the Ottoman legacy today? (3) Is there a temporal watershed clearly marking the time after which the workings of the legacy as continuity are transformed into legacy as perception?

Beginning with the political sphere, in one of its important aspects, the formation of state boundaries, there were several contending factors: the Ottoman administrative tradition; the aspirations of the national movements based on two (quite often incompatible) criteria: historic rights and self-determination; and the strategic interests of the European powers who, as a whole, treated the Ottoman Empire as a pillar and the young Balkan states as a serious threat to the European balance of power. The internal Ottoman provincial divisions had followed closely the boundaries of the numerous Balkan principalities in the fourteenth and fifteenth centuries; in this respect they seem to provide a clear, though not immobile, continuity from the pre-Ottoman period (down to preserving the toponymy), a par excellence example of the Ottoman legacy as the complex product of local Balkan, Islamic, and Turkish components.[14] In some instances, internal provincial frontiers were turned into state boundaries (like the vassal provinces of Wallachia and Moldavia, or Albania and Montenegro). In other cases an administrative unit, the Belgrade paşalık, became the nucleus for the future Serbian nation-state.

Still, neither historic rights (based on the territorial zenith of the medieval Balkan states) nor issues of self-determination were, in the final account, instrumental in delineating frontiers. At the very most, these elements shaped the controversial and incompatible Balkan irredentist programs. The size, shape, stages of growth, even the very existence of the different Balkan states were almost exclusively regulated by great power considerations following the rules of the balance-of-power game. As Bismarck hastened to inform the Ottoman delegates at the Congress of Berlin in 1878: "If you think the Congress has met for Turkey, disabuse yourselves. San-Stefano would have remained unaltered, if it had not touched certain European interests."[15] The other Balkan delegates were not given even this attention but were completely ignored. Disregarding valuative judgements, the Treaty of Berlin fatefully determined the political development of the Balkans in the century to follow.

A case like Bosnia is at first glance the obvious candidate to illustrate the workings of the Ottoman legacy in the political field. It was one of the important administrative units (vilayets) within the empire formed on the basis of the medieval kingdom of Bosnia. Its complex religious/ethnic structure is comprehensible only within the Ottoman framework, although even in the pre-Ottoman period, different religions could peacefully coexist (the Christian Bosnian church, Catholicism, and Orthodoxy), and belonging to the dominant religion was not a necessary criterion for political status.[16] Yet, aside from the Ottoman legacy in the demographic sphere, the Bosnian problem as a political issue should not be attributed principally to the Ottoman legacy; instead, it has been the immediate result of great and small power considerations. It was upheld, as no-man's-land, not because of the precarious mixture of its population, but because first Austro-Hungary was looking for an outpost in the Balkans, and later, because its quasi independence served to prevent the upsetting of a power balance between Serbs and Croats.

The case of Albania can be argued in a similar line of reasoning. Albania was not a clear-cut secessionist case like all other Balkan nations. The reason for this was the special status of the Albanians in the Ottoman Empire and their comparatively later effort to attain cultural autonomy. By the first decade of the twentieth century, when their movement for emancipation had gained considerable momentum, they had become the object of expansionist aims on the part of their already independent neighbors. Thus, while chronologically its birth coincided with the passing away of the Ottoman Empire, Albania's struggle for survival and its irredenta developed against other Balkan nations, particularly Serbia and Greece. It was, however, first and foremost the pressure of Austro-Hungary and Italy that guaranteed Albania's independent existence.

The Ottoman legacy in the political sphere (as far as foreign policy and the question of boundaries are concerned) chronologically spans from the beginning of autonomous or independent statehood in the Balkans until World War I, which marked the end of the political presence of the Ottomans in the Balkans. Thus, the workings of the Ottoman political legacy lasted from a few decades to almost a century for the different regions (with the exception of Albania). After 1912–1923, the common terminus post quem, the anti-Ottoman irredentist programs (though not the national ones in general) were, more or less, attained. Henceforth the Ottoman period in the self-consciousness of the Balkan political elites became only a matter of historical reflection, with consequences in relation to the modernization process, and to attitudes toward minorities.[17] The latter remained the only continuing real element of the legacy; in all other aspects it had turned into perception.

The creation of autonomous and independent Balkan states was not only a break with but a rejection of the political past. This is evident in the attempt to substitute new European institutions for the Ottoman state institutions and forms of local self-government. This process was more abrupt or gradual in different regions. In Greece, the Bavarian regency immediately launched an elaborate program of educational, judicial, bureaucratic, economic, military, and religious reforms on a society "in which men did not in practice differentiate between spheres of human affairs, such as political, economic, social, or religious." In constructing their polity, the Greeks were looking for working models neither in their immediate Ottoman past, not in their Byzantine legacy, but to the contemporary West. Autonomous Serbia for more than a decade under Miloš Obrenović remained a *paşalık*, and only in the 1840s, during the reign of Alexander Karageorgiević, began to lay the basis for a Western type of state apparatus. In Bulgaria, despite the efforts for an immediate break, it took nearly two decades to consolidate the new institutions.[18] Because of its peculiar position toward its Ottoman suzerain, Romania's Europeanization drive was not immediately related to its political break from the empire but preceded it. In general, as far as political institutions were concerned, the Ottoman legacy was insignificant, and it was only the differential speed of overcoming it in the separate Balkan states that marked its presence for a relatively short period.

Even in the case of modern Turkey, the extent to which the Ottoman state legacy might have been, even unwillingly, integrated into the institutions of the republic should not be overstated. Yet as Feroz Ahmad has pointed out, a legacy with an important impact even today "is the tradition of the strong, centralized state, identified with the nation, regarded as neutral and standing outside society, and representing no particularist interests."[19] For the Balkan societies coming out of Ottoman tutelage, even this cannot be asserted without qualifications. Unlike Turkey, Balkan societies had an endemic distrust of the state, stemming to a great extent from the fact that the Ottoman state had been seen as an institution alien and opposed to them because of its explicit identification with Islam and its implicit identification with Ottoman/Turkish ethnicity. While the state was strong and overpowering in all Balkans countries, this should be attributed primarily to their social structure, rather than to the influence of the historical legacy.

The limited Ottoman political legacy can be explained not only with the conscious rejection of the Ottoman political tradition but also with the lack of continuity of political elites in the Balkans, at least such elites who had partaken in the Ottoman political process. The Balkan Christian locals were integrated in the bureaucracy only at the lowest level, if at all, and then mostly as intermediaries between the self-governing bodies and the Ottoman authorities. This was almost entirely the case for Bulgaria and Serbia, not to speak of Montenegro, which was practically independent. The unique position of the phanariotes, simultaneously Greek cultural elites and Ottoman bureaucrats, does not significantly change the picture among the Greeks. The sphere of their influence was primarily in Istanbul (and for a century the Danubian principalities), but despite their commanding cultural authority, their political ideals and goals set them apart from the mainstream of the Greek national movement. Even if the assertions that the phanariotes were cherishing a Byzantine ideal and nourishing the dream of restoring the Byzantine Empire are groundless, their political instincts made them rely heavily on the unifying authority of Orthodoxy and Russian support, thus effectively making them representatives of the ecumenical imperial tradition that estranged them from the newly espoused ideals of the nation-state. Even while a segment of the phanariote elite took an important part in the political and literary accomplishments of the independent Greek state, it did so on an individual basis and not as a social group. In fact, the rhetoric of the break with the phanariote past was as vehement in modern Greece as the one with the Ottoman past. In both cases it was the conflict between the old imperial tradition and the new tradition of nationalism. The only real exception in this respect was Romania, which had retained its local aristocracy despite a century of phanariote predominance; however, this is to be explained by the special status of the antecedent Danubian principalities as vassal territories, which also accounts for the peculiarities in Romania's social and economic structure.

Aside from the Patriarchate and the phanariotes, the Ottoman Empire did not create or support political elites among the non-Muslims who had strong vested interests in its existence, and even these two loyal institutions were alienated after the 1820s. It was mostly the Muslim Balkan population that saw its allegiances primarily associated with the Ottoman Empire, although the fact that so many Muslims remained in the Balkans attests that localism was a dominant loyalty more powerful than the imperial attachment. This was true in the case of the Muslim Bosnians, who constituted the social elite of their region, as well as of some other non-Turkish Muslims. They did not develop a national ideology aspiring for a separate state and their fluid consciousness bore the features of the millet structure for a longer period.

The Ottoman Empire left a more tangible legacy in the economic and social spheres. There are several characteristics common to almost all Balkan societies that can be attributed directly to the Ottoman presence. These fundamental traits were absent from the development of Balkan medieval societies which were moving along the lines of a more or less common European feudal development, not only in its Byzantine version but also with the direct presence of Western forms after the conquest of Constantinople in 1204. The first of these characteristics is the absence of a landed nobility. It is not merely the question of having obliterated the old local Christian aristocracies but also of hindering the tendency to form a landowning class that could evolve independently from (let alone against) the strong centralized state. The overwhelming control of the state over the land, resources, and subjects resulted in the fact that "private large estates, even when the owner was a member of the ruling elite, could not attain predominance in agricultural production, chiefly because the working force had to be won over from a relatively free peasant class, whereas the produce would be sold at low prices fixed by the mechanisms of a command economy."[20] The existence of a relatively free peasantry (at least free from personal dependence and serfdom) and the consequent predominance of small peasant holdings as the basic unit of production is the second characteristic trait with which all Balkan societies (with the exception of Romania) began their independence.[21] The absence of an aristocracy, however, did not guarantee a quick and intensive capitalistic development which, in theory at least, would not have been inhibited by an aristocratic domination over the bourgeoisie like in other parts of Eastern Europe.[22] In fact, at the time when the Ottoman Empire began to be incorporated into the expanding European economy, there was a distinct tension between the imperial bureaucratic elites and the new social groups, primarily in the sphere of commerce.

These characteristics of the Balkan structure also partly explain what has come to be considered a feature of the Balkan experience: a certain commitment to egalitarianism. One can add here that this was also due to what Anatoly Khazanov has in a different context so aptly attributed to nomadic societies: "a precariousness of fortune precluding stable and internalized inequality."[23] The argument that the existence of a relatively free peasantry is an Ottoman legacy and that the Ottoman Empire spared the Balkans the so-called second edition of serfdom is plausible. Less plausible is the argument that this particular result in the long run "proved to be an obstacle to substantial increases in agricultural productivity and rendered more difficult the transition to the capitalistic mode of production."[24] The only Balkan exception, Romania, which did not spare its peasantry the second serfdom, retained a powerful landowning nobility, and even experienced a certain degree of urban administrative and political autonomy, equally lingered on in the periphery of European capitalist development. In any case, the whole debate transposes the emphasis from the Ottoman legacy as continuity to the perception of the Ottoman legacy as an agent of backwardness.

Urban life in the Balkans had an uninterrupted tradition from antiquity and throughout the Byzantine period, yet (or, rather, because of that) never acquired the autonomous role it had in the West, with the concomitant evolution of a strong independent commercial and industrial class. The Balkan city was incorporated in the Ottoman system as a completely constructed feudal category and was entirely subordinated to the state, a tradition characteristic also of medieval Muslim urban life.[25] While guilds were restricted throughtout the whole Ottoman period, a feature that distinguished them fundamentally from their Western European counterparts, the system of state sanction and protection proved beneficial for producers among the subject non-Muslim population. This created the paradoxical situation, from a Western European point of view, of rising capitalist elements adapting their activities to the guild system and, at the same time, adapting the guilds to suit the needs of capitalist production.[26] The staple orientalist argument is based on the difference between the position of the West European and "Oriental" (in this case Balkan/Ottoman) cities vis-à-vis the central locus of political power, and a dogmatic opposition between the latter as owing "their existence to a pre-economic logic of political domination and the symbolism of power," and the Western city that ostensibly "obeyed an economic logic from its beginnings."[27] It is, of course, not the existence of difference and its depiction that is objectionable but how it is interpreted and harnessed in ideological models.

The social legacy of a de facto free peasantry, the lack of an aristocracy, a weak bourgeoisie, and the presence of a strong centralized state was important for the political development of the postindependence period. The absence of an independent nobility was a factor with momentous repercussions, especially with the rise of nationalism and the formation of nation-states. In the Balkans (with the partial exception of Romania), it was not the nonexisting aristocracy that was the prominent social group to promote nationalism as in Hungary or Poland. Instead, nationalism was championed by intellectuals and the bourgeoisie, although one has to very careful not to overstate the role and participation of the latter.[28]

Even with this strong common legacy, the results were very different due to factors extraneous to the Ottoman legacy but typical for local developments in the post–Ottoman era. In the case of the closest social parallel, Bulgaria and Serbia, the different role of the peasants (extremely important in the Bulgarian, rather docile and dependent in the Serbian case) was due to the different time these peasantries became politically charged in the late nineteenth century.[29] The question can be constructed also in a different way: did the central place of the peasants in the Ottoman state, which, according to Inalcik, saw its primary social function in the support of this class to the detriment of other productive classes (particularly the nascent bourgeoisie), remain a living legacy?[30] Was the presence of strong state bureaucracies in practically all Balkan independent states necessarily an Ottoman legacy? In both cases, the correlation is rather dubious. Despite the central place of the peasantry in the economic and social structure of all Balkan countries, nowhere did the new ruling political elites champion peasant interests. Even in the only instance of genuine advocacy of the peasant cause and a real peasant political experiment, that of Alexander Stamboliiski in Bulgaria, there was no intrinsically antiindustrial or antimodernizing policy (despite the strong antiurban overtones).[31] The similarities, rather than being attributed to the common Ottoman legacy, can be seen as similar structural responses to challenges presented by agrarian societies integrated into an urbanized and industrialized Europe. Likewise, the existence of statism, the over-whelming role of state bureaucracies and the grip they exerted over society, was cer-tainly not confined in Europe to the countries of the Ottoman *Kulturraum* and should be interpreted in the larger framework of European history. In a slightly different context, Alexandru Duțu has reached the same conclusion that "the regional identity is based less on common traits and a common heritage and more on the common issues that we all have to face. These issues were produced by the process of modern-ization which put a special imprint on all people living in this area."[32]

Most important in the social domain is the Ottoman legacy in the demographic sphere. This was a long-term development that proved impossible or very difficult to undo, with immediate repercussions today. The demographic history of the Ot-toman Empire comprises problems pertaining to the geographic movement of the population (colonization, migrations); demographic processes (fertility, mortality, nuptiality, and so on); and other types of population movements (religious shifts, social mobility, and so on). As far as long-term demographic processes characteris-tics are concerned, such as fertility, mortality, marriage patterns, family, and house-hold size and structure, there is no indication that the Ottoman Empire has left a unique imprint.[33]

The fundamental consequence of the establishment of the Pax Ottomana in the Balkans was the abolishment of state and feudal frontiers, which facilitated or en-hanced population movements and the interpenetration of different groups within a vast territory. Although there are no reliable aggregate figures before the nineteenth century, attempts have been made to assess the character and effects of these move-ments. One of the contentious problems of Ottoman demographic history is the question of Turkish, or rather Turkic, colonization. As with the great majority of simi-lar problems, its interpretation (and the impetus for research) has been to serve other issues, especially to give an explanation for the Ottoman conquest, the long-term Ottoman presence, and the sizable Muslim population in the Balkans. Turkish his-toriography postulated that, among the variety of factors accounting for the Ottoman success, the size of the Turkish masses arriving from Anatolia was decisive. In this view, the history of the Ottoman Empire can be reinterpreted as the history of mi-grations of great masses who had numerical superiority over the indigenous popula-tion, and the conscious and planned colonization of the Balkans on the part of the sultan's government held a central place. In contrast, Balkan historiography has made considerable efforts to refute the essential significance of Ottoman colonization in explaining both the success of the Ottoman conquest and the significant size of Muslims by the last centuries of Ottoman rule. This attempt has centered on the process of conversions to Islam as chiefly responsible for Muslim growth. The out-come of the debate between the two contending interpretations need not necessarily serve either one of the political causes they can be used to legitimize. The issue in both cases is the attempt to prove the "blood-kinship" of the contested groups to the larger nations in the area. The fact that the Islamization thesis can be scholarly sup-ported far better than the colonization one by no means gives support to any of the anti-Muslim or anti-Turkish manifestations, which at one time or another have been pursued in different parts of the Balkans.

The substantial population shifts during the nineteenth century, for which there are aggregate numbers, were due mainly to political events, most prominently the secession of the Balkan nation-states. More than one million Muslims left the Balkans during the last three decades of the nineteenth century and relocated to Istanbul, the remaining European possession of the Porte, and to Anatolia. In the same period, one million Christian inhabitants changed their residence with the outgoing Muslims. Even more drastic were the migrations in the long war decade, 1912–1922 (the two Balkan wars, World War I, and the Greek-Turkish war). Close to two-and-a-half million people were affected by dislocations (among them close to one-and-a-half million Greeks from Asia Minor, around one-half million Muslims who left the Balkans for Turkey, one-quarter million Bulgarian refugees, and so on).[34] Such massive emigrations were untypical for the rest of Europe, to be surpassed only by the events of World War II.

Despite these drastic population shifts, not a single Balkan country achieved the cherished ideal characteristics of the European nation-state: ethnic and religious homogeneity. In this respect, the Balkans share with the rest of Eastern Europe a common predicament. Ever since the fifteenth century (and in the case of England much earlier), Western Europe has embarked on a huge homogenization drive with various degrees of success (the Spanish reconquista, England's expulsion of the Jews in the twelfth century, the religious wars in France and Germany) which, in conjunction with the strong dynastic states, had laid the foundations of the future nation-states. The argument that the West's intrinsic value lay in the deepest roots of a "democratic way of organizing society . . . with autonomous cities, corporate freedoms, the system of Estates and a series of other structural characteristics which are difficult to depict visually,"[35] all of which allowed it to arrive teleologically at democracy, can be effectively revisited. In fact, democracy as a political form became an attribute of the West European nation-states only in the twentieth century (and for Germany only after World War II), after they had achieved in the previous centuries a remarkable, although not absolute, degree of ethnic and religious homogeneity and disciplined society, at an often questionable human and moral price.

Greece and Albania came closest to monoethnic states but they, too, had to handle minority problems: Greece that of its so-called Slavic-speaking and Muslim minorities; Albania its tiny Greek minority. Bulgaria was left with over 13% minorities (Turks, Pomaks, Gypsies, Tatars, Armenians, Jews, Russians, and so on), Yugoslavia had close to 15% (Germans, Magyars, Albanians, Romanians, Turks, and so on), but its national majority of 85% itself was composed of three recognized constituents (Slovenes, Croats, and Serbs, including the separately unrecognized Macedonians as well as the Serbo-Croatian-speaking Bosnian Muslims). Romania had the largest minority of about 27% (Magyars, Germans, Jews, Ukrainians, Russians, Bulgarians, Turks, Tatars, Gypsies, and so on). Turkey itself, which emerged from the Ottoman Empire reduced and revolving around an ethnic nucleus after the expulsion of the Greeks and the Armenian massacres, had to deal with substantial minorities, such as the Kurds, to mention but the largest group.

Most complex was the situation in the so-called contact zones: Macedonia, Bosnia, Dobrudzha, Kossovo, Vojvodina, Transylvania, and Istanbul itself. Just their enumeration shows that some of them were contact zones within the Austro-Hungarian empire. This suggests that the question of the Ottoman legacy in the demographic sphere has to be approached on a higher level of generalization: the problem of imperial legacies in a nation-state context. If compared to the other multi-or supranational imperial European legacies of the time, the Austrian and the Russian, the Ottoman legacy displays some essential differences. Apart from the obvious fact of being a Muslim empire, the crucial distinction was that, at a time of burgeoning nationalist ideas, the dominant groups in the Austrian and Russian Empires were composed of the ethnic elements with the highest degree of national consciousness, whereas in the Ottoman Empire the case was reverse. The Turks, from a Balkan (but not from a Middle Eastern) perspective, were the last group to develop their own Turkish nationalism. When this began in the latter decades of the nineteenth century, the greater part of the Balkans was already outside the Ottoman sphere and was not directly affected by it, except for Macedonia and Albania. Yet, the Ottoman Empire shared with its other two imperial counterparts many more fundamental similarities created by the incompatibility between the imperial system and the criteria of the nation-state resting on the principles of self-determination, as well as ethnic and religious homogeneity.

All Balkan countries (Turkey included) have resorted to similar solutions in trying to resolve minority problems: emigration and assimilation. The culmination of the first was the series of major population shifts following World War I, but there were also substantial population waves, both interstate and internal, in the interwar period and after World War II: Greek emigration from Istanbul in the 1950s, German and Jewish emigrations from Ceauşescu's Romania, Turkish emigrations from Bulgaria in the 1950s and 1980s, and so forth. As for assimilation, there were several relatively successful outcomes: the integration and assimilation of the so-called Slavophones in Northern Greece; the similar fate of the remaining Greek population on the Bulgarian Black Sea coast, and so on. Still, one can indicate many more failures: the unresolved minority issues are, essentially, the existing and potential crisis points in the Balkans: Bosnia, Macedonia, Kossovo, Transylvania, Thrace, Cyprus.

Insofar as the complex ethnic and religious diversity is a continuity from the Ottoman period, the apparent conclusion would be that in the demographic sphere the Ottoman legacy is persistent. Yet the issue becomes more complex when taking into account the different and competing ways of shaping group consciousness in general, and ethnic and national consciousness in particular; it becomes even more complicated when exploring the problem of whether, when, and how the Ottoman legacy as historical continuity in this sphere turned into the perception; and it becomes almost confusing when trying to draw the delicate line between the workings of the Ottoman legacy and the influence of Turkish nationalism.

Nationalism in the Balkans in the nineteenth century was constructed primarily around linguistic and religious identities. Language was perceived by all national and cultural leaders as the mightiest agent of unification. The efforts of the new states centered on the creation of secularized, centralized, and uniform educational systems as one of the most powerful agents of nationalism, alongside the army. Yet this very emphasis on the unifying potential of language stressed its exclusiveness and the rigidity of the ethnic boundaries it delineated. This precluded the integration (except assimilation) of different linguistic groups into a single nation: Albanians in Serbia, Turks in Bulgaria and Greece, Greeks in Albania, Magyars in Romania, Kurds in Turkey, and so forth.

Moreover, not only groups of linguistic backgrounds different from the dominant ethnic one in the nation-state proved impossible to integrate; so also did groups of identical ethnic backgrounds and speakers of the same language, like the Pomaks in Bulgaria, the Slavic Bosnian Muslims, the Torbesh in Macedonia, and so on. These latter cases invoke the general problem of religion as ethnic boundary, and that of Balkan Muslims in particular. Despite the fact that language had become the nucleus of different national identities among Balkan Christians (for the most part Orthodox), it could not raze the fundamental boundary between Muslims and Christians that had been established during the centuries of Ottoman rule. The reason for this was not, as the great bulk of Balkan and foreign historiography maintains, the fact that Orthodoxy played a major and crucial role in nation-building.[36] In fact, "religion came last in the struggle to forge new national identities" and in some cases "did not become a functional element in national definition until the nation-states had nationalized their churches." It never could be a sufficient component of national self-identity and, even in the national struggles, its primary contribution was to strengthen the opposition to the Muslim rulers. The exception is the Albanian case, possibly because nationalist ideas developed simultaneously among its different religious components of which the Muslims were the majority, and because the perceived danger from without came from Christian quarters (Greeks and Serbs) rather than from the Muslim center. Within the Orthodox ecumene, the process of nation-building demonstrated "the essential incompatibility between the imagined community of religion and the imagined community of the nation."[37]

This does not mean that the religious boundary between Christianity and Islam was the only divider. Clearly, the different Christian denominations, and particularly the opposition between Orthodoxy and Catholicism, presented additional frontiers of tension. Yet these frontiers did not prove as unsurmountable. This is especially true of the coexistence and cooperation between the Romanian Uniate and Orthodox churches where Romanianness became the dominant link. Despite anti-Catholic prejudice in Bulgaria, the small Bulgarian Catholic community (as well as the even smaller group of Protestants) were considered and perceived themselves as organic parts of the Bulgarian nation. The unbridgeable division between Catholic Croats and Orthodox Serbs can be explained, rather than by irreconcilable religious differences, by the fact that the two communities had for a long period developed within different historical traditions. During the nineteenth century, the notion of separateness, although not irreversible, had become internalized by significant groups of the respective populations who were cherishing separate state-building ideals, despite and alongside the substantial appeal and support for the Yugoslav idea.

Ironically, Balkan nationalism, which irrevocably destroyed the imagined community of Orthodox Christianity, managed to preserve a frozen, unchangeable, and stultifyingly uniform image of the Muslim community, and consistently dealt with it in millet terms. In other words, the Christian populations of the Balkans began speaking, among themselves, the language of nationalism, whereas their attitudes toward the Muslims remained in the realm of the undifferentiated religious communities discourse. A manifestation of this Christian attitude was the continuous and indiscriminate use of the name Turk to refer to Muslims in general, a practice still alive in many parts of the Balkans.[38] On the other hand, the Balkan Muslims, because they could not adapt to the national mode and were practically excluded from the process of nation formation, retained a fluid consciousness that for a longer time displayed the characteristics of a millet mentality, and thus the bearing of the Ottoman legacy. This does not mean that Islam, or for that matter religion, became an alternative form of national consciousness. What it meant was that on the one hand, the Muslims were marginalized in the face of a sphere that proved to be exclusionary to them; on the other hand, it induced them to look to the Muslim sphere as an acceptable assimilative alternative.

It would be incorrect to describe this Muslim sphere as part of the Ottoman legacy. The Ottoman legacy was possibly alive in the consciousness of a generation after World War I, and the immediate memories of a living empire were extinguished, more or less, by the eve of World War II. However, with the creation of the Turkish republic, the Ottoman legacy vanished increasingly in the realm of perception, and thereafter one should speak of the influence of Turkish nationalism on a substantial part of the Balkan Muslim population. Still, the conflation of Ottoman with Turkish makes this distinction difficult. Because of the predominant view of a complete break with an alien culture and polity, the Balkan countries willingly relinquished any claim on the Ottoman past and saw Turkey as its legitimate heir. Therefore, when dealing with Turkish nationalism, they often ascribe to it imperial, Ottoman ambitions. At the same time, despite the refutation of the Ottoman imperial past, the Turks still view themselves as its genuine successors. The present active Balkan policy of Turkey, which is articulating its geopolitical interests in the form of protection over Muslims, certainly does not help refute these perceptions.

In the cultural sphere, the most visible and immediate break occurred in what is known as high/elite culture. This break was facilitated by the combination of two important boundaries: religious and linguistic. Ottoman culture, that is, the high culture of the Ottoman Empire, was produced and consumed exclusively by educated Ottoman, Arabic, and Persian-speaking Muslims. This group, mostly concentrated in Istanbul and less numerous in the Balkans, disappeared entirely from the newly seceded states, leaving behind only the presence of Ottoman architectural monuments. The exceptions are the Bosnian-Slavic-speaking Muslims who, unlike their counterparts in Bulgaria, Greece, or Macedonia, occupied the highest places in the social hierarchy of their region.[39] On the other hand, the aristocratic and clerical elites of the medieval Christian Balkan states, who were the potential creators of a local high culture, had for the most part emigrated or perished. After the conquest, only a small part of the Balkan Christian aristocracies was integrated in the lower echelons of political power, but for practical purposes (i.e., from the point of view of the sphere of the ethnic or religious group) they were nonexistent. The Ottomans did not create local Balkan political or cultural elites and, outside the institution of the Patriarchate and the phanariotes, no high Christian elites were integrated in the empire that was constructed around its Muslim essence. A partial exception was the vassal Ottoman territories of the Danubian principalities and especially Dubrovnik, whose cultural elites, although not integrated, were tolerated. Thus, one can actually speak of a double break from the world of Ottoman high culture: one was persistently in place from the time of the conquest; the second occurred at the time of political independence in the nineteenth century.

Looked at from another angle, however, the Ottoman period provided a framework for a veritable flourishing of post-Byzantine Balkan culture: not in the sense of being the dominant culture or receiving state support, nor in the sense of the Ottoman system having integrated and perpetuated elements of the Byzantine legacy, but in the sense of creating a common *Raum* in which Byzantine culture operated for several centuries in ecumenical dimensions. The Byzantine cultural sphere had left its strong imprint on the literary and art production of the area, but this is not sufficient enough to explain its endurance and creativity several centuries after the demise of the Byzantine Empire. It can be understood only by taking into account the imperial space provided by the Ottoman Empire where a full-blooded exchange between the different regions could take place. All over the Balkans, one can find traces of this exchange: works of Greek and Romanian iconographers, woodcarvers and goldsmiths in Bulgaria, icons of the famous Bulgarian Tryavna school in Romanian monasteries and Serbian and Macedonian churches. In fact, the disruption of this cultural ecumene coincided with the disintegration of the Ottoman world along national lines. It is symptomatic that during the nineteenth century, Bulgarian religious art (especially mural painting and the art of the iconostasis) continued to produce works of a quality such as could hardly be found in Romania, Serbia, and even in Greece. This has been explained by the fact that Bulgaria's retreat from the post-Byzantine sphere came about several decades later than that of its neighbors.[40]

Similarly, the phanariotes cannot be treated simply as an Ottoman institution; they were also the main link to, and preservers of, the Byzantine legacy. Thus, the passionate break with the phanariote tradition at the outset of independent Greece, the pronounced enmity to everything Byzantine, the attempt at basically wiping off a millennium of historical development (at least in the dominant discourse of the followers of Korais) is, among others, the result of a realization of how much the Byzantine legacy was actually built into the Ottoman Empire. The desire for a break with the medieval past and development along the lines of the European Enlightenment in some cases overrode the purely ethnoreligious opposition to the Ottomans. This brings in the important question of ideas consumption in the Balkans and the channels of intellectual and ideological penetration. Because of the crucial division between Islam and Christianity, ideas in the Balkans came almost exclusively from the Christian West and Russia. The notion of the complete cultural isolation of the Balkans from the European mainstream because of the lengthy Ottoman rule and the Byzantine legacy and the widespread stereotype of the Balkans having skipped the crucial formative stages of European/Western civilization have been seriously challenged. Paschalis Kitromilides has sharply pointed out that "humanism did not simply emerge as a shared cultural outlook in the West but also developed as the confluence of the intellectual traditions of the two halves of Europe." Serious scholarship has long recognized "the seminal contribution of the Greek East to the making of Renaissance humanism," but it is usually passed over in suspicious silence in general works, let alone in popular ones.[41] Beginning with the Enlightenment, which, together with nationalism, exerted a major formative influence on the Balkans, the region has actively partaken in every cultural and ideological current in Europe. It is ironic that the stubborn assertion of Balkan nationalists that the Ottoman Empire had fatally and absolutely cut off the Balkans from the mainstream of European development is backfiring at a moment when they are trying to prove their legitimate belonging to the continent.

At the same time, on the level of popular culture and everyday life, the Ottoman legacy proved much more persistent. One can look for it in authentic Ottoman elements (architecture and urban structure, food, music, the institution of the coffee-house); follow it up through its influence via direct cultural contact (language, religious syncretism); finally, trace it in the reactive response and adaptation of indigenous institutions and cultural trends to the Ottoman system.[42] The zealous efforts at de-Ottomanization succeeded primarily in the material (visible and public) sphere. The most radical changes occurred in the overall appearance of cities, architecture, clothing. All Balkan countries (although with different degrees of intensity) attempted to purify their languages and toponomy from Turkisms. As a whole, the existence of bi- and multilingualism expired with the passing of the generations with immediate knowledge of life in the empire. More important was the socialization of the broad masses of people as citizens of the nation-states through such state institutions as schools and the army, which promoted the standardized literary language and were central in the process of homogenization of the respective nations.

However, when it came to such phenomena as food and diet, as well as music, the Ottoman legacy seemed to be much more tenacious. As regards food, there is an interesting observation about Bulgaria that can be successfully generalized for the whole Balkan area. The greater abundance and diversification of food made dishes that were previously confined only to the Muslim urban elites increasingly accessible to the whole urban population and large segments of the rural population. Thus, while the haute cuisine of the limited Bulgarian urban elites tended to become more Europeanized in the last decades of the nineteenth century, the general cuisine of Bulgaria (Christian and Muslim alike) became increasingly Ottomanized, as it were, after the end of Ottoman rule.[43]

In the sphere of *mentalité* (popular beliefs, customs, attitudes, value system), the efforts to de-Ottomanize proved much more strenuous. De-Ottomanization has been regarded as a process that was to achieve the coveted ideal of the polar opposite of being Ottoman (or Oriental), namely, steady Europeanization, Westernization, or modernization of society. It was supposed to bring in a new set of relations both in family and in society based on individuality and rationality, an entirely different position for women, a revised role for children and child rearing, a new work ethic. To take one of the most exploited themes, the position of women, it continues to be almost exclusively attributed to the influence of Islam. Yet it is impossible to distinguish between the workings of traditional patriarchal peasant morality, the influence of Orthodox Christianity, and the role of Ottoman culture per se (in this case the role of Islam).[44] The difficulty or even impossibility of differentiating between Ottoman and traditional local cultures, of which many researchers have been aware, has led to methodological solutions such as the treatment of "de-Ottomanization," "de-

Orientalization," "debalkanization," and "depatriarchalization" as synonyms.[45] Yet, this bypasses an essential methodological challenge: as long as research continues to ignore the important examination of the axis Balkan–Ottoman, and instead follows exclusively the two bipolar axes, Balkan traditional culture–the West, and Ottoman culture–the West, this important aspect of social history will be trivialized into the usual dichotomy traditional–modern.[46]

"Balkan mentality" has been one of the most exploited mythologemes in popular discourse and an operative term in many scholarly studies. In the best analysis of the methodological dimensions of the problem, Paschalis Kitromilides concludes that "all anthropological and social psychological arguments in favour of the existence of a shared Balkan 'mentality' are bound to turn into sociological metaphysics unless they provide convincing answers to the question as to what is specifically Balkan about it."[47] His analysis of how Jovan Cvijić introduced and utilized the category in *La peninsule balkanique* led him to posit the incompatibility between this category and any ethnic and national constructs. Yet it is precisely on ethnic lines that most research on "Balkan mentality" is done. There has been also an (unconvincing) attempt to postulate the linguistic basis of a specific "Balkan mentality" and *homo balcaninus*.[48] While Kitromilides rightly objects to the overgeneralizations of the mentality approach, he allows for the description of what he calls "mental and attitudinal structures" in a strictly historically specific context. This is a distinctive and historically plausible set of mental characteristics, valid for the eighteenth-century Balkan Christian Orthodox ecumene: "Historical specificity is therefore the critical factor in the description of such sets of recurrent and pervasive assumptions and norms that define the outlook of a collectivity. But to insist upon talking about a diachronic uniformity called 'Balkan mentality' is no more than an unverifiable historical legend, and it can turn into a perverse mythology as well."[49]

Methodological and semantic paucity notwithstanding, there is no doubt that the Balkans represent a cultural region, possibly a subregion of the larger Mediterranean area. This is not simply an ascriptive category; the Balkan peoples themselves, although often reluctantly and with pejorative accents, accede to belonging to it. Whether and to what extent one can attribute its existence to the workings of the Ottoman imperial legacy (or earlier to the Byzantine legacy), the least that can be asserted is that the Ottoman Empire played a crucial role as mediator in the course of several centuries, which permitted broad contacts, mutual influences, and cultural exchange in a large area of the Eastern Mediterranean. To summarize, the Ottoman legacy as continuity displayed different degrees of perseverance. In practically all spheres, except the demographic and the sphere of popular culture, the break was enacted almost immediately after the onset of political independence and, as a whole, was completed by the end of World War I; thereafter it was relegated to the realm of perception. In the demographic sphere, the Ottoman legacy continued for some time and became intertwined and gradually transformed into the influence of the Turkish nation-state.

Turning to the Ottoman legacy as perception, it has been and is being shaped by generations of historians, poets, writers, journalists, and other intellectuals, as well as politicians. What we are dealing with is the evolving perception of the Ottoman past within a specific social group and the transmission and dissemination of this perception in broader strata of the population. The first can be reconstructed from the numerous output in historiographical works, textbooks, belles lettres, journalistic pieces, and works of art, and represents, essentially, the dominant views of the intellectual and political elites of the moment. The second problem is more difficult to analyze as there are no systematic studies of how deep and successful the penetration of these hegemonic views has been. Even more submerged in the realm of hypotheses is the important question of possible counterperceptions or alternative perceptions coming from different ethnic, social, or age groups within the separate nation-states. That there have been no systematic studies in this respect whatsoever is an indirect indication of the strength of the hegemonic view.

Probably the most striking feature of the dominant discourses in the different Balkan countries is the remarkable similarity between them and the amazing continuity over time. Since the perception of the Ottoman legacy is at the center of securing present social arrangements, and above all legitimizing the state and searching for identity at all times, this similarity (if not identity) in treatment and approach is another aspect of the Balkans as a historical entity. Briefly summarized (and for practical purposes somewhat simplified), the argument runs as follows:

On the eve of the Ottoman conquest, the medieval societies of the Balkans had reached a high degree of sophistication that made them commensurate with, if not ahead of, developments in Western Europe. Despite the political fragmentation of the peninsula, a characteristic typical of the latest and most developed stages of European feudal medieval societies, there were symptoms that indicated possible developments in the direction of consolidating the medieval nations (perceived as proto-nations), of humanism and national cultures. In this respect, the arrival of the Ottomans was a calamity of unparalleled consequences because it disrupted the natural development of southeast European societies as a substantial and creative part of the overall process of European humanism and the Renaissance. The consolidation of Ottoman rule in the Balkans definitively isolated the peninsula from European developments and left it untouched by the great ideas and transformations of the Renaissance and the Reformation. It further brought a deep cultural regression and even barbarization and social leveling out. The conquerors put an end to the existence of Balkan political and intellectual elites, either by physically annihilating part of the aristocracy and clergy (all Balkan historiographies utilize the nineteenth-century concept "intelligentsia"), or by driving them into emigration, and, finally, by integrating them into their political structure and, thus, effectively denationalizing them. The only institutions that kept the religion and ethnic consciousness alive were the Orthodox church and the self-governing bodies, chief among them the village commune.

The only redeeming feature in the first centuries of Ottoman rule was the possible relaxation of the economic plight of the peasantry with the introduction of a uniform and regular tax burden. But, according to a widespread assertion, though difficult to substantiate, the pressure of foreign rulers is something drastically different from the exploitation of one's own elites. The Ottomans have been unanimously described as bearers of an essentially alien civilization characterized by a fanatic and militant religion, which introduced different economic and societal practices and brought about the pastoralization and agrarianization of the Balkans. In depicting this civilization, the emphasis has been laid on the excesses of violence, crimes, and cruelty, something that reached unbearable proportions at the time of Ottoman decline, especially during the eighteenth century, and triggered the struggle for national emancipation.

This picture of "the saddest and darkest period"[50] in Balkan history makes the five centuries of Ottoman rule the historiographical counterpart of Western Europe's "Dark Ages" before the advent of historical revisionism. Modern Balkan historiographies were shaped in the century of the national idea and under the strong influence of the then dominant trends of romanticism and positivism. These historiographies acquired their institutional standing in the respective nation-states, of which they perceived themselves and were considered to be one of the most important pillars.[51] The predominantly ethical-didactic and religious orientation of historical writing until the eighteenth century was translated into an equally single-minded mission: to shape national consciousness, legitimize the nation-state, and thus fulfill an important social function. The fact that Balkan historiographies developed primarily as national historiographies accounts for their relative parochialism with little knowledge of the history of their neighbors in the same period. It is, moreover, not simply ignorance of the history of the neighboring nations but a conscious effort to belittle, ignore, distort, deride, and even negate. In this effort the mutual enmity of Balkan historiographies, which developed into a passionate polemical tradition, very often overshadowed even the hostility against the Ottoman Empire and Turkey. At the same time, for all the stereotypes about virulent Balkan nationalism, most Balkan nationalisms are essentially defensive, and their intensity is the direct result of problems of unconsolidated nation-states and social identities in crisis. This nervousness about identity accounts, among others, for the unique preoccupation with ethnogenesis in the Balkans. Within the persisting continuum of the nation-state and with different degrees of intensity (the shrill nationalism of many works of the interwar decade having remained, luckily, unsurpassed), this is the predominant mode of historical writing in the Balkans.

Thus, the Ottoman legacy as perception is firmly built in the discourse of Balkan nationalism as one of its most important pillars. While its intensity fluctuates with the consecutive waves of nationalism, it is nevertheless one of its permanent characteristics. At the same time, the Ottoman legacy as continuity has been in a process of decline for the past century. The countries defined as Balkan (i.e., the ones that participated in the historical Ottoman sphere) have been moving steadily away from their Ottoman legacy, and with this also from their balkanness, a statement that is devoid of any evaluative element. The most important conclusion that follows from this argument is that legacies are not perennial, let alone primordial. The three imperial legacies (Habsburg, Ottoman, and the Romanov cum Soviet) for all their prolonged and profound impact, are historical phenomena with their *termini post quem* and *ante quem*. Any reifying of their characteristics along immobile and unreformable civilizational fault lines can be, of course, the object of ideological propaganda or superficial political science exercises, but cannot be a legitimate working hypothesis for history.

Conclusion

Yet, like the poor, the Balkans shall always be with us.

Konrad Berkovici[1]

Perhaps the best solution would be to plow under every third Balkan.

Howard Brubaker[2]

"The Balkans are usually reported to the outside world only in time of terror and trouble; the rest of the time they are scornfully ignored. Kipling epitomized this attitude by exclaiming in *The Light That Failed*: 'Speaking of war, there'll be trouble in the Balkans in the spring.'" This was the opening paragraph of a book written in 1940.[3] It can be the opening paragraph to a book written in 1995. To the ones who reproduce an essentialist image of the Balkans, it would be simply another proof that nothing has changed in the past fifty, one hundred, and even one thousand years. Yet, as I have argued, the Balkans have a powerful ontology that deserves serious and complex study, and it is an ontology of constant and profound change.

If one were to make more of the frozen vision of the Balkans than merely define it as the product of casual, dismissive, or hectoring journalism, one could argue that this image is more than a stereotype. It appears as the higher reality, the reflection of the phenomenal world, its essence and true nature, the "noumenon" to the "phenomenon," to use the Kantian distinction. None of the politicians, journalists, or writers who have specialized in passing strictures on the Balkans have ever made a claim for a philosophical basis of their argument, yet this is what they have achieved. The frozen image of the Balkans, set in its general parameters around World War I, has been reproduced almost without variation over the next decades and operates as a discourse.

To come around full circle and link the Kennan prelude of the introduction with a Kennan coda, what one can hear in his piece are motives of a distinct and well-known earlier melody with some fresh improvisations. It is the American patrician version of the old aristocratic European paradigm garnished with nineteenth century Victorian righteousness. It manifests an evolutionary belief in the superiority of orderly civilization over barbarity, archaic predispositions, backwardness, petty squabbles, unconforming and unpredictable behavior, that is, "tribalism." The very use of "tribal" relegates the Balkans to a lower civilizational category, occupied primarily by Africans, to whom the term is usually applied. Africa and Asia have been classified by Elie Kedourie, according to their alleged political tradition, as the legacy of tribal rule and Oriental despotism. Tribal society's central feature is its primitiveness, lack of complexity and, implicitly, weakness, because when confronted "with the demand of modernization for a sophisticated system of law and political representation, it merely collapses into tyranny." It is also intrinsically passive, incompatible with initiative and enterprise. The classification of people according to notions of (social and technological) complexity and activity is a fundamental principle of the imperial discourse that has been inherited primarily by the press.[4] It also releases the "civilized world" from any responsibility or empathy that it might otherwise bestow on more "reasonable" people.

Thus, responding to the question "What is to be done?" Kennan concluded that "no one—no particular country and no group of countries—wants, or should be expected, to occupy the entire distracted Balkan region, to subdue its excited peoples, and to hold them in order until they calm down and begin to look at their problems in a more orderly way."[5] Ivo Banac interpreted this declaration of Balkan un-Europeanness as the basis for the politics of noninvolvement:

> In fact, his essay, which recommends noninvolvement, would be of no particular interest were it not for his candid opinion on the apartness of the Balkans from the European civilization. That is no small matter and, though hidden under wraps of cultural taboos, probably is the chief reason for Western aloofness and indifference to the area itself and to any action or involvement in it.[6]

There were many more practical reasons for the initial Western noninvolvement, but this is certainly no small matter. The alleged non-Europeanness of the Balkans might have been used to legitimize noninvolvement but it was not its cause. After all, the same West did not falter in its involvement in non-European, non-Christian, but oily Kuwait. Besides, Western noninvolvement itself is a problematic category. Understandably reluctant as the West was to involve itself directly in a war in Yugoslavia, it was certainly neither aloof, nor indifferent, nor inactive, nor even unanimous at the time of the country's breakdown and throughout its ugly divorce. It is preposterous to refuse to face the responsibility of both internal and external thugs and missionaries who plunged Yugoslavia into disintegration, and explain the ensuing quagmire by "Balkan mentalities" and "ancient enmities." There are equally important practical reasons for the West's final involvement in Yugoslavia. Most of them are prompted by extra-Balkan considerations: the place and future of NATO, the role of the Unites States as the global military superpower and especially its strategic stake in European affairs, and so forth. All of this is euphemistically enveloped in the favorite word in recent American diplomatic vocabulary: credibility. If ancient examples are any good, perhaps the most evocative is the behavior of the deities in the Trojan war who followed their own game when tipping the scales without, however, pretending they were doing it for the sake of humankind. But they were deities, after all.

There is an additional nuance that separates the West Europeans from their American counterparts. In the non-Yugoslav Balkans, the war in the former Yugoslavia is referred to exclusively as the Yugowar or the war in Bosnia. In Western

Europe, it is usually defined as the war in ex-Yugoslavia or in Bosnia, although there is occasional mention of a Balkan war. In the United States, the war is usually generalized as "the Balkan war," although there is occasional mention of the war in the former Yugoslavia. Some journalists have gone so far as to eradicate all Balkan history and reduce it to Serbian history. So, one reads that in June 1389 on the plain of Kosovo "occurred the primal act of slaughter from which all Balkan history since has flowed."[7] It is insubstantial that, except for the Serbs, the battle of Kosovo does not mean much for the rest of the Balkan nations who have had their own and quite different Kosovos. One of the charms of the Balkan nations, but also their curse, is that they have incredibly rich and dense histories, but they are usually self-contained. Save for historians, Kosovo came to the attention of the other Balkan publics at the same time that it reached their American contemporaries.

Why does the war need to be Balkan? The Spanish civil war was Spanish, not Iberian or Southwest European; the Greek civil war was never Balkan; the problem of Northern Ireland is fittingly localized—it is called neither Irish, nor British, not even English, which it precisely is. Why is it, then, that "Balkan" is used for a country at war that, before the sad events, insisted it was not Balkan and was previously not labeled Balkan but considered to be the shining star of Eastern Europe by its Western supporters? Has "Balkan" become so much of a *Schimpfwort* that it is hoped that those to whom it is applied would be horrified? Psychology should persuade politicians and journalists that bearing the brunt of collective stigma has never been a good deterrent. Studies on social policies dealing with stigma have shown that integration, rather than isolation, is the adequate solution.[8]

It would do much better if the Yugoslav, not Balkan, crisis ceased to be explained in terms of Balkan ghosts, ancient Balkan enmities, primordial Balkan cultural patterns and proverbial Balkan turmoil, and instead was approached with the same rational criteria that the West reserves for itself: issues of self-determination versus inviolable status quo, citizenship and minority rights, problems of ethnic and religious autonomy, the prospects and limits of secession, the balance between big and small nations and states, the role of international institutions.[9] It is paradoxical to read American journalists bemoan the split of their society (which they call "balkanization") while their politicians and their allies sealed the virtual, not potential, balkanization of Yugoslavia by embracing unconditionally the principle of self-determination. This is not to deny the legitimate nature of processes of secession and self-determination, but to call on giving phenomena their proper names and on having a clear perspective of their repercussions. It is, of course, a sublime irony to observe leaders of the cleansed societies of Western Europe fifty years after their ugliest performance raise their hands in horror and bombard (in words and in deed, and safely hidden behind American leadership) the former Yugoslavs in preserving "ethnic diversity" for the sake of securing a *Volksmuseum* of multiculturalism in a corner of Europe, after having given green light to precisely the opposite process.

There is another component, relevant in illuminating geopolitical choices and explicating balkanism as a discourse different from orientalism. As illustrated earlier, before the twentieth century, there existed an ambiguous attitude toward the Turks: an almost unconscious empathy with the rulers mingled with traditional sympathy for fellow-Christians. Britain, in particular, with its dominant anti-Russian attitude, upheld the Ottoman Empire as a barrier against further Russian expansion. This geopolitical configuration was in many ways inherited by the United States, and Turkey became an important element in the cold war anti-Soviet alliance. But there was no longer the admonishing figure of the suffering Balkan Christian. The former Christians were now all, with the exception of Greece, under the "evil empire" of communism. Besides, the central discourse had shifted from religion to ideology.

Additionally, since World War II, it has become illegitimate to openly bash nonwhite races, non-Christian religions, and non-European societies. Kennan's introduction accordingly downplays the role of the Ottoman Empire and the Turks for the historical fate of the Balkans: current problems stem from their "distant tribal past," and have roots that "reach back, clearly, not only into the centuries of Turkish domination." Finally, "one must not be too hard on the Turks"; after all, "there was more peace when they were still under Turkish rule than there was after they gained their independence. (That is not to say that the Turkish rule was in all other respects superior to what came after.)"[10]

There is, actually, nothing objectionable in this, either academically or politically. For one thing, the virtues of empires will be critically reassessed after close to two centuries of dubious performance of the nation-states. Epithets as "anomaly" for empires will probably fall into disuse in academic writing. It is time to reconsider with humility the effects of exporting the nation-state to societies that are ethnic and religious mosaics, and creating a mosaic of nation-states in place of the mosaic of nations.[11] The humility is even more imperative given the so-called "organic" growth of West European societies into nation-states. This outcome was the result of several centuries of social engineering—ethnic and religious wars and expulsions (i.e., ethnic cleansing) accompanying the process of centralization—triggered by a fundamental hostility to heterogeneity, which in the end brought about relatively homogeneous polities that "organically" grew into the modern nation-states. While this is an obvious reduction of a complex process, it is necessary in order to expose the moral pretensions that inform it. At the same time, putting the West European record straight certainly does not exempt the Balkans from their responsibilities. And it is absolutely not valid for Balkan politicians and intellectuals to use the Ottoman Empire and Turkey as the convenient scapegoat for all their misfortunes and misconducts, to attempt to define themselves against a demonized other, in this case very literally resorting to orientalism. What is objectionable, though, is that Kennan has essentialized the Balkans: virtually transforming Herder's Balkan "Volksgeist" into Kaplan's "Balkan ghosts."

Yet it is objectionable on epistemological grounds only insofar as one deals with the intellectual hypostasis of Kennan. If he is contextualized in the structure of an imperial geopolitical continuity, he would not be seen (or not seen only) as the hostage of a tradition of stereotypes. Certainly, Kennan is in the same relationship to "Balkanist" texts that all readers, according to Wolfgang Iser, are with written texts. The text, in his formulation, is bracketed off from the world it represents and "what is within the brackets is separated from the reality in which it is normally embedded." The ensuing continual oscillation between both worlds produces a twofold doubling—one affecting the recipient, the other the world of the text itself. While this duality serves to aestheticize the fictionality in literature because it is an essentially staged discourse, fiction in philosophical (or other) discourse remains veiled and, therefore, can be subject to rules of practical application, can be designed for a specific purpose, in a word, can be falsified.[12] Indeed, "the challenge of orientalism is precisely the challenge of a discursive formation that has complicated extratextual and nondiscursive implications and consequences."[13] One might also add, sources. From this perspective Kennan could be conceived also as the important architect as well as *porte-parole* of a power-political attitude. In this pattern, it is authority that shapes representation (or appropriates existing types of representation) whenever the political expediency arises. That someone operates entirely within the conceptual apparatus of a certain discourse is not, then, the result of the constraints of this discourse but a conscious and deliberate choice. In Iser's terms, it is an "intention-led mobilization" on the part of the activator.[14]

Kennan is thus an example of one at an intersection, or in the midst of a complex and dialectical chain reaction, between knowledge as power, of "discourse as a violence we do to things or, at all events, as a practice that we impose on them," and a configuration where (political) power yields knowledge, for the two are "rigorously indivisible."[15] To resort to the vocabulary of social psychology, John French and Bertram Raven differentiate between six bases of social power: coercive, reward, legitimate, reference, expert, and informational.[16] Expert power is based on the perception, on the part of the target, that the agent possesses superior power and ability, whereas informational power depends entirely on the quality of the agent's message, its persuasiveness, and the logic of the argumentation. The expert and informational power that someone like Kennan exerts is enhanced by, and at the same time bears a double responsibility because of, the dual target of his agency: policy makers and the public. Faced with stark political realities, and working within the confines and with the modest means of academe, one can hope only to subvert the informative power of expert authority.

By being geographically inextricable from Europe, yet culturally constructed as "the other" within, the Balkans have been able to absorb conveniently a number of externalized political, ideological, and cultural frustrations stemming from tensions and contradictions inherent to the regions and societies outside the Balkans. Balkanism became, in time, a convenient substitute for the emotional discharge that orientalism provided, exempting the West from charges of racism, colonialism, eurocentrism, and Christian intolerance against Islam. After all, the Balkans are in Europe; they are white; they are predominantly Christian, and therefore the externalization of frustrations on them can circumvent the usual racial or religious bias allegations. As in the case of the Orient, the Balkans have served as a repository of negative characteristics against which a positive and self-congratulatory image of the "European" and the "West" has been constructed. With the reemergence of East and orientalism as independent semantic values, the Balkans are left in Europe's thrall, anticivilization, alter ego, the dark side within. Reflecting on the European genius, Agnes Heller maintained that "the recognition of the accomplishment of others has always been part and parcel of the European identity," that "the myth of Occident and Orient is not a juxtaposition of civilization with barbarism but rather of one civilization with another," and that "European (Western) cultural identity has been conceived as both ethnocentric and anti-ethnocentric."[17] If Europe has produced not only racism but also antiracism, not only misogyny but also feminism, not only antiSemitism, but also its repudiation, then what can be termed Balkanism has not yet been coupled with its complementing and ennobling antiparticle.

Afterword to the
Updated Edition

Since the publication of *Imagining the Balkans* over a decade ago, political events in Europe have eloquently illustrated the law of unintended consequences. After 1989, Central Europe's emancipatory ideology (over which much scholarly ink was spilled) became a device entitling its participants to a share of privileges, most importantly accession to NATO and front seats for the European Union. While the final historical verdict may legitimize this strategy, an unintended consequence has been the death of "Central Europe" as an idea. Extending a protective arm around the old centers of the Habsburg Empire, the West, motivated in part by sentiment, neatly followed the new trench lines of Samuel Huntington's clash of civilizations.[1] Tony Judt wrote in 1997 that this would create "a sort of depressed Eurosuburb beyond which 'Byzantine Europe' would be made to fend for itself, too close to Russia for the West to make an aggressive show of absorption and engagement."[2]

Things changed almost overnight with the beginning of NATO expansion in 1997. Since 1989, the question of the alliance's mission has never ceased to be high on both the European and U.S. agenda. With the disbanding of the Warsaw pact in 1991 and the disintegration of the Soviet Union in 1992, NATO's main adversaries and targets had ceased to exist, and with them its raison d'être. There were serious plans in Europe to disband NATO and build alternative security systems confined to the continent. Yet NATO remained the only truly transatlantic institution in which the United States continued to play the role of a European great power, and it was reluctant to lose this position. The United States was and continues to be the chief advocate for further NATO expansion, despite a 1990 pledge that NATO would not expand beyond German borders, while Europe's proximity to and dependence on Russian natural resources make it more circumspect.[3] In 1997 three former Warsaw Pact countries — Poland, Hungary and the Czech Republic — were invited to join the alliance and became members in 1999. The invitation was extended to Lithuania, Latvia, Estonia,

Slovenia, Slovakia, Bulgaria, and Romania in 2002, all of which joined in 2004. In 2008 another two Balkan countries—Croatia and Albania—were invited, and Macedonia is bound to follow soon.

This trajectory of NATO's evolution, alongside the development of events that led to the disintegration of Yugoslavia, brought about the unexpected intersection of two processes. Until 1999, the international community confined its pressure on and involvement in Yugoslavia almost exclusively to the United Nations. There were a few minor UN-sanctioned NATO operations after the Srebrenica massacre and before the Dayton accord, including the maritime enforcement of the arms embargo and the brief bombing of Republika Srpska in Bosnia in 1995. However, this intervention as well as contemporaneous events in Somalia and even the First Gulf War were aimed at restoring or preserving the status quo.[4] Even the ethnic cleansing of Krajna, the secessionist Serb enclave in Croatia, where hundreds of thousands of Serbs were swept away by the Croatian army in 1995, was done with the active approval and tacit participation of the United States.

The three-month-long NATO bombing of Yugoslavia in 1999, on the other hand, for all intents and purposes carried out by the United States, marked a new precedent. It effectively underwrote the secessionist claims of a minority population and set the stage for Kosovo's full independence some nine years later, another precedent, whose ominous repercussions play out in the Caucasus today. As Charles King aptly comments: "Even at the time of the NATO air strikes, it was difficult to distinguish an intervention to prevent genocide, from one intended to support the long-term political aims of a guerilla army."[5] This became a fundamental departure from the treatment of similar conflicts (between Palestinians and Jews in Israel, Kurds and Turks in Turkey, Kurds and Arabs in the First Gulf War, and others) where sovereignty and territorial integrity had been the dominant principle since the end of the Second World War. In another respect the Kosovo war saw what one observer has called "the rise of humanitarian hawks" and became the dress rehearsal for American unilateralism that culminated in the Second Gulf War.[6] In this respect, to borrow from Norman Davies's history of Poland, the Balkans once again became "God's playground," a laboratory for experimentation with new approaches and solutions.

There were a host of political and moral considerations for the 1999 intervention, not least among them the desire to revive the last European organization in which the United States played a leading role.[7] Whatever the motivations, the bombing clearly had unintended consequences. Before the Kosovo war, the dominant paradigm applied to the Balkans translated into the practical ghettoization of the region. The pre-Kosovo European Union visa regime accepted Central Europe but not the rest of Eastern Europe and the Balkans, where restrictions were placed on the movement of populations. This was "balkanism" in action. The rhetorical legitimization of the 1999 intervention—as defense of universal human rights—effectively brought the Balkans back into the sphere of Western politics. Both the bombing and its aftermath bound Europeans and Americans much more closely—even inextricably—to the Balkans. Through KFOR, the NATO-led force under UN mandate, both Americans and Europeans began running two de facto protectorates (Kosovo and Bosnia-Herzegovina). There emerged, for the first time, a significant lobby among Eurocrats who believed that it would be in Europe's best interests to bring the Balkans into the

European sphere, rather than ghettoize them. Eight East European countries (Poland, Hungary, the Czech Republic, Slovakia, Slovenia, Estonia, Latvia, and Lithuania) were admitted to the EU in 2004. Visa restrictions were suspended for two Balkan countries—Bulgaria and Romania—and they were admitted in 2007. Although a general EU expansion fatigue has set in, it is likely that Croatia, one of the three official Balkan candidates alongside Macedonia and Turkey, will be admitted in due time. Albania and the other remaining Yugoslav splinters have all been recognized as potential candidates. All of this has been accompanied by the curious but predictable subsiding of the balkanist rhetoric, though it is still encountered abundantly in journalism and fiction, as well as scholarship.[8] Even the vocal and often spiteful objections to Turkey's accession focus on Islam, Middle Eastern culture, or women's and human rights; but they are not clad in the balkanist rhetoric.

When I originally conceived of and wrote *Imagining the Balkans,* my motives were manifold, but I was and continue to be very open about my political agenda: I resented the ghettoization of the Balkans, and the book was, among other things, a response to that. I refrained from generalizing on scholarly output, maintaining that, in principle, the scholarly project moves along a different line from the production of popular mythology, and only occasionally intersects with it. I did not deny that a great number of the scholarly practitioners of Balkan studies might privately share a staggering number of prejudices; rather, as a whole, the rules of scholarly discourse restrict the open articulation of these prejudices. I still believe this to be true, and if I have erred, it is only in the direction of too much lenience.[9] Now journalists too are becoming more careful of how they articulate opinions about the Balkans. We even have a new politically correct designation: the Western Balkans. While during the Cold War Yugoslavia was neatly exempt from any connection to the Balkans, its civil war in the 1990s was generalized as a Balkan war, although none of the other Balkan countries—Greece, Bulgaria, Romania, Turkey, even Albania—were in danger of entering it. Now, with the changed political conjuncture, one speaks only about the Western Balkans as a problematic zone, and the rest of the Balkans are exempt from the designation. Thus, while the balkanist rhetoric is still with us, conveniently submerged but readily at hand, it no longer serves power politics. Balkanism has not disappeared, but has shifted, for the time being, from the center stage of politics.

This may allow us to reflect more calmly on the scholarly project of making sense of the Balkans. In what follows, I would like to focus on the theoretical relevance of the book in light of my own further research and refinement of my conceptual thinking, particularly as related to the continuous elaboration of the categories of analysis suggested in *Imagining the Balkans.* I argued that a specific discourse, "balkanism," molds attitudes and actions toward the Balkans and could be treated as the most persistent form or "mental map" in which information about the Balkans is placed, most notably in journalistic, political, and literary output. In introducing the category of balkanism, I was directly inspired by—and at the same time invited critical comparison to—Said's "orientalism," as well as the subsequent literature on postcolonialism. While, understandably, most readers' attention was dedicated to the six chapters of the book that described, exposed, and critiqued the balkanist discourse, the seventh chapter, dealing with the *realia* of the Balkans, remained overshadowed; and the book was perceived by some as solely a deconstructivist exercise. Others, conversely, felt that this final chapter, in which I introduced the concept of historical legacy, deviated from a modernist approach back to a realist and empirical one. Here I will try to address two topics relevant to this discussion: one is the further elaboration of my reluctance to subsume balkanism within postcolonialism; the other to develop the general relevance of the notion of historical legacy.

A day before Edward Said's death, Gayatri Spivak wrote the preface to the Serbian translation of her book *A Critique of Postcolonial Reason*, which she later dedicated to her "friend and ally, the founder of postcolonial studies, Edward Said."[10] The opening phrase of this preface established a powerful link between balkanism and postcolonialism: "The translation of *A Critique of Postcolonial Reason* into Serbian is an instructive event for me. The relationship of postcolonial theory to the Balkan as metaphor is a critical task for our world."[11] In response to Spivak, Obrad Savi?, translator of her work and acting president of the Belgrade Circle, wrote that with the passing of Said, the "great 'burden' of spreading postcolonial theory has now fallen on your back. What I can promise at this moment is that you can always count on complete and unconditional support from your friends in and around the Belgrade Circle. We are small, but we never let go!"[12]

This emotional pledge and assertion of a correlation between balkanism and postcolonialism, as well as my earlier reluctance to link them together, prompted Dušan Bjeli?, another prominent member of the Belgrade Circle, to organize a panel at the 2004 convention of the Association for the Study of Nationalities to address the relationship between these two categories. At the conference, I discussed two broad issues: first, the meeting points (if any) between the categories and phenomena of balkanism and postcolonialism; second, the appropriateness or utility of approaching balkanism from a postcolonial perspective. Simply put: are there intersections between balkanism and postcolonialism, and if so, are they productive?

When I started writing this book, whose working title was *Balkanism*, I found to my surprise and delight that balkanism was an uninhabited category, something exceptionally rare in the humanities. This circumstance allowed me to use the term as both a mirror and foil of orientalism, to both pay homage to Edward Said and to argue for a substantive difference between the two categories and phenomena. To put it succinctly, "balkanism" expresses the idea that explanatory approaches to phenomena in the Balkans often rest upon a discourse or a stable system of stereotypes that place the Balkans in a cognitive straightjacket.[13] I argued for the historicity of balkanism, which was shaped as a discourse in the early decades of the twentieth century, but whose genealogy can be traced to patterns of representation from the sixteenth century onward. I thus insisted on the historical grounding of balkanism in the Ottoman period, when the designation "Balkan" first entered the peninsula. Arguably, some aspects of the balkanist discourse grew out of the earlier schism between the churches of Rome and Constantinople, but the most salient aspects emerged from the Ottoman period.

The Balkans have a number of different incarnations or manifestations, which can be roughly grouped into four categories. At its simplest, "Balkan" is a name: initially, the name of a mountain, used increasingly since the fifteenth century when it first appeared, until the nineteenth century, when it was applied to the peninsula and region as a whole. "Balkan" is also used as a metaphor. By the beginning of the twentieth

century, it became a pejorative, triggered by the events accompanying the disintegration of the Ottoman Empire and the creation of small, weak, economically backward
and dependent nation-states, striving to modernize. The difficulties of this modernization process and the accompanying excesses of nationalism created a situation in
which the Balkans began to serve as a symbol for the aggressive, intolerant, barbarian,
semi-developed, semi-civilized, and semi-oriental. It is this use and its present utilization in the real world of politics—"balkanism"—that shapes attitudes and actions
toward the Balkans. If there is a tentative connection to postcolonial theory, it is with
this aspect of the Balkans, and Spivak is correct in carefully linking it only to the Balkan
as metaphor.[14] Unlike the Orient, however, the Balkans can be addressed as a scholarly category of analysis—a concrete geographic region—and in this capacity it is
currently most often used as a synonym of Southeastern Europe. Finally, the Balkans
can be approached and interpreted through the notion of historical legacy, which is
intimately intertwined with the character of the Balkans as region and, thus, linked to
its concreteness.

There are obvious similarities between balkanism and orientalism. First and foremost, they are both discursive formations. Very much like orientalism, the Balkans
can serve as a powerful metaphor. Yet, the main difference between the two concepts
is the geographic and historical concreteness of the Balkans versus the mostly metaphorical and symbolic nature of the Orient. The lack of a colonial predicament for
the Balkans also distinguishes the two, as do questions of race, color, religion, language, and gender. The most important distinction, however, is what I perceive as the
pull of other essential aspects of the Balkans, which challenge the scholar to deal with
the ontology of the Balkans, rather than simply with its metaphoric functions. In a
way, Said's orientalism, too, was a concrete historically-inspired discussion: it was the
Palestinian predicament in the era of late imperialism. However, it was clad in such
a generalizing discourse that it proved to be transportable and became metaphori-
cally appropriate for designating the postcolonial as a whole. I would argue that, among
others, the circumstance that allowed Said to do so was the elastic nature of the Orient. Granted, one could also note the authors' different approaches and backgrounds:
orientalism exposed by a literary critic, balkanism analyzed by a historian. Here we
can already see the first methodological distinction (albeit not necessarily incompatible): one a structuralist (or, rather, poststructuralist) theory; the other an essentially
historical approach and interpretation.[15]

As a whole, one may generalize that the quarter-century after the appearance of
Orientalism saw a disciplinary shift in third world scholarship from sociological and
economic analysis to cultural and theoretical/semiotic/discursive analysis, and the
simultaneous appearance and maturation of postcolonial and global studies.
Postcolonial studies challenged the theoretical models and metanarratives built on
the earlier dominant paradigms of modernization, development, and world systems
theory. The problem is that postcolonialism itself became a new metanarrative, though
it is only fair to say that, despite some conservative hysteria, it has never been truly
institutionalized. There are only a handful of departments, centers, or programs in
postcolonial studies, whereas the study of globalization receives much more attention and funding. Nonetheless, postcolonial studies have undoubtedly achieved an
honorary status even if some are positing a melancholic phase[16] or at least are seriously

scrutinizing where, if anywhere, postcolonial studies are heading. It is quite interesting to note that it is precisely at this moment that some East European intellectuals are beginning to pose the question of their relation to the postcolonial.[17] To return to the most general understanding of postcolonialism as a cultural discipline dedicated to the analysis of discourse, the central question is: can the interpretation (mine or someone else's) of balkanism as a discourse be treated as a concrete historical/geographic version of postcolonial studies? What are the benefits of comparison? And, if some (as I do) maintain that this is difficult and not necessarily fortuitous, why the insistence on the distinction?

David Spurr offers two definitions of the postcolonial: first, as a historical situation marked by the dismantling of traditional institutions of colonial power; second, as a search for alternatives to the discourses of the colonial era. "While the first is the object of empirical knowledge, the second is both an intellectual project and a transnational condition that includes, along with new possibilities, certain crises of identity and representation."[18] My objections to the application of postcolonialism to the Balkans mostly concern the first meaning of postcolonialism. Postcolonial studies are a critique of postcoloniality, the condition in areas of the world that were colonies. I do not believe the Ottoman Empire, whose legacy has defined the Balkans, can be treated as a late colonial empire. First, there was no abyss or institutional/legal distinction between metropole and dependencies. Second, there was no previous stable entity which colonized. The Ottoman Empire became an elaborate state machine and an empire in the course of shaping itself as an expanding polity, which was an organic whole in all its territories. Third, there was no civilizing mission comparable to the French or the English colonial project. Fourth, there is no hegemonic cultural residue from the Ottoman Empire comparable to the linguistic and general cultural hegemony of English in the Indian subcontinent and elsewhere, or of French in Africa and Indochina. There is also the issue of self-perceptions. Subjectivity matters, after all, and contemporaries in the Balkans under Ottoman rule did not describe themselves as colonial subjects. The only party that insisted on its semicolonial status was the Ottoman Empire itself, as voiced by some intellectuals at the time and others during Turkey's Republican Era. These factors also apply as a whole to the Habsburgs. The Romanov Empire, while colonial empire par excellence in the East and in the South, was different in its relations to the Balkans, where the above patterns mostly held true. I would extend the same verdict to the Soviet Union in relation to its East European satellites (a case of a possible empire, although not uncontested historiographically),[19] though its relationship with Central Asia or the Caucasus might qualify as a colonial empire.[20] In light of this, up to now postcolonial studies have not really made methodological inroads in the Balkans and in Eastern Europe as a whole, in contrast to Wallerstein's world-systems theory, immensely popular in Greece and Turkey and widely read in some East European countries even before 1989.

Should one be pedantic about defining empire and colonialism? Maybe not. For structuralists of any kind, the Spanish empire is not much different from the Roman, the Ottoman, the British, or the Russian. In a way, they are all empires, and they are all colonial. But I would be surprised if any scholarly convention held a panel on the postcolonial sensibilities of fifth-century Gaul or sixth-century Iberia after the collapse of the Roman Empire. Despite its universalist articulation, postcolonialism's development is closely linked to the Indian subcontinent and Africa of the nineteenth and twentieth centuries. Even the nature of Latin American postcolonialism is contested.[21] The difference between the postimperial and the postcolonial is primarily the concern of the historian, yet each case requires a very different theoretical framing.

In an otherwise positive review of *Imagining the Balkans*, Gregory Jusdanis took me to task for refusing to consider Balkan societies as postcolonial: "While it is true that the social, political and economic relationships between the European imperial powers and their overseas possessions differed from those between the Ottoman state and the Balkans, why could the wars of independence against this rule not be considered postcolonial?" He further pointed out that attempts by nationalist historiographies to cleanse their traditions from the Ottoman legacy can be read as postcolonial endeavors to deny the cultural influence of the former ruler, and asked: "Is this not also the typical reaction of every nationalist movement—to distinguish itself from the polity against which it rebels?"[22] Certainly it is, but this presents a methodological conundrum: is every national movement necessarily anticolonial, and does it always produce a postcolonial situation? Time-bound and place-bound specificity matters, not only in order to avoid cognitive fallacies, but on ethical grounds as well. The emancipatory mantle of postcolonialism all too often serves as a cover for the perpetual lament of self-victimization.

Finally, any meaningful scholarly analysis has to do with the questions we ask, and the most adequate framing of the responses. The question that had interested me, and continues to interest me, is the ontology of the Balkans. I developed the idea of the Balkans as the Ottoman legacy, after a lengthy deconstruction of the discourse, in an effort to offer a reconstruction. This produced, I am afraid, misunderstanding by some; so I will rephrase it as a question with serious scholarly, political, and moral implications: How do we study historical regions?

Regions and regional identities have attracted much scholarly attention in recent years and are now studied with all the seriousness once conferred primarily on national identities.[23] Where regional allegiances were once seen simply as leftovers of provincial mentalities not yet co-opted by the nation-state, today they are often seen as places of resistance to centralized authority and harbingers of reform and democracy. They can also be seen as a more adequate structural base to accommodate ethnic or economic differences. There are many definitions of what constitutes a region in the literature, but the "lowest common denominator is that it is a territory or an area in some way demarcated or at least spatially defined."[24] Today, the category is utilized for territorial expanses of different sizes, and regions are studied as both subnational entities and supranational formations. In today's increasingly interdependent world (defined by some as globalization) certain regions may supersede the nation-state, or at least attempt to do so. Such is the ongoing experiment with the European Union, primarily an economic unit but with growing political and cultural ambitions, which symbolically appropriated the name of the larger geographic region: Europe. The project *Europa* was, in fact, the major impetus to the accumulation of a vast body of literature on regions and regionalism.

Some scholars, in an effort to move beyond the territorial tautology, point out that in order to be marked from the outside world, regions have to possess some internal similarities, cohesion, and affinity.[25] Europe can be approached as the component of different intersecting regional formations, of which the geography is but one aspect (and not always the most important): the region of Western Christianity; of contact and complex historical interplay between the three monotheistic world religions (Christianity, Islam, Judaism); of nations; the core-region of world colonization and industrialization. Numerous other definitions might be applied within the framework of different disciplines or approaches. Historians in particular are crucified between two poles: Marc Bloch's position that French history does not exist, there is only European history, against a position of well-argued skepticism that European history could ever be approached holistically in any methodologically convincing way.[26]

Eastern Europe should not simply be identified as a territorial subregion of Europe, though this often happens—and neither should Southeastern Europe or the Balkans be treated as subregions of the subregion. As territorial subregions, they are locked in a hierarchical matrix where they become, to utilize some Jakobsonian terminology, *marked* categories.[27] As an example of the complex notion of Europe, at American universities there are numerous departments of European studies. There is also, and usually not as an integral part of European studies, the field of East European studies. To this day, American universities as a rule advertise separate positions for East Europeanists. If a general position in European history is opened, it is usually specified as British, German, French, Italian, Spanish, Russian, even Irish history, while Polish, Czech, Hungarian, Romanian, Bulgarian, Serb, Croatian, Macedonian, Latvian, Estonian, Albanian, and other national histories are subsumed under the umbrella of East European history. "Eastern European," then, is a marked category as a subfield of European history. "Central European," or rather "East Central European," and "Southeast European" history and literature occasionally emerge as marked subcategories within this marked subfield. The rest of Europe, however, is not represented by commensurate categories and the appropriate specialists on "Northeastern Europe," "West Central Europe," nor even "Western Europe." These are, then, *unmarked* categories. Marked categories become different while unmarked categories retain power as the standard against which the rest must be positioned. In the case of Europe, this central notion is implicitly hierarchical, as Europe forms the nexus of several complex networks of meaning in which it plays quite different and far from commensurate roles: the role of geographic area but also those of economic and administrative powerhouse, of historical and intellectual idea, and, increasingly, of an ideal.

Since differentiation or disentanglement of entities takes place at the edge, for a long time borders were the preferred object of analysis, especially in examinations of identity and when defining regions. Identity and alterity (otherness) clearly exist in a symbiotic relationship, and their most sharply defined characteristics are best articulated at this border encounter. Consequently, otherness became a fundamental category of both social experience and social analysis, and it has made a powerful inroad in historical studies. Borders, however, turned out to be a problematic first choice. They are unstable and can be defined by a number of different criteria. More importantly, the excessive focus on borders imposed an unhealthy obsession with distinction and difference. Recently, there has been a powerful shift away from border studies toward the now-fashionable category of space, which allots due attention to the cohesive processes and structures within the entity. This approach, developed by geographers and anthropologists, stresses the links between knowledge, power, and spatiality and focuses on the metaphorical and material resonance of space.[28] While this theory has produced valuable works, it also has its dangers. Space is oftentimes uncritically linked to ethnicity or nation, and this either unintentionally replicates statist and nationalist claims under the guise of a new scholarly jargon, or produces static and ahistoric structural analyses.

It is against this background that I introduce the notion of historical legacy, which focuses attention on the element of time in order to answer a misleadingly simple question: What is a region? Historical legacy retains the valuable features of spatiality while simultaneously refining the vector of time, making it more historically specific. After all, as observed in the popular play about the Cold War, *A Walk in the Woods*, "history is only geography stretched over time."[29] Any region can be approached as the complex result of the interplay of numerous historical periods, traditions, and legacies; and of these categories, historical periods are the most straightforward. They delineate a length of time with some internal consistency and a more or less well-established beginning and end, based most often on (a cluster of) meaningful events.

Tradition and legacy are less straightforward. Raymond Williams observed that "tradition in its most general modern sense is a particularly difficult word."[30] Of its manifold meanings throughout the centuries, the general process of handing down knowledge and ideas survived, and was soon linked to the idea of respect and duty to the forebears. We have in this popular understanding of tradition several components: an active attitude, a conscious selection, and an evaluative elevation of elements created in an accumulative process of handing down. Legacy is a broadly used word, but it has not entered the specialized vocabulary of historians or other social scientists (barring the legal profession). Alongside its legal use (as a bequest), it is very similar to tradition: both designate the processes (and artifacts) of handing down. Yet, while tradition involves a conscious selection of elements bequeathed from the past, legacy encompasses everything—chosen or not—that is handed down from the past. In this sense, legacy neither betrays the past nor surrenders it to active meddling. Legacy may be exalted or maligned by successors, but this comes as a secondary process. Legacy as an abstract signifier is neutral. It is, then, my choice to make *historical legacy* the receptacle of a meaning on which I will elaborate below.

For purely cognitive purposes I distinguish between legacy as continuity and legacy as perception. Legacy as continuity is the survival (and gradual decline) of some of the characteristics of the entity immediately before its collapse. Legacy as perception, on the other hand, is the articulation and rearticulation of how the entity is thought about at different times by different individuals or groups. These should not be interpreted as "real" versus "imagined" characteristics: the characteristics of continuity are themselves often perceptual, and perceptions are no less a matter of continuous real social facts. In both cases, the categories designate social facts, which are at different removes from experience; but in the instance of perception, the social fact is removed yet a further step from immediate reality.

Let me provide two concrete examples from the Balkans and Eastern Europe to illustrate each type of legacy. If we look at the numerous historical periods, traditions, and legacies that shape Southeastern Europe, some periods and legacies overlap and others are completely segregated;[31] some have played themselves out in the same geographic space while others have involved different macroregions of southeast Europe.[32] These periods and legacies can also be classified according to their influence in different spheres of social life, such as political, economic, demographic, or cultural. In the religious sphere, one can single out the Christian, Muslim, and Judaic traditions, along with their numerous sects and branches. In the sphere of art and culture, there are the legacies of the pre-Greeks, the Greeks, and numerous ethnic groups that settled the peninsula. In social and demographic terms, we have the legacies of large and incessant migrations, ethnic diversity, seminomadism, a large egalitarian agricultural sphere, and late urbanization alongside a constant continuity of urban life.

Of the political legacies that have shaped the southeast European peninsula as a whole (Roman, Byzantine, Ottoman, and communist), two can be singled out as crucial before the nineteenth century. One is the Byzantine millennium, with its profound political, institutional, legal, religious, and cultural impact. The other is the half millennium of Ottoman rule that gave the peninsula its name and established its longest period of political unity. The Ottoman elements—or those perceived as such—have contributed to most current Balkan stereotypes. In the narrow sense of the word, then, one can argue that the Balkans are, in fact, the Ottoman legacy.

This legacy is different from the Ottoman polity or the Ottoman period; it is a process that began after the Ottoman Empire ceased to exist, and is the aggregate of characteristics handed down chiefly from the eighteenth and nineteenth centuries. I have attempted a systematic review of the workings of the Ottoman legacy as continuity in the political, cultural, social, and economic spheres where it displayed different degrees of perseverance. In practically all spheres, the break began almost immediately after the onset of political independence in the separate Balkan states and, as a whole, was completed by the end of World War I; in the realms of demography and popular culture, however, the Ottoman legacy continued for some time and was gradually transformed into the influence of the Turkish nation-state. After World War I, the Ottoman legacy as perception became the process of interaction of an ever-evolving and accumulating past with ever-evolving and accumulating perceptions of generations of people who are redefining the past. This legacy is not a reconstruction, but rather a construction of the past in works of historiography, fiction, journalism, and everyday discourse. The legacy as perception is one of the most important pillars in the discourse of Balkan nationalism and displays striking similarities in all Balkan countries. The Ottoman legacy is at the center of securing present social arrangements, above all legitimizing the state; and it is bound to be reproduced for some time to come.

The countries defined as Balkan (i.e. those in the historical Ottoman sphere) have been moving steadily away from their Ottoman legacy, and with this also from their "balkanness." I want to strongly emphasize here that this statement is devoid of any evaluative element. I argue that what we are witnessing today in the geographic Balkans—namely, the eradication of the final vestiges of a historical legacy of ethnic multiplicity and coexistence,[33] and its replacement by institutionalized ethnically homogeneous bodies—may well be an advanced stage of the final Europeanization of the region, and the end of the historic Balkans and the Ottoman legacy.

Let us now take the larger concept of Eastern Europe to further illustrate the concept of historical legacy. Geographically, Eastern Europe encompasses the Balkans, yet in a politico-historical sense it actually divided them during the period of the Cold War. If we look at the historical periods, traditions, and legacies that shape what constitutes Eastern Europe today, we see that some of these periods and legacies have overlapped, while others were completely segregated; some encompassed the whole region, while others involved only some of the area's constituent parts. Eastern Europe's communist legacy, the most recently created one and based on the shortest period of rule, is usually neglected, most often by those who insist on the permanence of the previous imperial legacies. It is preposterous to look for a socialist legacy *in* Eastern Europe: Eastern Europe, as a political space today, is the socialist legacy. After World War II, Eastern Europe's nineteenth-century role as an intermediary space balancing between two centers of political and economic expansion (Western Europe and Russia), which in the interwar period had given way to the function of a cordon sanitaire against bolshevism, had dramatically changed. Anyone who lived in pre-1989 Eastern Europe would concur that this notion made sense only as a political synonym for Warsaw Pact Europe. The moment the socialist period ended, around 1989, it turned into a legacy. Under the rubric of legacy as continuity, the socialist heritage in the political, economic, and social spheres is strikingly similar in all postcommunist countries. Whether they like it or not, most "transitologists" prefer Eastern Europe as a logical sphere of reference. The socialist legacy as continuity displays different degrees of perseverance in separate spheres and countries, but like any legacy, it is bound to subside. After this happens it will be relegated to the realm of perception. As a long-term process, Eastern Europe is gradually fading away. Integration with the European institutional framework may occur over the next few decades, but in the realm of perception, we are speaking of the discrete experience of two or three generations. Eastern Europe will soon disappear as a category, though attitudes will be more difficult and slow to change. Unlike the Ottoman legacy, which bears only the characteristics of the last two centuries of the Ottoman era, the socialist legacy, because of its relative brevity, reflects the characteristics of the whole period. But the socialist period is itself a subcategory of a larger phenomenon. I am referring to what came in the wake of the Ottoman period, which, depending on the preferred paradigm or terminology, has been defined as the capitalist world economy (Wallerstein), the capitalist mode of production (Marx), the "iron cage" of capitalist modernity (Max Weber), the age of industrialism, urbanism, modernization, or globalization. For Zygmunt Bauman, capitalism and socialism are "married forever in their attachment to modernity," and modernity itself is turning into a legacy.[34]

While thinking in terms of historical legacies is an acceptable and fruitful answer to the question of how best to approach historical regions, framing it within the postcolonial paradigm does not deliver some deeper insights. I am in favor of alternative framing paradigms and continue to admire many postcolonial works, but I do not think that exchanging one metanarrative for another grand theory provides any solution. In the end, this may be splitting hairs, but I believe that an excessive emphasis on abstract knowledge-power patterns stands in the way of the effort to recognize and recover the more determinate, more concrete, and ultimately more messy activities of history. I also disagree that theoretically informed empiricism (or simply put, intelligent, rigorous scholarship) is a counter or challenge to the theoretical array of studies. My objections refer primarily to the way we assess postcoloniality as a historical phenomenon. Things get more complicated if we search for alternative discourses of the colonial era, something that is both an intellectual project and a transnational condition that includes, along with new possibilities, certain crises of identity and representation. Here, the Balkans provide an interesting twist, particularly in the understanding of subjectivity. While self-understanding as colonial subjects was absent in the Balkans, contemporary East European intellectuals (in the post-1989 world) increasingly see themselves in a subordinate position vis-à-vis the centers of knowledge production and dissemination in the West, and some speak explicitly of intellectual neo-imperialism, neocolonialism, or self-colonization. This, I argue, produces an opening through which postcolonial theory finds an attentive ear among a new intellectual clientele. There is an unquestionable link between a number of East European intellectuals and postcolonialism, and while this link is not effectuated via balkanism, it does merit analysis.

John Dunham Kelly has identified three powerful antinomies in postcolonial theory, which can be identified with the work of their most influential theoreticians. Concerning the agency of dominated groups, Gayatri Spivak raised the question "Can the subaltern speak?" which addressed whether subalterns have the power to represent themselves, or whether it is precisely the lack of that power that makes them subalterns. Dipesh Chakrabarty's call for "provincializing Europe" refers to the power and possible inevitability of western paradigms. This particular antinomy poses difficulty for East European (Balkan inclusive) studies. It has been noted by some scholars outside the field (mostly those in Middle Eastern or South Asian studies) that among East Europeans there is a specific kind of ontological angst to "de-center" Europe. That may be so, but I submit to a very materialist bias: it simply reflects the physical fact that Europe (in a very elastic but mostly geographic understanding) is the natural geographic and historical background against which developments in one of its subregions in particular time periods can be most adequately projected.

Centered on the boundary issues between postcoloniality and globalization, Kelly's third antinomy focuses on when and how postcoloniality might end,[35] which relates directly to the positionality of contemporary East European intellectuals. Some argue that globalization is the successor of postcoloniality and "the late capitalist liberator from postcoloniality, as the globe moves from Western modernity to modernity at large or to alternative modernities, negating all vestiges of asymmetric colonial relations." Kelly's counterargument asserts that "postcoloniality and globalization can be seen as two sides of the same coin, the coin of American power." In his vision, "postcoloniality could end only when American power is as thoroughly confronted as European power has been, and the limitations intrinsic to the formal symmetries of the political present are as fully overcome as have been the formal asymmetries of the colonial past."[36] It is within this context that Judit Bodnar highlights the marginalization of Eastern Europe and argues persuasively about the similarities between postcolonial and postsocialist theory. Without stretching the meaning of coloniality to accommodate Eastern Europe, Bodnar nonetheless calls for opening up of categories that were hitherto used almost exclusively to conceptualize the non-western experience.[37]

With this text, I have tried to elaborate on the heuristic qualities of the concept of historical legacies for general historical analysis. Thinking in terms of historical legacies—characterized by simultaneous, overlapping, and gradually waning effects— allows us to emphasize the complexity and plasticity of the historical process. In the case of the Balkans and Eastern Europe, it allows us to rescue the region from a debilitating diachronic and spatial ghettoization, and insert it into multifarious cognitive frameworks over space and time. Europe, in this vision, emerges as a complex palimpsest of differently shaped entities, not only exposing the porosity of internal frontiers, but also questioning the absolute stability of external ones. In this respect, the task for balkanists and East Europeanists consists not so much of "provincializing" Europe but of "de-provincializing" Western Europe, which has heretofore expropriated the category of Europe with concrete political and moral consequences. In the academic sphere, this translates as the continuing necessity on the part of East Europeanists to have a good grasp of the West European fields, as well as to challenge the sanctioned ignorance of West Europeanists about developments in the eastern half of the continent. If this project comes to fruition, we will actually succeed in "provincializing" Europe effectively for the rest of the world, insofar as the European paradigm will have broadened to include not only a cleansed, abstract, and idealized version of power, but also one of dependency, subordination, and messy struggles. Perhaps, at that juncture, there could be a genuine and fruitful confluence of aims between postcolonial theory and anti-balkanism.

Notes

Preface

    1. Edward W. Said, *Representations of the Intellectual*, New York: Pantheon, 1994, xii.
    2. David Spurr, *The Rhetoric of Empire: Colonial Discourse in Journalism, Travel Writing, and Imperial Administration*, Durham, N.C., and London: Duke University Press, 1993, 196.

Introduction

    1. *Report of the International Commission to Inquire into the Causes and Conduct of the Balkan Wars*, Washington, D.C.: Carnegie Endowment for International Peace, 1914, 1.
    2. Ibid., 4–5, 19, 273.
    3. *The Other Balkan Wars. A 1913 Carnegie Endowment Inquiry in Retrospect with a New Introduction and Reflections on the Present Conflict by George F. Kennan*, Washington, D.C.: Carnegie Endowment for International Peace, 1993, 1.
    4. Ibid., 9.
    5. Ibid., 4.
    6. Hannah Pakula, *The Last Romantic. A Biography of Queen Marie of Romania*, New York, Simon and Schuster, 1984.
    7. *The Other Balkan Wars*, 4, 6, 11, 13.
    8. Mary Edith Durham, *Twenty Years of Balkan Tangle*, London: George Allen & Unwin, 1920, 238.
    9. *The Other Balkan Wars*, 12–13.
    10. Roger Cohen, "A Balkan Gyre of War, Spinning Onto Film," *New York Times*, section 2, 12 March 1995, 24.
    11. *The Other Balkan Wars*, 243, 395; John G. Heidenrich, "The Gulf War: How Many Iraqis Died?" *Foreign Policy*, no. 90, no. 91, 1993, 108–125.
    12. George Kenney, "The Bosnia Calculation," *New York Times Magazine*, 23 April 1995, 42–43; "George Kenney, "Steering Clear of Balkan Shoals," *Nation*, vol. 262, no. 2, 8/15 January 1996, 21–24; "Credit McNamara in Winning the Cold War," *New York Times*, 14 April 1995, A14; Philip Shenon, "20 Years After Victory, Vietnamese Communists Ponder How to Celebrate," *New York Times*, 23 April 1995, 12.
    13. Hugo Dyserinck and Karl Ulrich Syndram, *Europa und das nationale Selbstverständnis. Imagologische Probleme in Literatur, Kunst und Kultur des 19. und 20. Jahrhunderts*, Bonn: Bouvier, 1988; Munasu Duala-M'bedy, *Xenologie: Die Wissenshaft vom Fremden und die Verdrängung der Humanität in der Anthropologie*, Freiburg and Münich: Verlag Karl Alber, 1977; Alexandru Duțu, "Die Imagologie und die Entdeckung der Alterität," *Kulturbeziehungen in Mittel- und Osteuropa in 18. und 19. Jahrhundert*, Berlin, 1982, 257–263; Alexandru Duțu, "The Mental Substratum of the Cultural Activity," *Revue des études sud-est européennes*, vol. 28, nos. 1–4, 1990, 3–10; Nadja Danova, Vesela Dimova, and Maria Kalitsin, eds., *Predstavata za "drugiya" na Balkanite*, Sofia: Akademichno izdatelstvo "Marin Drinov," 1995; Klaus Roth, ed. *Mit der Differenz leben: Europäische Ethnologie und Interkulturelle Kommunikation*, Munich and New York: Waxmann Münster, 1996.

14. Edward W. Said, *Orientalism*, New York: Pantheon, 1978, 3.

15. Edward W. Said, "East isn't East," *Times Literary Supplement*, 3 February 1995, 3.

16. A paraphrase of the excellent article of Milica Bakić-Hayden and Robert Hayden, "Orientalist Variations on the Theme 'Balkans': Symbolic Geography in Recent Yugoslav Cultural Politics," *Slavic Review*, vol. 51, no. 1, Spring 1992, 1–15. It was only during the copyediting phase that I came across John B. Allcock's valuable article on constructing the Balkans. While I disagree with the notion that we should look at the image of the Balkans as a subtheme to Said's study (p. 179), I would like to express my great satisfaction over the numerous instances where our interpretation coincides. See John B. Allcock, "Constructing the Balkans," John B. Allcock and Antonia Young, eds., *Black Lambs and Grey Falcons: Women Travellers in the Balkans*, Bradford, England: Bradford University Press, 1991, 170–191.

17. Aijaz Ahmad, *In Theory: Classes, Nations, Literatures*, London and New York: Verso, 1992, 169–170, 177–178.

18. Asaf Hussain, Robert Olson, and Jamil Qureshi, *Orientalism, Islam, and Islamists*, Brattleboro, Vt.: Amana, 1984; David Kopf, "Hermeneutics Versus History," Journal of Asian Studies, vol. 39, no. 3, 1980, 495–506; Robert A. Kapp, "Introduction: Review Symposium: Edward Said's Orientalism," *Journal of Asian Studies*, vol. 39, no. 3, 1980, 481–484; Carol A. Breckenridge and Peter van der Veer, eds., *Orientalism and the Postcolonial Predicament: Perspectives on South Asia*, Philadelphia: University of Pennsylvania Press, 1993.

19. Bernard Lewis, *Islam and the West*, New York and Oxford: Oxford University Press, 1993, 99–118; Bernard Lewis, "Eurocentrism Revisited," *Commentary*, vol. 98, no. 6, December 1994, 47–61; Said, "East isn't East," 4.

20. J. S. F. Parker, "From Aeschylus to Kissinger," *Gazelle Review*, vol. 1, 1980, 4–16; Andrea Fuchs-Sumiyoshi, *Orientalismus in der deutschen Literatur, Untersuchungen zu Werken des 19. und 20. Jahrhunderts, von Goethes "West-östlichem Diwan" bis Thomas Manns "Joseph"-Tetralogie*, Germanistische Texte und Studien, Bd. 20, Hildesheim, Zurich, and New York: Georg Olms Verlag, 1984; Lisa Lowe, *Critical Terrains: French and British Orientalisms*, Ithaca, N.Y. and London: Cornell University Press, 1991; Laura Nader, "Orientalism, Occidentalism and the Control of Women," *Cultural Dynamics*, vol. 2, no. 3, 1989; Bryan S. Turner, *Orientalism, Postmodernism and Globalism*, London and New York: Routledge, 1994, 4–8.

21. Michael Richardson, "Enough Said. Reflections on Orientalism," *Anthropology Today*, vol. 6, no. 4, August 1990, 16–19; Edward W. Said, "Representing the Colonized: Anthropology's Interlocutors," *Critical Inquiry*, vol. 15, no. 2, Winter 1989, 225.

22. Said, *Orientalism*, 20–21, 55–59.

23. Ahmad, *In Theory*, 163–168; James Clifford, *The Predicament of Culture, Twentieth Century Ethnography, Literature and Art*, Cambridge: Cambridge University Press, 1988, 264–265.

24. Said, "East isn't East," 5.

25. The 1960s and 1970s produced intellectually important, and often scholarly more rigorous, contributions: Jonah Ruskin, *The Mythology of Imperialism*, New York: Random House, 1971; V. G. Kiernan, *The Lords of Human Kind: European Attitudes to the Outside World in the Imperial Age*, Harmondsworth, Middlesex, England: Penguin, 1972; Talal Asad, ed., *Anthropology and the Colonial Encounter*, London: Ithaca, 1973; Bryan Turner, *Marx and the End of Orientalism*, London: George Allen and Unwin, 1978.

26. Breckenridge and van der Veer, *Orientalism*, 1–2.

27. Said, *Orientalism*, 45.

28. Cited in Mary Douglas, ed., *Rules and Meanings. The Anthropology of Everyday Knowledge*, Harmondsworth, Middlesex, England: Penguin, 1973, 201.

29. James G. Carrier, "Occidentalism: The World Turned Upside-Down," *American Ethnologist*, vol. 19, no. 2, May 1992, 207.

30. Clifford, "On Orientalism," 272.

31. Carrier, "Occidentalism," 197.

32. Milica Bakić-Hayden, "Nesting Orientalisms: The Case of Former Yugoslavia," *Slavic Review*, vol. 54, no. 4, Winter 1995, 917–931; Elli Skopetea, *I Disi tis Anatolis. Ikones apo to*

telos tis Othomanikis Avtokratorias, Athens, Greece: Gnosi, 1992, 97–98; Elli Skopetea, "Orientalizam i Balkan," *Istorijski časopis*, vol. 38, 1991, 131–143.

33. The term is used in linguistics to denote characteristics such as the phonetical, morphological, and syntactic, characteristics that define the Balkan linguistic union; only occasionally has it had a pejorative meaning.

34. Said, "East isn't East," 3.

35. Clifford, "On Orientalism," 260.

36. Thierry Hentsch, *Imagining the Middle East*, Montréal and New York: Black Rose, 1992, 7.

37. Larry Wolff, *Inventing Eastern Europe, The Map of Civilization on the Mind of the Enlightenment*, Stanford, Calif.: Stanford University Press, 1994.

38. Roderic H. Davison, "Where is the Middle East?" *Foreign Affairs*, July 1960, 665–675.

39. Akbar S. Ahmed, *Postmodernism and Islam: Predicament and Promise*, London and New York: Routledge, 1992.

40. Semra Germaner and Zeynep Inankur, *Orientalism and Turkey*, Istanbul: Turkish Cultural Service Foundation, 1989, 21.

41. Richard Martin and Harold Koda, *Orientalism: Visions of the East in Western Dress*, New York: Metropolitan Museum of Art, 1994, 55.

42. Turner, *Orientalism*, 98.

43. Germaner and Inankur, *Orientalism and Turkey*, 42.

44. Arthur D. Howden Smith, *Fighting the Turks in the Balkans, An American's Adventure with the Macedonian Revolutionaries*, New York and London: G. P. Putnam's, 1908, 1–3, 24.

45. Ibid., 10–11.

46. Herbert Vivian, *The Servian Tragedy, with Some Impressions of Macedonia*, London: Grant Richards, 1904, 252–253, 267.

47. Smith, *Fighting the Turks*, 315–316.

48. Ibid., 311.

49. Ibid., 9.

50. Durham, *Twenty Years*, 12, 44, 53.

51. Said, "East isn't East," 6.

52. Z. Duckett Ferriman, *Greece and the Greeks*, New York: James Pott, 1911, 132, a point made earlier by Karl Emil Franzos, *Aus Halb-Asien, Culturbilder aus Galizien, der Bukowina, Südrusland und Rumänien*, Leipzig: Verlag von Breitkopf und Härtel, 1878.

53. Mary Edith Durham, *The Sarajevo Crime*, London: George Allen and Unwin, 1925, 11.

54. W. E. B. Du Bois, *Color and Democracy: Colonies and Peace*, New York: Harcourt, Brace, 1945, 58, 67.

55. Samir Amin, *Eurocentrism*, New York: Monthly Review, 1989, vii.

56. Mary Douglas, *Purity and Danger. An Analysis of Concepts of Pollution and Taboo*, Harmondsworth, Middlesex, England: Penguin, 1970, 12, 48–50, 115–116, 191–192.

57. William Miller, *Travels and Politics in the Near East*, London: T. Fisher Unwin, 1898, xvi.

58. Arnold van Gennep, *The Rites of Passage*, Chicago: University of Chicago Press, 1960; Victor Turner, *The Ritual Process: Structure and Anti-Structure*, Chicago: Aldine, 1969; Nathan Schwartz-Salant and Murray Stein, eds., *Liminality and Transitional Phenomena*, Wilmette, Ill.: Chiron, 1991, 40–41.

59. Skopetea, *I Disi*, 97–98.

60. Stephen C. Ainlay, Gaylene Becker, and Lerita M. Coleman, eds., *The Dilemma of Difference, A Multidisciplinary View of Stigma*, New York and London: Plenum, 1986, 21.

61. Clifford, "On Orientalism," 264; Said, *Orientalism*, 92–94.

62. Friedrich Nietzsche, *The Gay Science*, cited in Bakić-Hayden, "Nesting Orientalisms," 917.

63. Roland Barthes, "Bichon chez lez les nègres," *Mythologies*, Paris: Editions du Seuil, 1957, 72–73.

64. Spurr, *The Rhetoric*, 73, 75.
65. Martin Bernal, *Black Athena: The Afroasiatic Roots of Classical Civilization*, vol. 1, *The Fabrication of Ancient Greece 1785–1985*, New Brunswick, N.J.: Rutgers University Press, 1987, 189–215, 440–441.

Chapter 1. The Balkans: Nomen

1. Madan Sarup, *Post-Structuralism and Postmodernism*, Athens, Ga.: University of Georgia Press, 1993, 33.
2. Simon During, ed., *The Cultural Studies Reader*, London and New York: Routledge, 1993, 6–7.
3. John B. S. Morritt of Rokeby, *A Grand Tour. Letters and Journeys 1794–96*, ed. G. E. Marindin, London: Century, 1985, 65.
4. See Maria Todorova, *Angliiski pîtepisi za Balkanite, XVI-pîrvata chetvîrt na XIX v.*, Sofia: Nauka i izkustvo, 1987.
5. Edward Brown, M.D., *A Brief Account of Some Travels in Diverse Parts of Europe*, . . . , London: Benj. Tooke, 1685.
6. *Philippi Callimachi Experientis ad Innocentium octavum Pontificem maximum . . . de bello Turcis inferendo oratio*, Frankfurt, 1601. Cited in Michail Jonov, *Evropa otnovo otkriva bîlgarite*, Sofia: Narodna Prosveta, 1980, 43.
7. Hana Hynková, *Europäische Reiseberichte aus dem 15. und 16. Jahrhundert als Quellen für die historische Geographie Bulgariens*, Sofia: Verlag der Bulgarischen Akademie der Wissenschaft, 1973, 38.
8. Michail Jonov, ed.,*Nemski i avstriiski pîtepisi za Balkanite, XVII–XVIII v.*, Sofia: Nauka i izkustvo, 1986, 240.
9. Salomon Schweigger, *Eine newe Reysbeschreibung auss Teutschland nach Konstantinopel vnd Jerusalem. . . .* , Nuremberg: Johann Lantzenberger, 1608 (phototypic edition Graz, 1964), 46–47.
10. Jonov, *Nemski . . . XVII–XVIII*, 402.
11. *Beschreibung der Reisen des Reinhold Lubenau*, Herausgegeben von Wilhelm Sahm, 2 Teil, Königsberg, 1930, 109.
12. See Agop Ormandzhian, ed., *Armenski pîtepisi za Balkanite, XVII–XIX v.*, Sofia: Nauka i izkustvo, 1984, 16.
13. Bistra Cvetkova, ed., *Frenski pîtepisi za Balkanite, XV-XVIII v.*, Sofia: Nauka i izkustvo, 1975, 203.
14. Jonov, *Nemski . . .* , *XVII–XVIII v.*, 368, 397.
15. Rebecca West, *Black Lamb and Grey Falcon*, New York: Penguin, 1982, 244; R. J. Boscowich, *Journal d'un voyage de Constantinople en Pologne*, . . . , Lausanne: Grasset, 1772.
16. *Mémoires de Baron de Tott sur les Turcs et les Tartares*, vol. 2, Amsterdam, 1784, 154–155; Cvetkova, *Frenski . . .* , *XV–XVIII*, 333–336; Jean-Batiste Lechevalier, *Voyage de Propontide et du Pont Euxin*, . . . , vol. 2, Paris, 1801, 365–376; Felix Beaujour, *Voyage militaire dans l'Empire Ottoman*, . . . , vol. 1, Paris: Firmin Didot, 1829, 237–248; François Pouqueville, *Voyage en Morée*, . . . , vol. 3, Paris, 1805, 234–248.
17. Ormandzhian, *Armenski*, 74, 131.
18. *Carte der Europäischen Türkey nebst einem Theile von Kleinasien in XXI Blättern.* . . . , Vienna: Hrsg. von dem k.k. österreichischen Generalquartiermeisterstabe in Jahre, 1829.
19. Robert Walsh, *Narrative of a Journey from Constantinople to England*, London: F. Westley and A. H. Davis, 1828; James Edward Alexander, Esq., *Travels from India to England*; . . . , London: Purbury, Allen and Co., 1827; Captain James Edward Alexander, *Travels to the Seat of War in the East*, London: H. Colburn and R. Bentley, 1830; George Keppel, *Narrative of a Journey across the Balkans*, . . . , London: H. Colburn and R. Bentley, 1831; A. W. Kinglake, *Eothen*, London: Century, 1982.
20. *Dnevnyya zapiski poezdki v Konstantinopol' A.G. Krasnokutskogo v 1808 godu*, Moscow: V tipografii S. Selivanovskago, 1815, 6–9, 113–115.

21. Walsh, Narrative, 104–105, 112–114.

22. See "Haemos" in Paulys Real-Encyclopädie der Classischen Altertumswissenschaft — Neue Bearbeitung, Stuttgart: J. B. Metzler, 1912, 2221–2226; Konstantin Jireček, Die Heerstrasse von Belgrad nach Constantinopel und die Balkanpässe, Prague, 1877; Jovan Cvijić, La peninsule balkanique: géographie humaine, Paris: A. Colin, 1918, 1–6; Karl Kaser, Südosteuropäische Geschichte und Geschichtswissenschaft, Vienna and Köln: Böhlau Verlag, 1990, 94–95.

23. August Zeune, Goea: Versuch einer wissenschaftlichen Erdbeschreibung, Berlin, 1808, 11.

24. Francis W. Carter, "Introduction to the Balkan Scene," An Historical Geography of the Balkans, London: Academic, 1977, 7.

25. Ami Boué, La Turquie d'Europe, . . . , vol. 1–4, Paris: Arthus Bartrand, 1840.

26. James W. Redhouse, A New Turkish and English Lexicon, Beirut: Librarie du Liban, 1974; Redhouse Yeni Türkçe-Ingilizce Sözlük, Istanbul: Redhouse yayinevi, 1968. The Alps seem to present a similar case, where "alp" in Gaelic, "ailp" in Irish, means high mountain, particularly snow-capped.

27. Söz derleme dergisi, vol. 1, Istanbul, 1939, 159.

28. Halil Inalcık, "Balkan," The Encyclopedia of Islam, new edition, vol. 1, Leiden: E. J. Brill, 1960, 998–1000.

29. Machiel Kiel, "Gramota za osnovavaneto na grad Tryavna," Vekove, vol. 3, 1984, 72–75.

30. W. Barthold-B.Spuler, "Balkhan," The Encyclopedia of Islam, 1002.

31. Ihsan Gürkan, "Jeopolitik ve stratejik yönleriyle Balkanlar ve Türkiye geçmişin ışığında geleceğe bakiş," Balkanlar, Istanbul: EREN, 1993, 260.

32. Todor Nenov and Georgi Chorchomov, Stara planina. Pîtevoditel, Sofia: Meditsina i fizkultura, 1987, 7; Petîr Koledarov, "The Medieval Maps as a Source of Bulgarian History," Bulgarian Historical Review, no. 2, 1982, 96–110; Petîr Koledarov, Politicheska geografiya na srednovekovnata bîlgarska dîrzhava, Sofia, 1979; "Stara planina," Entsiklopediya Bîlgariya, vol.6, Sofia: Bîlgarska akademiya na naukite, 1988, 420; Plamen Tsvetkov, A History of the Balkans. . . . , vol.1, Lewiston, N.Y.: Edwin Mellen, 1993, 5.

33. Besim Darkot, "Balkan," Islâm Ansiklopedisi, Istanbul: Maarif Maatbasi, 1943, 280–283; Kaser, Südosteuropäische Geschichte, 91–92; P. Deliradev, Ot Kom do Emine (po biloto na Stara-planina), Sofia: n.p., 1934, 9–13.

34. Felix Ph. Kanitz, Donau-Bulgarien und der Balkan. . . . , Leipzig: H. Fries, 1875–1879; W. Tomaschek, "Zur Kunde der Hämus-Halbinsel," Sitzungsberichte der Kaiserlichen Akademie der Wissenschaften in Wien, 1887.

35. Samuel S. Cox, Diversions of a Diplomat in Turkey, New York: Charles L. Webster, 1887, viii.

36. Theobald Fischer, "Die südosteuropäische (Balkan) Halbinsel," ed. A. Kirchhoff, Landerkunde von Europa, vol. 2, part 2, Vienna, Prague, and Leipzig, 1893, 66; "Südosteuropäische Halbinsel oder Südosthalbinsel," A. Scobel, ed., Geographisches Handbuch. . . . , vol. 1, Bielefeld and Leipzig: Velhagen and Klasing, 1909, 713; Miller, Travels and Politics, ix, xiii, 87, 314.

37. Edward King, Europe in Storm and Calm. . . . , Springfield, Mass.: C. A. Nichols, 1885, vii–viii, 669–670, 688, 790.

38. Christo A. Dako, Albania. The Master Key to the Near East, Boston: E. L. Grimes, 1919, 132.

39. Otto Maull, "Länderkunde von Südosteuropa," Enzyklopedie der Erdkunde, Leipzig and Vienna: Franz Deuticke, 1929, 299.

40. Mathias Bernath, "Südosteuropäische Geschichte als gesonderte Disziplin," Forschungen zur osteuropäischen Geschichte, Berlin: Südosteuropa-Institut and Wiesbaden: O. Harassovitz, 1973, 142.

41. Kaser, Südosteuropäische Geschichte, 106; Paul Rohrbach, Balkan–Türkei: Eine Schicksalszone Europas, Hamburg: Hoffmann und Campe Verlag, 1940, 82.

42. Theodore I. Geshkof, Balkan Union: A Road to Peace in Southeastern Europe, New York: Columbia University Press, 1940.

43. Victor Papacostea, *Civilizaţie românească şi civilizaţie balkanică*, Studii istorice, Bucharest: Editura Eminescu, 1983, 346–347.

44. George W. Hoffman, *The Balkans in Transition*, Princeton, N.J.: D. Van Nostrand, 1963, 11–12.

45. Georg Stadtmüller, *Geschichte des Südosteuropas*, Munich: R. Oldenburg, 1950; *Südosteuropa unter dem Halbmond: Untersuchungen über Geschichte und Kultur der südosteuropäischen Völker wehrend der Türkenzeit*. . . . , Munich: Trofenik, 1975.

46. Nicolae Iorga, *Histoire des Etats balkaniques jusqu'à 1924*, Paris: J. Gamber, 1924; Jacques Ancel, *Peuples et nations des Balkans*, Paris: A. Colin, 1930; Leften S. Stavrianos, *The Balkans since 1453*, Hinsdale, Ill.: Dryden, 1958; Charles and Barbara Jelavich, *The Establishment of the Balkan National States, 1804–1920*, Seattle: University of Washington Press, 1977; Barbara Jelavich, *History of the Balkans: vol. 1. Eighteenth and Nineteenth Centuries. vol. 2. Twentieth Century*, New York: Cambridge University Press, 1983; Georges Castellan, *Histoire des Balkans: XIVe–XXe siècles*, Paris: Fayard, 1991; Daniel N. Nelson, *Balkan Imbroglio. Politics and Security in Southeastern Europe*, Boulder, Co.: Westview, 1991. A rare exception is Peter Sugar, *Southeastern Europe under Ottoman Rule, 1354–1804*, Seattle: University of Washington Press, 1977, who accepts the German distinction in his extensive treatment of Hungarian affairs.

47. Kaser, *Südosteuropäische Geschichte*, 9, 85, 112, 131.

48. Bernath, "Südosteuropäische Geschichte," 42.

49. Berkovici, Konrad, *The Incredible Balkans*, New York: Loring and Mussey, 1932, 217; Gabriella Schubert "Berlin und Südosteuropa," ed. Klaus Meyer, *Berlin und Osteuropa*, Berlin: Colloquium Verlag, 1991, 177; *The Balkans, Together with Hungary*. London: Royal Institute of International Affairs, 1945; Norbert Reiter, ed., *Die Stellung der Frau auf dem Balkan*, Wiesbaden: Otto Harrassowitz, 1987; Üstün Ergüder, "Türkiye ve Balkan Gerçeği," *Balkanlar*, Istanbul: EREN, 1993, 36.

50. N. G. Danchov and I. G. Danchov, *Bîlgarska entsiklopediya*, Sofia: Knigoizdatelstvo St. Atanasov, 1936; Rohrbach, *Balkan–Türkei*, 7.

51. Cvijić, *La peninsule balkanique*, 6–7.

52. Hoffman, *The Balkans in Transition*, 9–11.

53. Petîr Lazarov and Zhivko Zhelev, *Geografiya za 7. klas na srednite obshtoobrazovatelni uchilishta*, Sofia: Anubis, 1994, 68–69; *The New Encyclopaedia Britannica*, vol. 1, 1993, 833.

54. Carter, *An Historical Geography*, vol. 1; for different scopes of Balkan, see *Colliers Encyclopedia*, 1990; *Academic American Encyclopedia*, 1987; *The New Encyclopaedia Britannica*, 1994; *Encyclopedia Americana–International Edition*, 1993.

55. Fritz Viljavec, "Südosteuropa und Balkan," *Ausgewählte Aufsätze*, Munich: R. Oldenbourg, 1963.

56. *Balkanskite strani po pîtya na promenite*, Sofia: Markisa, 1993.

57. T. G. Masaryk, "Österreich und der Balkan," *Die Balkanfrage*, Munich and Leipzig: Verlag von Duncker and Humblot, 1914, 144.

58. Eric Hobsbawm, *Nations and Nationalism Since 1780*, Cambridge: Cambridge University Press, 1990, 31.

59. Roman Szporluk, *Communism and Nationalism: Karl Marx versus Friedrich List*, New York: Oxford University Press, 1988, 169–192.

60. *Grand Larousse de la langue française*, vol. 1, Paris: Librairie Larousse, 1971, 364; *Duden*. . . . , Mannheim: Bibliographisches Institut, 1976, 295; *Meyers Enzyklopädisches Lexikon*, Bd. 3, Mannheim, Vienna, and Zurich: Bibliographisches Institut, Lexiconverlag, 1971, 408; *Webster's New World Dictionary of the American English*, 3rd college edition, Cleveland and New York: Simon and Schuster, 1988, 105; *Webster's Ninth New Collegiate Dictionary*, Springfield, Mass.: Merriam-Webster, 1991, 126.

61. Norman Pound, "Balkans," *Academic American Encyclopedia*, vol. 3, Danbury, Conn.: Grolier, 1994, 40.

62. Alfredo Panzini, *Dizionario moderno*, Milan: Editore Ulrico Hoepli, 1950 (*balcanizzare*).

63. *New York Times*, 20 December 1918, p. 3.

64. *Oxford English Dictionary*, 903.

65. Paul Scott Mowrer, *Balkanized Europe: A Study in Political Analysis and Reconstruction*, New York: E. P. Dutton, 1921, vii, 34.

66. Michel Foucher, "The Geopolitics of Southeastern Europe," *Eurobalkans*, vol. 15, Summer 1994, 17.

67. M. E. Chamberlain, *Decolonization: The Fall of the European Empires*, Oxford: Basil Blackwell, 1985, 55–61.

68. Du Bois, *Color and Democracy*, 72.

69. Joseph-Roger de Benoist, *La balkanisation de l'Afrique occidentale française*, Dakar, Abidjan, and Lome: Les nouvelles éditions africaines, 1979, 148.

70. *Oxford English Dictionary*, 903.

71. Alexander Vodopivec, *Die Balkanisierung Österreichs. . . .* , Vienna and Munich: Verlag Fritz Molden, 1967, 7, 179.

72. *Washington Post*, "Book World," 2 April 1995, 1, 10; William H. Frey and Jonathan Tilove, "Immigrants In, Native Whites Out," *New York Times Magazine*, 20 August 1995, 44.

73. Richard Grant, "The World Beyond," *Washington Post*, 26 February 1995, 9.

74. John Steinbeck, *Travels with Charlie. In Search of America*, New York: Penguin, 1986, 220.

75. James Atlas, "Name That Era. Pinpointing A Moment On the Map of History," *New York Times*, 19 March 1995, E1–E5.

76. Patrick Glynn, "The Age of Balkanization," *Commentary*, vol.96, No 1, July 1993, 21–24.

77. Ellis Case, "He Hears America Sinking," *New York Times Book Review*, 27 March 1994, 11; David Patterson, "The Dangers of Balkanization," *Peace & Change*, vol. 20, no. 1, January 1995, 79; Stjepan G. Meštrović, *The Balkanization of the West. The Confluence of Postmodernism and Postcommunism*, London and New York: Routledge, 1994.

78. Harold Bloom, *The Western Canon. The Books and School of the Ages*, New York: Harcourt Brace, 1994, 517.

79. Dirlik, "The Postcolonial Aura," 347.

80. John Leonard, "C.I.A.—An Infinity of Mirrors," *Nation*, vol. 258, no. 12, March 28, 1994, 416.

Chapter 2. *"Balkans" as Self Designation*

1. Erving Goffman, *Stigma: Notes on the Management of Spoiled Identity*, Englewood Cliffs, N.J.: Prentice-Hall, 1963, 27.

2. Svetlozar Igov, *Istoriya na bîlgarskata literatura, 1878–1944*, Sofia: Izdatelstvo na Bîlgarskata akademiya na naukite, 1993, 104–115.

3. Miller, *Travels and Politics*, 58.

4. Aleko Konstantinov, *Do Chicago i nazad. Bay Ganyo*, Sofia: Bîlgarski pisatel, 1983, 109.

5. Igov, *Istoriya*, 108.

6. Lili Ilieva and Stiliyan Stoyanov, "Bay Ganyo kato 'Homo Balkanicus'—'svoya' i 'chuzhda' gledna tochka," *Balkanistic Forum*, No. 2, 1993, 67–68; Igov, 113.

7. Edward Shils, *Center and Periphery: Essays in Microsociology*, Chicago: University of Chicago Press, 1975, 7.

8. Igov, *Istoriya*, 111–112.

9. Vivian, *The Servian Tragedy*, 252.

10. A. Goff and Hugh A. Fawcett, *Macedonia: A Plea for the Primitive*, London and New York: John Lane, 1921, xv.

11. Igov, *Istoriya*, 111.

12. Ion Luca Caragiale, *Oeuvres Choisies: Theatre*, Bucharest: Editions "Le Livre," 1953, 20; Ion Dodu Bălan, *A Concise History of Romanian Literature*, Bucharest: Editura științifică și enciclopedică, 1981, 46–49.

13. Ion Luca Caragiale, *The Lost Letter and Other Plays*, London: Lawrence and Wishart, 1956, 9, 11.

14. Antun Barac, *A History of Yugoslav Literature*, Ann Arbor: Michigan Slavic Studies, 1976, 207–208.

15. Igov, *Istoriya*, 112.

16. Immanuel Wallerstein, *The Modern World-System*, 3 vols., New York: Academic, 1974–1989; Immanuel Wallerstein, *The Politics of the World-Economy: the States, the Movements, and the Civilizations; Essays*, New York: Cambridge University Press, 1984.

17. Ilieva, Stoyanov, "Bay Ganyo," 63.

18. Miller, *Travels and Politics*, XIII, 38–39.

19. Allen Upward, *The East and Europe: The Report of an Unofficial Mission to the European Provinces of Turkey on the Eve of the Revolution*, London: John Murray, 1908, 50.

20. Vivian, *The Servian Tragedy*, 289.

21. Robert Eisner, *Travels to an Antique Land: The History and Literature of Travel to Greece*, Ann Arbor: University of Michigan Press, 1991, 256.

22. Spyros Melas, "This is Greece!" *Modern Greek Literary Gems*, New York: R. D. Cortina, 1962, 47–49.

23. Stratis Myrivilis, "The Greek Waves," *Modern Greek Literary Gems*, New York: R. D. Cortina, 1962, 51–53.

24. Nikos Kazantzakis, "Crete, a Great and Noble Island," *Modern Greek Literary Gems*, New York: R. D. Cortina, 1962, 57.

25. George Papandreou, "Greece, the United States and their Mutual Common Interests in the Balkans," *The Southeast European Yearbook 1993*, Athens, Greece: ELIAMEP, 1994, 13–19.

26. Adamantia Pollis, "Greek National Identity: Religious Minorities, Rights, and European Norms," *Journal of Modern Greek Studies*, vol. 10, no. 2, 1992, 191.

27. Dako, *Albania: The Master Key*, 2, 28, 31, 128, 171.

28. *Ibid.*, 117, 120; Christo A. Dako and Dhimitri Bala, *Albania's Rights, Hopes and Aspirations. The Strength of the National Consciousness of the Albania People*, Boston: 1918, 8; Christo A. Dako and Mihal Grameno, *Albania's Rights and Claims to Independence and Territorial Integrity*, Boston: 1918.

29. Sali Berisha, "The Democratic Party Has Kept Its Word," *Rilindja Demokratike*, 7 March 1995; also in FBIS-EEU-95-049, 14 March 1995.

30. Arshi Pipa, "The Other Albania: A Balkan Perspective," Arshi Pipa and Sami Repishti, eds., *Studies on Kosova*, Boulder, Co.: East European Monographs, no. 155, New York: Columbia University Press, 1984, 244, 247, 251; Elez Biberaj, "Kosova: The Balkan Powder Keg," *Conflict Studies*, no. 258, London, 1993, 1–26; Gazmend Zajimi, "Historical Continuity of the Question of Kosova," *Kosova*, no. 1, 1993, 15–18; Arben Puto, "The London Conference in Two Editions," *Kosova*, no. 1, 1993, 19–22; Elez Biberaj, "Albania's Road to Democracy," *Current History*, vol. 92, no. 577, November 1993, 385.

31. Gramoz Pashko, "The Role of Christianity in Albania's Post-Communist Vacuum," *The Southeast European Yearbook 1993*, Athens, Greece: ELIAMEP, 1994, 47, 49, 53.

32. John Reed, *The War in Eastern Europe*, New York: Scribner's, 1919, 273.

33. Maria Mladenova and Nikolai Zhechev, *Rumînski pîtepisi ot XIX vek za bîlgarskite zemi*, Sofia: Izdatelstvo na Otechestveniya front, 1982.

34. Vladimir Tismaneanu and Dan Pavel, "Romania's Mystical Revolutionaries: The Generation of Angst and Adventure Revisited," *East European Politics and Societies*, vol. 8, no. 3, Fall 1994, 436.

35. Nicolae Iorga, *A History of Romania. Land, People, Civilization*, New York: AMS, 1970, 1.

36. Nicolae Iorga, *Histoire des Romains et de la Romanité Orientale*, vol.1, part 1, Paris: Librairie Ernest Laroux, 1937, 12.

37. Papacostea, "La péninsule balkanique," 345–357.

38. Joseph S. Roucek, *Balkan Politics. International Relations in No Man's Land*, Westport, Conn.: Greenwood, 1948, 9.

39. Vladimir Tismaneanu, "Romania's Mystical Revolutionaries," *Partisan Review*, vol. 61, no. 4, 1994, 600, 606.

40. Matei Calinescu, "Ionesco and *Rhinoceros*: Personal and Political Backgrounds," *East European Politics and Societies*, vol. 6, no. 3, 1995, 397–399.

41. Eugène Ionesco, *Présent passé: Passé présent*, Paris: Mercure de France, 1968, 181–182.

42. Emil M. Cioran, "A Little Theory of Destiny," *The Temptation to Exist*, trans. Richard Howard, Chicago: Quadrangle, 1968, 70–71.

43. Matei Calinescu, "'How can one be what one is?' Reflections on the Romanian and the French Cioran," manuscript, 1995, 34. Cited with the permission of the author.

44. Emil M. Cioran, *History and Utopia*, trans. Richard Howard, New York: Seaver, 1987, 34.

45. Matei Calinescu, "How Can One Be a Romanian," *Southeastern Europe*, vol. 10, no. 1, 1983, 25–36; Calinescu, "'How can one be what one is?'" 26–27.

46. Tismaneanu, "Romania's Mystical Revolutionaries," 602.

47. Katherine Verdery, *National Identity under Socialism: Identity and Cultural Politics in Ceausescu's Romania*, Berkeley: University of California Press, 1991, 256–301.

48. Scott L. Malcomson, *Borderlands: Nation and Empire*, Boston and London: Faber and Faber, 1994, 60–63.

49. Anette Insdorf, "A Romanian Director Tells A Tale of Ethnic Madness," *New York Times*, 6 November 1994, 422.

50. Victor Neumann, *The Temptation of Homo Europaeus*, Boulder, Co.: East European Monographs, no. 384, New York: Columbia University Press, 1993, 17, 33; Malcomson, *Borderlands*, 58.

51. Malcomson, *ibid.*, 116.

52. Bozkurt Güvenç, *Türk Kimliği. Kültür Tarihinin Kaynakları*, Ankara: Kültür Bakanlığı, 1993, 21.

53. Turgut Özal, *Turkey in Europe and Europe in Turkey*, Nicosia, Northern Cyprus: K. Rustem, 1991, viii.

54. *Ibid.*, 1, 22.

55. *Ibid.*, 349.

56. Tanıl Bora, "Turkish National Identity, Turkish Nationalism and the Balkan Problem," Günay Göksu Özdoğan and Kemâli Saybaşılı, eds., *Balkans: A Mirror of the New International Order*, Istanbul: EREN, 1995, 104, 110–112.

57. Yilmaz Çetinler, *Şu Bizim Rumeli*, Istanbul: Milliyet Yayınları, 1994.

58. Bora, "Turkish National Identity," 111–113.

59. Ibid., 114.

60. Nedim Gürsel, *Balkanlara dönüş*, Istanbul: Can Yayınlari, 1995, 123.

61. Quoted in Bora, "Turkish National Identity," 119.

62. Güvenç, *Türk Kimliği*, 26–30, 43.

63. Fazîl Hüsnü Dağlarca, *Selected Poems*, trans. Talât Sait Halman, Pittsburgh: University of Pittsburgh Press, 1969, 65, 103.

64. Dubravka Ugrešić, "Zagreb—Amsterdam—New York," *Cross Currents*, no. 11, 1992, 248–256.

65. Dubravka Ugrešić, *Have a Nice Day: From the Balkan War to the American Dream*, New York: Viking, 1993, 229–230.

66. Ugrešić, "Zagreb—Amsterdam—New York," 251.

67. Ibid., 253–254.

68. Ibid., 251, 252, 254.

69. Zrnka Novak, "Nema čistih ruku," *Oslobođenje*, 23 September 1990, 3.

70. Hohmeier, Jürgen, "Stigmatisierung als sozialer Definitionsprozess," Manfred Brusten and Jürgen Hohmeier, eds., *Stigmatisierung. Zur Produktion gesellschaftlicher Randgruppen*, Neuwied and Darmstadt: Hermann Luchterhand Verlag, 1975, 11.

71. Blagoje Babić, "Collapse of Yugoslav Self-Management Society and a Possible Alternative," *Međunarodni problemi*, vol. 66, no. 2, Belgrade, 1994, 205–227.

72. Miroslav Volf, "Exclusion and Embrace: Theological Reflections in the Wake of 'Ethnic Cleansing,'" *Communio Viatorum*, vol. 35, no. 3, 1993, 263–287.

73. Cited in Dževad Karahasan, *Sarajevo, Exodus of a City*, New York: Kodansha International, 1994, 114; Stephen Kinzer, "In Croatia, Minds Scarred by War. A Struggle to treat the trauma of the Balkan violence," *New York Times*, 9 January 1995, A6.

74. "Krlezas wilder Sohn. Interview mit Stabodan Snajder," *Ost-West Gegeninformationen*, vol. 8, no. 1, May 1996, 14.

75. Eva Hoffman, *Exit Into History: A Journey Through the New Eastern Europe*, New York: Penguin, 1993, 262.

76. Lyuben Karavelov, *Bîlgare ot staro vreme*, Sofia: Bîlgarski pisatel, 1981, 41. The original uses the noncapitalized "balkans" for mountains in general.

77. John Robert Colombo and Nikola Roussanoff, *The Balkan Range*, Toronto: Hounslow, 1976, 121.

78. *The Shade of the Balkans*, London: David Nutt, 1904, 31–32.

79. Iordan Iovkov, "Balkan," *Razkazi*, Sofia: Bîlgarski pisatel, 1974, 79–94.

80. *The Shade of the Balkans*, 27–28.

81. Petîr Mutafchiev, *Kniga za bîlgarite*, Sofia: Izdatelstvo na bîlgarskata akademiya na naukite, 1987, 66, 89.

82. Geshkof, *Balkan Union*, 47.

83. Ivan Slavov, "Balkanpolitikanstvo," *Edin zavet*, no. 1, 1993, 51.

84. *Kontinent*, 30–31 January 1993, 9.

85. Nikolai Todorov, *Development, Achievements, and Tasks of Balkan Studies in Bulgaria*, Sofia: Izdatelstvo na bîlgarskata akademiya na naukite, 1977; *Petnadeset godini institut za balkanistiska, 1964–1978: Istoricheska spravka i bibliografiya*, Sofia: CIBAL, 1979. Publications on Balkan problems include *Etudes balkaniques*, *Studia balkanica*, *Balkanistika*, *Bibliographie des études balkaniques*, Sofia, 1966– ; *Balkanistic Forum*.

86. Calinescu, "'How can one be what one is?'" 2–3; Calinescu, "How Can One Be a Romanian," 25–36.

87. Wolfgang Lipp, "Selbststigmatisierung," Brusten, Manfred and Jürgen Hohmeier, eds., *Stigmatisierung. Zur Produktion gesellschaftlicher Randgruppen*, Neuwied and Darmstadt: Hermann Luchterhand Verlag, 1975, 46–47.

88. Tomislav Z. Longinović, *Borderline Culture: The Politics of Identity in Four Twentieth-Century Slavic Novels*, Fayetteville: University of Arkansas Press, 1993, 13.

89. Tamas Hofer, ed., *Hungarians Between 'East' and 'West.' Three Essays on National Myths and Symbols*, Budapest: Museum of Ethnography, 1994.

90. György Konrád, "Central Europe Redivivus," *The Melancholy of Rebirth: Essays from Post-Communist Central Europe, 1989–1994*, San Diego: Harcourt Brace, 1995, 159.

91. Goffman, *Stigma*, 107.

92. Tsvetana Georgieva, "Khora i bogove na Balkanite," *Balkanistic Forum*, no 2, 1994, 33.

93. Thanos Veremis, "The Balkans in Search of Multilateralism," *Eurobalkans*, no 17, Winter 1994/95, 4.

94. Geshkof, *Balkan Union*, 4.

95. Hoffman, *Exit Into History*, 387.

96. Georgieva, "Khora i bogove," 41.

97. Roumiana Mihneva, "Notre Europe et 'l'autre Europe' ou 'européisation' contre évolution et certains problèmes du 'temps' transitoire dans les Balkans," *Etudes Balkaniques*, no. 3, 1994, 20.

98. Martha Forsythe, "Interes kîm bîlgarskiya folklor v SASHT," *Bîlgarski folklor*, no. 1, 1987, 80.

99. Lozanka Peicheva and Ventsislav Dimov, "Drugite v 'misteriyata' . . . ," *Balkanistic Forum*, no. 1, 1993, 39–45.

100. Tsvetan Todorov, "Zabelezhki otnosno krîstosvaneto na kulturite," *Literaturen vestnik*, no. 8, 1991, 3.

101. Dipesh Chakrabarty, "Postcoloniality and the Artifice of History: Who Speaks for 'Indian' Pasts?" *Representations*, vol. 37, Winter 1992, 342–369.

102. Gaylene Becker and Regina Arnold, "Stigma as a Social and Cultural Construct," *The Dilemma of Difference*, 56.
103. Lerita M. Coleman, "Stigma: An Enigma Demystified," *The Dilemma of Difference*, 227–228.
104. Carrier, "Occidentalism," 197.

Chapter 3. The Discovery of the Balkans

1. Helmuth von Moltke, *Briefe über Zustände und Begebenheiten in der Türkei aus den Jahren 1835 bis 1839*, Berlin: E. S. Mittler, 1911, letter of 21 May 1837.
2. Nicolae Iorga, *Les voyageurs français dans l'Orient Européen*, Paris: Boivin, J. Gamber, 1928, 112.
3. Edward Gibbon, *An Essai on the Study of Literature*, New York: Garland, 1970, 89–91.
4. Jean Copans and Jean Jamin, eds., *Aux origines de l'anthropologie française. . . .*, Paris: Le Sycomore, 1978, 77.
5. Joseph-Marie DeGérando, *The Observation of Savage Peoples*, Berkeley and Los Angeles: University of California Press, 1969, 63.
6. Eisner, *Travels*, 77.
7. "Robert Wood," *Dictionary of National Biography*, London: Oxford University Press, vol. 21, 1921–22, 844–846.
8. Raya Zaimova, *Bîlgarskata tema v zapadnoevropeiskata knizhnina XV–XVII vek*, Sofia: Universitetsko izdatelstvo "Sv. Kliment Okhridski," 1992, 209.
9. Ibid., 6.
10. Dorothy M. Vaughan, *Europe and the Turk: A Pattern of Alliances, 1350–1700*, Liverpool: University Press, 1954, vii–viii.
11. Carl Göllner, *Die Türkenfrage in der öffentlichen Meinung Europas im 16. Jahrhundert*, Baden-Baden: Bibliotheka Aureliana, 70, 1978.
12. Lucette Valensi, "The Making of a Political Paradigm: The Ottoman State and Oriental Despotism," Anthony Grafton and Ann Blair, eds. *The Transmission of Culture in Early Modern Europe*, Philadelphia: University of Pennsylvania Press, 1990, 199; Zdenko Zlatar, *Our Kingdom Come: The Counter-Reformation, the Republic of Dubrovnik, and the Liberation of the Balkan Slavs*, Boulder, Co.: East European Monographs, no. 342, New York: Columbia University Press, 1992, 15, 20.
13. Zlatar, *Our Kingdom Come*, 4, 21.
14. Zaimova, *Bîlgarskata tema*, 10, 139–144.
15. Franco Venturi, *The End of the Old Regime in Europe, 1768–1776*, vol. 1, Princeton, N.J.: Princeton University Press, 1989, 111–132.
16. Paschalis Kitromilides, "John Locke and the Greek Intellectual Tradition: An Episode in Locke's Reception in South-East Europe," G. A. J. Rogers, ed., *Locke's Philosophy: Content and Context*, Oxford: Clarendon, 1994, 222, 226, 231.
17. Karl Vocelka, "Das Türkenbild des christliched Abenlandes in der frühen Neuziet," Erich Zöllner and Karl Gutkas, eds., *Österreich und die Osmanen—Prinz Eugen und seine Zeit*, Vienna: Österreichischer Bundesverlag, 1988, 22–26.
18. Senol Özyurt, *Die Türkenlieder und das Türkenbild in der deitschen Volksüberlieferung vom 16. bis zum 20. Jahrhundert*, Munich: Wilhelm Fink Verlag, 1972.
19. Jonov, *Nemski . . . , XV–XVI v.*, 29; *Nemski . . . , XVII–XVIII v.*, 9.
20. Jonov, *Nemski . . . , XV–XVI v.*, 183–184.
21. Ibid., 461–562.
22. Ibid., 219.
23. Cvetkova, *Frenski . . . , XV–XVIII v.*, 135.
24. Vocelka, "Das Türkenbild," 30.
25. Jonov, *Nemski . . . , XVII–XVIII v.*, 22.
26. Gabriella Schubert, "Berlin und Südosteuropa," Klaus Meyer, ed., *Berlin und Osteuropa*, Berlin: Colloquium Verlag, 1991, 185–186.
27. Özyurt, *Die Türkenlieder*, 143.
28. Vocelka, "Das Türkenbild," 31.

29. Jonov, *Nemski* . . . , XVII–XVIII *v.*, 232.

30. Ibid., 363.

31. Gabriella Schubert, "Das Bulgaren-Bild deutscher Reisender in der Zeit der Osmanenherrschaft," *Zeutschrift für Balkanologie*, vol. 26, 1990, 115.

32. Vocelka, "Das Türkenbild," 31.

33. C. M. Woodhouse, *The Philhellenes*, London: Hodder and Stoughton, 1969, 9.

34. Eisner, *Travels*, 120.

35. Nikolai Todorov and Vesselin Traikov, eds., *Bîlgari uchastnitsi v borbite za osvobo-zhdenieto na Gîrtsiya, 1821–1828*, Sofia: Bîlgarska akademiya na naukite, 1971.

36. Schubert, "Berlin und Südosteuropa," 190.

37. Helmuth von Moltke, *Briefe über Zustände und Begebenheiten in der Türkei aus den Jahren 1835 bis 1839*, Köln: Verlag Jakob Hegner, 1968, 24, 27, 150–151.

38. Schubert, "Das Bulgaren-Bild," 120.

39. Felix Philipp Kanitz, *Donau-Bulgarien und ʽ r Balkan: Historisch-geographisch-ethnographische Reisestudien aus den Jahren, 1860–1878*, Leipzig: H. Fries, 1875–1879.

40. Karl Krumbacher, *Griechische Reise*, . . . , Berlin: August Hettler, 1886, 7–8, 10–11, 48–49, 253–255, 311–313, 340–343, 389.

41. Julius Stettenheim, *Bulgarische Krone gefällig? Allen denen, welche Ja sagen wollen, als Warnung gewidmet*, Leipzig: L. Freund, Buch-und Kunst-Verlag, 1888 (Zweite Auflage), 22.

42. Richard Ebermann, *Die Türkenfurcht, ein Beitrag zur Geschichte der öffentlishen Meinung in Deutschland während der Reformationszeit*, Halle: C. A. Kraemmerer, 1904, 69.

43. Gerhard Klussmeier and Hainer Plaul, eds., *Karl May. Biographie in Dokumenten und Bildern*, Hildesheim and New York: Olms, 1978, 104; Schubert, "Das Bulgaren-Bild," 118; Schubert, "Berlin und Südosteuropa," 195–196.

44. Craig Jonathan Saper, *Tourism and Invention: Roland Barthes's "Empire of Signs,"* dissertation, University of Florida, 1990.

45. Hartmut Albert, "Kosova 1979, Albania 1980, Observations, Experiences, Conversations," Arshi Pipa and Sami Repishti, eds., *Studies on Kosova*, Boulder, Co.: East European Monographs, no. 155, New York: Columbia University Press, 1984, 105.

46. Schubert, "Berlin und Südosteuropa," 196.

47. Cvetkova, *Frenski* . . . , XV–XVIII, 51–52, 58.

48. E. Kafé, "Le mythe turc et son déclin dans les relations de voyage des européen de la Renaissance, *Oriens*, 1968–1969, vol. 21–22, 159–195; Iorga, *Les voyageurs français*, 21–48.

49. Cvetkova, *Frenski* . . . , XV–XVIII, 73, 84.

50. Clarence Dana Rouillard, *The Turk in French History, Thought, and Literature* (1520–1660), Paris: Boivin, 1940 (reprint, New York: AMS, 1973).

51. Hans Sturmberger, "Das Problem der Vorbildhaftigkeit des türkischen Staatswesens im 16. und 17. Jahrhundert und sein Einfluss auf den europäischen Absolutismus," Comité international des sciences historiques, *XIIe congrès international des sciences historiques*, *Vienne 29 aout–5 septembre 1965. Rapport IV*, Horn and Vienna: (no publ., no year), 201–209.

52. Pierre Belon du Mans, *Les observations de plusieurs singularitez et choses mémorables*, . . . , Paris, 1553, 180–181.

53. François Rabelais, *Gargantua and Pantagruel*, Chicago: Encyclopaedia Brittanica, 1952, 40–41, 92–94.

54. Cvetkova, *Frenski* . . . , XV–XVIII, 13.

55. Auguste Boppe, *Journal et correspondence de Gédoyn "le Turc," consul de France à Alep (1623–1625)*, Paris: s.n., 1909, 47, 53.

56. Jean Coppin, *Le bouclier de l'Europe ou la guerre sainte*, . . . , Lyon: 1660.

57. Cvetkova, *Frenski, XV-XVIII*, 255.

58. Ibid., 229.

59. Jonov, *Evropa otnovo otkriva bîlgarite*, 79.

60. Charles de Peyssonnel, *Traité sur le commerce de la Mer Noire*, Paris, 1787; Esprit-Mary Cousinéry, *Voyage dans la Macédoine contenant des recherches sur l'histoire, la géographie et les antiquité de ce pays*, Paris: Imprimerie royale, 1831; *Mémoires de Baron de Tott sur les Turcs et les Tartares*, Amsterdam, 1784.

61. Iorga, *Les voyageurs français*, 109.

62. Melvin Richter, "Despotism," *Dictionary of the History of Ideas*, vol. 2, New York: Scribner's, 1973, 7, 10–12.

63. Ferrières de Sauveboeuf, *Mémoires historiques et politiques de mes voyages* . . . , vol. 2, Maestrücht and Paris, 1790, 302–303.

64. Pouqueville, *Voyage en Morée*, vol. 1, 350–358, vol. 2, 142; Guillaume-Antoine Olivier, *Voyage dans l'Empire Ottoman* . . . , vol. 1, Paris, 1801, 334–338.

65. Beaujour, *Voyage*, vol. 2, 589; "Journal inédit d'un voyage de Constantinople à Jassi, capitale de la Moldavie dans l'hiver de 1785," *Memoriu asupra vechei și actualei a Moldovei presentat lui Alexandru Voda Ipsilante domnul Moldovei la 1787 de comitele d'Hauterive*, Bucharest: L'Institut d'arts graphiques Carol Göbl, 1902, 311–312.

66. Venturi, *The End of the Old Regime*, 138–139; Hellen Hill Miller, *Greece Through the Ages. As Seen by Travelers from Herodotus to Byron*, New York: Funk and Wagnalls, 1972, 16; Eisner, *Travels*, 80–81.

67. Olga Augustinos, *French Odysseys. Greece in French Travel Literature from the Renaissance to the Romantic Era*, Baltimore: Johns Hopkins University Press, 1994, 61, 281, 285.

68. Ibid., xii, 185, 216–218.

69. M.-L.-J.-A.-C., Vicomte de Marcellus, *Souvenirs de l'Orient*, . . . , vol. 2, Paris: Debécourt, 1839, 542–545.

70. Paul Lucas, *Voyage du sieur Paul Lucas fait par ordre du roy dans la Grèce, l'Asie Mineure, la Macédoine et l'Afrique*, Paris, 1712, 240–259.

71. Beaujour, *Voyage militaire*, vol. 1, 242–245.

72. Pouqueville, *Voyage en Morée*, vol. 3, 234–240.

73. Jonov, *Evropa*, 79.

74. Cvetkova, *Frenski* . . . , *XIX v.*, 8–9.

75. William Fortescue, *Alphonse de Lamartine. A Political Biography*, London and Canberra: Croom Helm, New York: St. Martin's, 1983, 72–73, 75–76.

76. Lamartine, *Voyage en Orient*, Paris, 1887, 525.

77. Ibid., 248–265, 531–532.

78. Ami Boué, *La Turquie d'Europe* . . . , vols. 1–4. Paris: Arthus Bertrand, 1840; Ami Boué, *Recueil d'itinéraires dans la Turquie d'Europe*. . . . , Vienna: W. Braumüller, 1854.

79. Boué, *La Turquie d'Europe*, vol. 1, vii–xvii.

80. Ibid., vol. 4, 449–469.

81. Emile de Laveleye, *The Balkan Peninsula*, London: T. Fisher Unwin, 1887; Cyprien Robert, *Le monde slave. Son passé, son état présent et son avenir*, vol. 1, Paris: Passard, 1852, 4, 45–46; Louis Léger, *La Save, le Danube et le Balkan*. . . . , Paris: E. Plon, Nourrit, 1884, 194–195, 234.

82. *Opisanie Turetskoi imperii, sostavlennoe russkim, byvshim v plenu u turok v XVII veke*, Saint Petersburg, 1890; "Povest' i skazanie o pokhozhdenii v Ierusalim i Tsarigrad Troitsko-Sergieva monastyria, chernogo dyakona Iony po reklomu Malen'kogo," *Pamiatniki drevnei pis'mennosti i isskustva*, vol. 35, Saint Petersburg, 1882.

83. *Russkii posol v Stambule: Petr Andreevich Tolstoy i ego opisanie Osmanskoi imperii nachala XVIII v.*, Moscow: Glavnaya redaktsiia vostochnoi literatury izdatel'stva "Nauka," 1985.

84. F. P. Fonton, *Yumoristicheskie, politicheskie i voennye pis'ma iz glavnoi kvartiry Dunaiskoi armii v 1828 i 1829 godakh*, Leipzig, 1862 (Quoted in Kozhuharova, *Ruski pîtepisi*, 84).

85. Yurii I. Venelin, *Drevnye i nyneshnie bolgare* . . . vols. 1–2, Moscow, 1829–1841; Venelin, *O kharaktere narodnykh pesen u zadunaiskikh slavyan*, Moscow: 1835; Venelin, *O zarodyshe novoi bolgarskoi literatury*, Moscow, 1838.

86. P. Bezsonov, *Nekotorye cherty puteshestviya Yu.I.Venelina v Bolgariyu*, Moscow, 1857, 12–19.

87. Fonton, *Yumoristicheskie*; E. Kovalevskii, "Balkany. Nish," *Biblioteka dlya chteniya*, no. 80, Saint-Petersburg, 1847, razd. 3, 1–13; V. Grigorovich, *Ocherk puteshestviya po Evropeiskoi Turtsii*, Kazan, Sofia: Izdatelstvo na Bîlgarskata akademiya na naukite, 1978; E.

Yuzhakov, "Mesyats v Bolgarii," Kozhuharova, *Ruski pîtepisi*, 260–293; O. M. Lerner, "Vospominaniya o Bolgarii . . . ," *Zapiski grazhdanina*, Odessa, 1876, no. 8, 8–11, no. 9, 26–31, no. 11, 77–80; Inok Partenii, "Skazanie o stranstvii . . . ," Kozhuharova, *Ruski pîtepisi*, 182–196.

88. Friedrich Engels, "The Turkish Question," Karl Marx and Frederick Engels, *Collected Works*, vol. 12, New York: International, 1975, 23.

89. Kozhukharova, *Ruski pîtepisi*, 97, 102.

90. M. F. Karlova, "Turetskaya provintsiya i ee sel'skaya i gorodskaya zhizn'," *Vestnik Evropy*, no. 6, Saint Petersburg, 1870, 721–753.

91. Kozhukharova, *Ruski pîtepisi*, 367, 373.

92. Ibid., 267.

93. O. M. Lerner, "Vospominaniya o Bolgarii," *Zapiski grazhdanina*, no. 8, Odessa, 1876, 8.

94. Jelena Milojković-Djurić, *Panslavism and National Identity in Russia and the Balkans, 1830–1880, Images of the Self and Others*, Boulder, Co.: East European Monographs, no. 394, New York: Columbia University Press, 1994, 98–99.

95. Barbara Jelavich, *Russia's Balkan Entanglements, 1806–1914*, Cambridge: Cambridge University Press, 1991; Hugh Ragsdale, ed., *Imperial Russian Foreign Policy*, New York: Woodrow Wilson Center Press and Cambridge University Press, 1993; Irina S. Dostyan, *Rossiya i balkanskii vopros. . . .*, Moscow: Nauka, 1972.

96. Jovan Cvijić, *Makedonskie slavyane, . . .*, Petrograd: Slavyanskaya biblioteka, 1906, ii–iii.

97. Konstantine Leont'ev, "V svoem krayu," *Sobranie sochinenii*, vol. 1, Moscow: Izd. V. M. Sablina, 1912–1914, 306.

98. Nicolas Berdyaev, *Leontiev*, London: Geoffrey Bless, Centenary, 1940, 67–108; Konstantin Leontiev, *Vizantinizmît i slavyanstvoto*, Sofia: Slavika, 1993, 5–20.

99. Konstantin Leont'ev, "Vizantinism i slavyanstvo," *Vostok, Rossiya i slavyanstvo, Sbornik Statei*, vol. 1, Osnabrück: Otto Zeller, 1966, 114, 120–124.

100. Ibid., 106 and "Pis'ma otshel'nika," 267.

101. Leont'ev, "Vizantinism," 118, 188–189.

102. Ibid., 112, 188–189, 125–127, 112 and "Pis'ma otshel'nika," 266.

103. Leont'ev, "Egipetskii golub," *Sobranie sochinenii*, vol. 3, 392–393.

104. Leont'ev, "Vizantinism," 102, 129–130 and "Pis'ma otshel'nika," 274–275.

105. Leont'ev, "Russkie, greki i yugo-slavyane," *Vostok, Rossiya i slavyanstvo*, 204, 222.

106. Kozhukharova, *Ruski pîtepisi*, 378 and "Russkie, greki i yugo-slavyane," 203, 218.

107. Leont'ev, "Vizantinism," 130.

Chapter 4. Patterns of Perception until 1900

1. *The Cambridge History of English Literature*, vol. 14, Cambridge, 1922, 255.

2. Eisner, *Travels*, 20.

3. C. J. Heywood, "Sir Paul Rycaut, A Seventeenth-Century Observer of the Ottoman State: Notes for a Study," *English and Continental Views of the Ottoman Empire, 1500–1800*, Los Angeles: William Andrews Clark Memorial Library, 1972, 35.

4. Brandon H. Beck, *From the Rising of the Sun: English Images of the Ottoman Empire to 1715*, New York, Berne, Frankfurt-am-Main, and Paris: Peter Lang, 1987, 40.

5. Eisner, *Travels*, 52.

6. Beck, *From the Rising of the Sun*, 62.

7. A *Voyage into the Levant*, London: Andrew Crooke, 1636, 2.

8. John Walter Stoye, *English Travellers Abroad, 1604–1667*, London: Jonathan Cape, 1952, 177.

9. A *Voyage into the Levant.*, 2, 97.

10. Ibid., 103–104.

11. Ibid., 2.

12. Heywood, "Sir Paul Rycaut," 50–51.

13. Ibid., 55.

14. *The Complete Letters of Lady Mary Wortley Montagu*, vol. 1, Oxford: Clarendon, 1965, 313–314, 320.

15. Jeremy Black, *The British and the Grand Tour*, London: Croom Helm, 1985; Geoffrey Trease, *The Grand Tour*, London: Heinemann, 1967; William Edward Mead, *The Grand Tour in the Eighteenth Century*, Boston: Houghton Mifflin, 1914.

16. Eisner, *Travels*, 89.

17. Morritt, *A Grand Tour*, 245.

18. Ibid., 109.

19. Ibid., 171, 179.

20. Woodhouse, *The Philhellenes*, 13–14.

21. Edward Daniel Clarke, *Travels in Various Countries of Europe, Asia and Africa*, vol. 3, London: Cadell and Davies, 1814, 483–484.

22. "Edward Dodwell," *The Dictionary of National Biography*, vol. 5, 1921–1922, 1083.

23. Morritt, *A Grand Tour*, 136, 156, 180.

24. Woodhouse, *The Philhellenes*, 31–34, 37.

25. Ibid., 10, 38–39.

26. Ibid., 73–74, 120–123, 159–160.

27. Sarah Searight, *The British in the Middle East*, London: Weidebfeld and Nicolson, 1979, 16–20.

28. John Howes Gleason, *The Genesis of Russophobia in Great Britain*, New York: Octagon, 1972; Maria Todorova, *Angliya, Rossiya i Tanzimat*, Moscow: Glavnaya redaktsiya vostochnoi literatury izdatel'stva "Nauka," 1983.

29. Jack Snyder, *Myths of Empire. Domestic Politics and International Ambition*, Ithaca, N.Y. and London: Cornell University Press, 1991, 160.

30. Barbara Jelavich, "The British Traveller in the Balkans: The Abuses of Ottoman Administration in the Slavonic Provinces," *Slavonic and East European Review*, vol. 33, no. 81, June 1955, 412.

31. Upward, *The East and Europe*, 321.

32. David Urquhart, *The Spirit of the East: a Journal of Travels through Roumali*, vol. 1, London: H. Colburn, 1838, 195.

33. Woodhouse, *The Philhellenes*, 151.

34. Richard Shannon, "David Urquhart and the Foreign Affairs Committees," ed. Patricia Hollis, *Pressure From Without in Early Victorian England*, London: Edward Arnold, 1974.

35. Susan Hyman, ed., *Edward Lear in the Levant, Travels in Albania, Greece and Turkey in Europe 1848–1849*, London: John Murray, 1988, 26.

36. Kinglake, *Eothen*, 15.

37. Eisner, *Travels*, 138–139.

38. Kinglake, *Eothen*, 16.

39. Eisner, *Travels*, 145.

40. *Edward Lear in Greece*. A loan exhibition from the Gennadius library, Athens, Greece and Meriden, Conn.: Meriden Gravure, 1971; Edward Lear, *Journal of a Landscape Painter in Greece and Albania*, London, 1851; Lear, *Journal of a Landscape Painter in Southern Albania*, London: R. Bentley, 1852.

41. Hyman, *Edward Lear in the Levant*, 25; Eisner, *Travels*, 159.

42. Alice H. Eagly and Shelly Chaiken, *The Psychology of Attitudes*, Orlando, Fla.: Harcourt, Brace, Jovanovich, 1993, 634.

43. Skopetea, *I Disi*, 134, 150–152.

44. Dorothy P. Anderson, *Miss Irby and Her Friends*, London: Hutchinson, 1966, 20–21.

45. *Travels in the Slavonic Provinces of Turkey-in-Europe. By G. Muir Mackenzie and A. P. Irby*, 2nd ed. revised, London: Daldy, Isbister, 1877, 154.

46. Anderson, *Miss Irby*, 50–51, 38, 202.

47. *Travels in the Slavonic Provinces*, viii.

48. Anderson, *Miss Irby*, 134.

49. William Forsyth, *The Slavonic Provinces South of the Danube. A Sketch of Their History and Present State in Relation to the Ottoman Porte*, London: John Murray, 1876, 183–194.

50. *Travels in the Slavonic Provinces*, xi, xii.

51. "Smythe, Perce Ellen Frederick William, eighth viscount Strangford," *The Dictionary of National Biography*, vol. 18, 605–606; Viscountess [Emily] Strangford, *Report of the Expenditure of the Bulgarian Peasant Relief Fund*, London: Hardwicke and Bogue, 1878, 1.

52. Strangford, *Report*, 2–3, 25.

53. Ibid., 3, 21–22, 26.

54. Sheila Mary Smith, *The Other Nation: The Poor in English Novels of the 1840s and 1850s*, Oxford: Clarendon, 1980, 36.

55. Skopetea, *I Disi*, 136–137.

56. Harry C. Thomson, *The Outgoing Turk: Impressions of a Journey through the Western Balkans*, New York: D. Appleton, 1897, 209, 212, 221.

57. Cecil F. Melville, *Balkan Racket*, London: Jarrolds, 1941, 98–99.

58. Richard Shannon, *Gladstone and the Bulgarian Agitation 1976*, Hamden: Nelson, 1975; Richard Millman, *Britain and the Eastern Question, 1875–1978*, Oxford: Clarendon, 1979.

59. John L. C. Booth, *Trouble in the Balkans*, London: Hurst and Blackett, 1905, 115.

60. Anderson, *Miss Irby*, 136–137.

61. *Residence in Bulgaria*, London: John Murray, 1869, 412. *Twelve Years' Study or The Eastern Question in Bulgaria*, London: Chapman and Hall, 1877, 311.

62. *Residence*, 306–307.

63. Ibid., 10, 14–15.

64. Ibid., 78–79, 394–397.

65. Ibid., 237–238, 335, 409.

66. Stephen E. Larrabee, *Hellas Observed: The American Experience of Greece, 1775–1865*, New York: New York University Press, 1957; Marcia Jean Pakake, *Americans Abroad: A Bibliographical Study of American Travel Literature, 1625–1800*, Ph.D. dissertation, University of Minnesota, 1975.

67. The first was Joseph Allen Smith. R. A. McNeal, ed., *Nicholas Biddle in Greece. The Journal and Letters of 1806*, University Park, Penn.: Pennsylvania State University Press, 1993, 99.

68. Ibid., 9.

69. Ibid., 215, 225–228.

70. Ibid., 101–102.

71. Ibid., 149, 155–156, 178, 181, 226, 231.

72. Ibid., 31–33.

73. Ibid., 26.

74. Woodhouse, *The Philhellenes*, 23–24.

75. Mark Twain, *The Innocents Abroad or the New Pilgrim's Progress*, New York: Grosset and Dunlap, 1911, 288.

76. William Goodell, *Forty Years in the Turkish Empire*, New York: Robert Carter, 1883.

77. Leland James Gordon, *American Relations with Turkey, 1830–1930*, Philadelphia: University of Pennsylvania Press, 1932, 221–222.

78. James F. Clarke, *Bible Societies, American Missionaries, and the National Revival of Bulgaria*, New York: Arno, 1971; J. Clarke, *The Pen and the Sword: Studies in Bulgarian History*, Boulder, Co., East European Monographs, no. 252, New York: Columbia University Press, 1988; Tatyana Nestorova, *American Missionaries among the Bulgarians, 1858–1912*, Boulder, Co., East European Monographs, no. 218, New York: Columbia University Press, 1987.

79. Samuel S. Cox, *Diversions of a Diplomat in Turkey*, New York: Charles L. Webster, 1887, 184, 658; Ivan Ilchev, "Robert kolezh i formiraneto na bîlgarskata inteligentsiya (1863–1878), *Istoricheski pregled*, no. 1, 1981, 50–62.

80. Miller, *Travels and Politics*, 415.

81. Douglas Dakin, *British and American Philhellenes*, Thessaloniki: Idryma Meleton Hersonesou tou Aimou, 1957.

82. *Encyclopedia of American Foreign Policy*, New York: Scribner's, 1978, 764.

83. Gordon, *American Relations with Turkey*, 10–12.

84. David Porter, *Constantinople and its Environs . . .* , vol. 2, New York: Harper and Brothers, 1835, 317–318.

85. G. A. Perdicaris, *The Greece of the Greeks*, New York: Paine and Burgess, 1946.

86. *Encyclopedia of American Foreign Policy*, 273.

87. Marin V. Pundeff, *Bulgaria in American Perspective. Political and Cultural Issues*, Boulder, Co.: East European Monographs, no. 318, New York: Columbia University Press, 1994, 205–216, 219–221.

88. Januarius Aloysius MacGahan, *The Turkish Atrocities in Bulgaria*, Geneva: n.p., 1966; Pundeff, "Schuyler and MacGahan," 218–219, 221.

89. Anderson, *Miss Irby*, 126–127.

90. King, *Europe in Storm*, vii–viii, 734, 776–777, 790.

91. Edward King, *Echoes from the Orient*, London: C. Kegan Paul, 1880. vii.

92. King, *Europe in Storm*, 680, 705.

93. Ibid., 222–224; Michael Boro Petrovich, "Eugene Schuyler and Bulgaria, 1876–1878," *Bulgarian Historical Review*, no. 1, 1979, 51–69.

94. Pundeff, *Bulgaria in American Perspective*, 233–242.

95. William Eleroy Curtis, *The Turk and His Lost Provinces*, Chicago, New York, and Toronto: Fleming H. Revel, 1903, 191, 203–206, 261–265.

96. Ibid., 325, 336, 68.

97. Cox, *Diversions of a Diplomat*, 111, 183–184, 642–643, 658.

98. Rebecca West, *Black Lamb and Grey Falcon*, New York: Penguin, 1969, 1095. In the same vein, Billie Mellman notes: "As aristocratic culture slowly gave way to bourgeois attack on corruption and sensuality, the cosmopolitan, hedonistic appreciation of the exotic and oriental was supplanted by a preoccupation with 'propriety', accompanied by intolerance" (*Women's Orients: English Women and the Middle East, 1718–1918. Sexuality, Religion and Work*. Ann Arbor: The University of Michigan Press, 1995, 311).

99. Miller, *Travels and Politics*, 118, 279, 295–297, 319.

100. Duckett Ferriman, *Greece and the Greeks*, 150.

101. West, *Black Lamb and Grey Falcon*, 1089.

102. King, *Europe in Storm*, vii–ix.

103. Karl Marx and Friedrich Engels, "Manifesto of the Communist Party," *Collected Works*, trans. Richard Dixon et al., vol. 6., New York: International, 1976, 488.

104. Billie Melman, *Women's Orients: English Women and the Middle East, 1718–1918. Sexuality, Religion and Work*, Ann Arbor: University of Michigan Press, 1995, 311.

105. Ahmad, *In Theory*, 229.

106. Martin Meisel, *Shaw and the Nineteenth-Century Theatre*, Princeton, N.J.: Princeton University Press, 1963, 186, 194.

107. George Bernard Shaw, *Collected Plays with Their Prefaces*, vol. 1, New York: Dodd, Mead, 1975, 481–482.

108. Vesna Goldsworthy, *Inventing Ruritania: The Imperialism of the Imagination*, New Haven, Ct.: Yale University Press, 1998, 114.

109. Ibid., 475–477.

110. Ibid., 417.

111. Ibid., 506–507.

112. Ibid., 490.

113. Ibid., 490–491.

114. Ibid., 384–385.

115. Richard J. Crampton, *A Short History of Bulgaria*, New York: Cambridge University Press, 1987, 103.

116. John Reed, *The War in Eastern Europe*, New York: Scribner's, 1919, 38.

117. *Tsentralen dirzhaven arkhiv* (Central State Archives), Fond 176, Opis 4, a.e. 65, line 14, Report of Pancho Dorev to the minister of foreign affairs, N. 1495, 16 June 1921. My thanks to Rositsa Gencheva, who kindly drew my attention to this document.

118. Ivan D. Shishmanov, "Stari pîtuvaniya prez Bîlgariya v posoka na rimskiya voenen pît it Belgrad za Tsarigrad," *Sbornik za narodni umotvoreniya*, vol. 4, Sofia 1891, 324–325.

Chapter 5. From Discovery to Invention, from Invention to Classification

1. Count Hermann Keyserling, trans. Maurice Samuel, *Europe*, New York: Harcourt, Brace, 1928.
2. Sarup, *Post-structuralism*, 179.
3. Ainlay and Crosby, "Stigma, Justice," 20.
4. Jerome S. Bruner, Jacqueline J. Goodnow, and George A. Austin, *A Study of Thinking*, New Brunswick, N.J. and Oxford: Transaction, 1986, 2, 6, 12–15, 232.
5. Douglas, *Purity and Danger*, 49; Ainlay and Crosby, "Stigma, Justice," 20–21.
6. Ahmad, *In Theory*, 99.
7. Douglas, *Purity and Danger*, 49, 189, 191.
8. William Le Queux, *The Near East . . .* , New York: Doubleday, Page, 1907, 6; John Foster Fraser, *Pictures From the Balkans*, London: Cassel, 1906, 3, 16.
9. Harry De Windt, *Through Savage Europe . . .* , London: T. Fisher Unwin, 1907, 15.
10. Goff and Fawcett, *Macedonia*, 10.
11. Laura Sherman, *Fire on the Mountain: The Macedonian Revolutionary Movement and the Kidnapping of Miss Stone*, Boulder, Co.: East European Monographs, no. 62, New York: Columbia University Press, 1980; Duncan Perry, *The Politics of Terror: The Macedonian Liberation Movements*, Durham, N.C.: Duke University Press, 1988.
12. Berkovici, *The Incredible Balkans*, 90.
13. Bakić-Hayden, "Nesting Orientalisms," 6–7.
14. Zeman, "The Balkans and the Coming War," 27.
15. H. N. Brailsford, *Macedonia: Its Races and Their Future*, London: Methuen, 1906, xi.
16. Robert W. Seton-Watson, *The Southern Slav Question and the Habsburg Monarchy*, London: Constable, 1911, viii–ix, 336–337; Seton-Watson, *The Rise of Nationality in the Balkans*, London: Constable, 1917.
17. De Windt, *Through Savage Europe*, 45.
18. Cornelia Bodea and Hugh Seton-Watson, eds., *R. W. Seton-Watson şi Românii, 1906–1920*, vol. 2, Bucharest: Editura ştiinţifică şi enciclopedică: 1988, 675.
19. Booth, *Trouble in the Balkans*, 2.
20. Gunther, *Inside Europe*, 437.
21. Robert D. Kaplan, *Balkan Ghosts. A Journey Through History*, New York: St. Martin's, 1993, xxiii.
22. Mechthild Golczewski, *Der Balkan in Deutschen und Österreichischen Reise-und Erlebnisberichten*, Wiesbaden: Franz Steiner Verlag, 1981, 63–67, 269.
23. De Windt, *Through Savage Europe*, 68.
24. Charles J. Vopicka, *Secrets of the Balkans . . .* , Chicago: Rand McNally, 1921, v.
25. Durham, *Twenty Years of Balkan Tangle*, 39, 42, 283.
26. Durham, *The Burden of the Balkans*, 3, 81, 90.
27. Ibid., 286–287.
28. Ibid., 284–285.
29. Mowrer, *Balkanized Europe*, 8.
30. Durham, *Twenty Years of Balkan Tangle*, 52, 57, 108, 160, 234, 291–292.
31. Rumyana Koneva, "Balkanskite voini v nemskiya periodichen pechat," *Balkanistic forum*, vol. 2, 1993, 76–78.
32. West, *Black Lamb and Grey Falcon*, 21.
33. "Balkan," *Oxford English Dictionary*, vol. 1, 1989.
34. Agatha Christie, The Secret of Chimneys, New York: Dell, 1975, 104–105.
35. Ibid., 9–10.
36. George L. Mosse, *Toward the Final Solution. A History of European Racism*, New York: Howard Fertig, 1978, xii, xv–xvi, 2, 8–19, 17.

37. Alexander Grau Wandmayer, *The Balkan Slavs in America and Abroad. An address delivered by Alexander Grau Wandmayer, formerly Commissioner Plenipotentiary of the Ukrainian Government with the International Commission for the Liquidation of Austria before Students of Racial Backgrounds at Columbia University, July 28th, 1922*, New York, 1922.

38. Booth, *Trouble in the Balkans*, 147.

39. Windt, *Through Savage Europe*, 82, 98–99.

40. Goff and Fawcett, *Macedonia*, xiv, 13–16.

41. Ibid., 10.

42. Keyserling, *Europe*, 319.

43. Ibid., 321–322.

44. Marcus Ehrenpreis, *The Soul of the East: Experience and Reflections*. Trans. Alfhild Huebsch, New York: Viking, 1928, 208–209.

45. Ibid., 11–13.

46. Eisner, *Travels*, 119.

47. Cited in George E. Mylonas, *The Balkan States: An Introduction to Their History*, Washington, D.C.: Public Affairs, 1947, 169.

48. Eugen Thurnher, ed., *Jakob Philipp Fallmerayer: Europe zwischen Rom und Byanz*, Bozen: Athesia, 1990; Eugen Thurnher, ed., *Jakob Philipp Fallmerayer: Wissenschaftler, Politiker, Schriftsteller*, Innsbruck: Universitätsverlag Wagner, 1993.

49. Eisner, *Travels*, 119.

50. Josephine Wtulich, *American Xenophobia and the Slav Immigrant: A Living Legacy of Mind and Spirit*, Boulder, Co.,: East European Monographs, no. 385, New York: Columbia University Press, 1994, 40–41.

51. Wandmayer, *The Balkan Slavs*, 4, 11.

52. Wtulich, *American Xenophobia*, 34–38.

53. Arthur Ellridge, *Mucha: The Triumph of Art Nouveau*, Paris: Editions Pierre Terrail, 1992, 183.

54. Ibid., 193.

55. Archibald Lyall, *The Balkan Road*, London: Methuen, 1930, 12, 164.

56. Ibid., 13, 153, 157–158.

57. Ibid., 121.

58. Ibid., 13, 135.

59. Roucek, *Balkan Politics*, 3, 7.

60. *Nationalism and War in the Near East (By a Diplomatist)*, Oxford: Clarendon, 1915, ix, xii, xvi.

61. *Dictionary of the History of Ideas*, vol. 1, 619, vol. 2, 178.

62. Hans-Dieler Döpmann, "Die Christenheit auf dem Balkan im Spiegel deutschsprachiger Literatur des 19. Jahrhundests," Josip Matešić and Klaus Heitmann, eds., *Südosteuropa in der Wahrnehmung der deutschen Öffentlichkeit vom Wiener Kongress (1815) bis zum Parieser Frieden (1856)*, Munich: Südesteuropa Gesellschaft, 1990, 26.

63. Wolff, *Inventing Eastern Europe*, 315.

64. Brailsford, *Macedonia*, 1.

65. Felix Borchardt, "Berlin–Bagdad . . . ," *Balkan und Orient*, Berlin: Verlag Fritz Hirschberg, 1916/1917, 8; *Nationalism and War* , 20, 22.

66. Bernard Newman, *Balkan Background*, New York: Macmillan, 1935, 72.

67. Joseph Rothschild, cited in Henry L. Roberts, *Eastern Europe: Politics, Revolution, and Diplomacy*, New York: Alfred A. Knopf, 1970, 180.

68. Immanuel Wallerstein, *Geopolitics and Geoculture: Essays on the Changing World-System*, Cambridge: Cambridge University Press, 1991, 231.

69. "Responses to Samuel P. Huntington's 'The Clash of Civilizations?'" *Foreign Affairs*, vol. 72, no. 4, Sept./Oct. 1993, 2–26; Samuel P. Huntington, "If Not Civilizations, What?" *Foreign Affairs*, vol. 72, no. 5, Nov./Dec. 1993, 186–194; Richard E. Rubenstein and Jalte Crocker, "Challenging Huntington," *Foreign Policy*, no 96, Fall 1994, 113–128.

70. Theodore A. Couloumbis and Thanos Veremis, "In Search of New Barbarians . . . ," *Mediterranean Quarterly*, Winter 1994, 36–44.

71. Samuel Huntington,"The Clash of Civilizations?" *Foreign Affairs*, vol. 72, no. 3, Summer 1993, 30–31.

72. Couloumbis and Veremis, "In Search of New Barbarians," 40.

73. *Nationalism and War*, 31.

74. Ibid., 20, 22, 37, 40–41.

75. De Windt, *Through Savage Europe*, 84.

76. Berkovici, *The Incredible Balkans*, 3–5, 264–265.

77. Roucek, *Balkan Politics*, 12–13, 289.

78. Newman, *Balkan Background*, 248.

79. Roucek, *Balkan Politics*, 7.

80. Laird Archer, *Balkan Journal*, New York: W. W. Norton, 1944, 78.

81. Henry Miller, *The Colossus of Maroussi*, New York: New Directions, 1941, 14, 47–48.

82. *The Durrell-Miller Letters, 1935–80*, New York: New Directions, 1988, 148, 207.

83. Lawrence Durrell, *Esprit de Corps: Sketches from Diplomatic Life*, London: Faber and Faber, 1990, 9–19, 35–40, 82–83.

84. *The Durrell-Miller Letters*, 243, 245, 251.

85. Stavrianos, *The Balkans since 1453*, 801–802.

86. Richard Basset, *Balkan Hours. Travels in the Other Europe*, London: John Murray, 1990, 132.

87. Quoted in Thanos Veremis, *Greece's Balkan Entanglement*, Athens, Greece: ELIAMEP-YALCO, 1995, 99.

88. Cristopher Cvijic, *Remaking the Balkans*, London: Royal Institute of International Affairs, 1991, 2, 107.

89. Robert J. Donia and John V. A. Fine, Jr., *Bosnia and Hercegovina: A Tradition Betrayed*, New York: Columbia University Press, 1994, 26–28, 38. I would like to stress that in all respects this is a serious and scholarly book. It is the challenge of analyzing stereotypes that appear even in works dedicated to fighting them which prompted me to single out this particular work on Bosnia.

90. Michael Weithmann, *Balkan Chronik: 2000 Jahre zwischen Orient und Okzident*, Graz, Vienna, and Köln: F. Pustet/Styria, 1995, 41; Michael Weithmann, ed., *Der ruhelose Balkan: Die Konfliktregionen Südosteuropas*, Munich: Deutscher Taschenbuch Verlag, 1993, 9.

91. Eugene Hammel, "Meeting the Minotaur," *Anthropology Newsletter*, vol. 35, no. 4, April 1994, 48.

92. "Töten mit Messer," *Österreichische Zeitschrift für Geschichtswissenschaften*, vol. 1, 1994, 106; Hannes Grandits and Joel M. Halpern, "Traditionelle Wertmuster und der Krieg in Ex-Jugoslavien," *Beiträge zur historischen Sozialkunde*, no. 3, 1994, 91–102.

93. Maria Todorova, "On the Epistemological Value of Family Models: The Balkans Within the European Pattern," Josef Ehmer and Marcus Cerman, eds., *Family History and New Historiography. Festschrift for Michael Mitterauer*, Vienna (in press).

Chapter 6. Between Classification and Politics: The Myth of Central Europe

1. Gunther, *Inside Europe*, 437.

2. George Baranyi, "On Truths in Myths," *East European Quarterly*, vol. 15, no. 3, September 1981, 354.

3. Gale Stokes, "East European History after 1989," John R. Lampe and Paula Bailey Smith, eds., *East European Studies in the United States: Making Its Own Tradition after 1989*, Washington, D.C.: Woodrow Wilson Center, 1993, 35.

4. Mary Douglas and David Hull, *How Classification Works*, Edinburgh: Edinburgh University Press, 1992, 2.

5. Longinović, *Borderline Culture*, 26.

6. Richard Holbrooke, "America, A European Power," *Foreign Affairs*, vol. 74, no. 2, March/April 1995, 41; William Safire, "Hello, Central," *New York Times Magazine*, 12 March 1995, 24–26.

7. Jenö Szücs, "The Three Historic Regions of Europe, An Outline," *Acta Historica Scientiarum Hungaricae*, vol. 29 (2–4), 1983, 134–135, 151.

8. Ibid., 142.

9. Adam B. Seligman, *The Idea of Civil Society*, New York: Free Press, 1992, 200.

10. Szücs, "The Three Historic Regions," 140–142, 145, 147, 177.

11. Iver B. Neumann, "Russia as Central Europe's Constituting Other," *East European Politics and Societies*, vol. 7, no. 2, Spring 1993, 356.

12. Szücs, "The Three Historic Regions," 134–135, 180–181.

13. George Schöpflin and Nancy Wood, eds., *In Search of Central Europe*, Cambridge, U.K.: Polity, 1989, 19.

14. Czeslaw Milosz, *The Witness of Poetry*, Cambridge, Mass.: Harvard University Press, 1983, 3, 6–7, 10–11.

15. Schöpflin and Wood, *In Search of Central Europe*, 19.

16. Milosz, *The Witness*, 5.

17. Ibid., 7.

18. Czeslaw Milosz, "Central European Attitudes," *Cross Currents*, vol. 5, no. 2, 1986, 101–108.

19. Ibid., 101, 103, 106.

20. Timothy Garton Ash, "Does Central Europe Exist," *New York Review of Books*, vol. 33, no. 15, 9 October 1986, 191–215.

21. Neumann, "Russia," 357–358.

22. Schöpflin and Wood, *In Search of Central Europe*, 140–141.

23. Milan Kundera, "The Tragedy of Central Europe," *New York Review of Books*, vol. 31, no. 7, 26 April 1984, 34, 37; Şimečka, "Another Civilization? An Other Civilization?" Schöpflin and Wood, *In Search of Central Europe*, 159; Joseph Conrad, *Notes on Life and Letters*, Freeport, N.Y.: Books for Libraries, 1972, 135.

24. Kundera, "The Tragedy," 34.

25. "'The Post-Communist Nightmare': An Exchange," *New York Review of Books*, vol. 41, no. 4, 17 February 1994, 28–30.

26. Zdĕnek David, "Bohemian Utraquism in the Sixteenth Century: . . ." *Communio Viatorum*, vol. 35, no. 3, 1993, 229.

27. George Schöpflin, "Central Europe: Definitions Old and New," *In Search of Central Europe*, 18–19, 27.

28. Ibid., 9–10, 12, 14–15, 27.

29. Ibid., 2, 20.

30. Hának, "Central Europe," *In Search of Central Europe*, 57–69.

31. Nelson Goodman, "Seven Structures on Similarity," *How Classification Works*, 21.

32. Winfried Eberhard, Hans Lemberg, Heinz-Dieter Heimann, and Robert Luft, eds., *Westmitteleuropa. Ostmitteleuropa. Vergleiche und Beziehungen: . . .* , Munich: R. Oldenburg, 1992.

33. Csaba G. Kiss, "Central European Writers about Central Europe . . . ," *In Search of Central Europe*, 128.

34. Mihály Vajda, "Who Excluded Russia from Europe?" *In Search of Central Europe*, 175.

35. Schöpflin and Wood, *In Search of Central Europe*, 183, 188–189.

36. Radu Stern and Vladimir Tismaneanu, "L'Europe centrale: Nostalgies culturelles et réalités politiques," *Cadmos*, no. 39, 1987, 42, 44.

37. Jacques Rupnik, *The Other Europe*, London: Weidenfeld and Nicolson, 1988, 5, 21–22.

38. Neumann, "Russia," 350.

39. H.-P. Burmeister, F. Boldt, and Gy. Mészáros, eds., *Mitteleuropa — Traum oder Trauma? . . .* , Bremen, 1988.

40. Ferenc Fehér, "On Making Central Europe," *Eastern European Politics and Societies*, vol. 3, no. 3, Fall 1989, 443.

41. Ferenc Fehér and Agnes Heller, *Eastern Left, Western Left: Totalitarianism, Freedom and Democracy*, Atlantic Highlands, N.J.: Humanities, 1987, 17–18.

42. Henry Cord Meyer, *Mitteleuropa in German Thought and Action, 1815–1945*, Hague: Martinus Nijhoff, 1955.

43. Friedrich Naumann, *Mitteleuropa*, Berlin: G. Reimer, 1915; Naumann, *Bulgarien und Mitteleuropa*, Berlin: G. Reimer, 1916.

44. Joseph Partsch, *Mitteleuropa*, Gotha: J. Perthes, 1904.

45. Ash, "Does Central Europe Exist," *In Search of Central Europe*, 196.

46. Henry Cord Meyer, "*Mitteleuropa* in German Political Geography," *Collected Works*, vol. 1, Irvine, Calif.: Charles Schlacks, Jr., 1986, 123–124.

47. Oscar Halecki, *The Limits and Divisions of European History*, London and New York: Sheed and Ward, 1950, 202; Halecki, *The Millennium of Europe*, Notre Dame, Ind.: University of Notre Dame Press, 1963, xv–xvi, 333, 389.

48. Halecki, *The Millennium*, 3, 5, 39, 43–44, 372, 377 and *The Limits*, 13, 35, 121.

49. Halecki, *The Millennium*, 233, 307 and *The Limits*, 93, 99.

50. Halecki, *The Millennium*, 7–8, 43–44, 231 and *The Limits*, 78.

51. Halecki, *The Limits*, 78, 120.

52. Halecki, *The Millennium*, 335.

53. Ibid., 376.

54. Neumann, "Russia," 368.

55. Rupnik, *The Other Europe*, 3.

56. Wolff, *Inventing Eastern Europe*, 364.

57. Schöpflin and Wood, *In Search of Central Europe*, 194–195.

58. Ibid., 195, 197, 210, 212, 214.

59. Ibid., 198.

60. Ibid., 214.

61. Timothy Garton Ash, Michael Mertes, and Dominique Moisi, "Let the East Europeans In!" *New York Review of Books*, vol. 38, no. 17, 24 October 1991.

62. Neumann, "Russia," 364; Dušan Třestik, "We are Europe," *Iztok-Iztok*, nos. 9–10, 1993, 106; Hans Agnus Enzensberger, Ryszard Kapuściński, and Adam Krzemiński, "Back to the Future," *New York Review of Books*, 17 November 1994; Peter Hának, "The Danger of Burying Central Europe," *Magyar Lettre Internationale*, 1991, 4, quoted from *Iztok-Iztok*, nos. 9–10, 1993, 111–118.

63. Konrád, *The Melancholy of Rebirth*, 158–166, 177.

64. Ibid., vii, 195.

65. Vladislav Todorov, *Red Square . . . , Black Square*, Albany: State University of New York Press, 1995.

66. Neumann, "Russia," 364–365.

67. Vaclav Havel, "New Democracies for Old Europe," *New York Times*, 17 October 1993, E17.

68. Michael Waller, "Groups, Parties and Political Change in Eastern Europe from 1977," Geoffrey Pridham and Tatu Vanhanen, eds., *Democratization in Eastern Europe*, London and New York: Routledge, 1994, 38.

69. Enzensberger, Kapuściński, and Krzemiński, "Back to the Future."

70. Timothy Garton Ash, "Prague: Intellectuals and Politicians," *New York Review of Books*, vol. 42, no. 1, 12 January 1995, 34.

71. Vladimir Tismaneanu, "NYR, TLS, and the Velvet Counterrevolution," *Common Knowledge*, vol. 3, no. 1, 1994, 130–142.

72. R. C. Longworth, "Bulgaria, Romania Resist Pull of the West," *Chicago Tribune*, 10 October 1994, 1, 6.

73. Michael Ignatieff, "On Civil Society," *Foreign Affairs*, vol. 74, no. 2, March/April 1995, 134.

74. Paul Hockenos, *Free to Hate. The Rise of the Right in Post-Communist Eastern Europe*, New York: Routledge, 1993.

75. RFE/RL Daily Report, no. 183, 26 September 1994.

76. William Safire, "Baltics Belong in a Big NATO," *New York Times*, 16 January 1995, A17; Safire, "Hello, Central," *New York Times Magazine*, 12 March 1995, 24.

77. Robert D. Kaplan, "The Middle East is a Myth," *New York Times Magazine*, 20 February 1994, 42–43.

78. "Balkan Brinkmanship," *New York Times*, 10 March 1995, A28.

79. *Foreign Policy*, no. 97, Winter 1994–95, 183; Fouad Ajami, "In Europe's Shadows," *New Republic*, vol. 211, no. 21, 21 November 1994, 37.

80. *The MacNeill-Lehrer News Hour* broadcast, 7 February 1994.

81. Henry Kissinger, "Expand NATO Now," *Washington Post*, 19 December 1994; Kissinger, "Ready for Revitalizing," *New York Times*, 9 March 1995, A21.

82. Richard Holbrooke, "America's Stake in Europe's Future," discussion at the Woodrow Wilson International Center for Scholars, 10 February 1995.

83. Scott Malcomson, *Borderlands*, 120–121.

84. Sami Nair, "Le differend mediterranéen," *Lettre Internationale*, vol. 30, 1991, trans. in *Iztok-Iztok*, nos. 9–10, 1993, 55–63.

85. Egon Schwarz, "Central Europe—What It Is and What It Is Not," *In Search of Central Europe*, 143.

86. Neumann, "Russia," 364.

87. RFE/RL Daily Report, no. 57, 24 March 1993.

88. Heiner Müller, "Stirb schneller, Europa," *Iztok-Iztok*, nos. 9–10, 1993, 47.

89. David Bidney, "Myth, Symbolism, and Truth," Thomas A. Sebeok, ed., *Myth: Symposium*, Philadelphia: American Folklore Society, 1955, 12.

Chapter 7. The Balkans: Realia. *Qu'est-ce qu'il y a de hors-texte*

1. Cioran, *History and Utopia*, 34.

2. E. D. Hirsch, Jr., *Cultural Literacy: What Every American Needs To Know*, New York: Vintage, 1988.

3. Ronelle Alexander, "On the Definition of Sprachbund Boundaries: The Place of Balkan Slavic," Norbert Reiter, ed., *Ziele und Wege der Balkanlinguistik. . . .*, Berlin: Otto Harrassowitz, 1983, 16–17. See also Kristian Sandfeld, *Linguistique balkanique. Problème et résultat*, Paris: Librairie ancienne Honoré Champion, 1930; *Linguistique balkanique. Bibliographie*, Sofia: Institut d'études balkaniques, CIBAL, 1983.

4. John R. Lampe and Marvin R. Jackson, *Balkan Economic History, 1550–1950: From Imperial Borderlands to Developing Nations*, Bloomington: Indiana University Press, 1982; Iván Berend and György Ránki, *Economic Development in East-Central Europe in the Nineteenth and Twentieth Centuries*, New York and London: Columbia University Press, 1974.

5. The ensuing analysis is a revised version of my chapter "The Ottoman Legacy in the Balkans," L. Carl Brown, ed., *Imperial Legacy: The Ottoman Imprint in the Balkans and the Middle East*, New York: Columbia University Press, 1995. After my book came out, Fikret Adanir published "The Tolerant and the Grim: The Ottoman Legacy in Southeastern Europe," *Culture and Reconciliation in Southeastern Europe. International Conference, Thessaloniki, Greece, June 26–29, 1997*, Thessaloniki: Paratiritis, 1998, 107–119. There is basic agreement in our assessment of the Ottoman legacy.

6. Hans Georg Majer, ed., *Die Staaten Südosteuropas und die Osmanen*, Munich: Selbstverlag der Südosteuropa-Gesellschaft, 1989; Costas Hatzidimitriou, "From Paparrigopoulos to Vacalopoulos: Modern Greek Historiography on the Ottoman Period," A. Lily Macrakis and P. Nikiforos Diamandouros, eds., *New Trends in Modern Greek Historiography*, Hanover, N.H.: The Modern Greek Studies Association Occasional Papers 1, 1982, 13–23.

7. Benjamin Braude and Bernard Lewis, eds., *Christians and Jews in the Ottoman Empire. . . .*, vol. 1. New York and London: Holmes and Meier, 1982; Speros Vryonis, Jr., "The Experience of Christians under Seljuk and Ottoman Domination, Eleventh to Sixteenth Century" Michael Gervers and Ramzi Jibran Bikhazi, eds., *Conversion and Continuity. . . .*, Toronto: Pontifical Institute of Mediaeval Studies, 1990, 185–216; Şerif Mardin, "The Just and the Unjust," *Daedalus*, vol. 120, no. 3, Summer 1991, 118.

8. Niyazi Berkes, *The Development of Secularism in Turkey*, Montreal: McGill University, 1964; Şerif Mardin, *The Genesis of Young Ottoman Thought*, Princeton, N.J.: Princeton University Press, 1962; Yurii A. Petrosyan, *Mladoturetskoe dvizhenie* . . . , Moscow: Izdatel'stvo Nauka, 1973.

9. Semih Tezcan, "Kontinuität und Diskontinuität der Sprachentwicklung in der Türkei," *Die Staaten Südosteuropas* . . . , Munich: Selbstverlag der Südosteuropa-Gesellschaft, 1989, 215–222; Güvenç, *Türk Kimliği*, 263–272.

10. Nicolae Iorga, *Byzance après Byzance* . . . , Bucharest: A l'institut d'etudes byzantines, 1935.

11. Paschalis Kitromilides, *Enlightenment, Mationalism, Orthodoxy* . . . , Aldershot, Hampshire, England: Variorum, 1994; Kitromilides, *The Enlightenment as Social Criticism: Iosipos Moisiodax and Greek Culture in the Eighteenth Century*, Princeton, N.J.: Princeton University Press, 1992; Richard Clogg, ed., *Balkan Society in the Age of Greek Independence*, London: Macmillan, 1981; Dimitrije Djordjevic and Stephen Fischer-Galati, *The Balkan Revolutionary Tradition*, New York: Columbia University Press, 1981.

12. Paschalis Kitromilides, "The Enlightenment East and West: A Comparative Perspective on the Ideological Origins of the Balkan Political Traditions," *Canadian Review of Studies in Nationalism*, vol. 10, no. 1, Spring 1983, 55, 66.

13. Tom Nairn, *The Enchanted Class: Britain and Its Monarchy*, London: Radius, 1988, 129.

14. H. J. Kornrumpf, "Zur territorial Verwaltungsgliederung des Osmanischen Reiches, ihrem Entstehen und ihrem Einfluss auf die Nachfolgestaaten," K.-D. Grothusen, ed., *Ethnogenese und Staatsbildung in Südosteuropa*, Göttingen, 1974, 52–61.

15. R. W. Seton-Watson, *Disraeli, Gladstone and the Eastern Question*, London, 1935, 450.

16. John V. A. Fine, Jr., *The Late Medieval Balkans*. . . . , Ann Arbor: University of Michigan Press, 1987, 484.

17. Gunnar Hering, "Die Osmanenzeit im Selbstverständnis der Völker Südosteuropas," *Die Staaten* . . , Munich: Selbstverlag der Südosteuropa-Gesellschaft, 1989, 361.

18. John Petropulos, *Politics and Statecraft in the Kingdom of Greece, 1833–1843*, Princeton, N.J.: Princeton University Press, 1968, 501; Petropulos, "The Modern Greek State and the Greek Past," Speros Vryonis, Jr., ed., *The "Past" in Medieval and Modern Greek Culture*, Malibu, Calif.: Undena, 1978, 166; Michael Boro Petrovich, *A History of Modern Serbia, 1804–1918*, New York: Harcourt, Brace, Jovanovich, 1976; Bernard Lory, *Le sort de l'heritage ottoman en Bulgarie, 1978–1900*, Istanbul: Isis, 1985, 62–78.

19. Feroz Ahmad, *The Making of Modern Turkey*, London and New York: Routledge, 1993, 17.

20. Fikret Adanir, "Tradition and Rural Change in Southeastern Europe During Ottoman Rule," Daniel Chirot, ed., *The Origins of Backwardness in Eastern Europe*. . . . , Berkeley: University of California Press, 1989, 155.

21. Çaglar Keyder, "Small Peasant Ownership in Turkey: Historical Formation and Present Structure, *Review*, vol. 7, no. 1, Summer 1983, 53–107; Çaglar Keyder, Y. Eyüp Özveren, and Donald Quaetert, "Port-Cities in the Ottoman Empire. Some Theoretical and Historical Perspectives, *Review*, vol. 16, no. 4, Fall 1993, 541–542.

22. Jacek Kochanowicz, "The Polish Economy and the Evolution of Dependency," *The Origins of Backwardness in Eastern Europe*, 119.

23. Anatoly M. Khazanov, *Nomads and the Outside World*, Madison: University of Wisconsin Press, 1994, xi.

24. Adanir, "Tradition and Rural Change," 156.

25. Nikolay Todorov, *The Balkan City, 1400–1900*, Seattle and London: University of Washington Press, 1983, 3–8.

26. *Ibid.*, 460; Nikolay Todorov, "Les tentatives d'industrialisation précoces dans les provinces balkaniques de l'Empire Ottoman, Jean Batou, ed., *Between Development and Underdevelopment*. . . . , Genèva: Librairie Droz, 1991, 381–394.

27. Szücs, "The Three Historic Regions," 135–137.

28. Keyder, Özveren, and Quaetert, "Port-Cities," 551.

29. Gale Stokes, "The Social Origins of East European Politics," *The Origins of Backwardness*, 238.

30. Halil Inalcik, "Village, Peasant and Empire," *The Middle East and the Balkans under the Ottoman Empire*, vol. 9, Bloomington: Indiana University Turkish Studies, 1993, 141, 144. For a critique, see John Haldon, "The Ottoman State and the Question of State Autonomy: Comparative Perspectives," Halil Berktay and Suraiya Faroqhi, eds., *New Approaches to State and Peasant in Ottoman History*, London: Frank Cass, 1992, 53–77.

31. John D. Bell, *Peasants in Power: Alexander Stamboliski and the Bulgarian Agrarian National Union, 1899–1923*, Princeton, N.J.: Princeton University Press, 1977.

32. Alexandru Duţu, "National and Regional Identity in Southeast Europe," *Balkans: A Mirror of the New International Order*, 78.

33. Maria Todorova, *Balkan Family History and the European Pattern. Demographic Developments in Ottoman Bulgaria*, Washington, D.C.: American University Press, 1993.

34. Dimitrije Djordjevic, "Migrations During the 1912–1913 Balkan Wars and World War One," *Migrations in Balkan History*, Belgrade: Serbian Academy of Sciences and Arts, 1989.

35. Szücs, "The Three Historic Regions," 135.

36. George G. Arnakis, "The Role of Religion in the Development of Balkan Nationalism," *The Balkans in Transition*, 115–144.

37. Paschalis Kitromilides,"Imagined Communities and the Origins of the National Question in the Balkans," *European History Quarterly*, vol. 19, no. 2, April 1989, 177, 184.

38. Eran Fraenkel, "Urban Muslim Identity in Macedonia: . . . ," Eran Fraenkel and Christina Kramer, eds., *Language Contact — Language Conflict*, New York: Peter Lang, 1993, 29–44.

39. Darko Tanaskovic, "Les thèmes et les traditions Ottomans dans la littérature Bosniaque," *Die Staaten Südosteuropas*, 299–307.

40. Ivanka Gergova, "Medieval and Contemporary Art of the Balkans," *Vek 21*, no. 41, 19–25 October 1994.

41. Paschalis Kitromilides, review of *Europe: A History of its Peoples, European History Quarterly*, vol. 24, no. 1, January 1994, 126; Deno John Geanakoplos, *Byzantine East and Latin West . . .* , Oxford: Basil Blackwell, 1965; Geanakoplos, *Greek Scholars in Venice . . .* , Cambridge, Mass.: Harvard University Press, 1962; Geanakoplos, *Constantinople and the West. . . .* , Madison: University of Wisconsin Press, 1989; Robert Byron and David Talbot Rice, *The Birth of Western Painting . . .* , New York: A. A. Knopf, 1931.

42. Klaus Roth, "Osmanische Spuren in der Alltagskultur Südosteuropas," *Die Staaten Südosteuropas . . .* , 319–332; Wayne S. Vuchinich, "Some Aspects of the Ottoman Legacy," Charles and Barbara Jelavich,eds., *The Balkans in Transition . . .* , Berkeley and Los Angeles: University of California Press, 1963, 89–95.

43. Lory, *Le sort de l'heritage*, 138.

44. Ibid., 166–167.

45. Roth, "Osmanische Spuren," 323.

46. Lory, *Le sort de l'heritage*, 194–196.

47. Paschalis Kitromilides, "'Balkan mentality': History, Legend, Imagination," *Nations and Nationalism*, vol. 2, part 2, July 1996, 168.

48. Hans-Michael Miedlig, "Probleme der Mentalität bei Kroaten und Serben," *Septième Congres International . . .* , Athens: Association Internationale d'Etudes du Sud-Est Européen, Comité National Grec, 1994, 393–424; Miedlig, "Patriarchalische Mentalität als Hindernis für die staatliche und gesellschaftliche Modernisierung in Serbien . . . ," *Südost-Forschungen*, vol. 50, 1991, 163–190; Miedlig, "Gründe und Hintergründe der aktuellen Nationalitätenkonflikte in den jugoslawischen Ländern," *Südosteuropa*, vol. 41, 1992, 116–130; Tat'iana V. Tsiv'ian, *Lingvisticheskie osnovy balkanskoi medeli mira*, Moscow: Nauka, 1990; G. D. Gachev, "Balkany kak kosmos khaidutstva. . . ." *Sovetskoe slavianovedenie*, vol. 4, 1989, 171–173.

49. Kitromilides, "'Balkan mentality,'" 186–187.

50. Konstantin Jireček, *Geschichte der Bulgaren*, Prague, 1876.
51. Gerasimos Augustinos, "Culture and Authenticity in a Small State: Historiography and National Development in Greece," *East European Quarterly*, vol. 23, no. 1, 1989, 17–31.

Conclusion

1. *The Incredible Balkans*, 3.
2. Gunther, *Inside Europe*, 437.
3. Geshkof, *Balkan Union*, xi.
4. Spurr, *The Rhetoric*, 61–68, 71–73.
5. *The Other Balkan Wars*, 14.
6. Ivo Banac, "Misreading the Balkans," *Foreign Policy*, no. 93, Winter 1993–1994, 181.
7. Michael Kelly, "Surrender and Blame," *New Yorker*, vol. 30, no. 42, 19 December 1994, 44.
8. Chaim I. Waxman, *The Stigma of Poverty. A Critique of Poverty Theories and Policies*, New York: Pergamon, 1977, 124.
9. Susan L. Woodward, *Balkan Tragedy: Chaos and Dissolution after the Cold War*, Washington, D.C.: Brookings Institution, 1995.
10. *The Other Balkan Wars*, 14–15.
11. Esther Benbassa, "Balkans: sortir du cadre des État nations," *Liberation*, 16–17 January 1993, 5.
12. Wolfgang Iser, *Prospecting: From Reader Response to Literary Anthropology*, Baltimore and London: Johns Hopkins University Press, 1989, 238–241; Susan R. Suleiman and Inge Crosman, eds., *The Reader in the Text: Essays on Audience and Interpretation*, Princeton, N.J.: Princeton University Press, 1980.
13. Breckenridge and van der Veer, *Orientalism and the Postcolonial Predicament*, 5.
14. Wolfgang Iser, *The Fictive and the Imaginary. Chartering Literary Anthropology*, Baltimore and London: Johns Hopkins University Press, 1993, xvii.
15. Michel Foucault, *The Archaeology of Knowledge and The Discourse on Language*, New York: Pantheon, 1972, 229; Foucault, "Space, Power and Knowledge," Simon During, ed., *The Cultural Studies Reader*, London and New York: Routledge, 1993, 169.
16. J. Richard Eiser, *Social Psychology: Attitudes, Cognition and Social Behavior*, Cambridge: Cambridge University Press, 1986, 39; Alice H. Eagly and Shelly Chaiken, *The Psychology of Attitudes*, Orlando, Fla.: Harcourt, Brace, Jovanovich, 1993, 635–636.
17. Agnes Heller, "Europe: An Epilogue?" Brian Nelson, David Roberts, and Walter Veit, eds., *The Idea of Europe: Problems of National and Transnational Identity*, New York and Oxford: Berg, 1992, 14.

Afterword

1. Samuel Huntington, *The Clash of Civilizations and the Remaking of World Order*, New York: Simon & Schuster, 1996.
2. Tony Judt, "A Grand Illusion? An Essay on Europe," quoted in *New York Times*, January 24, 1997, A2.
3. Scholars argue about whether there was a formal commitment, but Mikhail Gorbachev in a recent interview was unequivocal that such a commitment was made (Adrian Blomfield and Mike Smith, "Gorbachev:US could start a new Cold War," *The Daily Telegraph*, 7 May 2008; available at: http://www.telegraph.co.uk/news/worldnews/europe/russia/1933223/Gorbachev-US-could-start-new-Cold-War.html). See also Stephen F. Cohen, "Gorbachev's Lost Legacy," *The Nation*, February 24, 2005; Robert B. Zoellick, "The Lessons of German Unification," *The National Interest*, September 22, 2000.
4. This point is made by Charles King, "The Kosovo Precedent," *NewsNet: The Newsletter of the AAASS*, May 2008, 48: 3, 1–3.
5. Ibid., 1.

6. Mathew Yglesias, "Kosovo and the Rise of the Humantiarian Hawks," *The American Prospect*, February 21, 2008 (available at: http://www.prospect.org/cs/article-kosovo_and_the rise_of_the_humanitarian_hawks.

7. See Maria Todorova, "The Balkans: From Invention to Intervention," in William J. Buckley, ed., *Kosovo: Contending Voices on Balkan Interventions*, Grand Rapids/London: Eerdmans, 2000, 159–169.

8. The Balkans as a name clearly continues to evoke the darkest of associations. A recent novel by Barbara Shenouda, about a Canadian novelist who has suffered the horrors of the Second World War, confronts the dark secrets of her past, and uncovers a deadly conspiracy to resurrect Hitler, is entitled *The Balkan Secret Conspiracy* (Lincoln, NE, 2007).

9. For a critique of the persistent presence of balkanism in academic studies, see Maria Todorova, "The Mausoleum of Georgi Dimitrov as Lieu de Mémoire," *Journal of Modern History*, vol.78, N.2, June 2006, 374–411.

10. Gayatri Chakravorty Spivak, "In Memoriam: Edward W. Said," *Comparative Studies of South Asia, Africa and the Middle East*, 23: 1&2, 2003, 6–7.

11. Spivak, 6.

12. Ibid., 7.

13. Here I am using Southeastern Europe and the Balkans as synonyms. On the nuanced differences between the two, see my treatment in "Historische Vermächtnisse als Analysekategorie. Der Fall Südosteuropa," in Karl Kaser, ed., *Europa und die Grenzen im Kopf*, Wieser Verlag, 2003, 221–246.

14. Spivak was alluding to the title of *Balkan As Metaphor: Between Globalization and Fragmentation*, ed. by Dušan Bjelić and Obrad Savić. Cambridge, Mass: MIT Press, 2002. This collection of essays, while accepting the difference between balkanism and orientalism, explicitly posits balkanism "as a critical study of colonial representation" (p.4).

15. It is symptomatic that there is not one single historian among the 15 authors of *Balkan as Metaphor*. Seven are literary scholars, six philosophers, one an anthropologist, and one a feminist antiwar activist. To my knowledge, the only historian who works on the premise that the Ottoman Empire was a colonial formation and the Balkans have a postcolonial predicament is Mary Neuburger, in *The Orient Within: Muslim Minorities and the Negotiation of Nationhood in Modern Bulgaria* (Cornell University Press, 2004).

16. The expression belongs to Kaplana Seshadri-Crooks, "At the Margins of Postcolonial Studies: Part 1," in Fawzi Afzal-Khan and Kaplana Seshadri-Crooks, eds., *The Pre-Occupation of Postcolonial Studies*. Durham, N.C.: Duke University Press, 2000, 3–4.

17. In the case of *Balkan as Metaphor*, there may also be another correlation that helps to explain the special predisposition for postcolonial theory in the former Yugoslavia, even before and apart from the wars for the Yugoslav succession in the 1990s. Of the fourteen articles in the volume, nine have been written by ex-Yugoslavs of the generation socialized under Tito, who had distinct ambitions and successfully maneuvered for the leadership of the Third World, and under whose rule Yugoslavia maintained special relations with India. Many Yugoslavs either studied in India or visited, and in any case have kept open a tradition of intellectual contacts. Apart from this case, which makes an explicit link between balkanism and postcolonialism, the other examples of applying postcolonial theory by East Europeans refer mostly to the postsocialist period and the involvement of Eastern Europe in the process of globalization: József Böröcz, "Empire and Coloniality in the 'Eastern Enlargement' of the European Union," in József Böröcz and Melinda Kovács, eds., *Empire's New Clothes: Unveiling EU Enlargement*. Published by *Central Europe Review*, 2001, 4–50 (http://www.ce-review.org); Henry F. Carey and Rafal Raciborski, "Postcolonialism: A Valid Paradigm for the Former Sovietized States and Yugoslavia?" in *East European Politics and Societies*, 18:2, 2004, 191–235.

18. David Spurr, *The Rhetoric of Empire: Colonial Discourse in Journalism, Travel Writing and Imperial Administration*, Durham, N.C.: Duke University Press, 1993, 6.

19. On the imperial and colonial nature of Russia and the Soviet Union, see Daniel R. Brower and Edward J. Lazzerini, eds., *Russia's Orient: Imperial Borderlands and Peoples, 1700–1917*, Bloomington: Indiana University Press, 1997; Theodore R. Weeks, *Nation and*

State in Late Imperial Russia: Nationalism and Russification on the Western Frontier, 1863–1914, DeKalb: Northern Illinois University Press, 1996; Alexandre Benningsen, "Colonization and Decolonization in the Soviet Union," *Journal of Contemporary History*, 4, 1969, 141–151; Hélène Carrère d'Encausse, *The End of the Soviet Empire: The Triumph of the Nations*, London: Basic Books, 1994; Ronald Grigor Suny, *The Revenge of the Past: Nationalism, Revolution and the Collapse of the Soviet Union*, Stanford: Stanford University Press, 1994; Robert Strayer, "Decolonization, Democratization and Communist Reform: The Soviet Collapse in Comparative Perspective," *Journal of World History*, 12, 2001, 375–406.

20. This is not the opinion of Carey and Raciborski, "Postcolonialism: A Valid Paradigm for the Former Sovietized States and Yugoslavia?" *East European Politics and Societies*, 18:2, 2004, 191–235. They apply the postcolonial paradigm not only to the former Soviet Union but to all ex-Soviet satellites and even to Yugoslavia and Albania on the grounds that "the communist system was indirectly exported by the Soviets, even if they were expelled from much of the Balkans" (200). This absurd argument can be twisted by saying that the Soviet Union itself may have been colonized by a western ideology like Marxism.

21. See, in particular, L. Klor de Alva, "Colonialism and Postcoloniality as (Latin) American Mirages," in *Colonial Latin American Review*, 1, 1992, 3–23.

22. *Journal of Modern Greek Studies*, 16:2, 1998, 376.

23. Celia Applegate, "A Europe of regions: Reflections on the Historiography of Subnational Places in Modern Times," *American Historical Review*, 104:4, 1999, 1157–1182; E. A. Swyngedouw, "The Heart of the Place: The Resurrection of Locality in the Age of Hyperspace," *Geografiska Annaler*, 71b, 1989; Michael Keating, *The New Regionalism in Western Europe*, Cheltenham: Edward Elgar, 1998; Richard Baldwin, "The causes of regionalism," *The World Economy*, 20:7, 1997, 865–888; Wilfred Ethier, "Regionalism in a multilateral world," *The Journal of Political Economy*, 106: 6, 1998, 1214–1245; Donald and Theresa Davidson, "Regionalism," *Modern Age*, 37: 2, 1995, 102–115; Sajal Lahiti, "Controversy: Regionalism versus multilateralism," *The Economic Journal*, 108: 449, 1998, 1126–1127.

24. Rune Johansson, "The Impact of Imagination: History, Territoriality and Perceived Affinity," in Sven Tägil, ed., *Regions in Central Europe. The Legacy of History*, London: Hurst & Company, 1999, 4.

25. Rune Johansson, "The Impact of Imagination," 4. The criteria of cohesion and affinity clearly introduce identity as a decisive factor. Accordingly, some authors speak separately of economic regions as functional entities that are not associated with feelings of affinity and identification. They also distinguish between economic regions and networks, where the latter are less clearly demarcated territorially, and often extend across borders (Ibid., 5).

26. Etienne François, Hannes Siegrist and Jakob Vogel, eds., *Nation und Emotion. Deutschland und Frankreich im Vergleich 19. und 20. Jahrhundert*, Göttingen: Vandehoeck & Ruprecht, 1995, 105; Michael Müller, "European History—a *façon de parler*," in *European Review of History*, 10: 2, 2003, 409–414.

27. As developed by N. S. Trubetzkoy, *Grundzüge der Phonologie*, Göttingen 1967. For a comment on the role of the "marked-unmarked" opposition in culture, see Zygmunt Bauman, *Culture as Praxis*, London: Sage Publications, 1999, 80–81.

28. See Derek Gregory, *Geographical Imaginations*, Cambridge, MA: Blackwell, 1994, 63, and especially chapters 1 and 6; Gregory, "Social Theory and Human Geography," in Gregory, Martin, Smith, eds., *Human Geography*; D. Gregory and J. Urry, eds., *Social Relations and Spatial Structure*, London: Macmillan, 1985; L. Lefebvre, *The Production of Space*, trans. D. Nicholson-Smithe, Oxford: Basil Blackwell, 1991; R. Butlin, *Historical Geography. Through the Gates of Time and Space*, London: Edward Arnold, 1993; Dodgshon, Society in Time and Space. For an anthropological take on the notion of space, see Rudolf zur Lippe, "Raum," in Christoph Wulf, Hrsg., *Vom Menschen. Handbuch Historischer Antrhopologie*, Weinheim und Basel: Beltz Verlag, 1997, 169–79.

29. Lee Blessing, *A Walk in the Woods. A Play in Two Acts* (1998), quoted in William Wallace, *Central Europe: Core of the continent, or periphery of the West?* London: Eleni Nakou Foundation, 1999, 5.

30. Raymond Williams, *Keywords. Vocabulary of Culture and Society*, Revised edition, New York: Oxford University Press, 1985, 318.

31. One could speak of synchronic and overlapping periods, by taking the example of the late Roman, Byzantine, and early Ottoman empires, and the period of great migrations from Central Asia (with is numerous political legacies as well as the social legacy of seminomadism), which peaked in the fourth and fifth centuries and whose spurts were felt until the fifteenth and sixteenth centuries. The same goes for the synchronic workings of the whole variety of different religious systems in the region, both as legacies and ongoing processes. An instance of ceasura between periods, and little if any overlap between legacies is, for example, the Hellenistic and communist period and legacy. Otherwise, legacies fade away in intensity with the passage of time but, in principle, they would be overlapping by definition.

32. An example of the first would be the Byzantine and the Ottoman period and legacy. Until the sixteenth century, there was an almost complete spatial coincidence between the spheres of influence of the Byzantine and Ottoman empires, both in Europe and in Asia Minor. After the early sixteenth century, the Ottoman Empire expanded its space in North Africa and elsewhere, but in Southeastern Europe both the space of the historical periods and that of the legacies are coincidental. For an example of the second sort, one can point to another two periods and legacies: the Roman Empire, which included Southeastern Europe in a space stretching from the British Isles to the Caspian and Mesopotamia (but excluding much of Northern and Central Europe), and the period and legacy of communism, which involved part of Southeastern Europe in a space encompassing the whole of Eastern Europe, and stretching through the Eurasian landmass to Central Asia (or including even China in some counts).

33. I wish to state strongly that I am not idealizing the imperial experience but simply pointing out that it had different organizational base lines from the nation-state. Any "imperial nostalgia" can be easily dispelled by a detailed knowledge of the citizens that felt oppressed, fought, and, finally, brought down the empires. This may seem obvious and trivial but I feel compelled to include this in view of the recent and growing trend to romanticize past empires that has permeated even much academic output.

34. Zygmunt Bauman, *Intimations with Postmodernity*, New York, 1992, 222.

35. *International Encyclopedia of the Social & Behavioral Sciences (IESBS)*, ed. by Neil J. Smelser, and Paul B. Bates. Amsterdam, New York: Elsevier Science, 2001, 11845–8.

36. *IESBS*, 11848. See also J. D. Kelly, "Time and the global: against the homogeneous, empty communities in contemporary social theory," in *Development and Change*, 29, 1998, 839–71. Likewise, Peter Hulme and Ali Behdad believe that postcolonial studies are finding their real critical vocation only in the age of globalization, by insisting on the structural links between the colonial and neocolonial forms of global hierarchy ("Introduction," in A. Loomba, S. Kaul, M. Bunzl, A. Burton, and J. Esty, eds., *Postcolonial Studies and Beyond*, Durham: Duke University Press, 2005).

37. Judit Bodnar, "Shamed by Comparison: Eastern Europe and the 'Rest,'" in Sorin Antohi and Larry Wolff, eds., *Europe's Symbolic Geographies*, CEU Press (forthcoming). I am grateful to the author for allowing me to consult her chapter in advance.

Bibliography

Adanir, Fikret, "The Tolerant and the Grim: The Ottoman Legacy in Southeastern Europe," *Culture and Reconciliation in Southeastern Europe. International Conference, Thessaloniki, Greece, June 26–29, 1997*, Thessaloniki: Paratiritis, 1998, 107–119.

———, "Tradition and Rural Change in Southeastern Europe During Ottoman Rule," Daniel Chirot, ed., *The Origins of Backwardness in Eastern Europe: Economics & Politics from the Middle Ages until the Early Twentieth Century*, Berkeley: University of California Press, 1989, 131–209.

Ahmad, Aijaz, *In Theory: Classes, Nations, Literatures*, London and New York: Verso, 1992.

Ahmad, Feroz, *The Making of Modern Turkey*, London and New York: Routledge, 1993.

Ahmed, Akbar S., *Postmodernism and Islam: Predicament and Promise*, London and New York: Routledge, 1992.

Ahrweiler, Hélène, *L'idéologie politique de l'Empire byzantin*, Paris: Presses universitaire de France, 1975.

Ainlay, Stephen C., Gaylene Becker, and Lerita M. Coleman, eds., *The Dilemma of Difference: A Multidisciplinary View of Stigma*, New York and London: Plenum Press, 1986.

Ajami, Fouad, "In Europe's Shadows," *New Republic*, vol. 211, n. 21, 21 November 1994, 29–37.

Akinian, P. Nerses, ed., *Das Armeniers Simeon aus Polen Reisebeschreibung Anlagen und Kolofone, Zusammenfassung in deutscher Sprache*, Vienna: Mechitarist Press, 1936.

Albert, Hartmut, "Kosova 1979, Albania 1980: Observations, Experiences, Conversations," Arshi Pipa and Sami Repishti, eds., *Studies on Kosova*, Boulder: East European Monographs No. 155, New York: Columbia University Press, 1984, 103–124.

Alcoranus Mahometicus . . . in die teutsche Sprache gebracht durch Salomon Schweigger, Nuremberg, 1616.

Alexander, James Edward, *Travels from India to England; comprehending a visit to the Burman Empire, and a journey through Persia, Asia Minor, European Turkey, &c. In the years 1825–26. Containing a chronological epitome of the late military operations in Ava; an account of the proceedings of the present mission of the Supreme Government of India to the Court of Tehran, and a summary of the causes and events of the existing war between Russia and Persia; with sketches of natural history, manners and customs, and illustrated with maps and plates*, London: Purbury, Allen, 1827.

Alexander, James Edward, *Travels to the Seat of War in the East, through Russia and the Crimea, in 1829. With Sketches of the Imperial Fleet and Army, Personal Adventures, and Characteristic Anecdotes*, London: H. Colburn and R. Bentley, 1830.

Alexander, Ronelle, "On the Definition of Sprachbund Boundaries: The Place of Balkan Slavic," Norbert Reiter, ed., *Ziele und Wege der Balkanlinguistik: Beiträge zur Tagung vom 2.–6. März 1081 in Berlin*, Berlin: Otto Harrassowitz, 1983, 13–26.

Alexandresku-Derska Bulgaru, Marie Mathilde, "La politique démographique des sultans à Istanbul (1453–1496)," *Revue des études sud-est européennes*, 28, 1–4, Bucharest, 1990, 45–56.

Allcock, John B, and Antonia Young, eds., *Black Lambs and Grey Falcons: Women Travellers in the Balkans*, Bradford, England: Bradford University Press, 1991.

Amin, Samir, *Eurocentrism*, New York: Monthly Review Press, 1989.

——, *Unequal Development: An Essay on the Social Formations of Peripheral Capitalism*, New York and London: Monthly Review Press, 1976.

Ancel, Jacques, *Peuples et nations des Balkans*, Paris: A. Colin, 1930.

Anderson, Dorothy P., *Miss Irby and Her Friends*, London: Hutchinson, 1966.

Anderson, Matthew S., *The Eastern Question, 1774–1923*, New York: Macmillan, 1966.

Andrić, Ivo, *The Bridge on the Drina*, Chicago: University of Chicago Press, 1977.

Angelomatis-Tsougarakis, Helen, *The Eve of the Greek Revival: British Travellers' Perceptions of Early Nineteenth-Century Greece*, London: Routledge, 1990.

Antonin, Archim, *Poezdka v Rumeliyu*, Saint Petersburg, 1879.

Antonov-Poljanski, Hristo, *Britanska bibliografija na Makedonija*, Skopje: Institut za natsionalna istorija, 1966.

Arato, Györg, ed., *Ot Karpatite do Balkana. Dnevnitsi I memoari za Bîlgariya ot ungarski emigranti 1849–1850*, Sofia: Izd.k.' "Ogledalo," Ungarski Kulturen institut, 2002.

Archer, Laird, *Balkan Journal*, New York: W. W. Norton, 1944.

Arnakis, George G., "The Role of Religion in the Development of Balkan Nationalism," *The Balkans in Transition: Essays on the Development of Balkan Life and Politics Since the Eighteenth Century*, Charles and Barbara Jelavich, eds., Berkeley and Los Angeles: University of California Press, 1963, 115–144.

Asad, Talal, ed., *Anthropology and the Colonial Encounter*, London: Ithaca Press, 1973.

Ash, Timothy Garton, "Does Central Europe Exist," *New York Review of Books*, vol. 33, n. 15, 9 October 1986, 45–52 (reprinted in George Schöpflin, and Nancy Wood, eds., *In Search of Central Europe*, Cambridge, U.K.: Polity Press, 1989, 191–215).

——, "Eastern Europe: Après Le Déluge, Nous," *New York Review of Books*, vol. 37, n. 13, 16 August 1990, 51–57.

——, "Prague: Intellectuals & Politicians," *New York Review of Books*, vol. 42, n. 1, 12 January 1995, 34–41.

Ash, Timothy Garton, Michael Mertes, and Dominique Moisi, "Let the East Europeans In!" *New York Review of Books*, vol. 38, n. 17, 24 October 1991, 19.

Atlas, James, "Name That Era: Pinpointing A Moment On the Map of History," *New York Times*, 19 March 1995, E1–E5.

Auerbach, Erich, *Mimesis: the Representation of Reality in Western Literature*, Princeton, N.J.: Princeton University Press, 1968.

Augustinos, Gerasimos, "Culture and Authenticity in a Small State: Historiography and National Development in Greece," *East European Quarterly*, vol. 23, n. 1, 1989, 17–31.

Augustinos, Olga, *French Odysseys: Greece in French Travel Literature from the Renaissance to the Romantic Era*, Baltimore: Johns Hopkins University Press, 1994.

Ayverdi, Samiha, *Ne Idik Ne Olduk*, Istanbul: Hülbe Yaynlar, 1985.

Babić, Blagoje, "Collapse of Yugoslav Self-Management Society and a Possible Alternative," *Meðunarodni problemi*, vol. 46, n. 2, Belgrade, 1994, 205–228.

Badie, Bertrand, and Pierre Birnbaum, *The Sociology of the State*, Chicago and London: University of Chicago Press, 1983.

Babinger, Franz, *Die Geschichtsschreiber der Osmanen und ihre Werke*, Leipzig, 1927.

Bakić-Hayden, Milica, "Nesting Orientalisms: The Case of Former Yugoslavia," *Slavic Review*, vol. 54, n. 4, Winter 1995, 917–931.

Bakić-Hayden, Milica, and Robert Hayden, "Orientalist Variations on the Theme 'Balkans': Symbolic Geography in Recent Yugoslav Cultural Politics," *Slavic Review*, vol. 51, n. 1, Spring 1992, 1–15.

Bălan, Ion Dodu, *A Concise History of Romanian Literature*, Bucharest: Editura ştiinţifică şi enciclopedică, 1981.

"Balkan Brinkmanship," *New York Times*, 10 March 1995, A28.

"Balkanisierung, *Meyers Enzyklopädisches Lexikon*, Mannheim, Vienna and Zürich: Bibliographisches Institut, Lexiconverlag, 1971, 408.

The Balkans, Many Peoples, Many Problems, Madison, Wisc.: USAFI, 1944.

The Balkans, Together with Hungary, London: Royal Institute of International Affairs, 1945.

Balkanski pesni, Varna: Zora, 1913.

Balkanskite strani po pîtya ha promenite, Sofia: Markisa, 1993.

Banac, Ivo, "Milan Kundera i povratak Srednje Evrope," *Gordogan*, vol. 9, n. 1, 1987, 39–46.

———, "Misreading the Balkans," *Foreign Policy*, no. 93, Winter 1993–94, 173–182.

Barac, Antun, *A History of Yugoslav Literature*, Ann Arbor: Michigan Slavic Studies, 1976.

Baranyi, George, "On Truths in Myths," *East European Quarterly*, vol. 15, No. 3, September 1981, 347–355.

Barnard, Frederick M., "Culture and Civilization in Modern Times," *Dictionary of the History of Ideas*, New York: Scribner's, 1973, vol. 1, 613–621.

———, *Herder's Social and Political Thought from the Enlightenment to Nationalism*, Oxford: Clarendon Press, 1965.

Barthes, Roland, *Mythologies*, Paris: Editions du Seuil, 1957.

Barthold, W.-B. Spuler, "Balkhan," *The Encyclopedia of Islam*, vol. 1, Leiden: E. J. Brill, 1960, 1002.

Basset, Richard, *Balkan Hours: Travels in the Other Europe*, London: John Murray, 1990.

Beaujour, Felix, *Voyage militaire dans L'Empire Ottoman, ou description de ses frontières et des ses principales défenses, soit naturelles, soit artificielles, avec 5 cartes géographiques*, Paris: Firmin Didot, 1829.

Beck, Brandon H., *From the Rising of the Sun: English Images of the Ottoman Empire to 1715*, New York, Berne, Frankfurt-am-Main and Paris: Peter Lang, 1987.

Beck, Hans-George, Manoussos Manoussakas, and Agostino Pertusi, eds., *Venezia: Centro di mediazione tra Oriente e occidente (secoli XV–XVI): Aspetti e problemi*, Florence: L. S. Olschki, 1977.

Becker, Gaylene, and Regina Arnold, "Stigma as a Social and Cultural Construct," Stephen C. Ainlay, Gaylene Becker, and Lerita M. Coleman, eds., *The Dilemma of Difference: A Multidisciplinary View of Stigma*, New York and London: Plenum, 1986, 40–58.

Behar, Cem, *Nuptiality and Marriage Patterns in Istanbul (1885–1940)*, Istanbul: Boğaziçi University Research Papers, 1985.

———, "Polygyny in Istanbul, 1885–1926," *Middle Eastern Studies*, vol. 27, n. 3, July 1991, 477–486.

Bekhin'ova, Ventsislava, ed., *Bîlgariya prez pogleda na cheshki pîteshestvenitsi*, Sofia: Izdatelstvo na Otechestveniya Front, 1984.

Bell, John D., *Peasants in Power: Alexander Stamboliski and the Bulgarian Agrarian National Union, 1899–1923*, Princeton, N.J.: Princeton University Press, 1977.

Belon, Pierre, *Les observations de plusieurs singularitez et choses mémorables, trouvées en Grèce, Asie, Iudée, Egypte, Arabie & autres pays astranges, rédigées en trois livres, par Pierre Belon du Mans*, Paris, 1553.

Benbassa, Esther, "Balkans: sortir du cadre des État nations," *Liberation*, 16–17 January 1993, 5.

Benoist, Joseph-Roger de, *La balkanisation de l'Afrique occidentale française*, Dakar, Abidjan and Lome: Les nouvelles éditions africaines, 1979.

Berdyaev, Nicolas, *Leontiev*, London: Geoffrey Bless, Centenary, 1940 (first published as *Konstantin Leont'ev*, Paris: Y.M.C.A., 1926).

Berend, Iván, and György Ránki, *Economic Development in East-Central Europe in the Nineteenth and Twentieth Centuries*, New York and London: Columbia University Press, 1974.

Berisha, Sali, "The Democratic Party Has Kept Its Word," *Rilindja Demokratike*, 7 March 1995; also in FBIS-EEU-95-049, 14 March 1995.

Berkes, Niyazi, *The Development of Secularism in Turkey*, Montreal: McGill University Press, 1964.

——, *Turkish Nationalism and Western Civilization: Selected Essays of Ziya Gökalp*, Westport, Conn.: Greenwood Press, 1981.

Berkovici, Konrad, *The Incredible Balkans*, New York: Loring and Mussey, 1932.

Bernal, Martin, *Black Athena: The Afroasiatic Roots of Classical Civilization*, vol. 1, *The Fabrication of Ancient Greece 1785–1985*, New Brunswick, N.J.: Rutgers University Press, 1987.

Bernath, Mathias, "Südosteuropäische Geschichte als gesonderte Disziplin," *Forschungen zur osteuropäischen Geschichte*, Band 20, Berlin: Südosteuropa-Institut and Wiesbaden: O. Harassovitz, 1973, 135–145.

Beschreibung einer Legation und Reise, von Wien aus Osterreich auff Constantinopel... Itzund aber in Druck verfertiget durch M. Franciscum Omichium, Güstrow: Im Fürsterlichen Mecklenburgischen Hofflager, 1582.

Beschreibung der Reisen des Reinhold Lubenau, Herausgegeben von Wilhelm Sahm, 2 Teil, Königsberg, 1930.

Bezsonov, P., *Nekotorye cherty puteshestviya Yu.I.Venelina v Bolgariyu*, Moscow, 1857.

Biberaj, Elez, "Albania's Road to Democracy," *Current History*, vol. 92, no. 577, 19–22.

——, "Kosova: The Balkan Powder Keg," *Conflict Studies*, no. 258, 1993, 1–26.

Bibliographie d'études balkaniques, 1–20, Sofia: Institut d'éetudes balkaniques, CIBAL, 1968–1987.

Bidney, David, "Myth, Symbolism, and Truth," Thomas A. Sebeok, ed., *Myth: Symposium*, Philadelphia: American Folklore Society, 1955, 1–14.

Bisanzio e l'Italia: raccolta di studi in memoria di Agostino Pertusi, Milan: Vita e pensiero, 1982.

Black, Jeremy, *The British and the Grand Tour*, London: Croom Helm, 1985.

Bloom, Harold, *The Western Canon: The Books and School of the Ages*, New York: Harcourt Brace, 1994.

[Blount, Henry], *A Voyage into the Levant: A Breife relation of a Journey, lately performed by Master H.B. Gentleman, from England by the way of Venice, into Dalmatia, Sclavonia, Bosnah, Hungary, Macedonia, Thessaly, Thrace, Rhodes and Egypt, unto Gran Cairo: with particular observations concerning the moderne condition of the Turkes, and other people under that Empire*, London: Andrew Crooke, 1636.

Bodea; Cornelia, and Hugh Seton-Watson, eds., *R. W. Seton-Watson şi Românii, 1906–1920*, vol. 2, Bucharest: Editura şiiţifică şi enciclopediă: 1988.

Boliac, Cezar, *Libertatea*, no. 6, 13, 14, 15, 17 April 1871.

Bolintineanu, Dimitrie, *Călătorii pe Dunăre şi în Bulgaria*, Bucharest: Tipografia nationala a lui Josip Romanow, 1958.

Booth, John L. C., *Trouble in the Balkans*, London: Hurst and Blackett, 1905.

Boppe, Auguste, *Journal et correspondance de Gédoyn "le Turc," consul de France à Alep (1623–1625)*, Paris: n.p., 1909.

Bora, Tan'l, "Turkish National Identity, Turkish Nationalism and the Balkan Problem," Günay Göksu Özdoğan and Kemâli Saybaşılı, eds., *Balkans: A Mirror of the New International Order*, Istanbul: EREN, 1995, 101–120.

Borchardt, Felix, "Berlin–Bagdad. Mitteleuropa und der Nahe Orient," *Balkan und Orient*, Berlin: Verlag Fritz Hirschberg, 1916/1917, 7–10.

Boscowich, R. J., *Journal d'un voyage de Constantinople en Pologne, fait à la suite de son excellence Mr Jag. Porter, ambassadeur d'Angleterre par ...*, Lausanne: Grasset, 1772. (Boscovich Ruggiero Giuseppe, *Giornale di un Viaggio da Constantinopoli in Polonia dell'abate ...*, Milan: Giordano Editore, 1966).

Böttner, Helmut, *England greift nach Südost-Europa (Wirtschaftlicher Tatbestand und Folgerungen)*, Vienna and Leipzig: Adolf Luser Verlag, 1939.

Boué, Ami, *Recueil d'itinéraires dans la Turquie d'Europe: Détails géographiques, topographiques et statistiques sur cet empire*, Vienna: W. Braumüller, 1854.

——, *La Turquie d'Europe ou observations sur la géographie, la géologie, l'histoire naturelle, la statistique, les moeurs, les coutumes, l'archéologie, l'agriculture, l'industrie, le commerce, les gouvernements divers, le clergé, l'histoire et l'état politique de cet empire*, vol. 1–4, Paris: Arthus Bartrand, 1840.

Bracciolini, Francesco, *La Bulgheria Convertita: Poema Heroica*, Rome, 1637.

Brailsford, H. N., *Macedonia: Its Races and Their Future*, London: Methuen, 1906.

Braude, Benjamin, and Bernard Lewis, eds., *Christians and Jews in the Ottoman Empire: The Functioning of a Plural Society*, vol. 1, New York and London: Holmes & Meier, 1982.

Braun, M., *Die Slawen auf dem Balkan bis zur Befreiung von der türkischen Herrschaft*, Leipzig, 1941.

Breckenridge, Carol A., and Peter van der Veer, eds., *Orientalism and the Postcolonial Predicament: Perspectives on South Asia*, Philadelphia: University of Pennsylvania Press, 1993.

Brodsky, Joseph, and Václav Havel, "'The Post-Communist Nightmare': An Exchange," *New York Review of Books*, vol. 41, n. 4, 17 February 1994, 28–30.

Brooke, Michael Z., *Le Play, Engineer and Social Scientist: The Life and Work of Frédéric Le Play*, Harlow: Longmans, 1970.

Brown, Edward, M.D., *A Brief Account of Some Travels in divers Parts of Europe, Viz. Hungaria, Servia, Bulgaria, Macedonia, Thessaly, Austria, Styria, Carinthia, Carniola and Friuli. Through a great part of Germany, and The Low Countries. Through Marca Trevisana, and Lombardy on both sides of the Po. With some observations on the Gold, Silver, Copper, Quick-Silver Mines, and the Baths and Mineral Waters in Those Parts. As also, the Description of many Antiquities, Habits, Fortifications and Remarkable Places. The Second Edition with many Additions*, London: Benj. Tooke, 1685.

Brown, L. Carl, ed., *Imperial Legacy: The Ottoman Imprint in the Balkans and the Middle East*, New York: Columbia University Press, 1995.

Bruner, Jerome S., Jacqueline J. Goodnow, and George A. Austin, *A Study of Thinking*, New Brunswick, N.J. and Oxford: Transaction Books, 1986.

Brusten, Manfred, and Jürgen Hohmeier, eds., *Stigmatisierung: Zur Produktion gesellschaftlicher Randgruppen*, Neuwied and Darmstadt: Hermann Luchterhand Verlag, 1975.

Burmeister, H.-P., F. Boldt, Gy. Mészáros, eds., *Mitteleuropa—Traum oder Trauma? Überlegungen zum Selbstbild einer Region*, Bremen: Temmen, 1988.

Busbecq, Ogier de, *A. Gislenii Busbequii omnia quae extant: Legationes Turcicae epistolae quatuor*, Amsterdam: Ex officina Elzeviriana, 1660.

Byron, Robert, and David Talbot Rice, *The Birth of Western Painting: A History of Color, Form and Iconography, illustrated from the Paintings of Mistra and Mount Athos, of Giotto and Duccio, and El Greco*, New York: A. A. Knopf, 1931.

Calinescu, Matei, "How Can One Be a Romanian," *Southeastern Europe*, vol. 10, no. 1, 1983, 25–36.

——, "'How can one be what one is?' Reflections on the Romanian and the French Cioran," manuscript, 1995, 41 pp.

——, "Ionesco and *Rhinoceros*: Personal and Political Backgrounds," *East European Politics and Societies*, vol. 6, no. 3, 1995, 397–399.

——, "Romania's 1930's Revisited," *Salmagundi*, vol. 97, Winter 1993, 134–151.

Callimachus, Philippus, *Philippi Callimachi Experientis ad Innocentium octavum Pontificem maximum . . . de bello Turcis inferendo oratio*, Frankfurt, 1601.

Cambridge History of English Literature, vol. 14, Cambridge, 1922.

Caragiale, Ion Luca, *The Lost Letter and Other Plays*, London: Lawrence and Wishart, 1956.

——, *Oeuvres Choisies: Theatre*, Bucharest: Editions "Le Livre," 1953.

Carré, John le, *The Night Manager*, New York: Ballantine, 1993.

Carrier, James G., *Occidentalism: Images of the West*, New York: Oxford University Press, 1995.
——, "Occidentalism: the world turned upside-down," *American Ethnologist*, vol. 19, no. 2, May 1992, 195–212.
Carte der Europäischen Türkey nebst einem Theile von Kleinasien in XXI Blättern: Nach den besten Hülfsquellen entworfen und gezeichnet durch den k.k. Oberstlieutenant Franz von Weiss. Vienna: Herausgegeben von dem k.k. österreichischen General quartiermeisterstabe in Jahre, 1829.
Carter, Francis W., "Introduction to the Balkan Scene," *An Historical Geography of the Balkans*, London: Academic Press, 1977, 1–24.
Carver, Robert, "Despair among the dervishes: The role of fundamentalism in Turkey," *Times Literary Supplement*, 3 February 1995, 13.
Case, Ellis, "He Hears America Sinking," *New York Times Book Review*, 27 March 1994, 11.
Castellan, Georges, *Histoire des Balkans: XIVe–XXe siècles*, Paris: Fayard, 1991.
Çetinler, Yilmaz, *Şu Bizim Rumeli*, Istanbul: Milliyet Yanınları, 1994.
Cetnarowicz, Antoni, *Tajna diplomacja Adama Jerzego Czartoryskiego na Balkanach: Hotel Lambert a kryzys serbski 1840–1844*, Krakow: Nakladem Uniwersytetu Jagiellonskiego, 1993.
Chakrabarty, Dipesh, "Postcoloniality and the Artifice of History: Who Speaks for 'Indian' Pasts?" *Representations*, vol. 37, Winter 1992, 342–369.
——, "Radical Histories and Question of Enlightenment Rationalism: Some Recent Critiques of Subaltern Studies," *Economic and Political Weekly*, 8 April 1995, 751–759.
Chamberlain, M. E., *Decolonization: The Fall of the European Empires*, Oxford: Basil Blackwell, 1985.
Charanis, Peter. *Studies on the Demography of the Byzantine Empire*, London: Variorum, 1972.
Chateaubriand, François-René, vicomte de, *Itinéraire de Paris à Jérusalem et de Jérusalem à Paris*, Paris: Le Normant, 1812 (2nd ed.).
Chikhachev, P. A., *Stranitsa o vostoke*, Moscow: Glavnaya redaktsiya vostochnoi literatury izdatel'stva "Nauka," 1982.
——, *Asie Mineure: Description physique, climatologie, zoologie, botanique, géologie, statistique et archéologie de cette contrée*, Paris, 1853–1869.
——, *Une page sur l'Orient*, Paris, 1868.
Chishull, Edmund, *Travels in Turkey and back to England: By the late Reverend learned Edmund Chishull*, London: W. Boyer, 1747.
Christie, Agatha, *The Secret of Chimneys*, New York: Dell, 1975.
Christoff, Peter K., *An Introduction to Nineteenth-Century Russian Slavophilism: a study in ideas*, 4 vols., Gravenhage: Mouton, 1961–1991.
The Church in the Christian Roman Empire, New York: Macmillan, 1956.
Cioran, Emil M., *History and Utopia*, trans. Richard Howard, New York: Seaver, 1987.
——, *Schimbarea la față a României*, Bucharest: Humanitas, 1991.
——, *The Temptation to Exist*, trans. Richard Howard, Chicago: Quadrangle, 1968.
Clarke, Edward Daniel, *Travels in Various Countries of Europe, Asia and Africa*, London: Cadell and Davies, 1814.
Clarke, James F., *Bible Societies, American Missionaries, and the National Revival of Bulgaria*, New York: Arno, 1971.
——, *Bulgaria and Salonica in Macedonia*, Boston: American Board of Commissioners for Foreign Missions, 1895.
——, *The Pen and the Sword: Studies in Bulgarian History*, Boulder, CO.: East European Monographs, no. 252, New York: Columbia University Press, 1988.
The Clash of Civilizations? The Debate (A Foreign Affairs Reader), New York: Council on Foreign Relations, 1993.
Clifford, James, *The Predicament of Culture: Twentieth Century Ethnography, Literature and Art*, Cambridge: Cambridge University Press, 1988.
Clifford, James, and George E. Marcus, eds., *Writing Culture: The Poetics and Politics of Ethnography*, Berkeley and Los Angeles: University of California Press, 1986.

Clogg, Richard, "Benjamin Barker's Journal of a Tour in Thrace (1823)," *University of Birmingham Historical Journal*, vol. 12, no. 2, 1971.

Clogg, Richard, ed., *Balkan Society in the Age of Greek Independence*, London: Macmillan, 1981.

Codrescu, Teodor, *O calatorie la Constantinopol*, Iasi, 1844.

Cohen, Roger, "A Balkan Gyre of War, Spinning Onto Film," *New York Times*, section 2, 12 March 1995, 1, 24–25.

——, "In the Dock: Balkan Nationalism," *New York Times*, 30 April 1995, E5.

Coleman, Lerita M., "Stigma: An Enigma Demystified," Stephen C. Ainlay, Gaylene Becker, and Lerita M. Coleman, eds., *The Dilemma of Difference: A Multidisciplinary View of Stigma*, New York and London: Plenum Press, 1986, 211–232.

A Collection of Modern and Contemporary Voyages and Travels: Containing, I. Translations from foreign languages, of voyages and travels never before translated. II. Original voyages and travels never before published. III. Analyses of new voyages and travels published in England, London: R. Phillips, 1805–1809.

Colombo, John Robert, and Nikola Roussanoff, *The Balkan Range*, Toronto: Hounslow, 1976.

Connor, Walker, *The National Question in Marxist-Leninist Theory and Strategy*, Princeton, N.J.: Princeton University Press, 1984.

Conrad, Joseph, *Notes on Life and Letters*, Freeport, N.Y.: Books for Libraries Press, 1972 (reprint of 1921 edition from Doubleday).

Copans, Jean, and Jean Jamin, eds., *Aux origines de l'anthropologie française: Les mémoires de la Société des observateurs de l'homme en l'an VIII*, Paris: Le Sycomore, 1978.

Coppin, Jean, *Le bouclier de l'Europe ou la guerre sainte, contenant des avis politiques et chrétiens, qui peuvent servir de lumière aux rois et aux souverains de la Chrétienté, pour guarantir leurs estats des incursions des Turcs et reprendre ceux qu'ils ont usurpé sur eux. Avec une relation de voyages faits dans la Turquie, la Thébaide et la Barbarie*, Lyon: 1660.

Corradi, Giuseppe, "Balcanica, penisola," *Grande Dizionario Enciclopedoci UTET*, vol. 2, Turin: Unione Tipografico-Editrice Torinese, 1993, 786–790.

Couloumbis, Theodore A., and Thanos Veremis, "In Search of New Barbarians: Samuel P. Huntington and the Clash of Civilizations," *Mediterranean Quarterly*, Winter 1994, 36–44.

Cousinéry, Esprit-Mary, *Voyage dans la Macédoine contenant des recherches sur l'histoire, la géographie et les antiquité de ce pays*, Paris: Imprimerie royale, 1831.

Covel, John, *Early Voyages and Travels in the Levant. II. Extracts from the Diaries of Dr. John Covel, 1670–1679*. London: Hakluyt Society, 1893.

Cox, Samuel S., *Diversions of a Diplomat in Turkey*, New York: Charles L. Webster, 1887.

Crampton, Richard J., *Eastern Europe in the Twentieth Century*, London and New York: Routledge, 1994.

——, *A Short History of Bulgaria*, New York: Cambridge University Press, 1987.

"Credit McNamara in Winning the Cold War," *New York Times*, 14 April 1995, A14.

Curtis, William Eleroy, *The Turk and His Lost Provinces*, Chicago, New York and Toronto: Fleming H. Revel, 1903.

Cvetkova, Bistra, ed., *Frenski pîtepisi za Balkanite, XV–XVIII v.*, Sofia: Nauka i izkustvo, 1975.

——, *Frenski pîtepisi za Balkanite, XIX v*, Sofia: Nauka i izkustvo, 1981.

Cvijic, Cristopher, *Remaking the Balkans*, London: Royal Institute of International Affairs, 1991.

Cvijić, Jovan, *La peninsule balkanique: géographie humaine*, Paris: A. Colin, 1918 (Serbian translation: *Balkansko poluostrvo i južnoslovenske zemlje*, Belgrade, 1922).

——, *Makedonskie slavyane. Etnograficheskie isscledovaniya*, Petrograd: Slavyanskaya biblioteka, 1906.

Dağlarca, Fazîl Hüsnü, *Selected Poems*, trans. Talât Sait Halman, Pittsburgh: University of Pittsburgh Press, 1969.

Dakin, Douglas, *British and American Philhellenes*, Thessaloniki: Idryma Meleton Hersonesou tou Aimou, 1957.

Dako, Christo A., *Albania: The Master Key to the Near East*, Boston: E. L. Grimes, 1919.

Dako, Christo A., and Dhimitri Bala, *Albania's Rights, Hopes and Aspirations. The Strength of the National Consciousness of the Albanian People*, Boston: 1918.

Dako, Christo A., and Mihal Grameno, *Albania's Rights and Claims to Independence and Territorial Integrity*, Boston: 1918.

Danchov, N. G., and I. G. Danchov, *Bîlgarska entsiklopediya*, Sofia: Knigoizdatelstvo St. Atanasov, 1936.

Danova, Nadya, *Natsionalniyat vîpros v grîtskite politicheski programi prez XIX vek*, Sofia: Bîlgarska Akademiya na Naukite, 1980.

Danova, Nadja, Vesela Dimova, Maria Kalitsin, eds., *Predstavata za "drugiya" na Balkanite*, Sofia: Akademichno izdatelstvo "Marin Drinov," 1995.

Darkot, Besim, "Balkan," *Islâm Ansiklopedisi*, Istanbul: Maarif Maatbasi, 1943, 280–283.

David, Zděnek, "Bohemian Utraquism in the Sixteenth Century: The Distinction and Tribulation of a Religious 'Via Media,'" *Communio Viatorum*, vol. 35, no. 3, 1993.

Davison, Roderic H., "Britain, the International Spectrum, and the Eastern Question, 1827–1841," *New Perspectives on Turkey*, no. 7, Spring 1992, 195–231.

———, "The Image of Turkey in the West in Historical Perspective," *Turkish Studies Association Bulletin*, no. 1, 1981, 1–6.

———, "Where is the Middle East?" *Foreign Affairs*, July 1960, 665–675.

DeGérando Joseph-Marie, *The Observation of Savage Peoples*, Berkeley and Los Angeles: University of California Press, 1969.

Deliradev, P., *Ot Kom do Emine (po biloto na Stara-planina)*, Sofia: n.p., 1934.

Derrida, Jacques, *Of Grammatology*, trans. Gayatri Chakravorty Spivak, Baltimore and London: Johns Hopkins University Press, 1976.

———, *The Other Heading: Reflections on Today's Europe*, trans. Pascale-Anne Brault and Micahel B. Naas, Bloomington and Indianapolis: Indiana University Press, 1992.

———, *Speech and Phenomena, and Other Essays on Husserl's Theory of Signs*, trans. David B. Allison, Evanston, Ill.: Northwestern University Press, 1973.

———, *Writing and Difference*, trans. Alan Bass, Chicago: University of Chicago Press, 1978.

De Windt, Harry, *Through Savage Europe: Being the Narrative of a Journey Undertaken as Special Correspondent of the "Westminster Gazette" Throughout the Balkan States and European Russia*, London: T. Fisher Unwin, 1907.

Dimitrov, Strashimir, "Za yurushkata organizatsiya i rolyata ï v etnoasimilatsionnite protsesi," *Vekove*, vol. 1–2, 1982, 33–43.

Dimitrova, Snezhana, "Jovan Cvijić za periferiyata i tsentîra," *Balkanistic Forum*, vol. 3, no. 1, 1994, 5–16.

Dirlik, Arif, "The Postcolonial Aura: Third World Criticism in the Age of Global Capitalism," *Critical Inquiry*, vol. 20, Winter 1994, 328–356.

Djordjevic, Dimitrije, "Migrations During the 1912–1913 Balkan Wars and World War One," *Migrations in Balkan History*, Belgrade: Serbian Academy of Sciences and Arts, 1989, 115–130.

Djordjevic, Dimitrije and Stephen Fischer-Galati, *The Balkan Revolutionary Tradition*. New York: Columbia University Press, 1981.

Dnevnyye zapiski poezdki v Konstantinopol' A. G. Krasnokutskogo v 1808 godu, Moscow: V Tipografii S. Salivanovskago, 1815.

Donchev, Doncho, *Fizicheska i sotsialno-ikonomicheska geografiya na Bîlgariya*, Veliko Tîrnovo: Slovo, 1994.

Donia, Robert J., and John V. A. Fine, Jr., *Bosnia and Hercegovina: A Tradition Betrayed*, New York: Columbia University Press, 1994.

Döpmann, Hans-Dieter, "Die Christenheit auf dem Balkan im Spiegel deutschsprachiger Literatur des 19. Jahrhunderts," Josip Matešić and Klaus Heitmann, eds., *Südosteuropa in der Wahrnehmung der deutschen Öffentlichkeit vom Wiener Kongress (1815) bis zum Pariser Frieden (1856)*, Munich: Südosteuropa-Gesellschaft, 1990, 19–32.

Dostyan, Irina S., *Rossiya i balkanskii vopros. Iz istorii russko-balkanskikh politecheskikh svyazei v pervoi tret'e XIX v.*, Moscow: Nauka, 1972.

——, *Russkaya obshchestvennaia mysl'i balkanskie narody: or Radishcheva do dekabristov,* Moscow: Nauka, 1980.

Douglas, Mary, *Purity and Danger: An Analysis of Concepts of Polution and Taboo,* Harmondsworth, Middlesex, England: Penguin, 1970 (first published in 1966).

——, ed. *Rules and Meaning. The Anthropology of Everyday Knowledge,* Harmondsworth, Middlesex, England: Penguin, 1973.

Douglas, Mary, and David Hull, eds., *How Classification Works: Nelson Goodman among the Social Sciences,* Edinburgh: Edinburgh University Press, 1992.

Doyle, Michael W., *Empires,* Ithaca and London: Cornell University Press, 1986.

Draganov, Mincho, ed., *Narodopsikhologiya na bulgarite: Antologiya,* Sofia: Otechestven front, 1984.

Driesch, Gerardus Cornelius, *Historia magnae legationis Caesareae, aquam fortunatissimis Caroli VI, auspicius Augustus imperantis post beinalis belli confectionem suscepit ilustrissimus et excellentissimus S. R. I. comes Damianus Hugos Virmontius, maximi Caesaris primus nuper ad Passarovicium caduceator ejusdemque magnus postea ad Portam Orator,* Vienna, 1721.

Droulia, Loukia, "Les relations de voyages source historique pour les pays du Levant (XVe au XIXe s.), *Relations et influences réciproques entre grecs et bulgares, XVIIIe–XXe siècle,* Thessaloniki, 1991, 181–186.

——, "La révolution française et l'image de la Grèce," *La révolution française et l'hellenisme contemporaine,* Athens, 1989.

Duala-M'bedy, Munasu, *Xenologie: Die Wissenshaft vom Fremden und die Verdrängung der Humanität in der Anthropologie,* Freiburg and Munich: Verlag Karl Alber, 1977.

Duben, Alan, and Cem Behar, *Istanbul Households: Marriage, Family and Fertility, 1880–1940,* Cambridge and New York: Cambridge University Press, 1991.

Du Bois, W. E. B., *Color and Democracy: Colonies and Peace,* New York: Harcourt Brace, 1945.

Duden: Das grosse Wörterbuch der deutschen Sprache in sechs Bänden, Mannheim: Bibliographisches Institut, 1976.

Durham, Mary Edith, *The Burden of the Balkans,* London: Edward Arnold, 1905.

——, *The Sarajevo Crime,* London: George Allen and Unwin, 1925.

——, *Some Tribal Origins, Laws and Customs of the Balkans,* London: George Allen and Unwin, 1928.

——, *Twenty Years of Balkan Tangle,* London: George Allen and Unwin, 1920.

During, Simon, ed., *The Cultural Studies Reader,* London and New York: Routledge, 1993.

Duroselle, Jean-Baptiste, *Europe: A History of its Peoples,* London: Viking, 1990.

Durrell, Lawrence, *Esprit de Corps: Sketches from Diplomatic Life,* London: Faber and Faber, 1990.

The Durrell-Miller Letters, 1935–80, New York: New Directions, 1988.

van der Dussen, Jan, and Kevin Wilson, eds., *The History of the Idea of Europe,* New York: Routledge, 1995.

Duțu, Alexandru, "Die Imagologie und die Entdeckung der Alterität," *Kulturbeziehungen in Mittel- und Osteuropa in 18. und 19. Jahrhundert,* Berlin, 1982, 257–263.

——, "The Mental Substratum of the Cultural Activity," *Revue des études sud-est européennes,* vol. 28, nos. 1–4, 1990, 3–10.

——, "National and Regional Identity in Southeast Europe," Günay Göksu Özdoğan, Kemâli Saybaşılı, eds., *Balkans: A Mirror of the New International Order,* Istanbul: EREN, 1995, 75–84.

Dyserinck, Hugo, "Komparatistische Imagologie. Zur politischen Tragweite einer europäischen Wissenschaft von der Literatur," Hugo Dyserinck and Karl Ulrich Syndram, eds., *Europa und das nationale Selbstverständnis: Imagologische Probleme in Literatur, Kunst und Kultur des 19. und 20. Jahrhunderts,* Bonn: Bouvier, 1988, 13–38.

Eagly, Alice H., and Shelly Chaiken, *The Psychology of Attitudes,* Orlando, Fla.: Harcourt, Brace, Jovanovich, 1993.

Eberhard, Winfried, Hans Lemberg, Heinz-Dieter Heimann, and Robert Luft, eds., *Westmitteleuropa. Ostmitteleuropa. Vergleiche und Beziehungen: Festschrift für Ferdinand Seibt zum 65. Gebirtstag*, Munich: R. Oldenburg, 1992.

Ebermann, Richard, *Die Türkenfurcht, ein Beitrag zur Geschichte der öffentlishen Meinung in Deutschland während der Reformationszeit*, Halle: C. A. Kraemmerer, 1904.

Edward Lear in Greece. A loan exhibition from the Gennadius library, Athens, Greece and Meriden, Conn.: Meriden Gravure, 1971.

Ehrenpreis, Marcus, *The Soul of the East: Experience and Reflections*, trans. Alfhild Huebsch, New York: Viking Press, 1928 (original, Stockholm: Hugo Gebers Förlag, 1927).

Eickhoff, Ekkehard, *Seekrieg und Seepolitik zwischen Islam und Abendland*, Berlin: De Gruyter, 1966.

——, *Venedig, Wien und die Osmanen*, Munich, 1970.

Eiser, J. Richard, *Social Psychology: Attitudes, Cognition and Social Behavior*, Cambridge: Cambridge University Press, 1986.

Eisner, Robert, *Travels to an Antique Land: The History and Literature of Travel to Greece*, Ann Arbor: University of Michigan Press, 1991.

Elenkov, Ivan, and Rumen Daskalov, *Zashto sme takiva? V tîrsene na bîlgarskata kulturna identichnost*, Sofia: Prosveta, 1994.

Ellridge, Arthur, *Mucha: The Triumph of Art Nouveau*, Paris: Editions Pierre Terrail, 1992.

Encyclopedia of American Foreign Policy, New York: Scribner's, 1978.

Engel, Claire-Éliane, *Les écrivains à la montagne*, Paris: Delagrave, 1934.

——, *La littérature alpestre en France et en Angleterre aux 18e et 19e siècles*, Chambéry: s.p., 1930.

Engels, Friedrich, "The Turkish Question," Karl Marx and Frederick Engels, *Collected Works*, trans. Richard Dixon et al., vol. 12, New York: International Publishers, 1975, 22–28.

English and Continental Views of the Ottoman Empire, 1500–1800, Los Angeles: William Andrews Clark Memorial Library, 1972.

Enzensberger, Hans Agnus, Ryszard Kapuściński, and Adam Krzemiński, "Back to the Future," *New York Review of Books*, vol. 41, no. 19, 17 November 1994, 41–48.

Ergüder, Üstün, "Türkiye ve Balkan Gerçeği," *Balkanlar*, Istanbul: EREN, 1993, 35–38.

Etat économique des pays balkaniques, 2 vols., Belgrade: Édition de l-Institut balkanique, 1938.

Fabian, Johannes, *Time and the Other: How Anthropology Makes Its Object*, New York: Columbia University Press, 1983.

Federici, Silvia, ed., *Enduring Western Civilization: The Construction of the Concept of Western Civilization and Its "Others,"* Westport, Conn.: Praeger, 1995.

Fehér, Ferenc, "On Making Central Europe," *Eastern European Politics and Societies*, vol. 3, no. 3, Fall 1989, 412–447.

Fehér, Ferenc, and Agnes Heller, *Eastern Left, Western Left: Totalitarianism, Freedom and Democracy*, Atlantic Highlands, N.J.: Humanities, 1987.

Ferriman, Z. Duckett, *Greece and the Greeks*, New York: James Pott, 1911.

Filimon, Ioannis, *Dokimion peri tis Filikis Etairias*, Nauplion, 1834.

Fine, Jr., John V. A., *The Late Medieval Balkans: A Critical Survey from the Late Twelfth Century to the Ottoman Conquest*, Ann Arbor: University of Michigan Press, 1987.

Fischer-Galati, Stephen, Radu R. Florescu, and George R. Ursul, eds., *Romania Between East and West: Historical Essays in Memory of Constantin Giurescu*, East European Monographs, no. 103, New York: Columbia University Press, 1982.

Fisher, Sydney Nettleton, *The Foreign Relations of Turkey, 1481–1512*, Urbana: University of Illinois Press, 1948.

Florescu, Radu, *Dracula, Prince of Many Faces: His Life and His Times*, Boston: Little, Brown, 1989.

——, *Dracula, a Biography of Vlad the Impaler, 1431–1476*, New York: Hawthorn Books, 1973.

Fonton, F. P., *Yumoristicheskie, politicheskie i voennye pis'ma iz glavnoi kvartiry Dunaiskoi armii v 1828 i 1829 godakh*, Leipzig, 1862.

Forsyth, William, *The Slavonic Provinces South of the Danube: A Sketch of Their History and*

Present State in Relation to the Ottoman Porte, London: John Murray, 1876.

Forsythe, Martha, "Interes kîm bîlgarskiya folklor v SASHT," *Bîlgarski folklor* no. 1, 1987, 79–81.

Fortescue, William, *Alphonse de Lamartine: A Political Biography*, London and Canberra: Croom Helm, New York: St. Martin's, 1983.

Foster, Charles Thornton, and F. H. Blackburne Daniell, *The Life and Letters of Ogier Ghiselin de Busbecq, Seigneur of Bousbecque, Knight, Imperial Ambassador*, London, 1881.

Foucault, Michel, *The Archaeology of Knowledge and The Discourse on Language*, trans. A. M. Sheridan Smith, New York: Pantheon, 1972.

——, *Language, Counter-Memory, Practice: Selected Essays and Interviews,*.ed. Donald F. Bouchard, trans. Donald F. Bouchard and Sherry Simon, Ithaca, N.Y.: Cornell University Press, 1977.

——, *L'Ordre du Discours*, Paris: Gallimard, 1971.

——, *Power/ Knowledge: Selected Interviews and Other Writings, 1972–1977*, ed. Colin Gordon, trans. Colin Gordon et al., New York: Pantheon, 1980.

——, "Space, Power and Knowledge," Simon During, ed., *The Cultural Studies Reader*, London and New York: Routledge, 1993, 161–169.

Foucher, Michel, "The Geopolitics of Southeastern Europe," *Eurobalkans*, vol. 15, Summer 1994, 16–19.

Fox, Robin, *The Challenge of Anthropology*, New Brunswick, N.J.: Transaction, 1994.

Fraenkel, Eran, "Urban Muslim Identity in Macedonia: The Interplay of Ottomanism and Multilingual Nationalism," Eran Fraenkel and Christina Kramer, eds., *Language Contact—Language Conflict*, New York: Peter Lang, 1993, 27–42.

France, Anatole, *Les pensées*, ed. Eric Eugène, Paris: Cherche-Midi, 1994.

Frankland, Charles Colville, *Travels to and from Constantinople, in the years 1827 and 1828: or Personal Narrative of a Journey from Vienna, through Hungary, Transylvania, Wallachia, Bulgaria, and Roumelia, to Constantinople; and from that city to the capital of Austria, by the Dardanelles, Tenedos, the Plains of Troy, Smyrna, Napoli di Romania, Athens, Egina, Poros, Cyprus, Syria, Alexandria, Malta, Sicily, Italy, Istria, Carniola, and Styria*, London: H. Colburn, 1829.

Franzos, Karl Emil, *Aus Halb-Asien: Culturbilder aus Galizien, der Bukowina, Südrusland und Rumänien*, Leipzig: Verlag von Breitkopf und Härtel, 1878.

Fraser, John Foster, *Pictures From the Balkans*, London: Cassel, 1906.

Frey, William H., and Jonathan Tilove, "Immigrants In, Native Whites Out," *New York Times Magazine*, 20 August 1995, 44.

Fuchs-Sumiyoshi, Andrea, *Orientalismus in der deutschen Literatur: Untersuchungen zu Werken des 19. und 20. Jahrhunderts, von Goethes "West-östlichem Diwan" bis Thomas Manns "Joseph"-Tetralogie*, Germanistische Texte und Studien, Bd.20, Hildesheim, Zurich, and New York: Georg Olms Verlag, 1984.

Fugagnollo, Ugo, *Bisanzio e l'Oriente a Venezia*, Trieste: Lint, 1974.

Gachev, G. D., "Balkany kak kosmos Khaidutstva. Balkanskaia kartina mira v etnoiazykovom i kul'turno-istoricheskom aspekte, *Sovetskoe slavianovedenie*, vol. 4, 1989, 171–173.

Gagnon, Jr., V. P., "Serbia's Road to War," *Journal of Democracy*, vol. 5, no. 2, April 1994, 117–131.

Galt, John, *Voyages and Travels, in the Years 1809, 1810, and 1811; containing Statistical, Commercial, and Miscellaneous Observations on Gibraltar, Sardinia, Sicily, Malta, Serigo, and Turkey*, London: X. T. Cadell and W. Davies, 1812.

Geanakoplos, Deno John, *Byzantine East and Latin West: Two Worlds of Christendom in Middle Ages and Renaissance*, Oxford: Basil Blackwell, 1967.

——, *Constantinople and the West. Essays on the Late Byzantine (Paleologan) and Italian Renaissances and the Byzantine and Roman Churches*, Madison: University of Wisconsin Press, 1989.

——, *Greek Scholars in Venice: Studies in the Dissemination of Greek Learning from Byzantium to Western Europe*, Cambridge, Mass.: Harvard University Press, 1962.

Gellner, Ernest, "The Mightier Pen? Edward Said and the Double Standards of Inside-out

Colonialism," *Times Literary Supplement*, 19 February 1993, 3–4.

van Gennep, Arnold, *The Rites of Passage*, Chicago: University of Chicago Press, 1960.

Gent, John Burbury, *A Relation of a Journey of the Right Honourable My Lord Henry Howard, From London to Vienna, and thence to Constantinople; In the Company of his Excellency Count Lesley, Knight of the Order of the Golden Fleece, Councellor of State to his Imperial Majesty, etc. And Extraordinary Ambassadour from Leopoldus Emperour of Germany to the Grand Signior, Sultan Mahomet Han the Forthe*, London: T. Collins, I. Ford and S. Hickman, 1671.

Georgeon, François, *Aux origines du nationalisme turc: Yusuf Akçura (1876–1935)*, Paris: Éditions A.D.P.F., 1980.

Georgescu, Stefan, *Memorii din timpul resboiului pentru independenţa, 1877–1878*, Bucharest, 1891.

Georgieva, Tsvetana, "Khora i bogove na Balkanite," *Balkanistic Forum*, no. 2, 1994, 33–42.

Gergova, Ivanka, "Medieval and Contemporary Art of the Balkans," *Vek 21*, no. 41, 19–25 October 1994, 3.

Germaner, Semra, and Zeynep Inankur, *Orientalism and Turkey*, Istanbul: Turkish Cultural Service Foundation, 1989.

Geshkof, Theodore I., *Balkan Union: A Road to Peace in Southeastern Europe*, New York: Columbia University Press, 1940.

Gibbon Edward, *An Essay on the Study of Literature*, New York: Garland, 1970.

Gleason, John Howes, *The Genesis of Russophobia in Great Britain*, New York: Octagon, 1972.

Glenny, Misha, "Here We Go Again — Misha Glenny on the Coming Balkan war," *London Review of Books*, 9 March 1995, 21.

Glynn, Patrick, "The Age of Balkanization," *Commentary*, vol. 96, no. 1, July 1993, 21–24.

Goff, A., and Hugh A. Fawcett, *Macedonia: A Plea for the Primitive*, London and New York: John Lane, 1921.

Goffman, Erving, *Stigma: Notes on the Management of Spoiled Identity*, Englewood Cliffs, N.J.: Prentice-Hall, 1963.

Gökalp, Ziya, *Türkçülüğün Esasları*, Ankara: Türk Tarih Kurumu, 1924.

Gökbilgin, M. Tayyib, *Rumeli'de Yürükler, Tatarlar ve Evlâdi Fatihan*. Istanbul, 1957.

Golczewski, Mechthild, *Der Balkan in Deutschen und Österreichischen Reise-und Erlebnisberichten*, Wiesbaden: Franz Steiner Verlag, 1981.

Göllner, Carl, *Turcica: Die europäischen Türkendrücke des XVI. Jahrhunderts*, vol. 1–2, Bucharest and Berlin (Bibliotheka Aureliana, 23), 1961–1968, vol. 3, *Die Türkenfrage in der öffentlichen Meinung Europas im 16. Jahrhundert*, Baden-Baden (Bibliotheka Aureliana, 70), 1978.

Goldsworthy, Vesna, *Inventing Ruritania: The Imperialism of the Imagination*, New Haven and London: Yale University Press, 1998.

Goodell, William, *Forty Years in the Turkish Empire*, New York: Robert Carter, 1883.

Goodman, Nelson, "Seven Structures on Similarity," Mary Douglas and David Hull, eds., *How Classification Works*, Edinburgh: Edinburgh University Press, 1992, 13–23.

Gordon, Leland James, *American Relations with Turkey, 1830–1930. An Economic Interpretation*, Philadelphia: University of Pennsylvania Press, 1932.

Goudge, Thomas A., "Evolutionism," *Dictionary of the History of Ideas*, New York: Scribner's, 1973, vol. 2, 174–189.

Gramsci, Antonio, *Selections from the Prison Notebook*, New York: International, 1971.

Grandits, Hannes, and Joel M Halpern, "Traditionelle Wertmuster und der Krieg in Ex-Jugoslavien," *Beiträge zur historischen Sozialkunde*, no. 3, 1994, 91–102.

Grant, Richard, "The World Beyond," *Washington Post*, 26 February 1995, 9.

Grigorovich, V., *Ocherk puteshestviya po Evropeiskoi Turtsii*, Kazan', 1848 (1st ed.): Moscow: Tipografiya M. N. Lavrova, 1877 (2nd ed.); Sofia: clzdatelstvo na Bîlgarska akademiya na naukite, 1978 (phototype edition).

Grishina, R. P., "Balkany v planakh Kominterna," *Slavyanovedenie*, no. 5, 1994.

Grozdanova, Elena, *Bulgarskata narodnost prez XVII vek. Demografsko izsledvane*, Sofia, 1989.

Gunther, John, *Inside Europe*, New York: Harper, 1940.

Gürkan, Ihsan, "Jeopolitik ve stratejik yönleriyle Balkanlar ve Türkiye geçmişin ışığında geleceğe bakış," *Balkanlar*, Istanbul: EREN, 1993.

Gürsel, Nedim, *Balkanlara dönüş*, Istanbul: Can yayinlari, 1995.

Güvenç, Bozkurt, *Türk Kimliği. Kültür Tarihinin Kaynaklari*, Ankara: Kültür Bakanlığı, 1993.

Gyuzelev, Ivan, "Znachenieto na Balkana za istoricheskoto razvitie na Bîlgariya," *Yubileen sbornik po sluchai 25–godishninata ot pîrviya vipusk na Gabrovskata Aprilovska gimnaziya*, Plovdiv, 1900.

Gyuzelev, Vasil, "Razmishleniya vîrkhu bîlgarskata srednovekovna istoriya na prof. Petîr Mutafchiev," Petîr Mutafchiev, *Kniga za bîlgarite*, Sofia: Bîlgarska akademiya na naukite, 1987, 5–21.

"Haemos," *Paulys Real-Encyclopädie der Classischen Altertumswissenschaft—Neue Bearbeitung*, Stuttgart: J. B. Metzler, 1912, 2221–2226.

Hakov, Cengiz, "Natsionalniyat vupros v republikanska Turtsiya," *Aspekti na etnokulturnata situatsiya v Bulgariya*, vol. 1, Sofia: Tsentur za izsledvane na demokratsiyata i fonadatsia "Friedrich Naumann," 1991, 67–76.

Halbfass, Wilhelm, *India and Europe: An Essay in Understanding*, Albany: State University of New York Press, 1988.

Haldon, John, "The Ottoman State and the Question of State Autonomy: Comparative Perspectives," Halil Berktay and Suraiya Faroqhi, eds., *New Approaches to State and Peasant in Ottoman History*, London: Frank Cass, 1992, 18–108.

Halecki, Oscar, *The Limits and Divisions of European History*, London and New York: Sheed and Ward, 1950.

——, *The Millennium of Europe*, Notre Dame, Ind.: University of Notre Dame Press, 1963.

Hall, Derek, *Albania and the Albanians*, London and New York: Pinter, 1994.

Hall, James A., "The Watcher at the Gates of Dawn: The Transformation of Self in Liminality and by the Transcendent Function," Nathan Schwartz-Salant and Murray Stein, eds., *Liminality and Transitional Phenomena*, Wilmette, Ill.: Chiron, 1991, 33–51.

Hammel, Eugene, "Meeting the Minotaur," *Anthropology Newsletter*, vol. 35, no. 4, April 1994, 48.

Hának, Péter, "Central Europe: A Historical Region in Modern Times: A Contribution to the Debate about the Regions of Europe," George Schöpflin and Nancy Wood, eds., *In Search of Central Europe*, Cambridge, U.K.: Polity Press, 1989, 57–69.

——, "The Danger of Burying Central Europe," *Magyar Lettre Internationale*, vol. 4, 1991 (published in *Iztok-Iztok*, nos. 9–10, 1993, 111–118).

Harris, George S., ed. *The Middle East in Turkish-American Relations: Report of a Heritage Foundation Conference, October 3–4, 1984*, Washington, D.C.: Heritage Foundation, 1985.

Hatzidimitriou, Costas, "From Paparrigopoulos to Vacalopoulos: Modern Greek Historiography on the Ottoman Period," A. Lily Macrakis and P. Nikiforos Diamandouros, eds., *New Trends in Modern Greek Historiography*, (Modern Greek Studies Association, Occasional Papers 1), Hanover, N.H.: 1982, 13–23.

d'Hauterive, Alexandre-Maurice Blanc Lanautte, "Journal inédit d'un voyage de Constantinople à Jassi, capitale de la Moldavie dans l'hiver de 1785," *Memoriu asupra vechei și actualei a Moldovei presentat lui Alexandru Voda Ipsilante domnul Moldovei la 1787 de comitele d'Hauterive*, Bucharest: L'Institut d'arts graphiques Carol Göbl, 1902.

Havel, Václav, "Anti-Political Politics," John Keane, ed., *Civil Society and the State: New European Perspectives*, London and New York: Verso, 1988, 381–398.

——, "New Democracies for Old Europe," *New York Times*, 17 October 1993, E17.

——, *The Power of the Powerless: Citizens against the state in central-eastern Europe*, London: Hutchinson, 1985.

Heidenrich, John G., "The Gulf War: How Many Iraqis Died?" *Foreign Policy*, no. 90–91, 1993, 108–125.

Held, Joseph, ed., *The Columbia History of Eastern Europe in the Twentieth Century*, New York: Columbia University Press, 1992.

Heller, Agnes, "Europe: An Epilogue?" Brian Nelson, David Roberts, and Walter Veit, eds., *The Idea of Europe. Problems of National and Transnational Identity*, New York and Oxford: Berg, 1992, 12–25.

Hentsch, Thierry, *Imagining the Middle East*, Montreal and New York: Black Rose, 1992.

Henze, Paul B., *The Plot to Kill the Pope*, London and Canberra: Croom Helm, 1984.

Hering, Gunnar, "Die Osmanenzeit im Selbstverständnis der Völker Südosteuropas," Hans Georg Mayer, ed., *Die Staaten Südosteuropas und die Osmanen*, Munich: Selbstverlag der Südosteuropa-Gesellschaft, 1989, 355–380.

Herman, Edward S., and Frank Brodhead, *The Rise and Fall of the Bulgarian Connection*, New York: Sheridan Square, 1986.

Herzfeld, Michael, *Anthropology through the Looking-Glass: Critical Ethnography in the Margins of Europe*, Cambridge: Cambridge University Press, 1987.

Heyd, Uriel, *Foundations of Turkish Nationalism*, Westport, Conn.: Hyperion, 1979.

Heywood, C. J., "Sir Paul Rycaut, A Seventeenth-Century Observer of the Ottoman State: Notes for a Study," *English and Continental Views of the Ottoman Empire, 1500–1800*, Los Angeles: William Andrews Clark Memorial Library, 1972, 31–59.

Hirsch, Jr., E. D., *Cultural Literacy. What Every American Needs To Know*, New York: Vintage, 1988.

Hobsbawm, Eric, *Nations and Nationalism Since 1780*, Cambridge: Cambridge University Press, 1990.

Hobsbawm, Eric, and Terence Ranger, *The Invention of Tradition*, Cambridge: Cambridge University Press, 1983.

Hockenos, Paul, *Free to Hate: The Rise of the Right in Post-Communist Eastern Europe*, New York: Routledge, 1993.

Hofer, Tamas, ed., *Hungarians Between 'East' and 'West'. Three Essays on National Myths and Symbols*, Budapest: Museum of Ethnography, 1994.

Hoffman, Eva, *Exit Into History. A Journey Through the New Eastern Europe*, New York: Penguin, 1993.

Hoffman, George W., *The Balkans in Transition*, Princeton, N.J.: D. Van Nostrand, 1963.

Hohmeier, Jürgen, "Stigmatisierung als sozialer Definitionsprozess," Manfred Brusten and Jürgen Hohmeier, eds., *Stigmatisierung: Zur Produktion gesellschaftlicher Randgruppen*, Neuwied and Darmstadt: Hermann Luchterhand Verlag, 1975, 5–24.

Holbrooke, Richard, "America, A European Power," *Foreign Affairs*, vol. 74, no. 2, March/April 1995, 38–51.

Hopkins, Terence K., *World-systems Analysis: Theory and Methodology*, Beverly Hills, Calif.: Sage, 1982.

Hughes, Edward, *The Development of Cobden's Economic Doctrines and His Methods of Propaganda*, Manchester, 1938.

Hunger, Hubert, ed., *Das byzantinische Herrschenbild*, Darmstadt: Wissenschaftliche Buchgesellschaft, 1975.

Huntington, Samuel, *The Clash of Civilizations and the Remaking of World Order*, New York: Simon and Schuster, 1996.

Huntington, Samuel P., "The Clash of Civilizations?" *Foreign Affairs*, vol. 72, no. 3, Summer 1993, 23–49.

———, "If Not Civilizations, What?" *Foreign Affairs*, vol. 72, no. 5, Nov./Dec. 1993, 186–194.

Hussain, Asaf, Robert Olson and Jamil Qureshi, *Orientalism, Islam, and Islamists*, Brattleboro, VT.: Amana, 1984.

Hyman, Susan, ed., *Edward Lear in the Levant: Travels in Albania, Greece and Turkey in Europe 1848–1849*, London: John Murray, 1988.

Hynková, Hana, *Europäische Reiseberichte aus dem 15. und 16. Jahrhundert als Quellen für die historische Geographie Bulgariens*, Sofia: Verlag der Bulgarischen Akademie der Wissenschaft, 1973.

Ignatieff, Michael, "On Civil Society," *Foreign Affairs*, vol. 74, no. 2, March/April 1995, 128–136.

Igov, Svetlozar, *Istoriya na bîlgarskata literatura, 1878–1944*, Sofia: clydatelstvo naBîlgarska akademiya na naukite, 1993.

Il cathechisimo translato della lingua tedescha in la lingua italiana per Salomon Schweigger: Allemagno Wirt. predicatore del Evangelio in Constantinopoli, Tübingen, 1585.

Ilchev, Ivan, "Robert kolezh i formiraneto na bîlgarskata inteligentsiya (1863–1878), *Istoricheski pregled*, vol. 1, 1981, 50–62.

Ilieva, Lili, and Stiliyan Stoyanov, "Bay Ganyo kato 'Homo Balkanicus' — 'svoya' i 'chuzhda' gledna tochka," *Balkanistic Forum*, no. 2, 1993, 63–68.

Inalcık, Halil, "Balkan," *The Encyclopaedia of Islam*, new edition, vol. 1, Leiden: E. J. Brill, 1960, 998–1000.

——, "Notes on a Study of the Turkish Economy during the Establishment and Rise of the Ottoman Empire," Halil Inalcık, ed., *The Middle East and the Balkans under the Ottoman Empire*, Bloomington: Indiana University Turkish Studies, vol. 9, 1993, 205–263.

——, *The Ottoman Empire: The Classical Age 1300–1600*. London, Weidenfeld and Nelson, 1973.

——, "Türkler ve Balkanlar," *Balkanlar*, Istanbul: EREN, 1993, 9–32.

——, "Village, Peasant and Empire," Halil Inalc'k, ed., *The Middle East and the Balkans under the Ottoman Empire*, vol. 9, Bloomington: Indiana University Turkish Studies, 1993, 137–160.

Inden, Ronald, *Imagining India*, Oxford and Cambridge: Blackwell, 1990.

Inglis, K. S., *Churches and the Working Classes in Victorian England*, London: Routledge and K. Paul, 1963.

Insdorf, Anette, "A Romanian Director Tells A Tale of Ethnic Madness," *New York Times*, 6 November 1994, H22.

Ionesco, Eugène, *Présent passé: Passé présent*, Paris: Mercure de France, 1968.

Ionescu de la Brad, Ion, *Excursion agricole dans la plaine de la Dobrodja*, Istanbul: Imprimerie du journal de Constantinople, 1850.

Iorga, Nicolae, *Byzance après Byzance: continuation de l'Histoire de la vie byzantine*, Bucharest: A l'institut d'etudes byzantines, 1935.

——, *Formes byzantines et réalités balkaniques* Paris: J. Gamber, 1922.

——, *Histoire des États balkaniques jusqu'à 1924*, Paris: J. Gamber, 1924.

——, *Histoire des Romains et de la Romanité Orientale*, vol. 1, part 1, Paris: Librairie Ernest Laroux, 1937.

——, *A History of Romania: Land, People, Civilization*, New York: AMS, 1970.

——, *Istoria Romînilor din peninsula balcanica (Albania, Macedonia, Epir, Tesalia, etc.)*, Bucharest, 1919.

——, *Les voyageurs français dans l'Orient Européen*, Paris: Boivin, J. Gamber, 1928.

Iovkov, Iordan, *Razkazi*, Sofia: Bîlgarski pisatel, 1974.

Iser, Wolfgang, *The Fictive and the Imaginary: Charting Literary Anthropology*, Baltimore and London: Johns Hopkins University Press, 1993.

——, "Interaction Between Text and Reader," Susan R. Suleiman and Inge Crosman, eds., *The Reader in the Text. Essays on Audience and Interpretation*, Princeton, N.J.: Princeton University Press, 1980, 106–119.

——, *Prospecting: From Reader Response to Literary Anthropology*, Baltimore and London: Johns Hopkins University Press, 1989.

Jelavich, Barbara, "The British Traveller in the Balkans: The Abuses of Ottoman Administration in the Slavonic Provinces," *Slavonic and East European Review*, vol. 33, no. 81, June 1955, 396–413.

——, *History of the Balkans: Vol. 1. Eighteenth and Nineteenth Centuries. Vol. 2. Twentieth Century*, New York: Cambridge University Press, 1983.

——, *Russia's Balkan Entanglements, 1806–1914*, Cambridge: Cambridge University Press, 1991.

Jelavich, Charles, and Barbara, "Balkans," *Encyclopedia Americana. International Edition*, vol. 3.

——, *The Establishment of the Balkan National States, 1804–1920*, Seattle: University of Washington Press, 1977.

Jireček, Konstantin, *Geschichte der Bulgaren*, Prague, 1876.

——, *Die Heerstrasse von Belgrad nach Constantinopel und die Balkanpässe*, Prague, 1877.

Johnson, Lonnie R., *Central Europe: Enemies, Neighbors, Friends*, New York and Oxford: Oxford University Press, 1996.

Jonov, Michail, *Evropa otnovo otkriva bîlgarite*, Sofia: Narodna Prosveta, 1980.

——, ed., *Nemski i avstriiski pîtepisi za Balkanite, XV–XVI v.*, Sofia: Nauka i izkustvo, 1979.

——, ed., *Nemski i avstriiski pîtepisi za Balkanite, XVII-XVIII v.*, Sofia: Nauka i izkustvo, 1986.

Judt, Tony, "At Home in This Century," *New York Review of Books*, vol. 42, no. 6, 6 April 1995, 9–14.

Kadare, Ismail, *The Three-Arched Bridge*, Franklin, N.Y.: New Amsterdam, 1995.

Kafé, E., "Le mythe turc et son déclin dans les relations de voyage des européen de la Renaissance, *Oriens*, vols. 21–22, 1968–1969, 159–195.

Kaim, Julius Rudolf, *Westöstliche Welt unter Slawen, Griechen, Türken*, Berlin: Volksverband der Bücherfreunde, Wegweiser Verlag, 1930.

Kanitz Felix Philipp, *Donau-Bulgarien und der Balkan: Historisch-geographisch-ethnographische Reisestudien aus den Jahren 1860–1879*, vols. 1–3, Leipzig: H. Fries, 1875–1879.

Kant, Immanuel, *Schriften zur Anthropologie, Geschichtsphilosophie, Politik und Pedagogie*, vol. 12, Frankfurt: Suhrkamp Verlag, 1977.

Kaplan, Robert D., *Balkan Ghosts: A Journey Through History*, New York: St. Martin's, 1993.

——, "The Middle East is a Myth," *New York Times Magazine*, 20 February 1994, 42–43.

Kapp, Robert A., "Introduction: Review Symposium: Edward Said's Orientalism," *Journal of Asian Studies*, vol. 39, no. 3, 1980, 481–484.

Karahasan, Dževad, *Sarajevo, Exodus of a City*, New York: Kodansha International, 1994 (first appeared as *Dnevni selidbe*, Zagreb: Durieux, 1993).

Karavelov, Lyuben, *Bîlgare ot staro vreme*, Sofia: Bîlgarski pisatel, 1981.

Karlova, M. F., "Turekskaya provintsiya I ee sel'skaya I gorodskaya zhizn,'" *Vestnik Europy*, no. 6, Saint Petersburg, 1870, 721–753.

Karpat, Kemal, *Ottoman Population, 1830–1914*, Madison: University of Wisconsin Press, 1985.

——, ed., *The Ottoman State and Its Place in World History*, Leiden: Brill, 1974.

Kaser, Karl, *Südosteuropäische Geschichte und Geschichtswissenschaft*, Vienna and Köln: Böhlau Verlag, 1990.

Kazantzakis, Nikos, "Crete, a Great and Noble Island," *Modern Greek Literary Gems*, New York: R. D. Cortina, 1962, 54–57.

Kazhdan, Alexander, and Giles Constable, *People and Power in Byzantium*, Washington, D.C.: Dumbarton Oaks Center for Byzantine Studies, 1982.

Keane, John, ed., *Civil Society and the State: New European Perspectives*, New York: Verso, 1988.

Kelly, Michael, "Surrender and Blame," *New Yorker*, vol. 30, no. 42, 19 December 1994, 44–51.

Kelly, T. Mills, "America's First Attempt at Intervention in East Central Europe," *East European Quarterly*, vol. 24, no. 1, March 1995, 1–16.

Kenney, George, "The Bosnia Calculation," *New York Times Magazine*, 23 April 1995, 42–43.

——, "Steering Clear of Balkan Shoals," *Nation*, vol. 262, no. 2, 8/15 January, 1996, 21–24.

Keppel, George, *Narrative of a Journey across the Balkans, by the Two Passes of Selimno and Pravadi; also of a Visit to Azani, and other Newly Discovered Ruins in Asia Minor, in the Years 1829–1830*, London: H. Colburn and R. Bentley, 1831.

Keyder, Çaglar, "Small Peasant Ownership in Turkey: Historical Formation and Present Structure, *Review*, vol. 7, no. 1, Summer 1983, 53–107.

Keyder, Çaglar, Y. Eyüp Özveren, and Donald Quaetert, "Port-Cities in the Ottoman Empire: Some Theoretical and Historical Perspectives," *Review*, vol. 16, no. 4, Fall 1993, 519–558.

Keyserling, Count Hermann, *Europe*, Trans. Maurice Samuel, New York: Harcourt Brace, 1928.

Khazanov, Anatoly M., *Nomads and the Outside World*, Madison: University of Wisconsin Press, 1994.

Kiel, Machiel, "Gramota za osnovavaneto na grad Tryavna," *Vekove*, vol. 3, 1984, 72–75.

Kiernan, V. G., *The Lords of Human Kind: European Attitudes to the Outside World in the Imperial Age*, Harmondsworth, Middlesex, England: Penguin, 1972.

King, Edward, *Echoes from the Orient*, London: C. Kegan Paul, 1880.

——, *Europe in Storm and Calm: Twenty Years' Experiences and Reminiscences of an American Journalist*, Springfield, Mass.: C. A. Nichols, 1885.

Kinglake, A. W., *Eothen*, London: Century, 1982.

Kinzer, Stephen, "In Croatia, Minds Scarred by War: A Struggle to Treat the Trauma of the Balkan violence," *New York Times*, 9 January 1995, A6.

Kirchhoff, Alfred, ed., *Länderkunde von Europa*, vol. 2, part 2, Vienna, Prague, and Leipzig: F. Tempsky, 1893.

Kiss, Csaba G., "Central European Writers about Central Europe: Introduction to a Non-Existent Book of Readings," George Schöpflin and Nancy Wood, eds., *In Search of Central Europe*, Cambridge, U.K.: Polity, 1989, 125–136.

Kissinger, Henry, "Expand NATO Now," *Washington Post*, 19 December 1994, A27.

——, "Ready for Revitalizing," *New York Times*, 9 March 1995, A21.

Kitromilides, Paschalis, "'Balkan Mentality': History, Legend, Imagination," *Nations and Nationalism*, vol. 2, part 2, July 1996, 163–191.

——, *Enlightenment, Nationalism, Orthodoxy: Studies in the Culture and Political Thought of South-Eastern Europe*, Aldershot, Hampshire, England: Variorum, 1994.

——, *The Enlightenment as Social Criticism: Iosipos Moisiodax and Greek Culture in the Eighteenth Century*, Princeton, N.J.: Princeton University Press, 1992.

——, "The Enlightenment East and West: a Comparative Perspective on the Ideological Origins of the Balkan Political Traditions," *Canadian Review of Studies in Nationalism*, vol. 10, no. 1, Spring 1983, 51–70.

——, *I Galliki Epanastasi ke i Motioanatoliki Evropi*, Athens, Greece: Diatton, 1990.

——, "Imagined Communities and the Origins of the National Question in the Balkans," *European History Quarterly*, vol. 19, no. 2, April 1989, 149–192.

——, "John Locke and the Greek Intellectual Tradition: An Episode in Locke's Reception in South-East Europe," G. A. J. Rogers, ed., *Locke's Philosophy. Content and Context*, Oxford: Clarendon, 1994, 217–235.

——, "La révolution française dans le sud-est de l'Europe: La dimension politique," *La révolution française et lhellenisme moderne*, Athens: FNRS and CNR, 1989, 223–245.

——, Review of *Europe: A History of Its Peoples*, *European History Quarterly*, vol. 24, no. 1, January 1994, 126.

Klussmeier, Gerhard, and Hainer Plaul, eds., *Karl May: Biographie in Dokumenten und Bildern*, Hildesheim and New York: Olms, 1978.

Knolles, Richard, *The Generall Historie of the Turks, from the first beginning of that Nation to the rising of the Othoman Familie, with all the notable Expeditions of the Christian Princes against them, together with the Lives and Conquests of the Ottoman Kings and Emperours; faithfullie collected out of the best Histories, both auntient and moderne, and digested into one continual Historie until this present yeare 1603*, London: Aislip, 1603.

Kochanowicz, Jacek, "The Polish Economy and the Evolution of Dependency," Daniel Chirot, ed., *The Origins of Backwardness in Eastern Europe: Economics & Politics from the Middle Ages until the Early Twentieth Century*, Berkeley: University of California Press, 1989, 92–130.

Koebner, R., and H. Schmidt, *Imperialism: The Story and Significance of a Political Word, 1840–1860*, Cambridge: Cambridge University Press, 1964.

Kohn, Hans, *Pan-Slavism, Its History and Ideology*, Notre Dame, Ind.: University of Notre Dame Press, 1953.

Koledarov, Petîr, "The Medieval Maps as a Source of Bulgarian History," *Bulgarian Historical Review*, no. 2, 1982, 96–110.

——, *Politicheska geografiya na srednovekovnata bîlgarska dîrzhava*, Sofia, 1979.

Koneva, Rumyana, "Balkanskite voini v nemskiya periodichen pechat," *Balkanistic forum*, vol. 2, 1993, 76–78.

Konrád, György, *Antipolitics: An Essay*, New York: Harcourt Brace Jovanovich, 1984.

——, *The Melancholy of Rebirth: Essays from Post-Communist Central Europe, 1989–1994*, San Diego: Harcourt Brace, 1995.

Konrád, György, and Ivan Szelenyi, "Intellectuals and Domination in Post-Communist Societies," Pierre Bourdieu and James S. Coleman, eds., *Social Theory for a Changing Society*, Boulder, Co.: Westview, New York: Russell Sage Foundation, 1991, 337–364.

Konstantinov, Aleko, *Do Chicago i nazad: Bay Ganyo*, Sofia: Bîlgarski pisatel, 1983.

Konstantinović, Zoran, "Bild und Gegenbild: Ein Beitrag zur Imagologie der südosteuropäischen Völker in der Phase ihrer nationalen Wiedergeburt," Hugo Dyserinck and Karl Ulrich Syndram, eds., *Europa und das nationale Selbstverständnis: Imagologische Probleme in Literatur, Kunst und Kultur des 19. und 20. Jahrhunderts*, Bonn: Bouvier, 1988, 283–294.

Kopf, David, "Hermeneutics Versus History," *Journal of Asian Studies*, vol. 39, no. 3, 1980, 495–506.

Kornrumpf, H. J., "Zur territorial Verwaltungsgliederung des Osmanischen Reiches, ihrem Entstehen und ihrem Einfluss auf die Nachfolgestaaten," K.-D. Grothusen, ed., *Ethnogenese und Staatsbildung in Südosteuropa*, Göttingen, 1974.

Koroğlu, Orhan, "Osmanl' döneminde Balkanlar," *Balkanlar*, Istanbul: EREN, 1993, 41–96.

Kovalevskii, E., "Balkany. Nish," Biblioteka dlya chtevriya, no. 80, Saint Petersburg, 1847.

Kozhuharova, Margarita, ed., *Ruski pîtepisi za bîlgarskite zemi XVII–XIX vek*, Sofia: Izdatelstvo na Otechestveniya front, 1986.

Krasnokutskii, Alexander Grigor'evich, *Dnevnyya zapiski poezdki v Konstantinopol' A.G. Krasnokutskogo v 1808 godu, samim im pisannyya*, Moscow: V tipografii S. Selivanovskago, 1815.

Krestovskii, Vsevolod, *Dvadtsat' mesyatsev v deistvuyushchei armii (1977–1878)*, vol. 1, Saint Petersburg, 1879.

Kritovoulos, *History of Mehmed the Conqueror*, trans. Charles T. Riggs, Princeton, N.J.: Princeton University Press, 1954.

Križan, Mojmir, "Postkommunistische Wiedergeburt ethnischer Nationalismen und der Dritte Balkan-Krieg," *Osteuropa*, vol. 45, no. 3, March 1995, 201–218.

"Krlezas wilder Sohn: Interview mit Slobodan Snajder," *Ost-West Gegeninformationen*, vol. 8, no. 1, May 1996, 12–15.

Krumbacher, Karl, *Griechische Reise: Blätter aus dem Tagebuche einer Reise in Griechenland und in der Türkei*, Berlin: August Hettler, 1886.

Kundera, Milan, "The Tragedy of Central Europe," *New York Review of Books*, vol. 31, no. 7, 26 April 1984, 33–38.

——, *Žert*, Prague: Ĉeskoslovensky Spisovatel, 1967.

Laber, Jeri, "Bosnia—Questions of Rape," *New York Review of Books*, vol. 40, no. 6, 25 March 1993, 3–6.

Lafore, Laurence, *The Long Fuse: An Interpretation of the Origins of World War I*, New York: J. B. Lippincott, 1971.

Lamartine, Alphonse-Marie-Louis de, *Souvenirs, impressions, pensées et paysages pendent un voyage en Orient (1832–1833), ou, Notes d'un voyageurs*, Paris: Charles Gosselin, 1835.

——, *Voyage en Orient*, Paris, 1887.

——, *Vues, discours et articles sur la question d''Orient, par . . . , membre de la Chambre des députés*, Paris: Charles Gosselin, 1840.

Lampe, John R., and Marvin R. Jackson. *Balkan Economic History, 1550–1950, From Imperial Borderlands to Developing Nations*, Bloomington: Indiana University Press, 1982.

Larrabee, Stephen E., *Hellas Observed: The American Experience of Greece, 1775–1865*, New York: New York University Press, 1957.

Laveleye, Emile de, *The Balkan Peninsula*, London: T. Fisher Unwin, 1887.

Lazarov, Petîr, and Zhivko Zhelev, *Geografiya za 7. klas na srednite obshtoobrazovatelni uchilishta*, Sofia: Anubis, 1994.

Leake, W. M., *Travels in Northern Greece*, London: J. Rodwell, 1835.

Lear, Edward, *Journal of a Landscape Painter in Greece and Albania*, London, 1851 (reprinted in London: Century, 1988).

——, *Journal of a Landscape Painter in Southern Albania*, London: R. Bentley, 1852.

——, *Views in the Seven Ionian Islands*, London, 1963, (facsimile edition in Odham, Lancashire: Hugh Broadbent, 1979).

Lechevalier, Jean-Batiste, *Voyage de Propontide et du Pont Euxin, avec la carte générale de ces deux mers, la description topographique de leurs rivages, le tableau des moeurs, des usages et du commerce des peuples qui les habitent; la carte particulière de la plaine de Brousse en Bythinie, celle du Bosphore de thrace, et celle de Constantinople accompagnée de la description des monuments anciens et moderned de cette capitale*, Paris, 1801.

Léger, Louis, *La Save, le Danube et le Balkan. Voyage chez les Slovènes, les Croates, les Serbes et les Bulgares*, Paris: E. Plon, Nourrit, 1884.

Lele, Jayant, "Orientalism and the Social Sciences," *Orientalism and the Postcolonial Predicament: Perspectives on South Asia*, Philadelphia: University of Pennsylvania Press, 1993.

Lemerle, Paul, "Byzance et les origines de notre civilisation," Agostino Pertusi, ed., *Venezia e l'Oriente fra tardo Medioevo e Rinascimento*, Florence: Sansoni, 1966.

Leonard, John, "C.I.A.—An Infinity of Mirrors," *Nation*, vol. 258, no. 12, March 28, 1994, 412–417.

Leont'ev, Konstantine, *Sobranie sochinenii*, Moscow: Izd. V. M. Sablina, 1912–1914 (Leont'ev, Konstantine, *Sobranie sochinenii K. Leont'eva*, Würzburg: Jal-reprint, 1975).

——, *Vostok, Rossiya i slavyanstvo. Sbornik statei*, vol. 1, Osnabrück: Otto Zeller, 1966.

Leontiev, Konstantin, "Vizantinizmît i slavyanstvo," Sofia: Slavica, 1993.

Le Queux, William, *The Near East: The Present Situation in Montenegro, Bosnia, Servia, Bulgaria, Roumania, Turkey and Macedonia*, New York: Doubleday, Page, 1907.

Lerner, O. M., "Vospominaniya o Bolgarii (Iz putevykh zametok)," *Zapiski grazhdanina*, Odessa, 1876, no. 8, 8–11, no. 9, 26–31, no. 11, 77–80.

Le voyage en Orient: anthologie des voyageurs français dans le Levant au XIXe siècle, Paris: R. Laffont, 1985.

Lewis, Anthony, "Are the Serbs Controlling Clinton?" *Gainesville Sun*, 14 March 1993, 2G.

Lewis, Bernard, *The Emergence of Modern Turkey*, New York: Oxford University Press, 1961.

——, "Eurocentrism Revisited," *Commentary*, vol. 98, no. 6, December 1994, 47–61.

——, "Islam," Denis Sinor, ed., *Orientalism and History*, Cambridge: W. Heffer and Sons, 1954, 16–33.

——, *Islam and the West*, New York and Oxford: Oxford University Press, 1993.

——, *Istanbul and the Civilization of the Ottoman Empire*, Norman: University of Oklahoma Press, 1989.

Linguistique balkanique: Bibliographie, Sofia: Institut d'études balkaniques, CIBAL, 1983.

Lipp, Wolfgang, "Selbststigmatisierung," Manfred Brusten and Jürgen Hohmeier, eds., *Stigmatisierung: Zur Produktion gesellschaftlicher Randgruppen*, Neuwied and Darmstadt: Hermann Luchterhand Verlag, 1975, 25–54.

Le livre noir de l'ex-Yugoslavie: Purification ethnique et crimes de guerre, Paris: Arléa, 1993.

Lloyd, G. E. R., *Demystifying Mentalities*, New York: Cambridge University Press, 1990.

Longinović, Tomislav Z., *Borderline Culture: The Politics of Identity in Four Twentieth-Century Slavic Novels*, Fayetteville: University of Arkansas Press, 1993.

Longworth, R. C., "Bulgaria, Romania Resist Pull of the West," *Chicago Tribune*, 10 October 1994, 1,6.

Lory, Bernard, *Le sort de l'héritage ottoman en Bulgarie: L'exemple des villes bulgares, 1878–1900*, Istanbul: Isis, 1985.

Lovinesco, Eugène, *Les voyageurs français en Grèce au XIX siècle (1800–1900)*, Paris, 1909.

Lowe, Lisa, *Critical Terrains: French and British Orientalisms*, Ithaca, N.Y. and London: Cornell University Press, 1991.

Lucas, Paul, *Voyage du sieur Paul Lucas fait par ordre du roy dans la Grèce, l'Asie Mineure, la Macédoine et l'Afrique*, Paris, 1712.

Lyall, Archibald, *The Balkan Road*, London: Methuen, 1930.

MacGahan, Januarius Aloysius, *The Turkish Atrocities in Bulgaria*, Geneva: n.p., 1966.

MacKenzie, David, *The Serbs and Russian Pan-Slavism*, Ithaca, N.Y.: Cornell University Press, 1967.

[Mackenzie, Georgina Muir, and Adelina Irby], *Travels in the Slavonic Provinces of Turkey-in-Europe by Miss Muir Mackenzie and Miss Irby*, London: Bell and Daldy, 1867.

———, *Travels in the Slavonic Provinces of Turkey-in-Europe. By G. Muir Mackenzie and A.P. Irby. With a Preface by the Right Hon. W. E. Gladstone, M.P.*, 2nd ed. revised, London: Daldy, Isbister, 1877.

Macmichael, William, *Journey from Moscow to Constantinople. In the Years 1817, 1818*, London: J. Murray, 1819.

The MacNeill-Lehrer News Hour broadcast, 7 February 1994.

Magaš, Branka, "Balkanization or Lebanization?" *The Destruction of Yugoslavia*, London and New York: Verso, 1993, 346–350.

Majer, Hans Georg, ed., *Die Staaten Südosteuropas und die Osmanen*, Munich: Salbstverlag der Südosteuropa-Gesellschaft, 1989.

Malcomson, Scott L., *Borderlands: Nation and Empire*, Boston and London: Faber and Faber, 1994.

Manoschek, Walter, *"Serbien is Judenfrei": Militärische Besatzungspolitik und Judenvernichtung in Serbien 1941–2*, Munich: R. Oldenburg, 1994.

Mans, Pierre Belon du, *Les observations de plusieurs singularitez et choses mémorables, trouvées en Grèce, Asie, Iudée, Egypte, Arabie & authres pays estranges, rédigées en trois livres, par . . . Le catalogue contenant les plus notables choses de ce present livre, est en l'autre part de ce feuillet*, Paris, 1553.

Marcellus, M.-L.-J.-A.-C., Vicomte de, *Souvenirs de l'Orient, par le Vicompte de Marcellus, ancien ministre plénipotentiaire*, Paris: Debécourt, 1839.

Marcus, George, and Michael Fischer, eds., *Anthropology as Cultural Critique: An Experimental Moment in the Human Sciences*, Chicago: University of Chicago Press, 1986.

Mardin, Şerif, *The Genesis of Young Ottoman Thought: A Study in the Modernization of Turkish Political Ideas*, Princeton Oriental Studies, vol. 21, Princeton, N.J.: Princeton University Press, 1962.

———, "The Just and the Unjust," *Daedalus*, vol. 120, no. 3, Summer 1991, 113–129.

Marglin, Stephen A. M., and Frederique Appfel Marglin, eds., *Dominating Knowledge: Development, Culture and Resistance*, Oxford: Clarendon, 1990.

Martin, Richard, and Harold Koda, *Orientalism: Visions of the East in Western Dress*, New York: Metropolitan Museum of Art, 1994.

Marx, Karl, and Friedrich Engels, "Manifesto of the Communist Party," *Collected Works*, trans. Richard Dixon et al., vol. 6., New York: International, 1976, 477–519.

Masaryk, T. G., "Österreich und der Balkan," *Die Balkanfrage*, Munich and Leipzig: Verlag von Duncker and Humblot, 1914.

Matanov, Khristo, and Rumyana Mikhneva, *Ot Galipoli do Lepanto: Balkanite, Evropa i osmanskoto nashestvie 1354–1571 g.*, Sofia: Nauka i izkustvo, 1988.

Matkovski, Aleksandar, ed., *Balkanot vo delata na stranskite patopisci vo vremeto na turskoto vladeenje: janicari, haremi, robovi*, Skopje: Kultura, 1992.

Matkovski, Alexander, "Bibliografija na patopisi za Balkanskiot poluostrov vo vreme ha turskoto vladeenje," *Glasnik na institutot za natsionalna istorija*, Skopje, 1971, vol. 15, no. 1 (1371–1600), 2 (1600–1800), 3 (1800–1912).

Matvejević, Predrag, "Central Europe Seen From the East of Europe," George Schöpflin and Nancy Wood, eds., *In Search of Central Europe*, Cambridge, U.K.: Polity Press, 1989, 183–190.

Maull, Otto, *Enzyklopedie der Erdkunde*, Leipzig and Vienna: Franz Deuticke, 1929.

McKechnie, Rosemary, "Becoming Celtic in Corsica," Sharon Macdonald, ed., *Inside European Identities: Ethnography in Western Europe*, Providence/Oxford: Berg, 1994, 118–145.

McNeal, R. A., ed., *Nicholas Biddle in Greece: The Journal and Letters of 1806*, University Park, Penn.: Pennsylvania State University Press, 1993.

Mead, William Edward, *The Grand Tour in the Eighteenth Century*, Boston: Houghton Mifflin, 1914.

Meisel, Martin, *Shaw and the Nineteenth-Century Theatre*, Princeton, N.J.: Princeton University Press, 1963.

Melas, Spyros, "This is Greece!" *Modern Greek Literary Gems*, New York: R. D. Cortina, 1962, 46–49.

Melchisedec, Episcop, *O excursine în Bulgaria de episcop Melchisedec*, Bucharest, 1885.

Mellor, Jane, "Is the Russian Intelligentsia European? (A Reply to Şimčka)," George Schöpflin and Nancy Wood, eds., *In Search of Central Europe*, Cambridge, U.K.: Polity Press, 1989, 163–167.

Melman, Billie, *Women's Orients: English Women and the Middle East, 1718–1918. Sexuality, Religion and Work*, Ann Arbor: University of Michigan Press, 1995.

Melville, Cecil F., *Balkan Racket*, London: Jarrolds, 1941.

Mémoires de Baron de Tott sur les Turcs et les Tartares, vol. 2, Amsterdam, 1784.

Mémoires du Sieur de la Croix, cy-devant secrétaire de l'Ambassade de Constantinople: Contenant diverses relations très curieuses de l'Empire Ottoman, Paris, 1684.

Meštrović, Stjepan G., *The Balkanization of the West: The Confluence of Postmodernism and Postcommunism*, London and New York: Routledge, 1994.

——, *Habits of the Balkan Heart: Social Character and the Fall of Communism*, College Station: Texas A&M University, 1993.

Meyer, Henry Cord, "*Mitteleuropa* in German Political Geography," *Collected Works*, vol. 1, Irvine, Calif.: Charles Schlacks, Jr., 1986, 109–126.

——, *Mitteleuropa in German Thought and Action, 1815–1945*, Hague: Martinus Nijhoff, 1955.

Miedlig, Hans-Michael, "Gründe und Hintergründe der aktuellen Nationalitätenkonflikte in den jugoslawischen Ländern, *Südosteuropa*, vol. 41, 1992, 116–130.

——, "Patriarchalische Mentalität als Hindernis für die staatliche und gesellschaftliche Modernisierung in Serbien im 19. Jahrhundert," *Südost-Forschungen*, vol. 50, 1991, 163–190.

——, "Probleme der Mentalität bei Kroaten und Serben," *Septième Congres International d'Etudes du Sud-Est Européen (Thessalonique, 29 août-4 septembre): Rapports*, Athens: Association Internationale d'Etudes du Sud-Est Européen, Comité National Grec, 1994, 393–424.

Mihneva, Roumiana, "Notre Europe at 'l'autre' Europe ou 'européisation' contre évolution et certains problèmes du 'temps' transitoire dans les Balkans," *Etudes balkaniques*, no. 3, 1994, 9–20.

Miller, Hellen Hill, *Greece Through the Ages: As Seen by Travelers from Herodotus to Byron*, New York: Funk and Wagnalls, 1972.

Miller, Henry, *The Colossus of Maroussi*, New York: New Directions, 1941.

Miller, William, *The Balkans: Roumania, Bulgaria, Servia, and Montenegro*, New York: G. P. Putnam's, 1896.

——, *Essays on the Latin Orient*, Cambridge: Cambridge University Press, 1921.

——, *The Ottoman Empire and Its Successors, 1801–1927*, Cambridge: Cambridge University Press, 1936.

——, *Travels and Politics in the Near East*, London: T. Fisher Unwin, 1898.

Millman, Richard, *Britain and the Eastern Question, 1875–1978*, Oxford: Clarendon, 1979.

Milojković-Djurić, Jelena, *Panslavism and National Identity in Russia and the Balkans, 1830–1880: Images of the Self and Others*, Boulder, Co.: East European Monographs, no. 394, New York: Columbia University Press, 1994.

Milosz, Czeslaw, "Central European Attitudes," *Cross Currents: A Yearbook of Central European Culture*, vol. 5, no. 2, 1986, 101–108.

———, *The History of Polish Literature*, New York: Macmillan, 1973.

———, *The Witness of Poetry*, Cambridge, Mass.: Harvard University Press, 1983.

Miyatev, Petîr, ed., *Madzharski pîtepisi za Balkanite, XVI–XIX v*, Sofia: Nauka i izkustvo, 1976.

Mladenova, Maria, and Nikolai Zhechev, *Rumînski pîtepisi ot XIX vek za bîlgarskite zemi*, Sofia: Izdatelstvo na Otechestveniya front, 1982.

Mohanty, S. P., "Us and Them: On the Philosophical Bases of Political Criticism," *Yale Journal of Criticism*, vol. 2, no. 2, 1989, 1–31.

Moltke, Helmuth von, *Briefe über Zustände und Begebenheiten in der Türkei aus den Jahren 1835 bis 1839*, Berlin: E. S. Mittler, 1911 (reprint, Köln: Verlag Jakob Hegner, 1968).

Mommsen, Wolfgang, *Theories of Imperialism*, New York: Random, 1980.

Montagu, Mary Wortley, *Letters of the Right Honorable Lady M . . . y, W . . . y, M . . . u, Written during her Travels in Europe, Asia and Africa to Persons of Distinction*, London, 1763.

Monumenta historica Hungariae: Ser. II: Verancsics Antal, Összes munkai, 1–72, t. 2–32, Budapest, 1857–1875.

Monumenta Poloniae historica, vol. 1, part 1 Warsaw: Panstwowe Wydawn, Naukowe, 1961.

Monumental Propaganda: A Travelling Exhibition Organized and Circulated by Independent Curators Incorporated, New York, 1994.

Morritt, John B. S. of Rokeby, *A Grand Tour: Letters and Journeys 1794–96*, G. E. Marindin, ed., London: Century, 1985.

Moser, Charles A., *A History of Bulgarian Literature, 865–1944*, Hague: Mouton, 1972.

Mosse, George L., *Toward the Final Solution: A History of European Racism*, New York: Howard Fertig, 1978.

Mouzelis, Nicos P., *Modern Greece: Facets of Underdevelopment*, London: Macmillan, 1988.

Mowrer, Paul Scott, *Balkanized Europe: A Study in Political Analysis and Reconstruction*, New York: E. P. Dutton, 1921.

Müller, Heiner, "Stirb schneller, Europa," *Iztok-Iztok*, nos. 9–10, 1993, 46–51.

Mutafchiev, Petîr, *Kniga za bîlgarite*, Sofia: Izdatelstvo na Bîlgarska akademiya na naukite, 1987.

Muzet, Alphonse, *Le monde balkanique: Roumains de Roumanie, de Transylvanie et de Bukovine, Serbes de Serbie, de Bosnie, de Croatie, de Dalmatie et de Monténégro, Bulgares, Grecs, Turcs et Albanais*, Paris: Ernest Flammarion, 1917.

Mylonas, George E., *The Balkan States: An Introduction to Their History*, Washington, D.C.: Public Affairs Press, 1947.

Myrivilis, Stratis, "The Greek Waves," *Modern Greek Literary Gems*, New York: R. D. Cortina, 1962, 50–53.

Nader, Laura, "Orientalism, Occidentalism and the Control of Women," *Cultural Dynamics: An International Journal for the Study of Processes and Temporality of Culture*, vol. 2, no. 3, 1989.

Nair, Sami, "Le differend mediterranéen," *Lettre Internationale*, vol. 30, 1991 (translated in *Iztok-Iztok*, nos. 9–10, 1993, 55–63).

Nairn, Tom, *The Enchanted Class: Britain and Its Monarchy*, London: Radius, 1988.

Nationalism and War in the Near East (By a Diplomatist), Oxford: Clarendon, 1915.

Naumann, Friedrich, *Bulgarien und Mitteleuropa*, Berlin: G. Reimer, 1916.

———, *Mitteleuropa* Berlin: G. Reimer, 1915.

Neale, Adam, M.D., *Travels through Some Parts of Germany, Poland, Moldavia and Turkey*, London: Longman, Hurst, Rees, Orme and Brown, 1818.

Nelson, Daniel N., *Balkan Imbroglio: Politics and Security in Southeastern Europe*, Boulder, Co.: Westview, 1991.

Nenov, Todor, and Georgi Chorchomov, *Stara planina: Pîtevoditel*, Sofia: Meditsina i fizkultura, 1987.

Nestorova, Tatyana, *American Missionaries among the Bulgarians, 1858–1912*, Boulder, Co.: East European Monographs, no. 218, New York: Columbia University Press, 1987.

Neumann, Iver B., "Russia as Central Europe's Constituting Other," *East European Politics and Societies*, vol. 7, no. 2, Spring 1993, 349–369.

Neumann, Victor, *The Temptation of Homo Europaeus*, Boulder, Co.: East European Monographs, no. 384, New York: Columbia University Press, 1993.

Newman, Bernard, *Balkan Background*, New York: Macmillan, 1935.

Nicolays, Nicolas de, *Les navigations, pérégrinations et voyages, faicts en la Turquie par Nicolas de Nicolays Daulphinoys Seigneur d'Arfeville, vallet de chambre et géographe ordinaire du Roy de France, contennants plusieurs singularitez que l'Auteur y a veu et observé*, En Anvers, 1576.

Nicolson, Marjorie Hope, "Literary Attitudes Toward Mountains," *Dictionary of the History of Ideas*, vol. 3., New York: Scribner's, 1973, 253–260.

——, *Mountain Gloom and Mountain Glory: The Development of the Aesthetics of the Infinite*, Ithaca, N.Y.: Cornell University Press, 1959.

Novak, Zrnka, "Nema čistih ruku," *Oslobođenje*, 23 September 1990, 3.

Nystazopoulou-Pelekidou, Maria, *Oi valkaniki laoi*, Ioannina, 1978.

Olivier, Guillaume-Antoine, *Voyage dans l'Empire Ottoman, l'Égypte et la Perse, fait par ordre du gouvernement, pendant les six premières années de la République*, Paris, 1801.

Opisanie Turetskoi imperii, sostavlennoe russkim, byvshim v plenu u turok v XVII veke, Saint Petersburg, 1890.

Ormandzhian, Agop, ed., *Armenski pîtepisi za Balkanite, XVII–XIX v.*, Sofia: Nauka i izkustvo, 1984.

Ortaylı, Ilber, *Imparatorluğun En Uzun Yüzyıl*, Istanbul: Hil Yayınları, 1983.

Oschlies, Wolf, "Ursachen des Krieges in Ex-Jugoslawien," *Aus Politik und Zeitgeschichte*, vol. 37/93, no. 10, September 1993.

Ostrogorski, Georgije, *History of the Byzantine State*, Oxford: Blackwell, 1956.

The Other Balkan Wars: A 1913 Carnegie Endowment Inquiry in Retrospect with a New Introduction and Reflections on the Present Conflict by George F. Kennan, Washington, D.C.: Carnegie Endowment for International Peace, 1993.

Özal, Turgut, *Turkey in Europe and Europe in Turkey*, Nicosia, Northern Cyprus: K. Rustem, 1991.

Özbaran, Salih, ed., *Tarih Öğretimi ve ders kitapları*, Istanbul: Tarih vakfı yurt yayınları, 1995.

Özyurt, Senol, *Die Türkenlieder und das Türkenbild in der deitschen Volksüberlieferung vom 16. bis zum 20. Jahrhundert*, (Motive, Freiburger folkloristische Forschungen, 4) Munich: Wilhelm Fink Verlag, 1972.

Page, Robert M., *Stigma*, London: Routledge and Kegan Paul, 1984.

Painton, Priscilla, "Who Could Have Done It," *Time*, vol. 141, no. 10, 8 March 1993, 33.

Pakake, Marcia Jean, *Americans Abroad: A Bibliographical Study of American Travel Literature, 1625–1800*, Ph.D. dissertation, University of Minnesota, 1975.

Pakula, Hannah, *The Last Romantic: A Biography of Queen Marie of Romania*, New York, Simon and Schuster, 1984.

Pamiatniki drevnei pis'mennosti i isskustva, vol. 35, Saint Petersburg, 1882.

Panayotov, Plamen, "Pîtuvane kîm Vizantion," Konstantin Leontiev, *Vizantinizmît i slavyanstvoto*, Sofia: Slavika, 1993, 5–20.

Pangelov, Boiko, "Foreign Policy is Strong When All Political Forces Rally in Support of National Interests," Interview with Deputy Minister of Foreign Affairs, *Kontinent*, 30–31 January 1993; also in FBIS-EEU-93-022, 4 February 1993.

Panzini, Alfredo, *Dizionario moderno*, Milan: Editore Ulrico Hoepli, 1950.

Papacostea, Victor, *Civilizaţie românească şi civilizaţie balkanică: Studii istorice*, Bucharest: Editura Eminescu, 1983.

Papadakis, Aristeides, "The Historical Tradition of Church-State Relations under Orthodoxy," Pedro Ramet, ed., *Eastern Christianity and Politics in the Twentieth Century*, vol. 1, Durham, N.C., and London: Duke University Press, 1988, 37–60.

Papadopoulos, S. I., *I kinisi tou Douka tou Never Karolou Gonsaga gia tin apeleftherosi ton valkanikon laon (1603–1625)*, Thessaloniki: Hidryma Meleton Chersonesou tou Haimou, Ekdoseis, 83, 1966.

Papandreou, George, "Greece, the United States and their Mutual Common Interests in the Balkans," *The Southeast European Yearbook 1993*, Athens, Greece: ELIAMEP, 1994, 13–22.

Papoulia, Basilike, "Die Osmanenzeit in der griechischen Geschichtsforschung seit der Unabhängigkeit," Hans Georg Majer, ed., *Die Staaten Südosteuropas und die Osmanen*, Munich: Selbstverlag der Südosteuropa-Gesellschaft, 1989, 113–126.

Pappazoglu, Maior D., *Călăudă pe riul Dunări din Porta de fier pînă in Marea Negri*, Bucharest: Tipografia statulni St. Sava si Nifon, 1863.

Parezanin, Ratko, *Za balkansko jedinstvo: osnivanje, program i rad Balkanskog instituta u Beogradu, 1934–1941*, Munich: s.n., 1976.

Parker, J. S. F., "From Aeschylus to Kissinger," *Gazelle Review*, vol. 1, 1980, 4–16.

Parry, V. J., "Renaissance Historical Literature in Relation to the Near and Middle East," B. Lewis and M. Holt, eds, *Historians of the Middle East*, London: Oxford University Press, 1962, 277–290.

Partenii, Inok, *Skazanie o stranstvii i puteshestvii po Rossii, Moldavii, Turtsii i Svyatoi zemle*, part. 4, Moscow, 1855.

Partsch, Joseph, *Mittaleuropa*, Gotha: J. Parthes, 1904.

Pashko, Gramoz, "The Role of Christianity in Albania's Post-Communist Vacuum," *The Southeast European Yearbook 1993*, Athens, Greece: ELIAMEP, 1994, 47–54.

Patterson, David, "The Dangers of Balkanization," *Peace & Change*, vol. 20, no. 1, January 1995, 76–81.

Paton, James Morton, *Chapters on Medieval and Renaissance Visitors to Greek Lands*, Princeton, N.J.: American School of Classical Studies in Athens, 1951.

Paulys Real-Encyclopädie der Classischen Altertumswissenschaft—Neue Bearbeitung, Stuttgart: J. B. Metzler, 1912.

Peicheva, Lozanka, and Ventsislav Dimov, "Drugite v'misteriyata' (Nablyudeniya vîrkhu bîlgarskata narodna muzika, interpretirana ot chuzhdentsi, vîv fonotekata na Bîlgarskoto natsionalno radio)," *Balkanistic Forum*, no. 1, 1993, 39–45.

Pelimon, A., *Impresiuni de kălătorie în Româniea*, Bucureşti: Imprimeria nationala alui Iosif Romanov et Comp., 1858.

Perdicaris, G. A., *The Greece of the Greeks*, New York: Paine and Burgess, 1946.

Perkin, Harold, *The Origins of Modern English Society 1780–1880*, London: Routledge and K. Paul, 1969.

Perry, Duncan, *The Politics of Terror: The Macedonian Liberation Movements*, Durham, N.C.: Duke University Press, 1988.

Pertusi, Agostino, *Storiografia umanistica e mondo bizantino*, Palermo: Instituto siziliano distudi bizantini e neoellenici, 1967.

Pertusi, Agostino, ed. *Venezia e il Levante fino al secolo XV*, Florence: L. S. Olschki, 1973–1974.

——, ed., *Venezia e l'Oriente fra tardo Medioevo e Rinascimento*, Florence: Sansoni, 1966.

Pesmazoglou, Stephanos, *Evropi-Tourkia: Andanaklaseis kai diathlaseis. I stratigiki ton keimenon*, vol. 1, Athens, Greece: Ekdoseis Themelio, 1993.

Petnadeset godini institut za balkanistiska, 1964–1978: Istoricheska spravka i bibliografiya, Sofia: CIBAL, 1979.

Petropulos, John, "The Modern Greek State and the Greek Past," Speros Vryonis, Jr., ed., *The "Past" in Medieval and Modern Greek Culture*, Malibu, Calif.: Undena, 1978, 163–176.

——, *Politics and Statecraft in the Kingdom of Greece, 1833–1843*, Princeton, N.J.: Princeton University Press, 1968.

Petrosyan, Yurii A., *Mladoturetskoe dvizhenie (vtoraya polovina XIX–nachalo XX v.)*, Moscow: Izdatel'stvo Nauka, 1973.

Petrovich, Michael Boro, *The Emergence of Russian Panslavism, 1856–1870*, New York: Columbia University Press, 1956.

——, "Eugene Schuyler and Bulgaria, 1876–1878," *Bulgarian Historical Review*, vol. 1, 1979, 51–69.

——, *A History of Modern Serbia, 1804–1918*, New York: Harcourt, Brace, Jovanovich, 1976.

Peyssonnel, Charles de, *Traité sur le commerce de la Mer Noire*, Paris, 1787.

Pfaff, William, "The Absence of Empire," *New Yorker*, vol. 68, no. 25, 10 August 1992, 59–69.

Picchio, Ricardo, *Relazioni storiche e culturali fra l'Italia e la Bulgaria*, Naples, 1982.

Pinson, Mark, "Ottoman Colonization of the Circassians in Rumili after the Crimean War," *Études balkaniques*, Sofia, 1972, N.3.

——, "Russian Policy and the Emigration of the Crimean Tatars in the Ottoman Empire 1854–1862," *Güney-Doğu Avrupa Araştirmalari Dergisi*, Istanbul, 1921, N.l.

Pipa, Arshi, "The Other Albania: A Balkan Perspective," Arshi Pipa and Sami Repishti, eds., *Studies on Kosova*, Boulder, Co.: East European Monographs, no. 155, New York: Columbia University Press, 1984, 239–254.

Pisarev, A., "Traditsii druzhby narodov kak yavlenie kul'tury: Osvobodite'naia bor'ba balkanskikh narodov protiv osmanskogo iga i rossiiskaya intelligentsiya," B. B. Piotrovskii, ed., *Sovetskaya kul'tura—70 let razvitiya. K 80-letiyu akad. M. P. Kima*, Moscow: Nauka, 1987, 258–261.

Pollis, Adamantia, "Greek National Identity: Religious Minorities, Rights, and European Norms," *Journal of Modern Greek Studies*, vol. 10, no. 2, 1992, 171–195.

Porter, David, *Constantinople and its Environs. In a Series of Letters, exhibiting the actual state of the manners, customs, and habits of the Turks, Armenians, Jews, and Greeks, as modified by the policy of Sultan Mahmoud. By an American, long resident at Constantinople*, New York: Harper, 1835.

"'The Post-Communist Nightmare': An Exchange" *New York Review of Books*, vol. 41, no. 4, 17 February 1994, 28–30.

Pounds, Norman, "Balkans," *Academic American Encyclopedia*, vol. 3, Danbury, Conn.: Grolier, 1994, 38–40.

"Povest' i skazanie o pokhozhdenii v Jerusalim i Tsar'grad Troitsko-Sergieva monastyria, chernogo dyakona Iony po reklomu Malen' kogo," *Pamiatniki drevnei pis'menmosti i isskustva*, vol. 35, Saint Petersburg, 1882.

Pouqueville, François, *Voyage en Morée, à Constantinople, en Albanie, et dans plusieurs autres parties de l'Empire Ottoman pendent les années 1789, 1799, 1800 et 1801*, Paris, 1805.

Pulaha, Selami, *Aspects de démographie historique des contrées albanais pendant les XVe–XVIe siècles*, Tirana, Albania, 1984.

——, "Wissenschaftliche Forschungen über die osmanische Periode des Mittelalters in Albanien (15. Jahrhundert bis Anfang des 19. Jahrhunderts), Hans Georg Majer, ed., *Die Staaten Südosteuropas und die Osmanen*, Munich: Selbstverlag der Südosteuropa-Gesellschaft, 1989, 163–178.

Pundeff, Marin V., *Bulgaria in American Perspective: Political and Cultural Issues*, Boulder, Co.: East European Monographs, no. 318, New York: Columbia University Press, 1994.

Puto, Arben, "The London Conference in Two Editions," *Kosova: Historical/Political Review*, no. 1, 1993, 19–22.

Rabelais, François, *Gargantua and Pantagruel*, Chicago: Encyclopedia Brittanica, 1952.

Ragsdale, Hugh, ed., *Imperial Russian Foreign Policy*, New York: Woodrow Wilson Center Press and Cambridge University Press, 1993.

Rallet, D., *Suvenire şi impresii de călătorie în România, Bulgaria, Constantinople*, Paris: Bouchet, 1858.

Ramet, Pedro, ed., *Eastern Christianity and Politics in the Twentieth Century*, vol. 1, Durham, N.C., and London: Duke University Press, 1988.

Recueil d'études sociales publié à la mémoire de Frédéric Le Play, Paris: A. et J. Picard, 1956.

Redhouse, James W., *A New Turkish and English Lexicon*, Beirut: Librarie du Liban, 1974.

Redhouse Yeni Türkçe-Ingilizce Sözlük, Istanbul: Redhouse yayinevi, 1968.

Reed, John, *The War in Eastern Europe*, New York: Scribner's, 1919.

Reiter, Norbert, ed., *Die Stellung der Frau auf dem Balkan*, Wiesbaden: Otto Harrassowitz, 1987.

Remak, Joachim, "1914—The Third Balkan War: Origins Reconsidered," *Journal of Modern History* vol. 43, 1971, 353–366.

Renda, Günsel, and Max Kortepeter, eds., *The Transformation of Turkish Culture: The Atatürk Legacy*, Princeton, N.J.: Kingston, 1986.

Répertoire d'études balkaniques, 1966–1975, 1–2, Sofia: Institut d'études balkaniques, CIBAL, 1983–1984.

Report of the International Commission to Inquire into the Causes and Conduct of the Balkan Wars, Washington, D.C.: Carnegie Endowment for International Peace, Division of Intercourse and Education, publication no. 4, 1914.

"Responses to Samuel P. Huntington's "The Clash of Civilizations?'" *Foreign Affairs*, vol. 72, no. 4, Sept./Oct. 1993, 2–26.

RFE/RL Daily Report, no. 183, 26 September 1994.

Richardson, Michael, "Enough Said. Reflections on Orientalism," *Anthropology Today*, vol. 6, no. 4, August 1990, 16–19.

Richter, Melvin, "Despotism," *Dictionary of the History of Ideas*, vol. 2, New York: Scribner's, 1973, 1–18.

Robert, Cyprien, *Le monde slave: Son passé, son état présent et son avenir*, vol. 1, Paris: Passard, 1852.

———, *Les Slaves de Turquie*, 2 vols., Paris: E. Depée et Sceaux, 1844.

Roberts, Henry L., *Eastern Europe: Politics, Revolution, & Diplomacy*, New York: Alfred A. Knopf, 1970.

Robinson, Gertrude, *David Urquhart: Some Chapters in the Life of a Victorian Knight-errant of Justice and Liberty*, Oxford: Blackwell, 1920.

Rohrbach, Paul, *Balkan — Türkei: Eine Schicksalszone Europas*, Hamburg: Hoffmann und Campe Verlag, 1940.

Roider, Jr., Karl A., *Austria's Eastern Question 1700–1790*, Princeton, N.J.: Princeton University Press, 1982.

Roth, Klaus, ed. *Mit der Differenz leben: Europäische Ethnologie und Interkulturelle Kommunikation*, Munich and New York: Waxmann Münster, 1996.

Roth, Klaus, "Osmanische Spuren in der Alltagskultur Südosteuropas," Hans Georg Majer, ed., *Die Staaten Südosteuropas und die Osmanen*, Munich: Selbstverlag der Südosteuropa-Gesellschaft, 1989, 319–332.

Rothschild, Joseph, *Return to Diversity: A Political History of East Central Europe Since World War II*, New York: Oxford University Press, 1989.

Roucek, Joseph S., *Balkan Politics: International Relations in No Man's Land*, Westport, Conn.: Greenwood, 1948.

Rouillard, Clarence Dana, *The Turk in French History, Thought, and Literature (1520–1660)*, Paris: Boivin, 1940 (reprint, New York: AMS, 1973).

Rubenstein, Richard E., and Jarle Crocker, "Challenging Huntington," *Foreign Policy*, no. 96, Fall 1994, 113–128.

Rufin, Jean-Christoffe, *L'Empire et les nouveaux barbares*, Paris, Hachettes-Pluriel, 1992.

Rupnik, Jacques, *The Other Europe*, London: Weidenfeld and Nicolson, 1988.

Ruskin, Jonah, *The Mythology of Imperialism*, New York: Random House, 1971.

Russel, Bertrand, *The Scientific Outlook*, New York: W. W. Norton, 1931.

Russkii posol v Stambule: Petr Andreevich Tolstoy i ego opisanie Osmanskoi imperii nachala XVIII v., Moscow: Glavnaya redaktsiia vostochnoi literatury izdatel'stva "Nauka," 1985.

Rycaut, Paul, *The Present State of the Ottoman Empire. Containing the Maxims of the Turkish Politie, the most Material Points of the Mahometane Religion, their Sects and Heresies, their Convents and Religious Votaries. Their military discipline, with an exact Computation of their Forces both by Land and Sea. Illustrated with divers Pieces of Sculpture representing the variety of Habits amongst the Turks*, London: John Starkey and Henry Brome, 1668.

Safire, William, "Baltics Belong in a Big NATO," *New York Times*, 16 January 1995, A17.

———, "Hello, Central," *New York Times Magazine*, 12 March 1995, 24–26.

Said, Edward W., *Culture and Imperialism*, London: Chatto and Windus, 1992.

———, "East Isn't East," *Times Literary Supplement*, 3 February 1995, 3–6.

———, *Orientalism*, New York: Pantheon, 1978.

———, "Representing the Colonized: Anthropology's Interlocutors," *Critical Inquiry*, vol. 15, no. 2, Winter 1989, 205–225.

——, *Representations of the Intellectual*, New York: Pantheon, 1994.

Sandfeld, Kristian, *Linguistique balkanique: Problème et résultat*, Paris: Librairie ancienne Honoré Champion, 1930.

Saper, Craig Jonathan, *Tourism and Invention: Roland Barthes's "Empire of Signs,"* Dissertation, University of Florida, 1990.

Sarup, Madan, *Post-Structuralism and Postmodernism*, Athens, Ga.: University of Georgia Press, 1993.

Saussure, Ferdinand de, *Course in General Linguistics*, London: Fontana/Collins, 1974.

Sauveboeuf, Ferrières, de, *Mémoires historiques et politiques de mes voyages faits depuis 1782 jusqu'en 1789, en Turquie, en Perse et en Arabie, melés d'observations sur le gouvernement, les moeurs, la religion et le commerce de tous les peuples de ces différents pays, avec les relations exactes de tous ces événements qui ont lieu dans l'Empire Ottoman depuis 1774 jusqu'à la rupture des Turcs avec les deux cours impériales; suivis de tous les détails de ce qui s'est passé de remarquable entre les deux armées de ces trois puissance belligérentes et d'un calcul raisonné des avantages que les Cours de Vienne et de Saint-Petersbourg peuvent retirer de leur victoires sur les Ottomans*, Maestrücht and Paris, 1790.

Sbornik za narodni umotvoreniya i narodopis, vol. 4, Sofia: Bîlgarska akademiya na naukite, 1891.

Schama, Simon, *Landscape and Memory*, New York: A. A. Knopf, 1995.

Schefer, Charles., ed., *Le voyage d'Outremer de Bertrandon de la Broquière, premier écuyer tranchant et conseiller de Philippe le Bon, duc de Bourgogne*, Farnborough: Gregg, 1972.

Schepper, C. D., "Missions diplomatiques de Corneiile Duplicius de Schepper dit Scepperus ambassadeur de Christien II, Charles V, de Ferdinand Ir et de Marie, reine de Hongrie, gouvernante des Pays-Bas, de 1523 à 1555. Par M. Le Bon de Saint Genois et G.-A. Issel de Schepper," *Mémoires de l'Academie royale des sciences, des lettres et des beaux arts de Belgique. Classe des lettres*, vol. 30, Bruxelles, 1857, 1–222.

Schöpflin, George, "Central Europe: Definitions Old and New," George Schöpflin and Nancy Wood, eds., *In Search of Central Europe*, Cambridge, U.K.: Polity, 1989, 7–29.

Schöpflin, George, and Nancy Wood, "Milan Kundera's Lament," George Schöpflin and Nancy Wood, eds., *In Search of Central Europe*, Cambridge, U.K.: Polity, 1989, 139–142.

Schubert, Gabriella, "Berlin und Südosteuropa," Klaus Meyer, ed., *Berlin und Osteuropa*, Berlin: Colloquium Verlag, 1991, 177–209.

——, "Das Bulgaren-Bild deutscher Reisender in der Zeit der Osmanenherrschaft," *Zeutschrift für Balkanologie*, vol. 26, 1990, 103–122.

Schwab, Raymond, *The Oriental Renaissance: Europe's Rediscovery of India and the East, 1680–1880*, New York: Columbia University Press, 1984 (translation of the French original *La Rénaissance Orientale*, Paris, 1950).

Schwarz, Egon, "Central Europe—What It Is and What It Is Not," George Schöpflin and Nancy Wood, eds., *In Search of Central Europe*, Cambridge, U.K.: Polity, 1989, 143–156.

Schwartz-Salant, Nathan, and Murray Stein, eds., *Liminality and Transitional Phenomena*, Wilmette, Ill.: Chirow, 1991.

Schweigger, Salomon, *Eine newe Reysbeschreibung auss Teutschland nach Konstantinopel vnd Jerusalem: Darinn die Gelegenheit derselben Laender/Staedt/Flecken/geben etc. der innwohnenten Voelker Art/Sitten/Gebraech/Trachten/Religion vnd Gottesdienst etc.* Nuremberg: Johann Lantzenberger 1608 (phototypic edition Graz, 1964).

Schwoebel, Robert, *The Shadow of the Crescent: The Renaissance Image of the Turk (1453–1517)*, Niewkoop: B. de Graaf, 1967.

Scobel, Albert, ed., *Geographisches Handbuch: Allgemeine Erdkunde, Länderkunde, und Wirtschaftsgeographie*, vol. 1, Bielefeld and Leipzig: Velhagen and Klasing, 1909.

Searight, Sarah, *The British in the Middle East*, London: Weidenfeld and Nicolson, 1979.

XVIe congres international des sciences historiques, Rapports, I, 2. Grands thèmes. L'image de l'autre: étrangers, minoritaires, marginaux, Stuttgart: Comité international des sciences historique, 1985.

Seligman, Adam B., *The Idea of Civil Society*, New York: Free Press, 1992.

Seton-Watson, Robert W., *Disraeli, Gladstone and the Eastern Question*, London, 1935.

——, *The Rise of Nationality in the Balkans*, London: Constable, 1917.

——, *The Southern Slav Question and the Habsburg Monarchy*, London: Constable, 1911.

Setton, Kenneth M., "The Byzantine Background to the Italian Renaissance," *Proceedings of the American Philosophical Society*, no. 100, 1956, 1–76.

——, *The Papacy and the Levant*, vol. 1 (1204–1402), vol. 2 (1402–1504), vol. 3 (1504–1552), vol. 4 (1551–1571), Philadelphia: American Philosophical Society, 1976–1984.

——, *Venice, Austria, and the Turks in the Seventeenth Century*, Philadelphia: American Philosophical Society, 1991.

Seydlitz, Melchior von, *Gründliche Beschreibung der Wallfahrt nach dem heiligen Lande neben Vermeldung der jemerlichen und langwierigen Gefengnuss derselben Gesellshaft: Gestellet durch den edlen ehrenvesten Melchior von Seydlitz aus Niklasdorf und Wirben in Schlesien, welcher persönlich solche Noth und Eleed ausgestanden*, Görlitz, 1580.

The Shade of the Balkans: Being a collection of Bulgarian folksongs and proverbs, here for the first time rendered into English, together with an essay of Bulgarian popular poetry, and another on the origin of the Bulgars, London: David Nutt, 1904.

Shannon, Richard, "David Urquhart and the Foreign Affairs Committees," Patricia Hollis, ed., *Pressure From Without in Early Victorian England*, London: Edward Arnold, 1974, 239–261.

——, *Gladstone and the Bulgarian Agitation 1976*, Hamden: Nelson, 1975.

Shashko, Filip, Beti Grinberg, Rumen Genov, eds., *Amerikanski pîtepisi za Bîlgariya prez XIX vek*, Sofia: Planeta3, 2001.

Shaw, George Bernard, *Collected Plays with their Prefaces*, vol. 1, New York: Dodd, Mead, 1975.

Shenon, Philip, "20 Years After Victory, Vietnamese Communists Ponder How to Celebrate," *New York Times*, 23 April 1995, 12.

Sherman, Laura, *Fire on the Mountain: The Macedonian Revolutionary Movement and the Kidnapping of Miss Stone*, Boulder, Co.: East European Monographs, no. 62, New York: Columbia University Press, 1980.

Shils, Edward, *Center and Periphery: Essays in Microsociology*, Chicago: University of Chicago Press, 1975.

Shismanov, Ivan D., "Stari pîtuvaniya prez Bîlgariya v posoka na rimskiya voenen pît ot Belgrad za Tsarigrad," *Sbornik za narodni umotvoreniya*, vol. 4, Sofia, 1891, 324–325.

Şimečka, Milan, "Another Civilization? An Other Civilization?" George Schöpflin and Nancy Wood, eds., *In Search of Central Europe*, Cambridge, U.K.: Polity, 1989, 157–162.

——, "Which Way Back to Europe? (A Reply to Mihály Vajda)," George Schöpflin and Nancy Wood, eds., *In Search of Central Europe*, Cambridge, U.K.: Polity, 1989, 176–183.

Simmons, Thomas W., *Eastern Europe in the Postwar Period*, New York: St. Martin's, 1991.

Simopoulos, Kyriakos, *Xenoi taxidiotes sten Hellada*, Athens, Greece: n.p., 1970–1975.

——, *Pos eidan oi xenoi tin Ellada tou 21*, Athens, Greece: n.p., 1979–1980.

Skilling, H. Gordon, "T. G. Masaryk, Arch-Critic of Austo-Hungarian Foreign Policy," *Cross Currents*, no. 11, 1992, 213–233.

Skopetea, Elli, *I Disi tis Anatolis: Ikones apo to telos tis Othomanikis Avtokratorias*, Athens, Greece: Gnosi, 1992.

——, "Orientalizam i Balkan," *Istorijski časopis*, vol. 38, 1991, 131–143.

Skowronek, Jerzy, *Polityka balkanska Hotelu Lambert (1833–1856)*, Warsaw: Uniwersytet Warszawski, 1976.

Slavov, Ivan, "Balkanpolitikanstvo," *Edin zavet*, no. 1, 1993, 51.

Söz derleme dergisi, vol. 1, Istanbul, 1939.

Smith, Arthur D. Howden, *Fighting the Turks in the Balkans: An American's Adventures with the Macedonian Revolutionaries*, New York and London: G. P. Putnam's, 1908.

Smith, Sheila Mary, *The Other Nation: The Poor in English Novels of the 1840s and 1850s*, Oxford: Clarendon, 1980.

Smochowska-Petrowa, Wanda, *Mikhail Chaikovski—Sadîk pasha i bîlgarskoto vîzrazhdane*, Sofia: Izdatelstvo na Bîlgarskata akademiya na naukite, 1973.

Snyder, Jack, *Myths of Empire: Domestic Politics and International Ambition*, Ithaca, N.Y. and London: Cornell University Press, 1991.

Sokoloski, M., "Islamizatsija u Makedonija u XV i XVI veku," *Istorijski Casopis*, 1975, 22.

Sorel, Georges, *The Illusion of Progress*, Berkeley: University of California Press, 1969.

Söz derleme dergisi, vol. 1, Istanbul, 1939.

Spurr, David, *The Rhetoric of Empire: Colonial Discourse in Journalism, Travel Writing, and Imperial Administration*, Durham, N.C., and London: Duke University Press, 1993.

Staar, Richard F., *The Communist Regimes in Eastern Europe*, Stanford, Calif.: Hoover Institution, 1971.

Stadtmüller, Georg, *Geschichte Südosteuropas*, Munich: R. Oldenburg, 1950.

——, "Osmanische Reichsgeschichte und balkanische Volksgeschichte," *Grundlagen der Europäischen Geschichte*, Munich and Vienna: R. Oldenbourg, 1965.

Stafford, Mark C., and Richard R. Scott, "Stigma, Deviance, and Social Control. Some Conceptual Issues," Stephen C. Ainlay, Gaylene Becker, and Lerita M. Coleman, eds., *The Dilemma of Difference: A Multidisciplinary View of Stigma*, New York and London: Plenum, 1986.

"Stara planina," *Entsiklopediya Bîlgariya*, vol. 6, Sofia: Bîlgarska akademiya na naukite, 1988, 415–420.

Stavrianos, Leften S., *The Balkans Since 1453*, Hinsdale, Ill.: Dryden, 1958.

——, *Balkan Federation: A History of the Movement Toward Balkan Unity in Modern Times*, 2nd ed., Hamden, Conn.: Archon, 1964.

——, "The Influence of the West on the Balkans," Charles and Barbara Jelavich, eds., *The Balkans in Transition. Essays on the Development of Balkan Life and Politics Since the Eighteenth Century*, Berkeley and Los Angeles: University of California Press, 1963, 184–226.

St. Clair, Alexandrine, *The Image of the Turk in Europe*, (Exhibition Catalogue), New York: Metropolitan Museum of Art, 1973.

St. Clair, Stanislas G. B., and Charles A. Brophy, *Residence in Bulgaria; or, Notes on the Resources and Administration of Turkey: The Condition and Character, Manners, Customs, and Language of the Christian and Mussulman Populations, with Reference to the Eastern Question*, London: John Murray, 1869.

——, *Twelve Years' Study or The Eastern Question in Bulgaria*, London: Chapman and Hall, 1877.

Steinbeck, John, *Travels with Charlie: In Search of America*, New York: Penguin, 1986.

Stern, Radu, and Vladimir Tismaneanu, "L'Europe centrale: Nostalgies culturelles et réalités politiques," *Cadmos. Cahiers trimestriel du Centre Européen de la Culture*, no. 39, 1987, 39–46.

Stettenheim, Julius, *Bulgarische Krone gefällig? Allen denen, welche Ja sagen wollen, als Warnung gewidmet*, Leipzig: L. Freund, Buch—und Kunst-Verlag, 1888 (Zweite Auflage).

Stewart, Cecil, *Serbian Legacy*, London: George Allen and Unwin, 1959.

Stiglmayer, Alexandra, ed., *Mass Rape: The War against Women in Bosnia-Herzegovina*, Lincoln: University of Nebraska Press, 1994.

Stoianovich, Traian, *Balkan Worlds: The First and Last Europe*, Armonk, N.Y. and London: M. E.Sharpe, 1994.

——, *Between East and West: The Balkan and Mediterranean Worlds*, 4 vols., New Rochelle, N.Y.: Aristide D. Caratzas, 1992–1995.

Stokes, Gale, "East European History after 1989," John R. Lampe and Paula Bailey Smith, eds., *East European Studies in the United States: Making Its Own Transition After 1989*, Washington, D.C.: Woodrow Wilson Center, 1993, 31–36.

Stokes, Gale, "The Social Origins of East European Politics," Daniel Chirot, ed., *The Origins of Backwardness in Eastern Europe: Economics & Politics from the Middle Ages until the Early Twentieth Century*, Berkeley: University of California Press, 1989, 210–251.

———, *The Walls Came Tumbling Down: The Collapse of Communism in Eastern Europe*, New York: Oxford University Press, 1993.

Stoneman, Richard, *Land of Lost Gods: The Search for Classical Greece*, London: Hutchinson; Norman: University of Oklahoma Press, 1987.

Stoye, John Walter, *English Travellers Abroad, 1604–1667*, London: Jonathan Cape, 1952.

Strangford, Viscountess, [Emily], *Report of the Expenditure of the Bulgarian Peasant Relief Fund*, London: Hardwicke and Bogue, 1878.

Sturmberger, Hans, "Das Problem der Vorbildhaftigkeit des türkischen Staatswesens im 16. und 17. Jahrhundert und sein Einfluss auf den europäischen Absolutismus," *Comité international des sciences historiques, XIIe congrès international des sciences historiques, Vienne 29 aout–5 septembre 1965. Rapport IV*, Horn and Vienna: (no publ., no year), 201–209.

Südosteuropa unter dem Halbmond. Untersuchungen über Geschichte und Kultur der südosteuropäischen Völker wehrend der Türkenzeit. Prof. Georg Stadtmüller zum 65. Geburtstag gewidmet, Munich: Trofenik, 1975.

Sugar, Peter, *Southeastern Europe under Ottoman Rule, 1354–1804*, Seattle: University of Washington Press, 1977.

Suleiman, Susan R., and Inge Crosman, eds., *The Reader in the Text: Essays on Audience and Interpretation*, Princeton, N.J.: Princeton University Press, 1980.

Suleri, Sara, *The Rhetoric of English India*, Chicago and London: University of Chicago Press, 1989.

Szamota, István, *Régi Utazások Magyarországon és a Balkán-félszigeten, 1054–1717*, Budapest: Franklin-Társulat, 1891.

Szporluk, Roman, *Communism and Nationalism: Karl Marx versus Friedrich List*, New York: Oxford University Press, 1988.

Szücs, Jenö, "The Three Historic Regions of Europe: An outline," *Acta Historica Scientiarum Hungaricae*, vol. 29 (2–4), 1983, 131–184. (Hungarian original published in *Történelmi Szemle*, no. 24, 1981, 313–369 and as *Vázlat Európa három régiójáról*, Budapest: Magvetó, 1983.)

Tanaskovic, Darko, "Les thèmes et les traditions Ottomans dans la littérature Bosniaque," Hans Georg Majer, ed., *Die Staaten Südosteuropas und die Osmanen*, Munich: Selbstverlag der Südosteuropa-Gesellschaft, 1989, 299–308.

Teplyakov, V. G., *Pis'ma iz Bolgarii*, Saint Petersburg, 1833.

Tezcan, Semih, "Kontinuität und Diskontinuität der Sprachentwicklung in der Türkei," Hans Georg Majer, ed., *Die Staaten Südosteuropas und die Osmanen*, Munich: Selbstverlag der Südosteuropa-Gesellschaft, 1989, 215–222.

Thomson, Harry C., *The Outgoing Turk: Impressions of a Journey through the Western Balkans*, New York: D. Appleton, 1897.

Thurnher, Eugen, ed., *Jakob Philipp Fallmerayer: Europa zwischen Rom und Byzanz*, Bozen: Athesia, 1990.

———, *Jakob Philipp Fallmerayer: Wissenschaftler, Politiker, Schriftsteller*, Innsbruck: Universitätsverlag Wagner, 1993.

Tismaneanu, Vladimir, "NYR, TLS, and the Velvet Counterrevolution," *Common Knowledge*, vol. 3, no. 1, 1994, 130–142.

———, "Romania's Mystical Revolutionaries," *Partisan Review*, vol. 61, no. 4, 1994, 600–609.

Tismaneanu, Vladimir, and Dan Pavel, "Romania's Mystical Revolutionaries: The Generation of Angst and Adventure Revisited," *East European Politics and Societies*, vol. 8, no. 3, Fall 1994, 402–438.

Todorov, Nikolai, *The Balkan City, 1400–1900*, Seattle and London: University of Washington Press, 1983.

———, "Les tentatives d'industrialisation précoces dans les provinces balkaniques de l'Empire Ottoman, Jean Batou, ed., *Between Development and Underdevelopment: The Precocious Attempts at Industrialization of the Periphery, 1800–1970*, Geneva: Librairie Droz, 1991, 381–394.

———, *Development, Achievements and Tasks of Balkan Studies in Bulgaria*, Sofia: Izdotelstvo na Bîlgarska akademiya na naukite, 1977.

———, "Social Structures in the Balkans during the Eighteenth and Nineteenth Centuries," *Etudes balkaniques*, vol. 4, 1985, 48–71.

Todorov, Nikolai, and Vesselin Traikov, eds., *Bîlgari uchastnitsi v borbite za osvobozhdenieto na Gîrtsiya, 1821–1828*, Sofia: Bîlgarska akademiya na naukite, 1971.

Todorov, Nikolai, and Asparukh Velkov, *Situation démographique de la péninsule balkanique (fin du XVe s. début du XVIe s.)*, Sofia, 1988.

Todorov, Tsvetan, "Reading as Construction," Susan R. Suleiman and Inge Crosman, eds., *The Reader in the Text: Essays on Audience and Interpretation*, Princeton, N.J.: Princeton University Press, 1980, 67–82.

——, "Zabelezhki otnosno krîstosvaneto na kulturite," *Literaturen vestnik*, no. 8, 1991, 3.

Todorov, Varban, *Greek Federalism During the Nineteenth Century (Ideas and Projects)*, Boulder, Co. and New York: Columbia University Press, 1995.

Todorov, Vladislav, *Red Square, Black Square: Organon for Revolutionary Imagination*, Albany: State University of New York Press, 1995.

Todorova, Maria, *Angliiski pîtepisi za Balkanite, XVI-pîrvata chetvîrt na XIX v.*, Sofia: Nauka i izkustvo, 1987.

——, "Afterthoughts on 'Imagining the Balkans,'" *Harvard Middle Eastern and Islamic Review*, 5, 1999–2000, 125–148.

——, *Angliya, Rossiya i Tanzimat*, Moscow: Glavnaya redaktsiya vostochnoi literatury izdatel'stva "Nauka," 1983.

——, "Der Balkan als Analysekategorie: Grenzen, Raum, Zeit," *Geschichte und Gesellschaft*, Heft 3, 2002, 470–492.

——, "The Balkans: From Discovery to Invention," *Slavic Review*, vol. 53, no. 2, Summer 1994, 453–482.

——, "The Balkans: From Invention to Intervention," William J. Buckley, ed., *Kosovo: Contending Voices on Balkan Interventions*, London: Eerdmans, 2000, 159–169.

——, *Balkan Family Structure and the European Pattern, Demographic Developments in Ottoman Bulgaria*, Washington, D.C.: American University Press, 1993.

——, "La Bulgarie—entre le discours culturel et la pratique politique," *Politique étrangère* (Paris), N.1, 1998, 125–139.

——, *Historische Vermächtnisse zwischen Europa und dem Nahen Osten/Historical Legacies Between Europe and the Near East*, Berlin: Brandenburgische Akademie der Wissenschaften, Wiisenschaftskolleg zu Berling, Fritz Thyssen Stiftung, 2007.

——, "Language as Cultural Unifier in a Multilingual Setting: the Bulgarian Case during the Nineteenth Century," *Eastern European Politics and Societies*, vol. 4, no. 3, 1990, 439–450.

——, "On the Epistemological Value of Family Models: the Balkans Within the European Pattern," Joseph Ehmer and Marcus Cerman, eds., *Family History and New Historiography: Festschrift for Michael Mitterauer*, Vienna (in press).

——, "Historische Vermächtnisse als Analysekategorie. Der Fall Südosteuropa," in Karl Kaser, Dagmar Gramshammer-Hohl and Robert Pichler, eds, *Europa und die Grenzen im Kopf*, Wieser Encyklopädie des Europäischen Ostens, Bd.11, Wieser Verlag, 2003, 221–246.

——, "Die Osmanenzeit in der Bulgarischen Geschichtsschreibung seit der Unabhängigkeit," Hans Georg Majer, ed., *Die Staaten Südosteuropas und die Osmanen*, Munich: Selbstverlag der Südosteuropa-Gesellschaft, 1989, 127–162.

——, "The Ottoman Legacy in the Balkans," L. Carl Brown, ed., *Imperial Legacy: The Ottoman Imprint in the Balkans and the Middle East*, New York: Columbia University Press, 1995, 45–77.

——, "Spacing Europe: What is a historical region" *East Central Europe/ECE*, 2006, vol. 32, N. 1–2, 7–55.

Todorova, Maria, and Nikolai Todorov, "The Historical Demography of the Ottoman Empire: Problems and Tasks," Richard B. Spence and Linda L. Nelson, eds., *Scholar, Patriot, Mentor: Historical Essays in Honor of Dimitrije Djordjević*, East European Monographs, no. 320, New York: Columbia University Press, 1992, 151–172.

Tomaschek, W., *Zur Kunde der Hämus-Halbinsel, Sitzungsberichte der Kaiserlichen Akademie der Wissenschaften in Wien*. Philosophischhistorische Klasse, Vienna, 1887.

"Töten mit Messer," *Österreichische Zeitschrift für Geschichtswissenschaften*, vol. 1, 1994, 100–110.

Trease, Geoffrey, *The Grand Tour*, London: Heinemann, 1967.

Treptow, Kurt W., ed., *Dracula: Essays on the Life and Times of Vlad Tepes*, New York: East European Monographs, no. 323, Columbia University Press, 1991.

Třestik, Dušan, "We in Europe," *Iztok-Iztok*, nos. 9–10, 1993, 106–110.

Tsimbaev, Nikolai I., *Slavianofil'stvo: Iz istorii russkoi obshchestvenno-politicheskoi mysli XIX veka*, Moscow: Moskovskii Gosudarstvennyi Universitet, 1986.

Tsiv'ian, Tat'iana V., *Lingvisticheskie osnovy balkanskoi medeli mira*, Moscow: Nauka, 1990.

Tsvetkov, Plamen, *A History of the Balkans: A Regional Overview from a Bulgarian Perspective*, vol. 1, Lewiston, N.Y.: Edwin Mellen, 1993.

Turner, Bryan S., *Marx and the End of Orientalism*, London: George Allen and Unwin, 1978.

——, *Orientalism, Postmodernism and Globalism*, London and New York: Routledge, 1994.

Turner, Victor, *The Ritual Process: Structure and Anti-Structure*, Chicago: Aldine, 1969.

——, *Dramas, Fields and Metaphors: Symbolic Action in Human Siciety*, Ithaca, N.Y.: Cornell University Press, 1974.

Twain, Mark, *The Innocents Abroad or the New Pilgrim's Progress*, New York: Grosset and Dunlap, 1911.

Ugrešić, Dubravka, *Have a Nice Day. From the Balkan War to the American Dream.* New York: Viking, 1993.

——, "Zagreb—Amsterdam—New York," *Cross Currents*, no. 11, 1992, 248–256.

Upward, Allen, *The East and Europe: The Report of an Unofficial Mission to the European Provinces of Turkey on the Eve of the Revolution*, London: John Murray, 1908.

Urquhart, David, *The Spirit of the East: A Journal of Travels through Roumeli*, London: H. Colburn, 1838.

——, *Turkey and Its Resources*, London: Saunders and Oatley, 1833.

Utin, Evgenii Issakovich, *Pis'ma iz Bolgarii v 1877 g.*, Saint Petersburg: Tipografiya M Stasyulevicha, 1879.

Vajda, Mihály, "Who Excluded Russia from Europe? (A Reply to Şimečka)," George Schöpflin and Nancy Wood, eds., *In Search of Central Europe*, Cambridge, U.K.: Polity, 1989, 168–175.

Vajda, Mihály, "East-Central European Perspectives," John Keane, ed., *Civil Society and the State. New European Perspectives*, London and New York: Verso, 1988, 333–360.

Valensi, Lucette, "The Making of a Political Paradigm: The Ottoman State and Oriental Despotism," Anthony Grafton and Ann Blair, eds. *The Transmission of Culture in Early Modern Europe*, Philadelphia: University of Pennsylvania Press, 1990, 173–203.

——, *Venise et la Sublime Porte*, Paris: Hachette, 1987.

Vaughan, Dorothy M., *Europe and the Turk: A Pattern of Alliances*, 1350–1700, Liverpool: University Press, 1954.

Venelin, Yurii I., *Drevnye i nyneshnie bolgare v politicheskom, narodopisnom, istoricheskom i religioznom ikh otnoshenii k rossiyanam*, vol. 1, no. 2, Moscow, 1829–1841.

——, *O kharaktere narodnykh pesen u zadunaiskikh slavyan*, Moscow: 1835.

——, *O zarodyshe novoi bolgarskoi literatury*, Moscow, 1838.

Venturi, Franco, *The End of the Old Regime in Europe, 1768–1776*, vol. 1, Princeton, N.J.: Princeton University Press, 1989.

Verdery, Katherine, *National Identity under Socialism: Identity and Cultural Politics in Ceausescu's Romania*, Berkeley: University of California Press, 1991.

Veremis, Thanos, "The Balkans in Search of Multilateralism," *Eurobalkans*, no. 17, Winter 1994/95, 4–9.

——, *Greece's Balkan Entanglement*, Athens, Greece: ELIAMEP-YALCO, 1995.

Viljavec, Fritz, *Ausgewählte Aufsätze*, Munich: R. Oldenbourg, 1963.

Vivian, Herbert, *The Servian Tragedy, with Some Impressions of Macedonia*, London: Grant Richards, 1904.

Vocelka, Karl, "Das Türkenbild des christliched Abenlandes in der frühen Neuzeit," Erich Zöllner and Karl Gutkas, eds., *Österreich und die Osmanen—Prinz Eugen und seine Zeit*, Vienna: Österreichischer Bundesverlag, 1988, 20–31.

Vodopivec, Alexander, *Die Balkanisierung Österreichs: Die grosse Koalition und ihr Ende*, Vienna and Munich: Verlag Fritz Molden, 1967.

Volf, Miroslav, "Exclusion and Embrace: Theological Reflections in the Wake of 'Ethnic Cleansing,'" *Communio Viatorum*, vol. 35, no. 3, 1993, 263–287.

Vopicka, Charles J., *Secrets of the Balkans: Seven Years of a Diplomatist's Life in the Storm Centre of Europe*, Chicago: Rand McNally, 1921.

Vostochnyi vopros vo vneshnei politike Rossii: Konets XVIII v.–nachalo XX v., Moscow: Nauka, 1978.

Vrančić Anton, "Iter Buda Hadrianopolim anno 1553 exaratum ab Antonio Verantio tunc Quinqueecclesiensi, mox Agriensi episcopo, ac demum archiepiscopo Strigoniensi, regio in Hungaria locumtenenti, magno regni cancellario atque S. R. E. Cardinali electo. Nunc primum e Verantiano cartophilacio in lucem editum," Abb. Fortis, *Viaggio in Dalmazia*, Venice, 1774.

Vranoussis, Leandros, *L'hellénisme postbyzantin et l'Europe: Manuscrits, livres, imprimeries*, Athens, Greece: Centre de recherches médiévales et neo-helléniques de l'Academie d'Athènes, 1981.

Vryonis, Jr., Speros, *The Decline of Medieval Hellenism in Asia Minor and the Process of Islamization from the Eleventh through the Fifteenth Centuries*, Berkeley: University of California Press, 1971.

———, "The Experience of Christians under Seljuk and Ottoman Domination, Eleventh to Sixteenth Century," Michael Gervers and Ramzi Jibran Bikhazi, eds, *Conversion and Continuity: Indigenous Christian Communities in Islamic Lands, Eighth to Eighteenth Centuries*, Toronto: Pontifical Institute of Mediaeval Studies, 1990, 185–216.

———, "Travelers as a Source for the Societies of the Middle East: 900–1600," A. E. Laiou-Thomadakis, ed., *Charanis Studies: Essays in Honor of Peter Charanis*, New Brunswick, N.J.: Rutgers University Press, 1980, 248–311.

Vuchinich, Wayne S., "Some Aspects of the Ottoman Legacy," *The Balkans in Transition: Essays on the Development of Balkan Life and Politics Since the Eighteenth Century*, Charles and Barbara Jelavich, eds., Berkeley and Los Angeles: University of California Press, 1963, 81–114.

Walicki, Andrzej, *The Slavophile Controversy: History of a Conservative Utopia in Nineteenth-Century Russian Thought*, Notre Dame, Ind.: University of Notre Dame Press, 1989.

Waller, Michael, "Groups, Parties and Political Change in Eastern Europe from 1977," Geoffrey Pridham and Tatu Vanhanen, eds., *Democratization in Eastern Europe*, London and New York: Routledge, 1994, 38–62.

Wallerstein, Immanuel, *The Capitalist World-Economy: Essays*, New York: Cambridge University Press, 1979.

———, *Geopolitics and Geoculture: Essays on the Changing World-System*, Cambridge: Cambridge University Press, 1991.

———, *The Modern World-System*, 3 vols., New York: Academic, 1974–1989.

———, *The Politics of the World-Economy: the States, the Movements, and the Civilizations; Essays*, New York: Cambridge University Press, 1984.

Walsh, Robert, *Narrative of a Journey from Constantinople to England*, London: F. Westley and A. H. Davis, 1828.

Walzer, Michael, ed., *Toward a Global Civil Society*, Providence and Oxford: Berghahn Books, 1995.

Wandmayer, Alexander Grau, *The Balkan Slavs in America and Abroad: An address delivered by Alexander Grau Wandmayer, formerly Commissioner Plenipotentiary of the Ukrainian Government with the International Commission for the Liquidation of Austria before students of racial backgrounds at Columbia University, July 28th, 1922*, New York, 1922.

Wandycz, Piotr S., *The Lands of Partitioned Poland, 1795–1918*, Seattle and London: University of Washington Press, 1974.

Ware, Ronald D., "Caesaropapism," Joseph Dunner, ed., *Handbook of World History*, New York: Philosophical Library, 1967, 136–138.

Washington Post, "Book World," 2 April 1995, 10.

Waxman, Chaim I., *The Stigma of Poverty: A Critique of Poverty Theories and Policies*, New York: Pergamon, 1977.

Weber, S. H., ed., *Voyages and Travels in the Near East during the XIX Century*, Princeton, N.J.: American School of Classical Studies in Athens, 1952–1953.

Weigand, Gustav, *Aleko Konstantinofs "Baj Ganju,"* Leipzig: Johann Ambrosius Barth, 1908.

Weithmann, Michael, *Balkan Chronik: 2000 Jahre zwischen Orient und Okzident*, Graz, Vienna, Köln: F. Pustet/Styria, 1995.

———, ed., *Der ruhelose Balkan: Die Konfliktregionen Südosteuropas*, Munich: Deutscher Taschenbuch Verlag, 1993.

West, Rebecca, *Black Lamb and Grey Falcon*, New York: Penguin, 1982.

Williams, Raymond, *Culture and Society, 1780–1950*, New York: Columbia University Press, 1958.

———, *Marxism and Literature*, Oxford: Oxford University Press, 1977.

Wolandt, Gerd, "Kants Völkeranthropologie als Programm," Hugo Dyserinck and Karl Ulrich Syndram, eds., *Europa und das nationale Selbstverständnis: Imagologische Probleme in Literatur, Kunst und Kultur des 19. und 20. Jahrhunderts*, Bonn: Bouvier, 1988.

Wolff, Larry, *Inventing Eastern Europe: The Map of Civilization on the Mind of the Enlightenment*, Stanford, Calif.: Stanford University Press, 1994.

Woodhouse, C. M., *The Philhellenes*, London: Hodder and Stoughton, 1969.

Woodward, Susan L., *Balkan Tragedy: Chaos and Dissolution after the Cold War*, Washington, D.C.: Brookings Institution, 1995.

Wtulich, Josephine, *American Xenophobia and the Slav Immigrant: A Living Legacy of Mind and Spirit*, Boulder, Co.: East European Monographs, no. 385, New York: Columbia University Press, 1994.

Zaimova, Raya, *Bîlgarskata tema v zapadnoevropeiskata knizhnina XV–XVII vek*, Sofia: Universitetsko izdatelstvo "Sv. Kliment Okhridski," 1992.

Zajimi, Gazmend, "Historical Continuity of the Question of Kosova," *Kosova*, no. 1, 1993, 15–18.

Zeman, Z. A. B., "The Balkans and the Coming War," *The Coming of the First World War*, R. J. W. Evans and Hartmut Pogge von Strandmann, eds., Oxford: Clarendon, 1988, 19–32.

Zeune, August, *Goea: Versuch einer wissenschaftlichen Erdbeschreibung*, Berlin, 1808.

Zhelyazkova, Antonina, *Razprostranenie na islyama v zapadnobîlgarskite zemi pod osmanska vlast, XV–XVIII vek*, Sofia: Bulgarian Academy of Sciences, 1990.

Zirojevic, Olga, "Die Bewahrung und Erforschung der osmanischen Hinterlassenschaft in Jugoslawien: Archive und Forschungseinrichtungen," Hans Georg Majer, ed., *Die Staaten Südosteuropas und die Osmanen*, Munich: Selbstverlag der Südosteuropa-Gesellschaft, 1989, 187–204.

Zlatar, Zdenko, *Our Kingdom Come: The Counter-Reformation, the Republic of Dubrovnik, and the Liberation of the Balkan Slavs*, Boulder, Co.: East European Monographs, no. 342, New York: Columbia University Press, 1992.

Zöllner, Erich, and Karl Gutkas, eds., *Österreich und die Osmanen—Prinz Eugen und seine Zeit*, Vienna: Österreichisches Bundesverlag, 1988.

Index